The 12 Moon Signs In Love

A Lover's Guide To Understanding Your Partner

By Vera Kaikobad

First published by Dog Ear Publishing
4010 W. 86th Street, Ste H
Indianapolis, IN 46268
www.dogearpublishing.net

ISBN: 1-59858-026-4
Library of Congress Control Number: 2005930395

This book is printed on acid-free paper.

Printed in the United States of America

for Armin
and
for those who have loved across lifetimes

Table of Contents

Chapter 14:

The Moon in Taurus Lover compared to a lover with:

Chapter 15:

The Moon in Gemini Lover compared to a lover with:

Chapter 16:

The Moon in Cancer Lover compared to a lover with:

Chapter 23:

The Moon in Aquarius Lover compared to a lover with:

Chapter 24:

The Moon in Pisces Lover compared to a lover with:

Acknowledgments

I am grateful to my beloved sister Armin who read and commented on the book in its early and final stages, and thank her for her author's wisdom, and for encouraging me. And since this book revolves around the theme of romance, I am also indebted to my parents Dolly and Dr. Homi Kaikobad who provided me with the best example, as well as a close up view of what a compatible marriage is and should be, over a span of more than three wonderful decades.

My final and biggest thanks goes to those of you who have enjoyed my personally written Astrology reports over the past decade and suggested the idea for this book. I hope that the information in this book will guide you to better understanding your life-partners by using the ancient and always available wisdom of the magical Moon.

Notes on Sources

Reluctance, by Robert Frost

Sonnet 116, by William Shakespeare

Maybe, by Carl Sandburg

Love Sonnet LXXIX, by Pablo Neruda

Translations From Diva-e-Shams, by Mevlana Jalal-ud-din Rumi

Sonnet XVII, by Pablo Neruda

i carry your heart, by e. e. cummings

Love Sonnet LXXIX, by Pablo Neruda

"I've got an arrow here", by Emily Dickinson

"Love is sufficient unto love", excerpt from the Prophet by Kahlil Gibran

He Wishes For The Cloths Of Heaven, by W. B. Yeats

How do I love thee? by Elizabeth Barrett Browning

Every selection of poetry used in this book is the sole property of the poet designated.

Introduction

Are you in love, dear reader? If you're reading this book, then there is surely someone who lives in your heart as your true beloved. How do you tell the difference between that truly compatible lover and the just-for-fun mate? If you've been wondering about how to relate to your lover on a higher, more <u>refined level</u> than only Sun sign Astrology, then the ancient and mystical Moon lies at the heart of your journey.

Ancient astrologers have also said that studying a man's Moon sign gives deep insights into *what kind of wife he will pick*. This book was written to help you with that delicate emotional matching process that occurs between two lovers.

Don't know your personal Moon sign? Find out today for FREE! Log onto Vera Kaikobad's http://www.astrologycompatibilityreports.com, email us your birth date and find out your Moon sign, or your lover's Moon sign within seconds!

Most people who are looking for real, lasting love agree that connecting with your soul mate requires more than just eyesight and pleasant conversation over coffee. Long term love flows more smoothly if your astrological Moon sign is compatible with your lover's Sun, Moon or Rising sign, and especially if you are willing to learn what your lover needs emotionally from you, but may not know how to ask for it.

Understanding your lover from the inside out has never been easier. *Part One* of this book describes each of the 12 astrological Moon signs, including their likes, dislikes in a relationship and includes information on the <u>10 specific traits the male and female of each Moon sign looks for in a lover</u>. Just read the section that analyzes your lover's Moon sign, get the invaluable insights you need to solidify your bond with your partner, and learn to speak to them in the emotional language that *they can understand easily*.

Part Two of this book contains 144 detailed, romantic Moon sign combinations, as well as helpful tips on how to avoid problems in your relationship according to the specific temperament of your lover's Moon sign. This section reveals the emotional triggers of each Moon sign to give you the maximum information on what your lover wants. Find out how your personal Moon sign blends with your lover's Sun, Moon and Rising sign for maximum compatibility.

Part Three of this book contains information on the romantic expectations of each Moon sign, information on what love means to each Moon sign from their own point of view and finally, a helpful Moon sign gift guide. Anyone can buy a gift for a lover based on their Sun sign, but giving them a present based on their secret, emotional make up will make a better impression on them, make them more responsive to your love and help them feel closer to you.

What does the faraway Moon have to do with love and romance? A lot, if you're hopelessly in love. Most of us know our Sun signs. Are you a flirtatious, go-getter Gemini? A sensitive and artistic Cancer or perhaps a sultry and mysterious Scorpio? Your Sun sign is the sign you look for in newspapers to read your weekly horoscope.

But what a majority of people don't know is that they also have a powerful, personal Moon sign, an equal player in the accurate interpretation of one's personality, moods and feelings. The Moon sign of a person can help explain the difference between one charismatic and flamboyant Sun sign Leo with a *Leo Moon sign* who revels in being the life of the party, and another privacy-loving Sun sign Leo with a *Cancer Moon sign,* shunning the public glare by choice and curling up in bed with a good book and a fresh cup of hot chocolate.

Knowing your lover's Sun sign but not their Moon sign is like knowing what your lover looks like but never hearing them speak. If you're deeply in love with a Sun sign Leo, for example, understanding their Moon sign can greatly affect your daily give and take with them in a relationship. Do you know how your lover's Moon sign colors their interactions with you?

Your Moon sign is determined by the position of the Moon at the time of your birth, and reserves an influential presence in the study of Compatibility Astrology. Your Sun sign reflects what the world perceives in you, while your Moon sign reflects what you see in yourself. Your Moon sign doesn't eclipse your Sun sign, instead it fine-tunes and modulates it according to the original rhythms of your natural emotions.

Have you ever gazed at the distant, milky white Moon, nestled against a raven night sky surrounded by millions of shivering, silvery stars, and wondered about your beloved, your true love? From Shakespeare to Rumi, from Keats to Browning, thousands of poets have poured out their heart's musings by simply gazing at the Moon. What is this ancient magic we feel when we look at the Moon?

Our personal Moon sign symbolizes our deepest emotions, our *unexpressed* desires and motivations, and is often a stand-alone guide to our true natures. The Moon reflects our individual comfort level within a love relationship. It is with the help of our Moon sign that we are able to undergo some of the biggest emotional migrations of our lives, successfully process the forgotten dreams of our childhood, understand the growing pains of our adolescence and anticipate our entry into the exciting world of love and attraction between the sexes.

The beautiful Moon conceals many secrets, and now you can learn to speak the language of the Moon in a few turns of the pages of this book. May your love flourish and may your relationship grow stronger. Happy bonding!

Note: The Sun/Moon conjunction and the Mars/Venus conjunction: keys to romantic compatibility.

If your Moon sign is the same as your lover's Sun sign, then this is a good sign of a particularly promising marriage or relationship. You may experience just as many ups and downs as other couples who don't share this aspect, but you will be able to weather the storms together more easily than others. (For example: your Moon is in Scorpio and your lover's Sun is in Scorpio, or your Sun is in Taurus and your lover's Moon is in Taurus.)

Another equally good aspect to have in a couple's chart is the conjunction of Mars and Venus, which means that one partner's Mars is in the same sign as the other partner's Venus. If this aspect is found, it could be a particularly blessed marriage or relationship. Mars and Venus blend male and female energies into perfect synchronicity, and increase emotional compatibility through physical intimacy. (For example: your Mars is in Gemini and your partner's Venus is in Gemini. This works best if the Mars is in the male's natal chart and the Venus is in the female's natal chart).

Part I:
The 12 Moon Signs in Love

Chapter 1
The Aries Moon Lover

Ruler: Mars
Element: Fire
Quality: Cardinal
Symbol: The Ram

"Ah, when to the heart of man
Was it ever less than a treason
To go with the drift of things,
To yield with a grace to reason,
And bow and accept the end
Of a love or a season?"
~ Robert Frost (Aries Poet)

Who could resist falling in love with an Aries Moon lover? Blend together the literary genius of Mark Twain, with the wacky humor of comedian Eddie Izzard and the intensity of character actor Kevin Spacey, and you have before you the intriguing Aries Moon persona.

Your trademark quality is bring-it-on optimism and an indefatigable thirst for life's many adventures. Any ups and downs in your destiny never cause you to give up or back down, and you will look for the same kind of fighting spirit in your partner. You cannot tolerate being restricted in any way and this is important for your lovers to know ahead of time. You like to do things your way and that means that while you may let a new lover enter your life, you may not permit too many partner-initiated changes in the way you live your life. Trust plays a major role in your relationships and you like it when the relationship is based on blind trust.

As an Aries Moon lover, your personality may fall into any one of the three, specific Aries Moon personality types. Which one of the following describes you best? You may either be dominant and aggressive, or a *ram type*; passive and non-confrontational, or a *lamb type*; or a balanced mixture of both, which is the *ram/lamb type* of Aries Moon personality. Learning to tell them apart can help your new lover figure out what you desire and how they can fulfill that emotional need.

When you are younger and initially entering the exciting and often tumultuous world of love, sex and dating, you will be a quick and eager learner. If you are male, you will find that female admiration is never lacking. Partners are drawn to your robust energy level, (Mars rules energy, action and pure passion) and your ability to make your lover laugh by looking very silly yourself. Ram type, Aries Moon author Mark Twain once said that *"History never repeats itself, but it does rhyme."* Well-timed witticisms and an original sense of humor are age-old aphrodisiacs, they say, and if this is true, then you are a fine example of it. An Aries Moon sign makes you an irresistible and persuasive lover.

Mark Twain is also a good example of the romantic side of the Aries Moon person. Let's take a peak into his heart and read the description of his feelings toward his future wife, Olivia Langdon, with these beautiful words: *"Out of the depths of my happy heart wells a great tide of love and prayer for this priceless treasure that is confided to my life-long keeping. You cannot see its intangible waves as they flow towards you, darling, but in these lines you will hear, as it were, the distant beating of the surf."* As an Aries Moon male, Mark Twain was an excellent example of the famously quick wit as well as privately tender nature of this Moon sign.

The ruler of your Moon sign is Mars, the most masculine and passionate planet in the solar system. Venus traditionally rules love, beauty and all things feminine, while machismo Mars supplies passion in a relationship. While you can confidently captivate lovers with your natural charm and vibrant personality, you are also quickly bored and may terminate a perfectly good relationship with great potential, only because you feel there is no novelty left in it. Aries is an impatient sign and you may give up on true love before you have fully experienced it. That would be a shame. After you enter your late thirties and early forties, you will take love more seriously than you do when you're younger.

If variety and excitement were once the major motivation for you in relationships, stability with one partner who can understand you and tolerate your slightly impatient nature (not everyone will), may prove to be the best match for you. You expect quick reciprocity from your lover. If you are female, Mars will give you added power, which is good to have in the arena of your profession. Picture the grace of Jacqueline Kennedy Onassis (a *ram/lamb type* Aries Moon person), the femininity of model Tyra Banks (a *ram type* Aries Moon person), the disarming humor of comedian Ellen Degeneres (a *ram type* Aries Moon person) and the delicate beauty of Angelina Jolie (another *ram type* Aries Moon person), and you can envision the hard-to-resist appeal of a woman with an Aries Moon sign. They are often successful and ambitious women who know exactly where they're going in life. A well-timed but sincere compliment will not go amiss with a beautiful and bright Aries Moon female.

This fiery Moon sign can juggle a lot of projects at a time and provide many good ideas at work, but bringing those projects to a successful conclusion may not always be their forte. If you're a female and your Moon sign is Aries, you are more likely to demand to be treated with respect and equality at work, and could easily be a pioneer for your sisters from all the other signs. But you must keep in mind that when you are in love, a strong persona might often cause you to be misunderstood as being too domineering for your love relationship to flourish comfortably. You're an active, self-motivated and memorable personality, and that is the most lovable thing about you. America's most elegant Aries Moon first lady Jacqueline Kennedy said it best: *"I want to live my life, not record it."* And as an Aries Moon woman, with self-confidence like that, you'd be very much in demand!

If you are a man with an Aries Moon sign, you may look to balance the different parts of your life. Use your forceful and charismatic persona at work to get the job done and achieve the success you desire, but make sure you let your partner get some of your attention when at home. As life begins to purify your love over time, there may be a tendency in you to place more emphasis on the active part of a relationship or the newness factor in a relationship, instead of enjoying the more mature, secure and stable levels of compatibility with a lover.

"Where's the excitement? Where's that brand new feeling of being in love that I like? Things just don't seem the same with my lover, have they changed or have I?" the Aries Moon male may wonder. The secret is that neither of you have changed,

but have become witness to your relationship growing into a closer, more emotionally significant bond. Yes, this is what real intimacy is. As a romantic idealist, you admire those couples who can stay together for decades and enjoy a marriage that the whole world looks up to as the best example of successful, long-term love.

Aries Moon mates enjoy the feeling of excitement in love, but confuse it with a desire for change, and end up sending their lover mixed signals. You may feel inexplicably bored with the pace of the relationship, and your mate might misinterpret this as your being bored with *them*. Clear up those lines of communication often to avoid trouble in love land. Your mate might really need to enjoy stability more than change in their connection with you, while you may feel as though your relationship is stuck and cannot progress any further.

The key would be to understand that those long-term unions that you wish you could enjoy don't necessarily guarantee excitement, but they do guarantee success. If your lover has to change their personality to keep your love or to compete to get your attention, they might feel left out. If you are continually too involved with the lighter aspects of bonding (concentrating on having fun instead of cultivating a serious connection) while ignoring the deeper aspects of it, your lover may stop trying all together, which could one day cost you the love of your life.

The impetuosity of Mars and the changeable influence of the Moon make for a slightly jumpy personality. Mars wants things done yesterday and the Moon functions out of an enormous emotional reservoir of feelings. Whether male or female, there is a restless element in your temperament that you have to deal with (as does your lover), and while you are passionate, romantic and loving, an inability to be patient and a tendency to jump to conclusions and make snap decisions can work against you, causing many a good match to throw up their hands in defeat and take off for greener, more patient pastures.

Mars, the great warrior planet, is also famous for his legendary temper, so use more diplomacy to sort out problems and things should move along beautifully. The nicest thing about you, unlike the fixed signs (Taurus, Leo, Scorpio, Aquarius), is that once someone (very respectfully) shows you what you did wrong, you will willingly change your attitude. The secret is to approach you in a non-threatening, friendly manner and when you are in the right mood.

People with Aries as their Moon sign fall in love many times in their lives, and they will give their heart away many times too. But they will give both their heart and soul only once or twice in a lifetime. So, pick your life partner wisely. While you are playful and young in outlook, you will often do well with a partner who can do what you may have trouble doing: expertly managing your finances, being frugal and planning intelligently for the future.

Some Aries Moon people are impulse-shoppers, so if your partner is careful about expenditures and you're not, there might be some interesting discussions at the kitchen table. Being reasonable and meeting your lover half way is the key to solving your dilemma. As an Aries Moon person, you may want sole control over what you spend, but hearing what your lover has to say about it is also a great idea.

An Aries Moon lover is very involved in standing apart from the masses. They want to be noticed as unique and powerful personalities, due to the highly *energizing* temperament of Mars. Willful and often acting out of a sense of urgency about what you want to do, it is very crucial that you find the proper direction or perfect outlet for your enormous reserves of energy. If, for example, you propose marriage to your lover, you will want to hear an immediate and resounding *yes* to your question. Therefore, Aries Moon folks should seriously study the differences between love and sex. Sexual compatibility very rarely results in long-term emotional compatibility. And you usually *do* want to wed for life.

Mars can make you aggressive and ambitious (the ram type Aries Moon personality), while the Moon can help soften up any hard edges in your persona. If you're a more mellow Aries Moon person (like the lamb type), you will draw toward yourself lovers who are more take-charge and outgoing than you are. They may unconsciously try to bring you out of your shell and bring you face to face with the more spirited side of your nature. You may be a quiet, thoughtful and beautiful blend of the lyrical Moon and go-getter Mars, embodying the best of both energies, giving you a rather smooth-flowing, pleasant and even-tempered personality.

As an Aries Moon lover, there is a purity and innocence about true love that reflects the purity in you. Quick to declare how you feel, you must also understand that once you build a love relationship, it will not be easy to dismantle. If you fall in love with a needy partner who cannot function independently of you and needs constant emotional reassurances from you, you will feel frustrated if you stay in the relationship and guilty if you leave it. Again, choose wisely and take your time.

You need a higher and consistent level of freedom in your love life than do other Moon signs, and your lover will have to deal with this aspect without taking it too personally. While you are honest about falling in love, you will also be honest about admitting that you no longer have any interest in your partner. And while you may think that a casual friendship between a former lover and yourself will still continue, don't be too sure that your partner will want that. It may take them some time to heal. Due to your friendly nature, you may not want to sever all ties to any lover. Your actions leave an indelible mark on your lovers, and keeping this in mind will give you a better insight into your partner as well as your own romantic nature.

In love relationships your motto should be go-slow, which means that you should not rush the normal pace of the relationship just because you are bored, excited or too eager. Give your lover time to study you and try to do the same, as this will keep your relationship from heating up too quickly and burning out. While you can fall in love at any age, you can sustain a good marriage if you marry later in life.

This is when you will have better grasped this multifaceted and sometimes complicated emotion called love, and tempered it into becoming something tangible that can support you when the seasons change and you begin to age. Yes, every young-hearted Aries Moon person also ages. Growing old with a trusted life-partner who has successfully and voluntarily acclimated to the unique rhythms of your Aries Moon personality, is supremely rewarding and something most couples would look forward to their whole lives. This dream is not beyond the reach of someone as idealistic as you.

You are driven by your heart more than your intellect (a romantic like you wouldn't have it any other way!) and true love will always be a shining prize that you will want to chase no matter what your age. You know you've found your soul mate when you feel like suggesting something extremely impractical or impossible to your lover (like quitting both your jobs and running off to Tibet for a year to learn Tibetan, or take off for Europe for six months to take photographs of rare, alpine wild flowers in the spring), and the words come out of your lover's mouth instead of yours. Your true soul companion will delight in your secret need to be a little wild and crazy (okay, *really* wild and crazy) and never try to change you, but will actually encourage your authentic, think-out-of-the-box personality. That's true love, Aries Moon style.

10 specific traits that a man with the Moon in Aries looks for in a lover

He wants a lover who:
1. Lets him express himself without restrictions
2. Can be emotionally secure and independent of him if need be
3. Will never criticize him in public or make a scene

4. Feels no need to compete with her lover
5. Will place her love for him far above her relatives; he should always be number one in her life
6. Understands that while he may have a temper, it also disappears just as quickly
7. Is not verbally combative or uses tears to manipulate him
8. Has her own life, favorite sport and circle of friends
9. Is not suspicious or controlling
10. Is more tolerant and patient than he is

10 specific traits that a woman with the Moon in Aries looks for in a lover

She wants a lover who:
1. Is athletic, health-conscious and dresses well in public
2. Is self-confident but not overbearing
3. Will not be a pushover for his relatives; she should always be number one in his life
4. Knows how to not take it personally when she gets angry; her annoyances pass quickly
5. Can be financially trusted with *her* money
6. Knows how to encourage her interests without patronizing her
7. Will not be jealous, possessive of her or competitive with her
8. Is not threatened by her fiery, independent nature
9. Has a calm but wise personality
10. Places his love for her above his friends

Find Your Perfect Moon Sign Love Match

If you have an Aries Moon sign, you will attract lovers who have either the Sun, Moon or Rising sign in these fire and air signs: **Aries, Leo, Sagittarius, Gemini, Libra and Aquarius.**

If you have an Aries Moon sign, you can still have a good relationship with a lover whose Sun, Moon or Rising sign is in the following earth and water signs: **Taurus, Virgo, Capricorn, Cancer, Scorpio and Pisces.** It might take adjustments, but it will be worth it!

Celebrities with the Moon in Aries: Mark Twain, Jacqueline Kennedy, Angelina Jolie, Ellen Degeneres, Pamela Anderson, Tyra Banks, Celine Dion, Meg Ryan, Bill Gates, Luciano Pavarotti, Kevin Bacon, Kevin Spacey, Anderson Cooper, Dr. Masaru Emoto (water scientist), John Voight, Aishwarya Rai and Eddie Izzard (comedian), Jennifer Lopez.

Chapter 2

The Taurus Moon Lover

Ruler: Venus
Element: Earth
Quality: Fixed
Symbol: The Bull

"Love alters not with his brief hours and weeks,
But bears it out...even to the edge of doom.
If this be error and upon me proved,
I never writ, nor no man ever loved."

~ William Shakespeare (Taurus Poet and Master Playwright)

The exquisite words of the Bard still ring true deep in the heart of every romantic Taurus Moon person. Mix together the charm of handsome screen legend Gregory Peck, the quiet machismo of Charles Bronson, the pioneering spirit of Sir Edmund Hillary and the grace of speed climber Dean Potter and you have before you best attributes of the Taurus Moon male. This is one of the most beautiful placements for the Moon because the Moon is exalted or well placed in this sign. If your Moon sign is Taurus, you give off a relaxed, peaceful and dependable energy to your lover. The energetic and restless signs will gravitate toward you without knowing why!

This Moon position confers a great ability to concentrate on a project and focus for hours at a time. And if the object of that intensity of focus is your partner, then romantic times are ahead! The Moon in Taurus is a wonderful placement where the stability of Taurus combines with the imagination of the responsive and soft-natured Moon. Symbolically, Venus (the ruler of Taurus) and the Moon are beloved sisters and get along famously.

The Taurus Moon personality is divided into two, distinct parts. Which one resonates more with you? The first type of Taurus Moon personality is the *builder type* and the second is the *stabilizer type*. The strong, dependable builder type does exactly what its title suggests; it builds a solid foundation in life and creates it with a hope that what they choose to pour their energies into will last a lifetime, be it a career, business, marriage or family. This type can be ambitious, dominant and driven, and may take failure, criticism or opposition very hard. The stabilizer type is more easy-going, romantic, poetic and will feel at total ease in the relationship, marriage or family setting, while handling career changes with grace. They will prefer to devote their energies toward more emotional and private avenues of self-expression, such as interpersonal relationships. Both types will feel a special draw toward nature and draw great sustenance from its eternal beauty and its ageless purity.

Let's take a closer look at this Moon sign. As a Taurus Moon person, the sensory impulses around you register more deeply in your subconscious than they do for other people. The intricate patterns on the trunk of a weather-beaten tree attract your attention while others walk right past it without noticing it. You will run your palms over the gray grain of an ancient rock (Taurus is very tactile), or ponder the exquisite color of a stormy sky while others run for cover. Of all the earth signs, Taurus is known as the most sensitive (many of the world's greatest singers and vocalists have the sign of Taurus prominently placed in their natal charts: Taurus rules the throat.) Nature speaks to you in a language all her own, and it is hauntingly beautiful. Naturalness and simplicity attract you and your lover might like to note this tip.

Earning the love and loyalty of a Taurus Moon lover take time and serious effort. *"Will he make a faithful spouse? Will he respect the bond we have created or carelessly take risks with it?"* a Taurus Moon female asks. *"Will she spend everything I earn on clothes and shoes, or will she wisely handle our joint financial resources?"* a Taurus Moon male wonders. He wants to know this because he wants to make sure he's getting the real deal, a jewel of a life-companion who will stand the test of time.

As a Taurus Moon lover, you might be tempted to test your lover from time to time. There might be a bit of insecurity hidden somewhere that might cause you to experience an occasional panic attack. Your partner should calm your fears and let you know that they're here to stay, come what may. Taurus Moon people need highly reciprocal, physically demonstrative partners and this may be the key to maintaining a long and happy connection with you.

You are steady, think carefully about things and come to a conclusion at your own pace. Anyone who wants to hurry you into a decision should first try pushing a mountain. No one will be able to rush you into something before you feel you are ready. Taurus (along with its polar opposite eighth sign of Scorpio) is a money sign and is connected to the second sector of personal income in all astrological natal charts. This position gives you an ability to manage your money, assets, resources and income better than others, as patience and pragmatism are your best qualities.

You tend to be responsible about taking out loans and making investments, and fancy, get-rich-quick schemes seldom have an effect on you. You are also suspicious about anyone who offers something for nothing (including a new lover who declares their love for you too soon). This suspicion keeps you safe and puts the pressure on other people to prove themselves to you. Taurus lends you an artistic, amiable temperament (Venus rules art) and writing, painting, photography come naturally to you. You have a strong creative urge, which could at some point bring you income.

The influence of Venus on Taurus Moon females is evident by the fact that some of the most alluring and compassionate women in the world have this Moon sign placement. Think of the sacrifice of Mother Teresa, the dark sensuality of Demi Moore, the velvet voice of country music singer Faith Hill and the magnetism of Cameron Diaz and you have created the perfect Taurus Moon female.

Delving deeper into the Taurus Moon female persona, Mother Teresa, once said: *"I ask of you one thing. Do not tire of giving, but do not give your leftovers. Give until it hurts, until you feel the pain."* This gives us a clear idea of the passion, resolve and commitment of this Moon placement, which in her case, includes feeling another's abject sorrow, changing your whole life for a cause, and awakening other people's sense of responsibility within the world community. Mother Teresa of Calcutta is truly the best example of this Moon sign.

As a Taurus Moon person, you are private by temperament and being amidst a big crowd for too long is sometimes uncomfortable for you. You prefer small, trusted groups of people, as few as three to six if possible, to socialize with. As a fixed sign, you do not weather change well and of all the other Moon signs, take any enforced change very hard. Flexibility is not something that comes to you easily, due to a trust in the safety felt in predictability and routine. When this ability is combined with the persistence and steady nature of Taurus, you have a person who thinks everything out very carefully and plans meticulously. Sir Edmund Hillary, the first man to reach Mt. Everest embodies the spirit of the Taurus Moon male with the following statement: *"I am a person of modest abilities, but I have a great deal of determination. And once started on a project that I want to do, I don't give up easily."*

As a Taurus Moon person, you may be inclined to take your own sweet time in finding a partner with the result that you usually make the right choice, even if the courtship takes a rather long time. However, waiting too long to declare your affection for a lover or being too reticent in accepting that love from someone, may cost you the love of your life. Patience is a good thing, if employed in moderation and in the most appropriate situations. Otherwise, it may create in you a fear of living your life fully, inclusive of all the risks taken in the path of love. Everybody makes mistakes, and while you don't approach love with the wild abandon of the fire (Aries, Leo, Sagittarius) or air (Gemini, Libra, Aquarius) signs, you do want to know that you're progressing along the right track at every step.

You may also sometimes experience difficulty in trusting a new lover. *"I love her, but is she really marriage material? If things don't work out, it may take me years to heal myself and come out of it. Should I risk loving her? Or wait for another, more compatible lover to come along?"* the suspicious Taurus Moon male wonders. The Taurus Moon female is also in the same boat. *"I adore him, but sometimes it feels like he's not really interested in getting serious. I want marriage and commitment; I want security and trust. I want what we have created together to last. Should I let him get emotionally close to me or will I regret it?"* Love is a strange phenomena, the right lover may creep up on you in the guise of the wrong one. You may like to use trust as a strength, not as a weakness.

Your fixity and desire for a stable routine in your life may go against you in one small way. If you ever find yourself in the wrong relationship (life is extremely changeable and usually at the exactly wrong time), or if you realize that your partner is not faithful to you, you are very likely to remain in that relationship or marriage for the sake of convention. A choice like that could cause you to feel depressed and withdrawn for years. Know when to stay and when to move on.

Also, the ultimate sign of love from you is when you allow your lover full and unrestricted access to your home and financial assets. You are careful about financial expenditures and will enjoy a partner more when you can trust them to stay within the bounds of what you, as a couple, can realistically afford. And while sometimes, your partner has to make the first move, once you are sure they have the qualities you have been looking for, you will devote your time and emotions to stabilizing the relationship into a solid marriage.

Taurus is a traditional sign and when it comes to marriage, you have dependable and old-fashioned values. Trusting someone enough to let them make a home in your heart is scary business for you, so once you have made a choice, you will stay with one partner for a long time. The late Ronald Reagan once wrote his wife Nancy a particularly beautiful love letter on the occasion of their thirty-first wedding anniversary, in which he told her: *"I told you once*

that it was like an adolescent's dream of what marriage should be like. That has-
n't changed. You know I love the ranch but these last two days made it plain I only
love it when you are there. When you aren't there I'm no place, just lost in time &
space. I more than love you, I'm not whole without you. You are life itself to me.
When you are gone, I'm waiting for you to return so I can start living again." Mr.
Reagan's Moon sign was Taurus.

You know you've found your soul mate when you can sit next to your lover for
hours and not utter a word. You don't have to. But you know your relationship
has entered the higher realms of communication between lovers when this
happens. Taurus feels everything acutely. Words have become superfluous.
Your internal rhythms have finally synchronized. That's true love, Taurus
Moon style.

10 specific traits that a man with the Moon in Taurus looks for in a lover

He wants a lover who:
1. Is all natural, dresses casually and is not excessively talkative
2. Respects his need for routine and order in certain parts of his life
3. Appreciates spending time in the wilds of nature like he does
4. Is cautious about money matters and spends wisely
5. Spends time with her friends but never divulges any of his personal secrets
   to them
6. Understands the secret and spiritual nature of monogamy
7. Places him above all other family members
8. Treats him with sensitivity and appreciates his tender side
9. Never pushes him to decide things when he is not ready
10. Will never shout at him or issue ultimatums (they never work on a Taurus
    Moon lover, but kindness always does)

**10 specific traits that a woman with the Moon in Taurus looks
for in a lover**

She wants a lover who:
1. Is financially stable and actively stays out of debt
2. Is careful with his money and hers, and will not become a financial burden
   on her
3. Is respectful toward those whom she idolizes (her family, parents, role mod-
   els)
4. Has a traditional but dependable side
5. Loves being in nature and uses that time to strengthen their bond

6. Will let her take her time and make important relationship decisions
7. Is not excessively talkative but comfortable with silence and peace
8. Understands her need for trust and true monogamy within their relationship
9. Places her above all other family members and respects her as much as he loves her
10. Will never issue ultimatums to get his way (they never work on a Taurus Moon lover, but tact and patience always do)

Find Your Perfect Moon Sign Love Match

If you have a Taurus Moon sign, you will attract lovers who will have either the Sun, Moon or Rising sign in these earth and water signs: **Taurus, Virgo, Capricorn, Cancer, Scorpio and Pisces.**

If you have a Taurus Moon sign, you can still have a good relationship with a lover whose Sun, Moon or Rising sign is in the following fire and air signs: **Aries, Leo, Sagittarius, Gemini, Libra and Aquarius**. It might take adjustments, but it will be worth it!

Celebrities with the Moon in Taurus: Mother Teresa, Sir Edmund Hillary, Bill Clinton, Jesse Jackson, Gregory Peck, Faith Hill, Jim Morrison, Bob Dylan, Lucy Liu, Christina Aguilera, Charles Bronson, Carl Jung, Matt Dillon, Ronald Reagan, Demi Moore, Galen Rowell (rock climber and photographer), Dean Potter (speed climber), Katherine Hepburn, Loretta Lynn, Elton John, Dr. Phil and Cameron Diaz.

Chapter 3

The Gemini Moon Lover

Ruler: Mercury
Element: Air
Quality: Mutable
Symbol: The Twins

"Maybe he believes me, maybe not.
Maybe I can marry him, maybe not.
Maybe the wind on the prairie,
The wind on the sea, maybe,
Somebody, somewhere, maybe can tell.
I will lay my head on his shoulder
And when he asks me I will say yes,
Maybe."
~ Carl Sandburg

Ah, the beautifully perplexing duality of the sign of the twins. Put together the brilliance of Issac Asimov (author of *I, Robot*, a moving story about positronic robots), the crazy genius of Jim Carrey, the grace of Fred Astaire, the agility of martial artist Jet Li and you have before you the fascinating Gemini Moon male. Gemini (the sign of the jokester, the mimic and teacher) is a mutable sign, which means that it can adapt to any person, experience or situation more easily than the fixed (Taurus, Leo, Scorpio, Aquarius), or cardinal (Aries, Cancer, Libra, Capricorn) signs. It can also change positions back just as quickly, therefore this Moon sign's lesson to learn is constancy.

The fascinating and dual natured (Gemini is the sign of the celestial twins) Gemini Moon personality is divided into two separate, versions. The first type of Gemini Moon personality is the *serious type* and the second is the *fun-loving type*. The serious type is mature, ambitious, organized, yearns to reach the top of their profession and will express its dominant leadership characteristics in love relationships. The second type of Gemini Moon personality is the fun-loving type; mental stimulation is crucial to them (boredom makes them irritable), this type is not as methodical as the serious type of Gemini Moon person, and may tend to scatter their energies easily. While they may lack the goal-oriented temperament of the serious type, they may be just as assertive and dominant in relationships or friendships. Both types must watch a tendency toward bossiness and learn to give other, gentler personalities an equal chance to voice their opinions (Mercury, the planet that rules speech, makes Gemini Moon people talkative and expressive). The fun-loving type will excel in the fields of stand up comedy, salesmanship, writing or teaching. Which one seems like a better match with your personality?

Let's take another look at the magic of this Moon sign. If your Moon is in the third sign of voluble Gemini, you have a flexible and easy-going temperament and are also a natural collector or processor of information on a variety of topics and in different formats. Like the other air signs of Aquarius and Libra, you love communication, and there is great appreciation in your heart for the written and spoken arts. You can also be moody like the Cancer Moon person, but it will alternate very quickly with cheerfulness. You have an irrepressible curiosity about life and the next adventure that may be headed your way. There is a restlessness about you that is very easy to spot, and usually the entire focus of your life lies outside of the home sector.

Your bright spirit and enthusiasm draws lovers to you, making them want to be a part of anything you deem worthwhile. You, the other hand, are attracted to lovers who can walk into a room, wake everyone up and shake things up a bit. Sigmund Freud had a Gemini Moon sign and he once stated that: *"Love and work are the cornerstones of our humanness."* As a Gemini Moon person, you are hungry to read and write books, and you want to understand the world around you, quickly absorbing all the impulses you receive from it. You are an erudite mixture of the legendary roaming tradesman of Samarkand, the traveling messenger of medieval Europe or the clever newsman on CNN. Ever observant, you eagerly lap up new bits of information and store them away for future reference in your mind.

What are Gemini Moon females like? Some of the world's most amazing women have Gemini as their Moon sign. Imagine the evergreen vivacity of Goldie Hawn, the chic appeal of Brooke Shields, the desire and drive of aviation pioneer Amelia Earhart, the brooding and hypnotic beauty of Jennifer Connelly and you have created the unforgettable, multi-talented Gemini Moon woman.

Forever questioning the *why* of things, Gemini Moon folks ask hundreds of questions and expect a hundred correct answers instantly. You want to be able to grasp any chain of thought, so that somewhere down the line you can use it to get along with any person from any walk of life. The idea is to be everyone's pal, but sometimes also actively keep people from getting too close too quickly. Ever sensitive to your environment and the art of perfect timing, the moment has to be just right for you, no matter what you're doing.

The transfer and translation of ideas lie in the domain of Mercury, the planet which rules your Moon sign. Experimental and exploratory by nature, the Gemini Moon lover is a raconteur par excellence, and you use speech, the written word and any other communicative medium to zero in on potential partners. You could sell a used car back to a used car salesman and come back with a coupon. So, with such a clever and sharp lover, your partner will have to be quick with words!

Initially, your lover might be very unsure about where you stand, and wonder if you love them, if you want a future with them. The twins are the symbol of this Moon sign and they may *both* decide to talk at the same time, or excitedly say two totally different things. But your lover shouldn't despair, gregarious as you are, you will probably tell them yourself how you feel about them. You may need to learn to be selective about how much information you give out, but you're sweetly romantic in your own special way too.

If you have a Gemini Moon sign, the influence of Gemini's ruler, Mercury, lends you a healthy interest in people, the latest news, debates, literature, art, music and particularly travel. Anything new and untried will instantly draw your attention. The words *actively versatile* describe you well, and rapid communication plays a very big role in your relationships. Movement and the cognitive act are governed by Mercury, as is speed. You bond through frequent and energetic exchanges of information and, a partner who understands this will be most loved by you. You experience an emotional release through frequent communication that you cannot through anything else. Your cell phone and your car are the two most important objects in your life; if they malfunction, it could send you into quite a frenzy.

The desire to communicate, no matter what one's life condition, is evidenced by the passion and dedication of one blind teacher who, thankfully for the world, had a Gemini Moon sign. There was a time long ago, when most people had given up on blind people ever learning to read. But there are many ways to read; the eyes are not the only tools. A small French boy named Louis

Braille thought he could make a difference and he earned a lot of good karma by doing so.

Blind due to an eye accident from the tender age of three, Louis was an intense little boy and really wanted to read. Even though, according to the world at that time, the joys of literature, poetry and other communicative mediums were denied him, he was convinced that he could bring this gift to blind people everywhere by creating the language of Braille. A true educator and inspiring communicator, he is the best example of the mental acuity and inventiveness of this Moon sign placement. Taking communication between vision-impaired human beings to a whole new level, this is just the kind of thing to expect with from a man with a Gemini Moon who could see into the future of human communication. He symbolizes the best attributes of this Moon placement.

When it comes to Gemini Moon folks being in love, there are two kinds of partners that find their way into your life. One is the quiet type who is comfortable in letting you take in the lead, *("I know you how you like Chinese food, honey, we'll go to that place on the corner that you like."* a timid lover might acquiesce), while the other is just expressive and assertive as you are, and may clash with you when you butt heads on certain issues *("Chinese food again? But I'm in the mood for Mexican food. Get in the car and we'll go get some tacos!"* an outspoken mate might say). Being listened to secretly thrills you and you love an audience, but if your lover is just as opinionated as you, it could get interesting in a hurry on the home front.

There will be debates and a healthy exchange of viewpoints between you and your lover, but that is all it should remain – a debate. If it gets out of hand, it might adversely affect your love relationship. Quick-witted and very easily pushed into boredom, you like to surround yourself with intelligent people who speak their mind and love to share information on everything from politics, free speech (truly your domain), religion, women's rights, men's rights and even the most taboo of subjects. Verbally clever, you love it when you are able to say anything without getting into trouble, especially around your partner. It is important for your lover to never judge your chosen philosophy in life, because criticizing that would be a vicarious criticism of you.

If your partner understands this, your relationship will proceed smoothly. You are mentally the most active sign, and it is very difficult for you to tune out this raucous world and relax. Intellectual by nature (the mental energy you give off is electric) you find it preferable to be around people from whom you can acquire information you can use and quickly apply to your life (teaching may also draw you.) This is good in a social sense, but it is these very people who will not see the more emotional side of you. No one emotion will ever control your thinking for too long and you will only show your tender, sensitive side to those who can be trusted to keep your secrets.

One of the best ways to bond with you is to make you laugh. The Moon sign of Gemini responds quickly and earnestly to anyone who is willing to look a little silly and make you break out in uncontrollable laughter. Humor is the key to opening the path toward a lover noticing you and walking up to you to make an introduction. You are assertive and attracted to happiness and merriment, so if your lover is a natural jokester or a comedian, they will earn extra points for this.

In love, you are quick to spot a potential partner and may try to speed the relationship up to your level of comfort (Mercury rules speed and rapid movement). You need a sense of mental stimulation almost constantly but being slightly nervous by temperament, will also need to have your own space. Partnering with someone who needs to be near their lover all the time and needs assurances of love frequently will drive you up the wall (excessive closeness causes a strange confusion in you), causing you to abruptly end the relationship before it even gets off the ground. You have a fear of your lover restricting your every movement and need someone who will not interfere with your need to frequently reinvent yourself. You might like to find someone who is independent as well as comfortable with closeness at intervals.

Cerebral as you are, your partner should know that you can be quite irritable or moody sometimes, and to leave you alone and give you some personal space when that occurs. This is due to the influence of the changeability of the Moon when filtered through the nervous, high-strung energy of Mercury. If your partner can take the many fluctuations of your temperament in their stride, it will be a wonderful relationship. A practical, responsible life partner, who is good at financial management and planning for the future would be a gift to you. You are changeable by temperament, and your lover should anticipate these shifts beforehand, and always keep the doors of communication open with you.

If you're a Gemini Moon person who is reading this chapter and wondering, *"What is Vera talking about? This Gemini Moon sign description doesn't fit me at all! I'm actually kind of shy and I hate standing up before a crowd to give a speech"*, you're probably a more toned-down, refined and introverted version of the aggressive and energetic Gemini Moon personality. When the energy of the soft-natured and changeable Moon mingles with the dominant and non-stop-go energy of Mercury, the result is a person who mirrors *either* the Moon part of this combination or the Mercury part.

The Moon is cool (focused on feelings, emotional, easily inspired or easily offended) while Mercury is super-charged and fast (assertive, restless to the extreme, focused on instant gratification and susceptible to believing rumors). Mercury can make you aggressive, bold and ambitious, while the Moon softens up any hard edges in your persona. If you're a more mellow Gemini Moon person, you will draw toward yourself lovers who are more take-charge and outgoing than you are. They may unconsciously try to bring you out of your shell and bring you face to face with the more spirited side of your nature. You may be a quiet, slightly emotional but thoughtful blend of the lyrical Moon and gregarious Mercury, embodying the best of both energies, giving you a personality that is either supportive or support-seeking.

As efficient multi-level communicators, this Moon sign is so communication-oriented, that even dreams can be used as communication tools between lovers. You know that you've found your soul mate when you both end up saying the same thing at the same time, or end up completing each other's sentences for one another. When both you and your lover secretly pick the same city to visit for your honeymoon, or end up buying the same book for each other, you've made a connection that is deep and significant. That's true love, Gemini Moon style.

10 specific traits that a man with the Moon in Gemini looks for in a lover

He wants a lover who:
1. Is highly communicative and curious about life
2. Is emotionally independent and can enjoy closeness as well as autonomy
3. Will understand his many fluctuating moods and know that each is temporary
4. Allows him to structure his life on his own terms
5. Gives him the gift of freely traveling or living on his own sometimes
6. Never tries force him into any routine at home
7. Understands his nervousness as a natural part of him
8. Will never judge his many friends or prevent him from interacting with them
9. Is familiar with his restless side but does not try to change him
10. Loves books, keeps up with the latest news and enjoys travel and an active social life

10 specific traits that a woman with the Moon in Gemini looks for in a lover

She wants a lover who:
1. Will not restrict her from expressing herself in any way
2. Lets her travel on her own or sometimes live by herself if she seeks solitude
3. Is careful about his finances and doesn't make decisions without consulting her
4. Is a well-rounded and well-traveled intellectual by temperament
5. Will not over-dramatize the relationship to get her attention
6. Is not too emotional or unreasonably suspicious about her male friends
7. Gives her the personal freedom she needs pursue her own goals
8. Respects her well-developed intelligence without patronizing her
9. Will adapt to her restlessness without trying to curb it
10. Is a good and interesting conversationalist and loves to travel

Find Your Perfect Moon Sign Love Match

If you have a Gemini Moon sign, you will attract lovers who have either the Sun, Moon or Rising sign in these air and fire signs: **Gemini, Libra, Aquarius, Aries, Leo and Sagittarius.**

If you have a Gemini Moon sign, you can still have a good relationship with a lover whose Sun, Moon or Rising sign is in the following earth and water signs: **Taurus, Virgo, Capricorn, Cancer, Scorpio and Pisces**. It might take adjustments, but it will be worth it!

Celebrities with the Moon in Gemini: John Kerry, John Edwards, Barack Obama, Sigmund Freud, Issac Asimov, Dr. Homi Kaikobad (master acupuncturist), Louis Braille, Dr. Nguyen Van Nghi (master acupuncturist), Amelia Earhart, Fred Astaire, Jim Carrey, Brooke Shields, Goldie Hawn, Mollie Sugden (Mrs. Slocombe on *Are You Being Served?*), Johannes Kepler (German author, astronomer, astrologer), Jet Li, Jackie Chan, Joe Lieberman, Kylie Minogue and Jennifer Connelly.

Chapter 4

The Cancer Moon Lover

Ruler: the Moon
Element: Water
Quality: Cardinal
Symbol: The Crab

"Because of this, love, tie me to a purer motion,
to the constancy that beats in your chest
with the wings of a swan underwater,
so that our sleep might answer all the sky's
starry questions with a single key,
with a single door the shadows had closed."
~ Pablo Neruda, (Poet with a Cancer Moon sign)

An enviably acute sense of perception is synonymous with the Moon in Cancer, as is a natural intuition about life and human nature. Blend together the lyricism of Willie Nelson, the masculinity of Harrison Ford, the humor of Mike Myers and the mysticism of Padre Pio, and you have before you the amazing Cancer Moon personality.

The Moon is at home in the fourth sign of Cancer and if this is your Moon sign, your personality will fall into one of two, signature Cancer Moon personality types. The first type of Cancer Moon personality is the *careerist type* and the second is the *nurturing type*. If you're like the nurturing type of Cancer Moon personality, part of you may be very concerned with the emotional relationships between people, and the effects of timely supporting and bonding. This special kind of supporting has many applications in the overall life of a Cancer Moon person, who can be either too dependent on a lover (for example, fearful or unable to function if their partner is not near them), or too worried about their welfare (like a mother would possessively worry about her baby).

The careerist type is a well-balanced version of the Cancer Moon personality and strikes a balance between caring for their lover and giving their lover lots of space, while retaining plenty of emotional space for themselves too, so that their professional goals don't suffer. The careerist type will spend more time finding their niche in the professional sphere and will derive great satisfaction from success while the nurturing type will derive the majority of satisfaction in life from a happy, supportive and loving family and relationship environment. Which one of these two Cancer Moon personalities is a match with you? Let's investigate further.

Cancer, the fourth sign, governs fertility, our past, the mother figure, our home, our basic life foundations and the automatic patterns of our early emotional conditioning. It also rules our ability to *feel* as well as our tendency to *fear* extreme tenderness between two people. The Moon in Cancer asks you, *"What is your deepest, unspoken need?"* or, *"What is your biggest fear in life?"* Functioning under the direct influence of the faraway but influential Moon, Cancer as a Moon sign may sometimes leave you emotionally wide open, which often makes you vulnerable.

If this is your Moon sign, there is a refined gentility about you, whether you are a male or female. Cancer is magnificently maternal in its most important relationships, which means that your natural reaction in most situations is to walk in, sympathize and clean up the mess other people make. This could be a major reason that people might take advantage of you, but you usually don't find out their motives until much later. When the time comes for them to return the favor, you may find that there is no reciprocity at all. A flood of emotions can blind you to reality, as can placing your trust in the wrong person at the wrong time.

You are very likely to need the emotional support system of at least one strong female (symbolically, the Moon which resonates to the female vibration) in your life, regardless of your gender. This could also be a non-aggressive male who is more like a mother figure, who is caring and nurturing toward you. More likely than other signs to stay in a debilitating relationship, family or marriage, or stay due to the children (or a pronounced sense of responsibility), you tend to hold on with a super-tight grip when it comes to what you want, and will fight to protect the rights of those whom you choose to love. Therefore, the best way to love you is to understand the magical patterns of your moods. And to do so, we must find out what makes you feel secure, and can gently bring your guard down.

No doubt you've heard about how the intuitionist Cancer Moon sign is moody and emotional. Your moods act in perfect rhythm with the phases of the Moon, and many times they may even react to other people's emotions as they respond to the lunar phases. This would create a clashing of the Moon's fantastical energies through different people. In love, you crave security in both its tangible (a secure home, a stable job, a regular income) as well as intangible (the unconditional love of your family and spouse, and supportive friends) forms. Indeed, this reflects in a very accurate way, how you see the world and what you want it to be. You want that rock-solid support system to always be there, as it may be the one thing that you tend to count on, no matter what other life-changes come your way.

So, what are female Cancer Moon personalities like? They are attractive and magnetic. Hollywood legend Cyd Charrise, the evergreen Suzanne Somers, the talented Aretha Franklin and the delicately beautiful Drew Barrymore exude the Cancer Moon essence. Whether it's a job, your beloved, your home, your friends and your belongings; you get attached very easily. The world tells you to analyze while your heart urges you to *feel*. Sometimes you will be attracted to people who are as detached toward you, as you are emotional about them. The more closeness you desire from them, the more space they will create between themselves and you. Ever had that perplexing experience, dear Cancer Moon reader?

Lovers like that may have their own emotional issues and can shatter your fragile calm, make you withdraw into your emotional shell and prevent you from opening your heart when the right person comes along. Both you and your partner have lessons to learn from one another. You have to learn to depend on your intellect more than your heart, while your partner must learn to trust their emotions more than their mind, as only then would you reach a common platform on which to communicate and take your love to the next level of true intimacy.

Let's discuss this further. You function from a primeval base of raw feelings and reactions and this may sometimes cause you to be misunderstood. While you can't change what you feel (and you shouldn't have to), you can understand it by looking at it from a different viewpoint. Your emotions (a certain wait-and-see, overly careful attitude or a tendency to care particularly when it is not appreciated) help you protect yourself, but can also cause you to sink into melancholia or become confused. An overload of emotions or fear can debilitate you and defeat you, blurring your path ahead. Go ahead and be supportive and protective of others. But be supportive and protective toward yourself first, only then can you be of help to others.

You are drawn to music and nature because the rhythms of sound and the rhythms of nature reflect the age old and ever dependable phases of the Moon, with which you have a very close tie. Tears (another form of the mighty oceans) are cathartic for you and may be an easy way to cleanse your heart of unpleasant daily interactions, or even some temporary confusion caused by an insensitive lover. Therefore, you must choose a partner who understands your emotional make-up and won't make demands on you to "*Stop being so emotional all time*". This would be highly dishonoring of you. You must have the freedom to weep when you want, enjoy your solitude and enjoy your personal space in any way you wish. Process and release what you feel and your natural equilibrium will return.

You have a deep recognition of the healing attributes of always being in touch your feelings and while you must never lose that, you might want to also try to let things go once in a while. It is hard for you to forgive and impossible for you to forget (your Moon sign is strongly memory-oriented), but this might help you more than you know. You can also exhibit a very strong possessiveness that could disrupt a perfectly good relationship, and may even interfere with your connection to your children, who may try to leave home and begin their lives while you try to find ways of delaying this eventual departure. A fear of being abandoned may lie at the heart of your reactions.

Your Moon position indicates that you are at your best when in a loving and undeniably secure marriage or relationship, where your loyalty and caring nature can take flight without interruption or excessive criticism. Companionship will be extremely vital in stabilizing your moods when you enter into your golden years. Being all alone, when you are in your seventies might prove too traumatic for your delicate emotions. Not that you are frail and can't manage life alone (you are far stronger than most Moon signs), but that it will be more pleasant for you if you can age with a partner who is gentle, kind and emotionally secure themselves. Unspoken reciprocity and security are the two things that you desire the most from your lover. You have an unutterable inner yearning to have someone *match* your incredible intuitionism.

You know you've found your true soul mate when they can tell what your reaction will be to a certain person or memory without your having to mention it. They will run to protect you, care for you and shield you from hearing hurtful words. They are sensitive to you, and your comfort-level is paramount to them and for once, you get to be pampered and told how much you are loved and valued. They will also stand up and tell you to your face when you are being too emotional about too inconsequential a matter.

Your true soul companion is fearless and lets your authentic emotions play themselves out on the chess board of life without interfering with them, and that's when you know that your journey to find your life partner has not been in vain. You finally found the one who is a perfect blend of stability and quiet wisdom. And you will love them back with a heart as pure as that pale, white orb, standing quietly in the night sky for millions of years. No questions asked. This is true love, Cancer Moon style.

10 specific traits that a man with the Moon in Cancer looks for in a lover

He wants a lover who:
1. Understands that he is deeply emotional but does not mention it
2. Will not suppress his moody spells but lets him ride them out on his own timetable
3. Does not have insecurity issues and can exist on her own should he need space
4. Respects his love of his family, his past (or culture) and his mother
5. Provides him with the kind of emotional security that never wavers
6. Understands that his need to collect things (even money) is a self-protective, emotional reaction
7. Will not use his sensitivity against him, no matter what the dispute
8. Encourages him to express himself, especially through humor or comedy
9. Always sides with him in any argument with another person, places him above her family
10. Knows about his imaginative side and helps him express it using art, music or writing

10 specific traits that a woman with the Moon in Cancer looks for in a lover

She wants a lover who:
1. Can calm her fears, even if he doesn't understand what triggered them
2. Can financially protect her and support her (and extend that support to her offspring)
3. Will show gratitude if she financially protects and supports him
4. Will respect her need for tenderness and emotional closeness
5. Helps her express her artistic, musical and imaginative side
6. Understands her moods and gives her the time and space to process them
7. Regularly and verbally appreciates the things she does for the relationship or family
8. Understands the connection between her need to mother her lover and her self-esteem

9. Encourages her to be fearlessly bold in any situation
10. Won't confuse her need for emotional proximity with physical proximity

Find Your Perfect Moon Sign Love Match

If you have a Cancer Moon sign, you will attract lovers who will have either the Sun, Moon or Rising sign in these water and earth signs: **Cancer, Scorpio Pisces, Taurus, Virgo and Capricorn.**

If you have a Cancer Moon sign, you can still have a good relationship with a lover whose Sun, Moon or Rising sign is in the following fire and air signs: **Aries, Leo, Sagittarius, Gemini, Libra, Aquarius**. It might take adjustments, but it will be worth it!

Celebrities with the Moon in Cancer: William Blake, Franklin Delano Roosevelt, Theodore Roosevelt, Willie Nelson, Aretha Franklin, Drew Barrymore, Eminem, Adam Sandler, Suzanne Somers, Cyd Charisse, Mary Todd Lincoln, Harrison Ford, Kurt Cobain, Condoleezza Rice, Mike Myers, Paul Petzoldt (mountaineer), Cecil John Rhodes, and Padre Pio (saint).

Chapter 5

The Leo Moon Lover

Ruler: The Sun
Element: Fire
Quality: Fixed
Symbol: The Lion

"My eyes no longer seek,
I am courageous,
no more meek. Daring lion,
far from weak,
Shine like Venus celestial."

~ Rumi

Very few can resist falling for the charms of a person with a Leo Moon sign. Combine the steely charisma of Clint Eastwood, with the spirituality of Mahatma Gandhi, the boyish good looks of Tom Cruise with the sensitivity of Keanu Reeves and you have created the magical Leo Moon persona. If your Moon sign is Leo, you are a true champagne-and-roses romantic and thoroughly enjoy being in a mutually satisfying relationship. Leo has the distinction of being the sign that rules the human heart! Romance, fun, risk-taking and having children come under the rulership of the fifth sign of Leo, and a Leo Moon person will take a romantic risk any day. You have a big heart and love is truly the elixir of life for you.

The Leo Moon personality is divided into two, separate versions. Let's see which one resonates more with your personality. The first one is the *lion type* of Leo Moon personality while the second is the *cub type*. The lion type is ambitious, dominant and charismatic, while the cub type is creative, emotional and non-aggressive. The cub type personality seeks out harmonic relationships and intimacy, and fares best with assertive lovers while the lion type needs to be with partners who will not challenge their authority or try to dominate them. Let's take an in-depth look at the overall nature of this Moon sign.

If you have a Leo Moon, you find it hard to be without a partner to love for too long. Coupling is natural for you and you thrive best when you're the center of your lover's world. Leo Moon folks also have a wonderfully unique sense of humor. This brings to mind a particularly hilarious quote by the lion type, Leo Moon politician Winston Churchill: *"Never hold discussions with the monkey when the organ grinder is in the room."* If this is your Moon sign, you are a happy, sunny personality who loves a good-looking life-partner on your arm, enjoys a quick repartee and revels in an evening full of joyous entertaining.

It's easy to fall under your love spell; your grand fire sign enthusiasm is so contagious! Mix up the sensuous voice of the legendary Barbra Streisand and the impishness of Renee Zellweger, with the exquisite balance of rock climber Lynn Hill and the comedic charm of Queen Latifah, and you have created the unforgettable Leo Moon woman. Women with this Moon placement are ambitious, passionate, love to be complimented and noticed, especially by the opposite sex. If you love a Leo Moon woman, make sure she can see that you have exquisite taste! She is discriminating and only expects the best from a lover. She's worth it and she knows it.

If you have a Leo Moon sign, you can make your partner feel as though they are the only worthwhile thing in your life. You fill them with a sense of euphoria and excitement that other signs cannot match. A romantic traditionalist, no one has to teach you to remember anniversaries, bring flowers, write love notes and remember your lover's birthday or the day you first met. If you are a male with the Moon in Leo, the ladies will give you extra points for important courtesies such as these.

No matter how old you get, you will always be an incorrigible romantic at heart. One thing you might like to watch out for when in love, is the pressure to marry a partner whom you have not fully tested out yet. The impulse to get to the alter and say your vows, as well as the attraction of post-marital bliss may stand in the way of your making a decision based on fact, logic and reason. What place does reason have in matters of the heart? Well, it may mean a lot when it comes to giving your heart away to the wrong person and having to live with the consequences (financial and emotional) for years to come.

For a trusting and eager Leo Moon person, there is always the risk of a partner taking advantage of your good nature (especially your tendency to lavish money and gifts on your love object, which makes them think that you have an inexhaustible supply of wealth). You are advised to take marriage more seriously than you take romance and love, and to always wait before rushing toward matrimony. If you're in love with the right person, it won't matter how long you wait. But if you're with the wrong one, a little time may bring to light any unsuitable qualities in your partner that you may have previously missed.

Being a true fire Moon sign, you may sometimes display that famous temper of yours. But as is the case with other fiery Moon signs (Aries, Sagittarius), it dissipates just as soon as its first appearance. You really can't remain annoyed with anyone forever, that's the beauty of your open heart and your ability to forgive quickly (although you must be appealed to in the right way). Freedom warrior Mahatma Gandhi, who had a Leo Moon sign, once eloquently said that: *"The weak can never forgive. Forgiveness is the attribute of the strong."* Trust, faith and a desire to see the good side of human nature is a profound part of your noble Leo Moon persona. How endearing is a lover who forgives easily? Why, extremely endearing! You won't want to hold that destructive tension in your heart, when you'd rather hold someone else's heart within your own.

You attract attention easily (can the Sun ever hide in the sky? The Sun rules your Leo Moon sign) and may find yourself in professions or vocations where you have to be front and center a lot, thus putting you squarely in the path of potential lovers who want to be seen with you. Ambitious and ever eager to prove your mettle to a cynical world that thinks you can't succeed, you will need the faith and support of a solid, faithful partner who can withstand the highs and lows of your professional endeavors with you.

Also, you will need a spouse or partner who will not mind you getting more attention than them. If your partner is resentful about this factor, it could create problems revolving around pride and control. Leo is a dominant sign and you may unconsciously take control of the relationship without asking your partner for any input. As goes the age-old adage, two dominant people cannot make a relationship work without at least one of them learning the invaluable art of compromise. Asking your mate for their opinion would be a step in the right direction, and this courtesy will go a long way in strengthening your bond.

You have a very deep-seated need to be evaluated, accepted and admired by your peers. Your natural self-confidence is charming (and *very* attractive to the opposite sex) but if it ever gets out of hand, it could be seen as conceit or self-absorption. A proud Leo Moon mate? No way! Well, actually a mate who knows the difference between pride and self-confidence will win on all fronts. And you do like to win.

If you're a typical Leo Moon person (or the lion type Leo Moon personality), non-combative, accommodating and easy-going partners are usually best for you, so that you can shine in front of the world and still have the love of your life standing next to you. Of all the signs, you in particular hope to be able to grow old with your soul mate. Stable companionship is crucial to getting the most out of life for you, and you really do prefer having your lover right next to you when you turn seventy-two and cut the birthday cake. Leo Moon folks never remain single for long, there will always be someone waiting in the wings to be noticed by you. Be tender, dear Leo Moon. You're in demand!

You know you've found the soul mate of your dreams when they get a chance to be center stage or strike it rich, and they give it up to be near you instead. When your lover does something touchingly sweet for you, especially at great personal cost to themselves, your enormous Leo Moon heart bursts open its great gates and floods your beloved with appreciation. As I mentioned above, Leo rules the human heart. And when the Leo Moon person wants to show their beloved how much they are appreciated, it is an amazing thing to watch. If your lover is selfless, you will mirror that in exactitude. If they show compassion, you will respond in kind. This produces in you the kind of emotion that has inspired hauntingly beautiful poetry throughout the ages. That's true love, Leo Moon style.

10 specific traits that a man with the Moon in Leo looks for in a lover

He wants a lover who:
1. Is loyal, faithful and optimistic even in the face of adversity
2. Takes the time to look physically attractive when they are seen together in public
3. Understands that his temper quickly dissolves over the slightest act of kindness
4. Will not compete with him and will spend his money wisely
5. Joins him in his eager pursuit of romance, excitement and fun
6. Comprehends his desire to be respected and accepted in the eyes of his male peers
7. Understands his secret desire to take risks
8. Will place her love for him above all other relatives
9. Will not over-dramatize the relationship to get his attention
10. Is firm in what she wants and what she will put up with, as Leo Moon males are attracted to beautiful but no-nonsense women who expect only the best behavior from a lover

10 specific traits that a woman with the Moon in Leo looks for in a lover

She wants a lover who:
1. Takes the time to look handsome and well-groomed when they are seen together in public
2. Has a strong, forceful personality she can respect, but is not overbearing
3. Lives by a strict honor code and is a thorough gentleman with good manners
4. Is wise and balanced in his judgments
5. Respects women and will not be domineering toward his lover
6. Will place his love for her above everyone else
7. Understands her need for faithfulness and will keep former lovers at a strict distance
8. Will never stand in the way of her personal ambition or desire for independent success
9. Appreciates her intensity in matters of the heart
10. Will respectfully let *her* decide when she wants to become a mother and raise a family with him

Find Your Perfect Moon Sign Love Match

If you have a Leo Moon sign, you will attract lovers who have either the Sun, Moon or Rising sign in these fire and air signs: **Aries, Leo, Sagittarius, Gemini, Libra and Aquarius.**

If you have a Leo Moon sign, you can still have a good relationship with a lover whose Sun, Moon or Rising sign is in the following earth and water signs: **Taurus, Virgo, Capricorn, Cancer, Scorpio and Pisces.** It might take adjustments, but it will be worth it!

Celebrities with the Moon in Leo: Mahatma Gandhi, Ansel Adams, Oscar Wilde, Walt Whitman, Paul McCartney, Keanu Reeves, Zubin Mehta, Renee Zellweger, Queen Latifah, Clint Eastwood, Carlos Santana, Gloria Steinem, Tom Hanks, Lynn Hill (rock climber), Dale Earnhardt Jr., Barbra Streisand, Winston Churchill and Tom Cruise.

Chapter 6

The Virgo Moon Lover

Ruler: Mercury
Element: Earth
Quality: Mutable
Symbol: The Virgin

"But this, in which there is no I or you,
so intimate that your hand upon my chest is my hand,
so intimate that when I fall asleep it is your eyes that close."
~ Pablo Neruda

The attention and consideration that a Virgo Moon lover showers on a lover can be hard to resist. Combine the inventive genius of Alexander Graham Bell, with the personal magnetism of Sean Connery, the poetry of Robert Frost and the emotional strength of Lance Armstrong, and you have before you the enigmatic Virgo Moon persona. Fastidious and brainy, Virgo Moon people are a usually delight to have a relationship with.

If you want your partner to be attentive, honest and have a sense of order to their lives, a lover with a Virgo Moon sign will seal the deal. Lovers who are flighty and lack focus or direction in life will be attracted to your grounded, let's-get-this-show-on-the-road persona. Relationships are somewhat of an enigma to practical-minded Virgo Moon folks, who usually place other important responsibilities in life over falling head over heels and pondering the mysteries of romance. *"Falling in love sounds nice, but I need to get on my feet first and finish my degree (or buy a house, or make sure the business succeeds), otherwise I won't be able to give my lover the time they need."* the Virgo Moon lover reasons.

It should be mentioned, however, that there are two distinct types of the Virgo Moon persona. The first is the *organizer type*, which is the true, traditional prototype of the Virgo Moon essence. This type is meticulous, clever and is visibly horrified by a messy home, dirty fingernails, an un-ironed shirt collar or a cluttered kitchen sink. They tend to dress well, are extremely goal-oriented, perfectly groomed and never late for an appointment or date. Particularly careful about their diet and personal hygiene, any disturbance in their family environment or at work will send them running to the medicine cabinet, hurriedly searching for that all important bottle of anti-acid. This type is famous for spending time vacuuming their car's carpets on the weekends and running up their charge cards at the bookstore. Virgo Moon people *love* books and music!

The second type of Virgo Moon person is the *easy-going type*. Indeed, you might be surprised if you entered their homes, as it may not look like the proverbial neat and tidy a-place-for-everything-and-everything-in-its-place Virgo abode. This type of Virgo Moon person somehow has difficulty in properly coordinating their life and therefore may be forever trying to catch up with the world. They may have many unfinished goals and may be careless about how they look in public. Important papers may lie scattered around their homes and they may have trouble find anything on time. *"Oh, I'll get to it when I get to it!"*, they explain. So, which type of Virgo Moon sign resonates better with you? Both exist, although the second type is more rare than the first, and both may be of a highly intellectual bent of mind.

Unlike the romantic Pisces, Cancer or Taurus Moon person who thinks love is what they should build their life around, as a work-is-worship Virgo Moon lover, you will think that anything that brings to the fore the more complicated, emotional issues of life, can wait until later. While you may be curious about love, you may delay falling in love, or you may desire what is known in Astrology as passionate chastity or a chaste passion. You can, in some cases, go without expressing your sensual side for long periods of time, and this may be because you will mistrust any emotion that brings you to the brink of losing control or making a mistake.

This changes once you find a loving partner who has proven their devotion to you over time, and who does not fear commitment like it was the Bubonic plague. If a partner refuses to commit to you but says they love you all the time, you are likely to get suspicious. *"If he can't commit now, how well will he commit after we're married? If he's not responsible now, how responsible will he be after we have a family of our own?"* the cautious Virgo Moon female wonders.

Once you have committed your heart to that one special person and have entered into the calm waters of a trusted partnership with your spouse, you can be as passionate as any other sign. No sign has a monopoly over the true expression of passion. And you can rival the Scorpio Sun or Moon person when it comes to being passionate. The only requirement is that your lover inspires in you an unspoken, unshakeable trust that will last a lifetime. You are highly analytical and detail-oriented, so if your partner is sloppy and lazy, you're looking at a quick hello and a quicker goodbye. A considerate, loving and cool-tempered partner, who understands your need to organize your life carefully, will bring out your romantic side and allow you to, at least once in a blue moon, throw caution the winds and let cupid take over.

Morph together the golden voice of Emmylou Harris, with the energy and ambition of Madonna, the intensity of Jodie Foster with the ethereal beauty of Michelle Pfeiffer and voila! Standing before you is the quintessential Virgo Moon lady. These women are expressive and sensuous, as well as very success-ful in their chosen fields. The Virgo Moon woman has often been accused of being a 'nag' to her partner. It should be said in her defense that in the begin-ning, she will always try to broach the subject with tact and diplomacy.

If this polite request is continually ignored, then she may take to repeating her requests over and over until they are heard. Generally, there is always a good reason for any request made by this Moon placement. Any person a Virgo Moon lover picks to spend their life with better be ready to be there for a life-time. Virgo is earthy and the earth is ancient. A Virgo Moon lover will be more eager than any other Moon sign to actively work to resolve any relationship problems and prevent clashes from occurring, which is excellent for the future health of the union.

It is also worth noting that as a Virgo Moon person, you will more often than not, attract or be attracted to partners who go all out emotionally when in love. Your partner will be able to do everything that you cannot: they will cry easily, they will perhaps use an element of drama to attract your attention (should you begin to lose yourself in work and neglect the relationship) and generally be able to be more free in letting it all hang out emotionally.

You have a veritable dread of emotional outbursts and dramatic scenes, and would prefer that these private issues be sorted out behind closed doors in soft whispers where the neighbors won't know that you're engaging in a full out 'couple's cat fight'. *"Why can't you control yourself? Why can't we discuss this at home?"* a Virgo Moon lover questions their partner. *"Why can't you express your love for me more openly? So what if people can hear us. I don't care!"* your partner shouts back.

In most cases, your partner was attracted to you because you truly have every-thing they dream of in a lover: you are true to your word, you're a good provider and supporter, you are not fussy about romance (but may be fussy about other things) and you are a calm and gentle partner, whose most prized quality is that they are there with a solid support system when things go terribly wrong. The best thing would be for you to find a partner who is just as poised and graceful in a crisis as you are, but can also bring out in you a sense of fun and ease without it letting it get out of hand.

You are careful about money, so your partner shouldn't spend unwisely, mismanage household funds and give you a panic attack every time the first of the month draws near. You like a clean house, so your lover shouldn't create an atmosphere of untidiness where you can't even think properly, because a home in constant disarray will affect your nerves and your digestive system (the digestive tract is ruled by Virgo). And most of all, they should accept you as you are without trying to overtly change you. You are an excellent choice for anyone who wants a no-nonsense, clean-cut, conventional relationship created within traditional gender roles.

Virgo is the sixth sign of service, hygiene, health and work. And more often than not, a person with the Moon in this sign will assume all responsibility for keeping the relationship afloat and making sure that the house is run efficiently. While it is good to serve your partner or relationship, be sure that you are not being made to do more than is fair. This sign is very likely to fall victim to a person who will use love (or an illness or frailty, as Virgo rules health) in order to control you and subtly use your kindness against you, all the while sweet-talking you into believing everything. Anyone with the Moon in Virgo is also highly deductive by nature and will quickly notice it if their lover is taking them for granted, but due to your earthy, stable nature, getting you to take some action and do something about it will take time.

Yes, you might be picky and yes, you might be seen as too critical at times. But then you are mercilessly critical of yourself too. Your lover should know that your need to point out things is not personal, but your way of *perfecting* your lover or the relationship. Perfection itself can be misleading and cause you to forget to celebrate the humanity and naturalness in people. For you, order and structure sometimes precede passion and merriment. Your guard won't go down until the last bill is paid and the last chore is completed to your complete satisfaction.

When it comes to settling down permanently, you like to have a predictable marriage so that each partner can weather any storm together and not have to face sudden disruptions in your love life. You provide a happy and stable marriage and in today's world, with a record high divorce rate, which person wouldn't appreciate that? No one likes to become a tragic statistic and bonding with you can usually assure that. You are an intellectual with a heart of gold and any person would be fortunate to have you in their life. You will make some adjustments in your personality (even if it is hard) if your lover has most of the qualities you want in a life-partner.

You know you've found the love of your life when your partner adjusts their habits according to your desires. This usually means doing certain things around the house (Virgo rules humble service, so there should be fairness in who does which chore, Virgo Moons shouldn't get stuck holding the vacuum cleaner all the time) or following certain rules that you yourself follow. It may be something as small and insignificant as turning off the lights in a room they're not using or not cutting their fingernails at the dinner table.

Detail-oriented Virgo Moon people will notice this extra effort; they never miss a thing. You're not a demanding lover (in fact you may tolerate more of your partner's idiosyncrasies than anyone should be allowed to), but organization and discipline somehow make you breathe easier. And anyone who truly loves you will not mind going that extra mile for you. Isn't that what all, true soul mates will obligingly do for each other?

Virgo is an earth sign, and your commitment to your relationship is rock-solid. So, when you find that your lover has gone beyond what was necessary to please you, it makes you feel the one emotion that is more important to you than all else: to be *appreciated*. Extremely devoted once you pledge your love, Virgo Moon people quickly respond to the slightest kindness, especially from lovers. This kindness (particularly if unexpected) brings out in you that passion some Astrologers always seem to think the quiet, introverted Virgo Moon mate is incapable of. And yet, it's real, it's palpable and it's always been there. Your devotion is as true, as pure and perfect as your beating heart. That's true love, Virgo Moon style.

10 specific traits that a man with the Moon in Virgo looks for in a lover

He wants a lover who:
1. Is frugal with money and resources and tries not to be an impulse shopper
2. Has simple tastes and is not a loud, aggressive personality
3. Loves books, music, art, literature and any other communicative medium
4. Will not take his criticism to heart
5. Never takes advantage of his ability to be a good, dependable provider
6. Will frequently and verbally appreciate what he does for her (this bolsters his self-esteem)
7. Will stand by him proudly even if he becomes a poor man
8. Understands his need for order, organization and cleanliness

9. Won't bicker with him in public or in front of family/friends
10. Respects his need for privacy and won't share his personal secrets with even the closest of her friends

10 specific traits that a woman with the Moon in Virgo looks for in a lover

She wants a lover who:
1. Is well-groomed and dresses simply but smartly in public
2. Is careful with finances, wise about expenditures and plans ahead for that rainy day
3. Is honest about his past and very committed to their future together
4. Understands and encourages her strong intellectual, artistic side (must love books!)
5. Will be discreet about their private life in front of family or strangers
6. Maintains clean personal habits and is hard-working
7. Frequently and verbally appreciates what she does for him, the house and the relationship
8. Will not become a burden on her financially for a prolonged period of time
9. Knows that she may sometimes hold back her feelings, but agrees to work through any impending emotional gridlock together
10. Handles emotionally charged issues with calmness and grace instead of hysterically

Find Your Perfect Moon Sign Love Match

If you have a Virgo Moon sign, you will attract lovers who will have either the Sun, Moon or Rising sign in these earth and water signs: **Taurus, Virgo, Capricorn, Cancer, Scorpio and Pisces.**

If you have a Virgo Moon sign, you can still have a good relationship with a lover whose Sun, Moon or Rising sign is in the following fire and air signs: **Aries, Leo, Sagittarius, Gemini, Libra and Aquarius.** It might take adjustments, but it will be worth it!

Celebrities with the Moon in Virgo: John F. Kennedy, Robert Frost, Lance Armstrong, Sean Connery, Gabriel Garcia Marquez, Michelle Pfeiffer, Bill Cosby, Courteney Cox, Raquel Welch, Jodie Foster, Madonna, John Travolta, Alexander Graham Bell (inventor), Emmylou Harris, the Dalai Lama, Wolf Blitzer (CNN anchorman), Mary Kate and Ashley Olsen, Robert Redford.

Chapter 7

The Libra Moon Lover

Ruler: Venus
Element: Air
Quality: Cardinal
Symbol: The Scales of Justice

"i carry your heart with me (i carry it in my heart)
i am never without it, anywhere i go you go, my dear;
and whatever is done by only me is your doing."

~ e. e. cummings (Libra Poet)

What happens when you blend together the faith and physical strength of mountaineer Erik Weihenmayer, with the intensity of Mel Gibson and Nicholas Cage, and the literary superpower of writer Agatha Christie? You get that elusive brains-and-brawn combination that is typical of the Libra Moon personality. Libra is the seventh sign of marriage and love relationships. As a Libra Moon person, you have a desire for harmonious and smooth-flowing relationships and tend to attract opportunities for love relationships more easily than other signs.

Venus' gift you as a Libra Moon person, is that you understand at a profoundly deep level, the true meaning of sharing your life with another human being, as well as the inevitable and sometimes uncomfortable compromises that go along with it. Like the other airy Moon signs of Gemini and Aquarius, you love books and revel in the literary arts.

The Libra Moon essence is embodied in women like the beautiful country music superstar Shania Twain, and literary mega-giants such as poetess Elizabeth Barrett Browning, author Jane Austen and the world famous mystery writer Agatha Christie. The latter three Libra Moon women have revolutionized the world of writing. Libra Moon people *love* books!

As a Libra Moon person, you are flirtatious and highly sensitive to attention from the opposite sex, and it is easy to catch you trying out your charms on any willing prospect. Not that you're seriously pursuing them, but this is your way of feeling attractive. If your love object gets too serious too soon (which is understandable, given the amount of attention you shower them with) you are likely to backtrack and make a run for it. When younger, you may chase elusive romance more than actually building a mature, adult relationship.

It should be mentioned for the sake of clarity that there are two distinct versions of the Libra Moon personality. One is the *marriage type* or more common kind of Libra Moon person, who, beginning at a very young age, is very interested in having and maintaining love relationships. They will make their relationship the focal point of their life, usually with such concentration that no other interests can provide a contrast to it. This kind of Libra Moon person, while sincerely devoted to their partner, will say things like *"Oh, I'd simply die if my lover wasn't with me!"* or *"I don't know if I could go on without him, he's my whole life"*. The slightest rejection from a partner will send them into panic mode.

The other type is the more intellectual Libra Moon person, the *thinker type*, who is more emotionally balanced than the marriage type of Libra Moon personality, and expresses detached, air sign tendencies in relationships, and may even choose to spend more time honing their intellectual talents instead of pursuing romance and neglecting their artistic and literary side. The artist or writer in them has to come out before the lover in them can be awakened, which is the key to relating to them. Intellectual relationships will make them very happy until the time has come to begin the search for an attractive lover.

The marriage type of Libra Moon person may spend a great part of their life thinking about finding that one person who will be their marriage mate, while the thinker type will devote more time to finding ways to bring forth all their mental energy in the form of writing or creativity. Both make flexible and accommodating life-mates once the knot is legally tied.

Let's delve deeper into the more common, marriage type of Libra Moon person. If this is your Moon sign, as a young person, you may have naively viewed marriage or relationships a sort of permanently blissful state of being, something that you could happily look forward to during young adulthood. But as you age and mature, you will realize that there are two important aspects of love that you must appreciate before you jump into the wild and crazy world of dating and relationships.

The first aspect of love is that you must first build a relationship with *yourself* from the ground up. Know who you are, know what you love and know what to leave alone. If you have low self-esteem, you must fortify it before falling in love. The second aspect is to build a relationship with the concept of love itself. Put aside what the media has taught you about romantic love for a moment. You may be impressionable about romance and love and may unconsciously take on qualities that don't suit you, in order to make your partner feel content and secure. This might cost you in the future, when you meet a potential partner who wants to love the authentic you but finds that this part of you doesn't exist anymore.

Ever the romantic integrator, Libra Moon folks can be very accommodating and can spin a whole new world into existence just to make their lover feel enthralled. Being in love is pretty heady stuff. But be mindful of the fact that perfect relationships do not exist. Many can come close, but very few are without flaws. You may be more attracted to the newness of romance than the actual act of looking for a life partner and then sticking to one lover, while letting your connection gradually progress toward a marriage.

You can coordinate your personality to effortlessly blend with your lover's. And while this makes you a highly desirable spouse, it must serve a purpose. You desire the total package when in love, and often your lover can supply some but not all the qualities you desire. The benefit of having the Moon in Libra is that it gives you the ability to be an excellent judge of fairness in a relationship. Your equality-radar quickly senses when your lover is not being fair to you (Libra rules the scales of justice, if one side dips, Libra is on alert). While you may be deeply in love, you can also tell when your relationship ceases to be an equal exchange of love.

You can sense this change even if it is to an imperceptible degree. This is both a blessing and a curse, because you will often see the end of a weak relationship approaching before your lover does. Use this wisdom wisely. You are naturally averse to completely terminating connections to lovers, which is in natural accordance with the wishes of Venus, the Goddess of harmonizing and blending many discordant energies into one. As the sign of the diplomat and negotiator, Libra produces a natural sense of balance in you and keeping everything on an equal footing is important to you.

Venus makes the Libra Moon person a social all-rounder, with a malleability of temperament that can forge a bond with the toughest opponent. If you are male, you will be influenced by Venus through your likes and dislikes and your overall personality. Women will enjoy being around you and will feel as though only you can appreciate their femininity. You will have excellent taste and will instinctively know what behavior women like and what they abhor.

If you are female, you will come across as smart and refined. Beware of being too 'nice', though. If you have to sound assertive once in a while to make an important point with an aggressive person, don't be shy about it. People will recover. But you will never recover if you give up your viewpoint all the time just to keep the peace. In the end, you'll feel like you lost your own voice.

The influence of charming Venus (the traditional Goddess of love and beauty) increases if you are a female with the Moon in Libra, producing a doubly feminine effect in your personality. While both the male and female Libra Moon folks are easy to fall in love with, they must watch out for a desire to fall in love too quickly. Once again, envision the scales of Libra and know that balance is important. Venus is an eternal matchmaker and does not like to see people in the single state (maybe she needs to spend some time with lone ranger Uranus! Uranus protects his autonomy like we watch over our wallets in a crowded mall). She'd much rather match up the most compatible lovers so that they can begin the process of falling in love and experiencing passion and getting married. Such is the highly integrative nature of Lady Venus.

As a person with a Libra Moon sign, you will usually have more than one love partner to choose from and this is why you must choose wisely. Just because there are potential lovers available to have relationships with, doesn't mean that you begin one out of sheer boredom. Libra marries for the long haul, so that another dream may come true: retiring with your soul mate. Also, you may have trouble deciding on which lover to finally pick. Too much fence sitting might cause your lover to give up on you and walk away. Be firm in making decisions and stick to the outcome.

Your desire for growing old with your partner, as you both age together and experience maturity together, becomes more important as you enter your forties and fifties. You will look for someone who is willing to walk through to the end of life as a unit, so that each is there for the other and neither will have to pass away alone in some cold, dark hospital room. As a romantic Libra Moon person, you look for a lover you can *realistically* live with. A well-read, articulate and physically graceful lover might tempt you.

You know you've found your true soul mate when your beloved does those little things that make a Libra Moon person's eyes brighten like stars. Hey, Lady Venus herself is watching, isn't she? Little, romantic formalities are of great significance to her. Your Venus-stamped and approved lover is courteous, sensitive and gallant (if male), even-tempered, delicate and feminine (if female), and understands the mystical relationship between secret love notes, wild, blooming roses and the haunting sound of rain falling on distant mountains. This is true love, Libra Moon style.

10 specific traits that a man with the Moon in Libra looks for in a lover

He wants a lover who:
1. Appreciates his considerate, relationship-oriented nature
2. Reciprocates promptly when he goes out of his way to do something nice for her
3. Is both feminine and fun-loving, as well as a solid intellectual
4. Will not press him to start a family until he is emotionally ready
5. Is fair-minded and gives him as much freedom as she needs herself
6. Maintains herself physically; he loves going out and being seen with a beautiful woman
7. Will not use drama to attract his attention and is emotionally secure
8. Will remain emotionally balanced and easy-going in the face of life's many changes
9. Will join him in actively avoiding emotional gridlock in the relationship
10. Is very communicative, social and enjoys travel, music, art and writing

10 specific traits that a woman with the Moon in Libra looks for in a lover

She wants a lover who:
1. Is a gentleman and well-versed in the subtle courtesies of romance
2. Maintains himself physically, works out and is never a couch potato
3. Loves books, is fond of poetry, music and is of a literary bent of mind
4. Is erudite and cultured as well as sentimental like she is
5. Will not pressure her to enter motherhood if she is not ready
6. Values the purity of a relationship once it turns into a marriage
7. Is willing to adjust to her periodic need for solitude
8. Is not jealous, possessive and judgmental about her friends and family
9. Encourages her carefree side
10. Allows her the freedom she needs to live her life and make her own decisions

Find Your Perfect Moon Sign Love Match

If you have a Libra Moon sign, you will attract lovers who have either the Sun, Moon or Rising sign in these air and fire signs: **Gemini, Libra, Aquarius, Aries, Leo and Sagittarius.**

If you have a Libra Moon sign, you can still have a good relationship with a lover whose Sun, Moon or Rising sign is in the following earth and water signs: **Taurus, Virgo, Capricorn, Cancer, Scorpio and Pisces**. It might take adjustments, but it will be worth it!

Celebrities with the Moon in Libra: Erik Weihenmayer (mountaineer), Emily Dickinson (American poet), Agatha Christie, Jane Austen, Elizabeth Barrett Browning, Edouard Manet, Oliver Wendell Holmes, Reinhold Messner (mountaineer), Brett Favre, Mel Gibson, Bruce Springsteen, Nicholas Cage, Ted Turner, George Bush Sr., George Bush, Ray Charles, Deepak Chopra, Kid Rock, Shania Twain, Nikola Tesla, Leonardo DiCaprio and Ashton Kutcher.

Chapter 8

The Scorpio Moon Lover

Ruler: Pluto
Element: Water
Quality: Fixed
Symbol: The Scorpion

"I don't love you as if you were the salt-rose, topaz
or arrow of carnations that propagate fire:
I love you as certain dark things are loved,
secretly, between the shadow and the soul."
~ Pablo Neruda

Weave together the imaginative genius of director Steven Spielberg, with the sensitivity of actor Jude Law, the passion of martial artist Bruce Lee with the charisma of Nelson Mandela, and you have created the charismatic Scorpio Moon persona. This is one of the most enigmatic placements for the Moon in your natal chart. The eighth sign conceals a great many mysteries; mysteries that revolve around complicated subjects like psychology, danger, regeneration, death, rebirth and human sexuality.

The Scorpio Moon personality is divided into two, specific personality types. The first type is the *ambitious type* and the second type is the *passionate type*. The ambitious type devotes their energies toward rising up in the world of professional prestige while the passionate type derives a large part of their fulfillment in life through love relationships, close friendships, happy, stable marriages and nurturing their families. Both types are private, secretive and dominant; they fall into the role of relationship manager very easily and usually, voluntarily. Which personality type fits you best? Let's analyze this Moon sign in greater detail.

If your Moon sign is Scorpio, you have a handful of close confidants (Scorpio always has confidants, friendship alone is not deep enough) with whom you can safely bare your soul. The sophisticated Scorpio Moon personality advances by the careful retention of secrets, information and volcanic energy, which is almost always fiercely internalized. The Scorpio Moon person's motto in life is envision and master.

You are usually in full control of your emotions and will not break under pressure. You keep secrets as well as know the secrets of others. Secrets often have a way of finding you, almost as though they trust you to keep them protected. The Scorpio Moon personality can wear two masks. One is worn for intimates whom you trust and one is worn to protect yourself from the 'riff raff' that you think makes up this crazy world. There is no such thing as a superficial Scorpio Moon person.

Refined, eloquent and deeply emotional, your sensitivity is evident in your likes and dislikes. A woman with a Scorpio Moon will automatically know the inner musings of her lover at any given time. Bring together the legendary beauty of violet-eyed screen legend Elizabeth Taylor, the perfectly graceful movements of rock climber Steph Davis, with the sensuous appeal of Elizabeth Hurley and the dedication of anchorwoman Christiane Amanpour, and you have before you the unforgettable Scorpio Moon lady.

Your partner in life should not be afraid of the rawness of authentic human emotion, and should know when to be near you and when to offer you space to think. Every Scorpio Moon person will need lots of space in order to process feelings and impressions and for that, you crave the refreshing nature of solitude. Scorpio is the sign of the brilliant psychologist who reads people like we read the sports section in the newspaper. If you pick a friend, you will pick them for life and expect that same loyalty back. This can give others some idea of how seriously you take relationships.

In love, a certain rock-solid stability is sought out by most Scorpio Moon lovers and that is often the first step toward building a solid relationship with you: your lover must be dependable without a shadow of a doubt. (If you love a Scorpio Moon person, get ready to be tested at every turn until your intense Scorpio Moon lover is absolutely positive that you are worth spending time and effort on.) Reliable and somewhat moody, you have a tendency to get yourself into situations where you end up bringing out the most extreme emotions in lovers.

Any lover who is light-hearted about love, thinks love is synonymous with casual fun and believes in promiscuity disguised as free love, will find themselves out of your life in an instant. And you never look back. You are usually profoundly monogamous, perhaps because you understand the spiritual aspects of how human sexuality blends with the subtle emotional regeneration of a person. You do not take human intimacy lightly. You expect perfect monogamy from your partner and unless you get it, they will never feel the legendary passion of the Scorpio Moon sign.

Generic horoscopes describe Scorpio as a highly sexual sign. This is incorrect because any sign can be sexual, but not every sign can grasp the unseen, karmic nature of the most intimate interactions between two human beings. One can be sexual without being sensual, but only a well-balanced Scorpio Moon person can be an authentic combination of both sexuality and sensuality. Sagacious Scorpio, as the eighth sign, rules money and any financial assets held jointly by a couple. So, serious financial discussions are a given in any relationship with a Scorpio Moon lover.

At some point or the other, the conversation will turn toward merging the bank accounts of two people into one, and allowing your lover access to all your assets. This is when the real test of your love relationship begins. Weak, immature relationships will bend, crumble and fall to the dust under the tension created by feelings of mistrust and suspicion. When you finally allow your lover full access to your credit cards and checkbooks, they know they have been accepted by you on a very intimate level. You want your lover to be frugal, be honest to the bone and extremely up front about any and everything they spend with your money, and if this occurs, the bond will solidify.

As a Scorpio Moon person, you know you've found your soul mate when your interactions over money or any jointly shared assets flow smoothly and without doubt. And particularly, when you know that the one you love will never taint the purity of your relationship by betraying you in any way. When blind trust takes the place of even the slightest suspicion in your relationship, its time to accept that the journey you set out on a long time ago, has finally ended: you found that one jewel of a person who places you above all else and would give up the world for you. When faced with rare devotion such as that, a Scorpio Moon lover will draw out every treasure out from inside the immeasurable earth and lay them at their lover's feet. The devotion they receive will be offered back ten times more intensely. That's true love, Scorpio Moon style.

10 specific traits that a man with the Moon in Scorpio looks for in a lover

He wants a lover who:
1. Is intense about life and people and is emotionally vibrant
2. Understands his slightly moody nature without trying to change him
3. Looks for a deep meaning in all her interactions

4. Comprehends the difference between sexuality and sensuality
5. Is monogamous and loyal
6. Spends money (especially his) wisely and is practical
7. Is respectful of him even if there is a disagreement
8. Respects his need for privacy and voluntarily keeps her former lovers at bay
9. Places her love for him above all other relationships in her life
10. Is deeply spiritual and wise as a life-partner

10 specific traits that a woman with the Moon in Scorpio looks for in a lover

She wants a lover who:
1. Is dependable and keeps true to his word even in the face of any major life changes
2. Understands and never mocks her sensitivity
3. Is not afraid of human emotions and their true expression
4. Is careful about the management of his finances as well as hers
5. Looks for true commitment in life and is not secretive
6. Will not use her emotions against her
7. Is even-tempered and easy to communicate with
8. Is willing to keep all his former lovers at a strict distance
9. Will place his love for her above all the other relationships in his life
10. Is well-mannered, kind and an intellectual (poetry, literature, music, art or nature lover)

Find Your Perfect Moon Sign Love Match

If you have a Scorpio Moon sign, you will attract lovers who will have either the Sun, Moon or Rising sign in these water and earth signs: **Cancer, Scorpio, Pisces, Taurus, Virgo and Capricorn.**

If you have a Scorpio Moon sign, you can still have a good relationship with a lover whose Sun, Moon or Rising sign is in the following fire and air signs: **Aries, Leo, Sagittarius, Gemini, Libra and Aquarius.** It might take adjustments, but it will be worth it!

Celebrities with the Moon in Scorpio: Nelson Mandela, Jude Law, Bruce Lee, Ben Affleck, Will Smith, Steven Spielberg, Bono, Elizabeth Taylor, Harry Truman, Meher Baba, Elizabeth Hurley, Alanis Morrisette, Viktor Yushchenko, Charlie Chaplin, Steph Davis (rock climber and mountaineer), Bob Marley, Judy Woodruff, Christiane Amanpour and Jimmy Carter.

Chapter 9

The Sagittarius Moon Lover

Ruler: Jupiter
Element: Fire
Quality: Mutable
Symbol: The Centaur

"I've got an arrow here,
Loving the hand that sent it
I, the dart revere
Fell, they say, in 'skirmish'
Vanquished, my soul will know
By but an arrow
Sped by an archer's bow."
~Emily Dickinson (Sagittarius Poet)

What happens when your lover becomes a philosopher, and a philosopher becomes your lover? Why, only good things, of course! Add together the ambition of Tiger Woods, the sheer genius of Mozart and Beethoven, with the intellect of Charles Dickens and the good looks of Richard Gere and presto! You've just conjured up the magnetic Sagittarius Moon male. If your Moon sign is Sagittarius, you are independent, openhearted and can adjust yourself to any type of lover. Sagittarius is a mutable sign, therefore it is easy for you to modulate your flexible personality and make your partner feel truly appreciated.

There are two, fascinating types of the Sagittarius Moon personality, which one represents you best? The first is the *sage type* while the second is the *adventurer type*. The sage type is wise, tolerant and has a professor-like quality about them. This type is intriguing because they thirst to drink in the knowledge of life; one is more likely to find this type at the library, thumbing through ancient texts at three in the morning, than at the dance club. The sage type adjusts well to the stability required in marriage and commitment, but will always place intellectual pursuits and personal freedom above all else.

The second type of Sagittarius Moon lover is the adventurer type. This type is humorous and easy to talk to, as well as extremely restless and is happiest while embracing risk. Hungering for adventure, the thrill of sport and new, exciting relationships, the adventurer type will love to travel and be free of responsibilities that don't make any sense to their view of life. Both the sage type and adventurer type of Sagittarius Moon personality are assertive and will tend to fall easily into the role of relationship manager. Let's take a deeper look at this Moon sign.

Like other fiery Moon signs (Aries and Leo), your enthusiasm for life's richest experiences is endearing. You are our cultural broker and our facile foreign ambassador. Sagittarius is connected to the ninth sector in Astrology, which rules ethics, law, foreign travel, justice, foreigners, languages, higher learning, philosophy and religion. If your Moon sign is Sagittarius, you will have many friends from all walks of life, especially people from foreign nations.

Always au fait on the latest news, you enjoy learning different, often exotic or extinct languages and travel around the world meeting intriguing people with whom you have absolutely nothing in common. Variety is the spice of life! Ever adaptable, you can dine with a king in the afternoon and break bread with a pauper at dinnertime without judging either. Your mind is pure and free of the ugliness of gender differences, racism or class bias.

When it comes to love, you are a lot like your fiery Moon sign counterparts (Aries Moon and Leo Moon), in that you end up in relationships where your lover sometimes becomes too attached to you too soon. While you're getting ready to finally confer upon them, the truly heartfelt title of close friend (Sagittarius Moon people take friendships more seriously than relationships because they often last longer and are less demanding), your partner will be getting ready to do some serious bouquet-tossing. Mind your head and be ready to duck if you're not ready, dear Sagittarius Moon! You function best when your potential partner gives you enough time to decide for yourself how you want your relationship to progress.

Be clear about what you want from a partner before things get serious. Sage type Sagittarius poet, Rainer Maria Rilke beautifully described how this fiery Moon sign looks upon the magic of human partnering: *"Once the realization is accepted that even between the closest human beings, infinite distances continue, a wonderful living side by side can grow, if they succeed in loving the distance between them, which makes it possible for each to see the other whole against the sky."*

Some of the most intelligent and attractive women have Sagittarius as their Moon sign. Incorporate the business savvy and vision of Oprah Winfrey, with the fragile beauty of Nicole Kidman, the trendy chic of Jennifer Anniston with the business genius of domestic diva Martha Stewart, and you have the Sagittarian Moon total-package female. Victor Hugo, a sage type of Sagittarius Moon personality, once said mysteriously that: *"When a woman is speaking to you, listen to what she is saying with her eyes."*

Women who have the ninth sign as their Moon sign are cheerful and intelligent life-companions who will want to be full and equal partners in their marriage or relationship, and will want a fair say in everything. Ever-mindful of the equality factor (Sagittarius rules law), they will choose a wise as well as light-hearted lover who is, as Jack London once put it, "temperamentally large" so that they can understand each other at a vast and expansive level.

Sagittarius makes for a versatile Moon sign, which means that you can take in a truly panoramic view of life, and all its multitudinous experiences much more easily than other, more rigid, routine-oriented signs. Born with a teacher's heart and a student's eagerness, you are the zodiac family's most beloved raconteur. Happy, positive personalities when in the public eye (attention and admiration from peers brightens your spirit like nothing else can and helps you feel like a vital part of the world community), you may also go through some blue spells privately. True to the style of Jupiter (the ruler of your Moon sign), if you're happy, you'll be euphoric, and if you're down in the dumps, it will be hard to drag you out of bed in the morning.

When you're blue, you're going to need a careful mixture of lots of TLC and lots of space from your lover. It is worthwhile to be mindful of what Jupiter can do to your emotions. You may fall in love at first sight and declare your love in an instant, and also get up the next day, and be face to face with the daunting task of having to slow down the relationship considerably before it heats up and burns out too quickly. Jupiter likes to make you jump in do things super-fast, and then just as quickly, make you rethink your strategy.

When the energy of the soft-natured and changeable Moon mixes with the let's-rock-n-roll energy of big, old Jupiter, the result is a person who feels each emotion in a big way. The giant planet Jupiter magnifies the emotion derived from each experience three times over. Each emotion is felt in an enormous, all-consuming wave. Why? Well, Jupiter just happens to be the largest planet in our solar system.

So when its time to declare your love, a little patience could save you a cartload of trouble, particularly if your partner is of a more emotional and sentimental variety. You are advised to take marriage more seriously then you take romance and love, and like other fiery Moon signs (Aries, Leo) to always wait before rushing toward matrimony. If you're in love with the right person, it won't matter how long you wait. But if you're with the wrong one, a little time may bring to light any unsuitable qualities in your partner that you may have previously missed.

Whether you're a typical Sagittarius Moon personality or a more introverted version of it, you are usually attracted to lovers who are both bookish and athletic, and while you enjoy dating a variety of wonderful and interesting people, your final choice in picking a marriage partner will be someone who understands your secret religious side. Surprised? Sagittarius rules the ninth house of religion and philosophy in astrological natal charts. So, some people with this Moon placement will have a very phase-oriented relationship with religion. They will go through times when they are very drawn to the scripture and ceremony aspect of religion, and then undergo a phase when they have a more, free flowing spiritual rather than religious bent of mind. Either way, you will always want to be connected to that age-old mystery that blends belief with mysticism.

No matter what your basic philosophy, your partner will sometimes have to be the stabilizing force in your life. Like all fiery Moon signs, you are young at heart. Your life partner should bring to the table all the qualities that you lack, but not be so different from you that you have nothing in common to chuckle about when you're both old and gray. Friendship will play a great part in picking a partner with whom to grow old, and if that friendship (more than passion or love) can be maintained, you will be more content in your golden years.

You know you've found your soul mate when you can open your heart in front of them and not be judged, but simply accepted with an equally open heart. You are honest about falling in or out of love at any given time of the day. This is because you know a great and powerful truth about love, which is that no person can remain in love twenty-four hours a day, nor can they remain out of it twenty-four hours day. Love is a beautiful but mysterious butterfly with its own moods and fancies, and it likes to come and go, fly in and fly out on its own, deciding its chosen course without considering other practical or societal factors.

World famous composer Beethoven, who had a Sagittarius Moon sign, once wrote an exquisitely beautiful love letter to someone he called his "immortal beloved". Let's take a peak into how this Moon sign expresses love: *"My angel, my all, my very self...If we were wholly united you would feel the pain of it as little as I! We shall surely see each other...ah! There are moments when I feel that*

speech is nothing after all, cheer up, remain my true, only treasure, my all as I am
yours; the Gods must send us the rest, that which shall be best for us."

You know that realistically, storybook love doesn't exist, but what does exist is
an ongoing and sacred friendship between two honest people who understand
that no one mood is constant and that human nature is a constantly evolving
entity. You understand that one can only experience true love when it is given
freely, *without reserve* and received freely, *without doubt*, like the wild winds
that roam the earth just before a magnificent lightning storm. For you,
authentic love is infused with raw freedom; the freedom to love, the freedom
to roam, and the freedom to return without judgment. That's true love, Sagittarius Moon style.

10 specific traits that a man with the Moon in Sagittarius looks for in a lover

He wants a lover who:
1. Is open-minded and prejudice free
2. Respects his need for freedom in all aspects of life
3. Will not try to change him or criticize his experimental attitude about life
4. Knows when to offer help and when to let it be requested (she shouldn't mother him)
5. Has an independent life of her own apart from her life with him
6. Is not clingy or excessively emotional and forgives easily
7. Will be open to adjusting to an unconventional relationship/marriage
8. Is health-conscious and physically fit
9. Will not issue ultimatums to get her way
10. Won't pressure him into becoming a father if he is not emotionally ready for it

10 specific traits that a woman with the Moon in Sagittarius looks for in a lover

She wants a lover who:
1. Is cultured, well traveled and is a citizen of the world in spirit
2. Respects her need for freedom in all aspects of her life
3. Is open-hearted, easy-going and forgives easily
4. Will not try to change her to make his own life easy
5. Takes care of his physique and works out to stay fit
6. Will not jump in and try to rescue her (she's tough and perfectly capable)
7. Is not jealous or suspicious of her male friends

8. Will not push her into a traditional family role before she is ready to accept it
9. Encourages her intellectual side
10. Is willing to talk through any problem that could lead them into occasional emotional gridlock

Find Your Perfect Moon Sign Love Match

If you have a Sagittarius Moon sign, you will attract lovers who have either the Sun, Moon or Rising sign in these fire and air signs: **Aries, Leo, Sagittarius, Gemini, Libra and Aquarius.**

If you have a Sagittarius Moon sign, you can still have a good relationship with a lover whose Sun, Moon or Rising sign is in the following earth and water signs: **Taurus, Virgo, Capricorn, Cancer, Scorpio and Pisces.** It might take adjustments, but it will be worth it!

Celebrities with the Moon in Sagittarius: Tiger Woods, Vincent Van Gogh, Thomas Jefferson, Henri Matisse, Victor Hugo, Micheal Jordan, Oprah Winfrey, Pablo Picasso, Jennifer Anniston, Nicole Kidman, Martha Stewart, Justin Timberlake, Albert Einstein, Donald Trump, Ludwig Van Beethoven, Johannes Brahms, Wolfgang Amadeus Mozart, Mariah Carey, Charles Dickens, Vin Diesel, Thomas Edison and Richard Gere.

Chapter 10

The Capricorn Moon Lover

Ruler: Saturn

Element: Earth

Quality: Cardinal

Symbol: The Mountain Goat

"Love gives naught but itself
and takes naught but from itself.
Love possesses not
nor would it be possessed;
For love is sufficient unto love."
~ Kahlil Gibran (Capricorn Poet)

Imagine a man who has the vision of Charles Darwin, the wisdom of President Abraham Lincoln, the creativity of Frederick Chopin and the good looks of Brad Pitt. Congratulations! You've just created the multifaceted Capricorn Moon male. If you have a Capricorn Moon sign, you're an intense individual and are loved by the planet of wisdom, Saturn. Saturn is seen as a truly powerful force in astrological charts because it rules time itself, as well as the ancient interplay between human karma and human desire.

There are two, specific versions of the amazing Capricorn Moon personality; can you tell which one suits you better? Capricorn Moon partners will either be like the *teacher type* of Capricorn Moon personality, a type that is very assertive, ambitious, protective and will instantly take charge of any love relationship by leading it subtly into the direction of their choosing, or they might be like the more soft-natured, amiable, *follower type* of Capricorn Moon personality, who may still be trying to figure out their role in the world, and will tend to submit to stronger personalities. Let's delve deeper into how this Moon sign approaches life.

When the energy of the soft-natured Moon is blended with the responsible, duty-conscious energy of old Saturn, the result is a person who is very aware of their responsibilities and may be a tad too strict with themselves in life.

Mature and wise beyond your years even as children, love is never casual or *fun* to you because you can often sense the karmic nature of falling love, as well as losing a loved one. Some people with Capricorn laced prominently through their natal charts will have learnt from great personal losses, some of them occurring at an extremely tender age.

These lines from Capricorn poet, Edgar Allen Poe's poem *'Annabel Lee'* are descriptive of Saturn's influence when it inter-mingles with the magic of the Moon*: "But our love was stronger, by far, than the love of those who were older than we, of many far wiser than we..."* Love is often a great spiritual and mystical movement in your life that colors everything it touches, and also creates in you an unspeakable confusion that you can't explain away.

You are attracted to clean-cut, orderly and efficient partners who have a definite plan for where they're going in life. Your search is one of high honor in life and the reason you work so hard, is because you can sense that glittering prize at the end of your journey. You're a cut above the rest, and you know it. A well-groomed, attractive person who is always on time for dates and presents you with tasteful gifts, is someone you identify with and can relax around. Any vagueness or fear of commitment from your partner can make you want to give up altogether. Your partner must use caution and extreme gentleness in handling your particular temperament.

Are you in love with a woman who has a Capricorn Moon sign? Then you should know that Capricorn Moon females are incredible women who combine the leadership ability of world class mountaineer Junko Tabei, the comedic genius of Lucille Ball, with the energy and femininity of Sarah Jessica Parker and the haunting beauty of Kim Basinger. These women are the very best in their fields and have successfully achieved the career goals that were so close to their hearts. Capricorn Moon women need to be proud of their spouses as well as children. Achievement and social acceptance lie close to their hearts.

As a Capricorn Moon person, you take falling in love seriously and hope that you don't have to try too hard to locate a partner who is the best match for your lifestyle and goals. Saturn, the ruler of your Moon sign endows you with an air of dependability, and people tend to trust that you are someone who can fix any problem anytime. Capricorn is a cardinal sign, and leadership abilities powered by a rock-solid willpower are ingrained in your nature.

A good example of the strict resolve that Capricorn Moon people subject themselves to is Junko Tabei, the first woman in the world to summit Mount Everest. She put it this way: *"Technique and ability alone do not get you to the top; it is the willpower that is the most important. This willpower you cannot buy with money or be given by others. It rises from your heart."*

While people place so much confidence in you, you sometimes paradoxically suffer from low self-esteem in private. Saturn (which is a serious planet) brings with it depression or a tendency to be melancholic at various times in your life. Sometimes there is a reason for it (a lover's insensitivity) and sometimes it hits you out of nowhere. There may even be a desire to savor your solitude in perfect silence. Some Capricorn Moon children can be very self-contained and quiet. Abraham Lincoln, who had a Capricorn Moon sign, once said of himself: *"I am rather inclined to silence, and whether that be wise or not, it is at least more unusual nowadays to find a man who can hold his tongue than to find one who cannot."* His legendary melancholia both endeared him to millions and also purified him emotionally.

Therefore, a partner who can gift you some space (physical and emotional) in which to deal with what you are feeling, would be ideal for you. Status plays a big part in how your life unfolds and there is usually a decidedly careerist streak in you. You hope to steadily move upward from that Nissan to a brand new Jag. You're not superficial (in fact, you may be too intense), but these objects are tangible reminders of how hard you worked and how far you've come. In your mind, anything worth doing, is worth doing superbly. What you do in life, what you *become as a result of your actions*, has to mean something.

You like watching successful people and are interested in how they made it to the top. There is a different kind of solace you derive emotionally from being looked up to by your peers, and being the best in your field, that you cannot get from relationships alone. Hard working and conscious of the proper management of resources, you would make an ideal spouse to someone who also dreams of bettering themselves and receiving true respect and acknowledgment from the world. The bottom line is that you admire success and more importantly, idealize it.

Your focus revolves around how to turn that success into *significance*. You understand that a lot of people are rich, but not all rich people have lived lives worthy of respect. Your ideal partner is one who can show you how not to be so serious all the time and can bring out your light-hearted, romantic side. Your love partners will usually be more carefree than you are and maybe even a little careless with money. They say opposites attract and since a Saturn-ruled, Capricorn Moon person is frugal and conserves resources, a partner who is spendthrift will cause you more heartburn than you'd care to admit in public.

A true logistician, you usually put work, ambition and responsibility above other things, but when you meet that one person who makes your heart do cartwheels, you will temporarily try to become like them. But as you get to know them better, your usual, careful self will pop out and try to secretly train your lover for the life that you have planned with them. Your secret motto is *"prepare for the future"*. Be responsible, but also be open to having fun once in a while. The poets are right, romance and love really are things worth enjoying forever. Being more easy-going without giving up your principles will help you bond with your partner, as well as help you achieve the best of both worlds.

You want to build a foundation that is strong enough to last a few lifetimes and most importantly, you want to leave behind a particular accomplishment or legacy that your descendants will be proud of. If both you and your partner understand this and work together toward it, you will feel more peaceful and content about your role in life and your place in this world. Whichever pinnacle you end up reaching in life, your partner will be with you. And as you begin to age, this non-judgmental companionship will be the greatest gift of all to you.

You know you've found your soul mate when your lover knows how seriously you take life, especially your work-life and agrees to work with you instead of complaining about how you're never at home. Saturn is the old timekeeper of the solar system, and strict though he is, he is also extremely mindful of sacrifices and adjustments made in the path of love. Your secret sensitive side responds quickly to a lover who is not combative but accommodating and reasonable. In return, you will give your partner every comfort in life, and a love that is stable and will last a lifetime. That's true love, Capricorn Moon style.

10 specific traits that a man with the Moon in Capricorn looks for in a lover

He wants a lover who:
1. Knows that he will often have to put work ahead of love
2. Will not mistake his involvement in his career for his disinterest in her
3. Learns to anticipate and work with his possible tendency toward depression
4. Allows him time and solitude to process his feelings
5. Appreciates his inclination toward order and structure
6. Recognizes his sweet, tender and privately passionate side
7. Knows that being appreciated by his peers is crucial to his self-esteem
8. Is patient and never verbally combative

9. Is passionate in private but graceful and restrained when in public

10. Remembers that he takes any rejection or loss very hard

10 specific traits that a woman with the Moon in Capricorn looks for in a lover

She wants a lover who:

1. Understands the subtle link between status and self-esteem

2. Is confident and knows where he's headed in life

3. Is strongly success-oriented and wants to accomplish something great in the world

4. Believes in order, propriety and is self-disciplined

5. Places work over wasting time and appreciates her devotion to their relationship

6. Is comfortable with the thought of a long and happy marriage with one woman

7. Is respectful and poised in public but easily expresses passion in private

8. Will be supportive of her, whether she chooses a career or her home as her life-focus

9. Keeps in mind that she does not weather rejection very well

10. Brings out her joyous and fun-loving side more than her duty-conscious side

Find Your Perfect Moon Sign Love Match

If you have a Capricorn Moon sign, you will attract lovers who have either the Sun, Moon or Rising sign in these earth and water signs: **Taurus, Virgo, Capricorn, Cancer, Scorpio and Pisces.**

If you have a Capricorn Moon sign, you can still have a good relationship with a lover whose Sun, Moon or Rising sign is in the following fire and air signs: **Aries, Leo, Sagittarius, Gemini, Libra and Aquarius.** It might take adjustments, but it will be worth it!

Celebrities with the Moon in Capricorn: Abraham Lincoln, George Washington, Indira Gandhi, Charles Darwin, Thomas Paine, Bruce Willis, Reese Witherspoon, Liv Tyler, Kim Basinger, Lucille Ball, Arnold Schwarzenegger, Napoleon Bonaparte, Cher, Junko Tabei (first woman to summit Mt. Everest), Fredrick Chopin, Johnny Depp, Sarah Jessica Parker, Leann Rimes, Matt Damon, Ray Romano, David Letterman and Brad Pitt.

Chapter 11

The Aquarius Moon Lover

Ruler: Uranus

Element: Air

Quality: Fixed

Symbol: The Water- Bearer

"Had I the heavens' embroidered cloths,
Enwrought with golden and silver light,
The blue and the dim and the dark cloths
Of night and light and the half-light,
I would spread the cloths under your feet:
But I, being poor, have only my dreams;
I have spread my dreams under your feet;
Tread softly because you tread on my dreams."
W. B. Yeats (Poet with the Moon in Aquarius)

Morph together the debonair style of Cary Grant, the tanned good looks of George Clooney, with the unforgettable voice of Merle Haggard and the phenomenal imagination of J. R. R. Tolkien, and you have just invented the classic formula for the magnetic Aquarius Moon male. The world is your friend and your friends are your world. If your Moon sign is Aquarius, then your trademark quality is friendliness and a lack of prejudice. Intellectually sensitive Aquarius rules the eleventh sector of friendship and humanity in astrological charts.

The Aquarius Moon personality comes in two, interesting shades; the first type is the *intellectual activist type* while the second is the *social butterfly type*. The first type is intelligent, dominant, charismatic and lives in the world of ideation and sometimes, humanitarianism. The second, social butterfly type of Aquarius Moon lover is fun-loving, less intense, loves mingling with their friends and enjoys a good romance. Freedom is extremely important to both types. Which Aquarius Moon personality suits you better?

Let's take a deeper look into the magic of this Moon sign. You are immune to race, gender and all other types of ugly human biases, which makes you a true citizen of the world. Progressive Aquarius is an air sign and when the Moon is in this sign, it approaches love, romance and intimacy with a strong emphasis on friendship first. In fact, sometimes even you may not be sure if you want your lover to be your friend, or if your friend should also be your lover. Choose wisely, because when two varying personalities match up in the game of love, changes might take you by surprise.

A true cosmopolite, you are an intellectual with a taste for the exotic and rare, and would rather trust the logical impulses of your mind than the muddy waters of your feelings. An over-emotional partner could easily upset the delicate equilibrium of your temperament. Invariably, you will attract lovers who are more involved in the feeling aspects of love, while you dwell more on the analytical and universal aspect of love.

The more mysterious you remain, the more your lovers want to hover near you. J. R. R. Tolkien, an intellectual activist type of Aquarian Moon author, once made the following quizzical but telling statement: *"I'm told I talk in shorthand and then smudge it."* Intense while also practicing firm detachment, you usually will disallow hysteria or drama from interfering with the way you live your life and make important decisions.

When the energy of the soft-natured and changeable Moon is filtered through the erratic and radical energy of the renegade planet Uranus, the result is a person who may sometimes have a tendency to suddenly change their mind about something, and take off on a completely new track. Be that as it may, Uranus is a logical planet. Drawn toward oft-neglected social causes, the words *freedom, equality, humanity, fact, reason, balance* and *brotherhood* resonate deep within your core. Abraham Lincoln, a famous Sun sign Aquarian once said that: *"Passion has helped us; but can do so no more. It will in future be our enemy. Reason, cold, calculating, unimpassioned reason, must furnish all the materials for our future support and defense."* Well said, Mr. President.

You have a prodigious memory, but also get bored easily and may not have the patience for relationships that drain you emotionally more than they excite you mentally. As you age, you will be more successful in picking partners who reflect your core values. You will then feel more confident about your choices in life, and could enjoy a marriage or relationship that lasts decades and will be the envy of all your friends and family.

An equally intellectual partner, who has their own well-structured life, is loyal but can function well independently of you, is ideal for you. There is a middle way and it can bring you that perfect mixture of proximity as well as personal space. An Aquarian Moon lover is answerable to no one, and your lover must accept that from the beginning. Communication will be the thread that strengthens your relationship, so find a partner who can talk about anything, anytime. A ready sense of comedy in your lover would be an added bonus; you have a dry and unique sense of humor and never travel without an extra satire in the trunk of your car.

So, what are Aquarian Moon females like? They are some of the most beautiful and intelligent women in the world. Combine the business savvy of Britney Spears, with the legendary beauty of Marilyn Monroe and the ethereal attractiveness of Uma Thurman and voila! You've just created the alluring Aquarian Moon lady. These women are ambitious, but also free thinkers who little value what society thinks about them. They have lived their lives according to their own desire, and make interesting and vibrant partners who will encourage lovers to also be free in expressing themselves and be particularly proud of their autonomy.

If you have this Moon sign, you are independent and possess an easy-going spirit, but sometimes that produces in you a loneliness that you superbly mask. Surrounding yourself with many people from all walks of life (Aquarius is the sign of universal brotherhood and unity amongst all people) proves healing, at least for a while. Uranus, the ruler of your Moon sign, is a planet of extremes. So, while you may be having fun hanging out with four of your best friends some evening, after a while, you will secretly feel like heading home to healing solitude and relaxing with a favorite book. If, on the other hand, you have spent too many back-to-back days with your lover, it may create a desire in you to balance it out by drifting away for a while. Why? One reason could be that your search is one of balance and authentic experiences of freedom within any one-on-one encounter.

Unless your interactions with the people in your life are spaced out and properly balanced, they may not feel quite as fulfilling. Your style of processing love is complicated and unique and this must be respected and honored. Your lover must allow you to retain all your friendships, and never place any restrictions on you under the guise of love. A lover who uses guilt to keep you bound in an unhappy relationship, will soon find themselves alone. The actions of Uranus are lightning fast but well thought out.

Love and romance are a sweet and tempting enigma to you and the lover you settle down with finally will be as unique a personality as you are. You may choose to be friends with them for a long time before you say *"I do"* because this is your way of making sure that you are not being used by an incompatible lover. When you tie the knot, you will be as surprised as your lover because the desire to merge destinies will come out of nowhere (thanks to Uranus, the planet of sudden, unplanned moves). But the fixity of your Moon sign will ensure that you pick the most emotionally flexible lover within your own age bracket to spend your days with.

When the energy of the passive and changeable Moon mingles with the dominant, bold and renegade energy of Uranus, the result is a person who mirrors *either* the Moon part of this combination or the Uranus part. The Moon is cool (yin, female, emotional and highly responsive), while Uranus is the lone ranger planet that will refuse to follow any leader, preferring to head out into the wilds alone.

Uranus can make you aggressive and actively defiant of society's rules, while the Moon softens up any hard edges in your persona. If you're a more mellow Aquarian Moon person, you will draw toward yourself lovers who are more take-charge and outspoken than you are. They may unconsciously try to bring you out of your shell and bring you face to face with the more spirited side of your nature. You may be a quiet and thoughtful blend of the lyrical Moon, and the bad-boy-genius of the solar system, Uranus. You embody the best of both energies, giving you an intellectual and highly original personality.

Intellectual activist type, Aquarius Moon people are strong-willed, charismatic and often dominant partners. Ever tuned in to friendship, you may not as a rule, place marriage on too high a pedestal. But if children do happen to come along, you will treat them with kindness and equality, as if they were your little best friends. Egalitarian at heart, Aquarian Moon moms will never talk down to their kids, but treat them with fairness. Many of you may also be drawn to being single in order to devote more time to personal goals and dreams, which may sometimes fall by the wayside if a life-partner enters the picture too soon. Your life-partner will have to be adaptable and able to understand as well as accept the unusual nature of the Aquarian Moon sign, never asking you to change, but secretly making many compromises themselves along the way.

You experience love through the medium of the highest realms of human thought. Like the other airy Moon signs of Gemini and Libra, you love communication and words, and there is an actual *taste* in your heart for the literary arts. More than how they dress and what they look like, the way your lover thinks, what your lover believes and what personal conviction they are willing to give up everything for, is what draws you magnetically to them. Your love must be premised on personal freedom, no matter how difficult this is to achieve with the average lover, you will achieve it with the right one effortlessly.

You know you've found your soul mate the day they tell you that the love you share must be totally unconditional. They will understand and be prepared for the fact that your relationship may be highly unconventional, it may undergo its own phases but will never be weak enough to crumble and fade away. They will never try to change its true, natural and beautiful state only to fit in with society's notion of how you should live your life. The world may tell you that love should be bound up in a box and tucked away on a shelf. But you must tell them that love lets you fly in the sky of your desire, setting you forever free. That's true love, Aquarius Moon style.

10 specific traits that a man with the Moon in Aquarius looks for in a lover

He wants a lover who:
1. Is independent, emotionally secure and comfortable with periodic autonomy from him
2. Considers solitude a precious gift and is not hyper-sensitive or clingy
3. Is not looking for a conventional, one-size-fits-all relationship
4. Has her own life, circle of friends and interests apart from him
5. Understands that climbing the social ladder may not be on his life-agenda, but living on the strength of his own principles is
6. Is an intellectual, a good conversationalist and is not a constant complainer
7. Encourages him to be unique and original and can be his best friend
8. Will not restrict him from spending time with his friends
9. Allows him the freedom to decide for himself if he wants a family
10. Is practical, frugal and does not spend his money unwisely

10 specific traits that a woman with the Moon in Aquarius looks for in a lover

She wants a lover who:
1. Is not threatened by a forward-thinking and independent woman
2. Is proud of her intellect, her grasp over many subjects and ability to express herself originally
3. Is mature and wise in all his dealings and is willing to be her best friend
4. Is free of any kind of ugly prejudice
5. Understands that she may need to spend time by herself sometimes

6. Isn't looking for a tradition-minded, run-of-the-mill soul mate, but is open to marriage if she is
7. Respects her views on life and refrains from altering her way of living it
8. Is not hyper-sensitive, critical or needy
9. Will not be suspicious of her male friends
10. Trusts her and will not pressure her into motherhood before she is ready

Find Your Perfect Moon Sign Love Match

If you have an Aquarian Moon sign, you will attract lovers who have either the Sun, Moon or Rising sign in these air and fire signs: **Gemini, Libra, Aquarius, Aries, Leo and Sagittarius.**

If you have an Aquarius Moon sign, you can still have a good relationship with a lover whose Sun, Moon or Rising sign is in the following earth and water signs: **Taurus, Virgo, Capricorn, Cancer, Scorpio and Pisces**. It might take adjustments, but it will be worth it!

Celebrities with the Moon in Aquarius: Cary Grant, Carl Sandburg, Jean Paul Sartre, Britney Spears, Tim McGraw, George Clooney, Marilyn Monroe, Merle Haggard, Uma Thurman, David Beckham, J. R. R. Tolkien, Mohammed Ali, Tony Blair, Arthur Conan Doyle, Sir Issac Newton, Colin Powell and Tobey McGuire.

Chapter 12

The Moon In Pisces

Ruler: Neptune

Element: Water

Quality: Mutable

Symbol: The Fish

"I love thee freely, as men strive for right
I love thee purely, as they turn from praise,
I love thee with the passion put to use,
In my old grief and with my childhood's faith.
I love thee with a love I seemed to lose
With my lost saints, I love thee with the breath,
Smiles, tears, of all my life — and, if God choose,
I shall but love thee better after death."

~ Elizabeth Barrett Browning (Pisces Poetess)

Imagine a man with the vision and compassion of Dr. Martin Luther King Jr., the appeal of rock and roll icon Elvis Presley, and the poetic soul of writer and rock climber/mountaineer John Muir. These are the amazing qualities present in the Pisces Moon male. Whether male or female, if you have this Moon placement, you're inspiring, sensitive and soulful. You have a magical connection to nature, art, water and dreams. Neptune, the ruler of Pisces, is traditionally associated with the untamable power of the oceans, and the element of water truly exhibits the awesome might of Mother Nature.

The Pisces Moon personality can be separated into two, distinct types. The first type of Pisces Moon personality is the *beauty seeker type*; this type is passionate, somewhat submissive in love relationships, takes what their lover says rather seriously and revels in their approval. The beauty seeker type acclimates to the marriage setting easily and makes a very accommodating spouse and lover. They seek beauty, and through beauty, they seek harmony. Their goal is to harmonize their inner world as much as possible, particularly through the avenue of intimate relationships.

The second type of the Pisces Moon persona is the *spirit seeker type*. This fascinating type is self-sufficient, smart and in control of their emotions. Managing a business, raising a family, pursuing their passion in life; they can do it all. This type seeks spiritual connectivity in life, and they may look for it through the mediums of nature, spirituality, religion, mysticism or humanitarian work, where the oceanic compassion of Neptune truly comes into its own. Let's study this Moon sign in greater depth.

While Pisces Moon people are artistic and poetic, they are also illusory and hard to define. With your Moon sign in Pisces, you will either love the feeling of physically being in the water, or be totally terrified of it. Nature will draw you with its purity and simplicity. John Muir, who had a spirit seeker type of Pisces Moon personality, eloquently described his appreciation of nature with the following words: *"Climb the mountains and get their good tidings. Nature's peace will flow into you as sunshine flows into trees. The winds will blow their own freshness into you, and the storms their energy, while cares will drop off like autumn leaves."* Pisces Moon readers will be nodding their heads in agreement to this great advice!

Generally, people will say that you have the gift of being able to get along with anyone, which is true. Mutable Pisces makes for a compassionate Moon sign, and this affords you a chance to put yourself in any situation or envision any experience. You are comfortable with change, because you know that with change comes another chance to observe life's fascinating and unpredictable landscapes.

If you're a beauty seeker type of Pisces Moon personality, you are emotionally flexible, but you may sometimes change too easily or give in too often to make your partner happy (or to avoid conflict). You are also likely to mimic (Pisces is the sign of the performer or mimic) your lover and change your personal preferences in order to create more similarities between you. This is not necessary, because you are a unique soul whose individuation should be encouraged and not eclipsed and altered.

The Moon's soft natured and trusting energy, when filtered through the easily moved Neptune influence, creates a person who is sometimes prone to being a victim of deception. Beware of becoming the focus of the emotional and spiritual 'pickpocket', or someone who uses you by manipulating your emotions, or perhaps more particularly, by breathing life into your deepest fears. With so many lunar as well as Neptune-influenced emotions welling up inside you, you will need a firm anchor in life to stabilize yourself and feel confident. You sometimes believe too easily, especially if the packaging is just right or if substance is lacking in your daily life.

So, what are women with this Moon placement like? They are indubitably some of the most alluring and beautiful in the world. Envision a cocktail that contains the refined and elegant beauty of Catherine Zeta Jones (beauty seeker type), the comedic talent of Sandra Bullock (beauty seeker type) and the eternal grace and humanitarian spirit of Audrey Hepburn (spirit seeker type). These traits embody the Pisces Moon sign, and your compassion is often your greatest strength. Pisces makes women with this placement delicately feminine and romantic, and they will feel drawn toward partners who are strong and masculine. The Moon in the water sign of Pisces creates a temperament where your sympathy is aroused easily.

This Moon position is also associated with possible communication problems with a partner, usually in the early stages of the relationship. Neptune sometimes creates a fog, a dense mist around you and as a result, you may try hard to say something and the other person may not hear you correctly. The solution is to articulate your thoughts more than once and with clarity and power. Don't expect your lover to read your mind, even though you can easily read theirs. A Pisces Moon position makes you a wonderfully helpful, attentive and loving mate. But beware of sacrificing too much of your personality in order to save your partner from working on the relationship, or fitting into your lover's idea of an ideal partner. Each partner should be equally concerned about the welfare of the love you share.

There may be things in your heart that you don't think your partner can deal with, but somehow expect them to know. An inability or refusal to give your lover all the facts could lead to problems later on, with you accusing your beloved that they don't make any effort to understand you. They do, dear Pisces Moon, but you may not have communicated all the details. And yes, that includes all the ugly ones too. Perfection is a nice word, but in real life relationships, it has no place at all. You have an ideal in your mind about what your relationship should be, but more often than not, you will be disappointed. Does this sound like your story, dear Pisces Moon?

Is there a solution? Yes! Learn to actively push away all the fear from your heart and don't try to be someone's perfect love, because, like everyone else, you too will undergo gradual emotional changes as the years wear on. Your true self is more beautiful than you think. And don't expect your lover to be your perfect love either, no one can fulfill expectations that high. Your opposite Moon sign of Virgo believes that love is devotion, and you believe that love is sacrifice. Neither of you may, therefore, understand the true, raw and often imperfect nature of human love. Love changes us, as should every healthy life experience. If it didn't, there would be so many life-lessons that we would never learn.

Remember, that you also have a secret tendency to give up too easily if things don't go well. Accept the changing tides of love and like the oceans that rule you, you will get into the flow of things. You partner should understand, that from time to time, you will need to leave the stressful world behind and run off into the wilds. Why? Because you live in your emotions and have created a private world there, that mirrors the deepest Neptunian waters where no one else is permitted entry. You need to escape the drudgery and chaos of suburbia so that you can recharge you emotional batteries and return to us afresh. At times such as that, your lover should step away from you and let you drift, because this proves healing to your very sensitive nervous system.

You know you've found your soul mate when your lover responds to your unspoken fears intuitively, before you have uttered a single word. Your fear of loneliness, your fear of being unloved will be tangibly felt by your true soul companion, who will also have the same fears and questions as you, but who will become the immovable rock of support in your life. Marie Curie had a Pisces Moon sign and she said something extremely beautiful in two, short, simple sentences: *"Nothing in life is to be feared. It is only to be understood."* A celebrated scientist, she was not only sensitive but also embodied the confident side of a Pisces Moon person. *"Life is not easy for any of us. But what of that? We must have perseverance and above all, confidence in ourselves. We must believe that we are gifted for something and that this thing must be attained."*

As a sensitive water sign, you need a firm anchor to bring back your faith in yourself from time to time. When you receive unconditional support like that from a lover, it awakens the power of the primeval and immeasurable oceans in you. The oceans are symbolic of pure emotion. Your romantic and trusting side comes out, flooding your lover with gratitude for understanding your beautiful, unveiled self. That's true love, Pisces Moon style.

10 specific traits that a man with the Moon in Pisces looks for in a lover

He wants a lover who:
1. Is feminine and passionate but strong-willed as well
2. Believes in him when he is too heartbroken to believe in himself
3. Is practical and frugal and appreciates his intensely romantic nature

4. Knows that self-doubt is his greatest enemy and reminds him of this without mothering him too much
5. Can adjust to an unconventional relationship or marriage
6. Reminds him that not everyone should be trusted too easily
7. Understands his emotions and their erratic patterns, while bringing him the gift of clarity
8. Grants him the gift of personal space and freedom when the world begins to close in on him
9. Allows him the freedom to decide for himself if he wants a family
10. Is artistic, imaginative with a fondness for music and spending time in nature near great bodies of open water.

10 specific traits that a woman with the Moon in Pisces looks for in a lover

She wants a lover who:
1. Is firm, serious and matter-of-fact with the world but treats her with much tenderness
2. Comprehends how her sensitive emotions color her decisions
3. Fulfills her need for regular attention from her partner
4. Can instill in her a personal sense of confidence when she begins to doubt herself
5. Remembers that her lover also has to be her emotional rock
6. Lets her independent and creative side take flight
7. Reminds her to not be too trusting of the wrong people
8. Gives her emotional 'breathing space' from time to time
9. Understands her spiritual attitude about love and relationships
10. Shares her philosophy about life and her core values

Find Your Perfect Moon Sign Love Match

If you have a Pisces Moon sign, you will attract lovers who will have either the Sun, Moon or Rising sign in these water and earth signs: **Cancer, Scorpio Pisces, Taurus, Virgo and Capricorn.**

If you have a Pisces Moon sign, you can still have a good relationship with a lover whose Sun, Moon or Rising sign is in the following fire and air signs: **Aries, Leo, Sagittarius, Gemini, Libra and Aquarius**. It might take adjustments, but it will be worth it!

Celebrities with the Moon in Pisces: Dr. Martin Luther King Jr., John Muir (author and rock climber), Benjamin Franklin, Michealangelo, Amadeo

Modigliani, Edgar Allen Poe, Paul Newman, Sandra Bullock, Joe DiMaggio, Alex Rodriguez (A-Rod), Elvis Presley, Catherine Zeta Jones, Audrey Hepburn, Micheal Jackson, Paul Cezanne, Hillary Clinton, Marie Curie, Robert De Niro, Ben Stiller, Leonardo da Vinci and Sarah Michelle Gellar.

Part II:
144 Romantic Moon Sign Combinations for Every Moon Sign

Chapter 13

The Aries Moon Sign Lover

Aries Moon vs. Aries Sun, Moon or Rising Sign
The Fire and Fire Relationship

Fire: "I need romance and passion to really enjoy my relationship. Will my boyfriend be a faithful mate for life?" the fiery female partner wonders. "I want an active and freedom-loving partner. Will my girlfriend understand my need for true freedom in life or will she be too controlling of what I want to do with my life?" the fiery male lover thinks to himself.

Aries Moon lovers get along exceptionally well with partners who have their Sun, Moon or Rising sign in their own fire sign of Aries, because fire encourages fire and helps it burn spectacularly bright for all the world to see. Each partner represents an element. Understanding that element helps us delve deeper into the real personality of that partner. Fire represents excitement, a burning passion and a soaring inspiration. Elementally, fire supports its own energy beautifully. A good example of this would be the magnificent fireworks that light up the night sky at New Year's Eve around the world.

The double fire relationship illuminates the worlds of two, loving soul mates and chases all those shadows away that may try to encroach on their love in the form of doubt. Fire is one of the most important of the four elements because without it, the world would freeze and cease to sustain life. With the gift of heat, frozen icebergs melt and create more water, the great oceans move and frozen hearts begin to feel the depth of human emotion once again. But the fire energy must always be maturely handled to bring forth its best attributes. A fire that burns too hot, dies away just as quickly. Therefore, the key is to let it burn *slowly and sustain it for a longer period of time*, changing it from a destructive fire to a productive fire. Too much fire can cause destruction, but if its power is controlled and tempered, it can turn into the comforting fireplace that keeps our homes so warm and cozy when the harshness of winter descends. Balancing the attributes of this useful element is key.

Fiery Aries Moon lovers, as well as Aries type partners are passionate and charismatic, and when they're truly in love, they glow and give off a certain positive energy. While sexual compatibility and emotional attachment may never be lacking in a double Aries romantic combination, sometimes tempers may flare and a temporary inability to understand each other may arise. Fire signs are dominant, and two willful Mars-ruled lovers might clash on occasion as passionately as they love. Forgiveness will come easily but after a while, the emotional wear and tear may begin to color the relationship. The Aries Moon lover as well as their Aries type partner, has strong opinions on almost everything, and they are quite candid about their observations. Words must be used with diplomacy because both these lovers will respond favorably to the slightest kindness.

It might help this pair if they can figure out what type of Aries energy they each symbolize. People with Aries as their Moon sign will be either aggressive (the *ram type* Aries personality), or soft-spoken and more passive (the *lamb type* Aries personality) or a balanced blend of both (the *ram/lamb* Aries personality). If the Aries Moon lover is of a dominant variety, they will get along best with the ram/lamb type Aries persona, because this one will provide the tenderness needed as well as refuse to be too tightly controlled by anyone.

If both the Aries Moon lover and their Aries type partner are mature in the ways of romantic love and well balanced emotionally, they may be able to endure many of life's ups and down with characteristic fire sign courage. A friendship may initially be the best testing ground for them, before they impulsively leap headlong into the world of love and life-long promises. Aries Moon lovers are active and energetic, as are Aries type partners, and both share the same mental circuitry. A natural sympathy will always be shared, and if both partners with this Aries essence can practice more tact without trying to reshape each other's lives, compatibility will be achieved quickly. Aries Moon lovers respond ardently to romantic overtures.

They might also like to watch that famous Martian temper with partners. Mars rules aggression and war, but most importantly, Mars like to draw our attention to the truth hidden behind problems that may have been lurking beneath the surface of a relationship, but have not been dealt with over many years. Unafraid of confrontation, Mars makes the Aries Moon lover come out and confront the pesky problem in order to be done with it forever. This brings the relationship up to the highest level of truth and honesty, which is always good for the overall health of the relationship in the long run.

One of these Aries energy lovers will have to regularly balance out any trigger areas; like financial issues, watching overspending and making the bigger and more important financial purchases as a team instead of unilaterally. Patience and strict honesty will be key in keeping a double Aries vibration relationship keep on expressing its best attributes for years to come.

This double Mars relationship will need stability and direction from the start. Mars is a volatile planet and unless its massive energies are properly channeled, they can easily get scattered. One of these two will undoubtedly be the more passive lover or more easy-going partner, because two forceful personalities cannot exist unless one of them learns to be the peacemaker and compromiser. It is this lover, upon whom depends the final direction of the relationship.

Their love depends on cooperation and the more accommodating they both become, the more success they will achieve. They will be friends for a lifetime as well as each other's fiercest protectors. An Aries Moon partner needs to be in love with a soul mate who lives by a strict honor code and keeps their promises, come what may. The Aries energy will keep them both idealistic and always willing to give love a second shot. A little emotional adjustment from both lovers will make this a love story to remember.

Aries Moon vs. Taurus Sun, Moon or Rising Sign
The Fire and Earth Relationship

Fire: "I need romance and passion to really enjoy my relationship. Will my boyfriend be a faithful mate for life?" the fiery female partner wonders. "I want an active and freedom-loving partner. Will my girlfriend understand my need for true freedom in life or be too controlling?" the fiery male lover thinks to himself.

Earth: "Does my boyfriend manage his finances maturely or will I end up paying his bills and supporting him? I need stability and true commitment before I can

enjoy the romance between us." the earthy female thinks to herself. "Will my
future wife spend my hard earned cash on frivolous items at the mall or be wise
enough to save up for our retirement?" the earthy male lover wonders.

Aries Moon lovers can easily co-exist with lovers who have their Sun, Moon or Rising sign in the stable and romantic earth sign of Taurus. Each partner symbolizes an element. Understanding that element helps us delve deeper into the real personality of that partner. Fire represents a zest for life, a passionate temperament and an easily inspired heart. Earth represents an unmatched stability and reliability: earth is a faith in love and an undying dedication to a relationship. Elementally, fire and earth can support each other wonderfully. Fire needs the earth so that it has support to burn on, while the earth needs fire to give it warmth, so that the winter's last frozen touch is melted away and spring can be reborn.

Fire, however, must be handled in a mature way, because it can cause destruction if not controlled, while the earth element can cause a landslide to occur and rearrange the map in one stroke. When these energies mingle in appropriate amounts, the fire element warms our homes and the earth element provides a stable base and foundation for us to create our lives on. Balancing the attributes of each element is key. As long as the Aries Moon lover controls their tendency to be impatient and make snap decisions, they will be able to enjoy their most passionate and emotionally uplifting relationship with their Taurus type lover.

The easily excited Aries Moon lover might say, *"Let's go on a romantic adventure! What are you waiting for, sweetheart?"* while the Taurus type lover might ask, *"Where's the plan? Show me your blueprint, honey. Love stories take time to create."* If the Taurus type person watches their tendency toward pessimism or unnecessarily stalling the making of important decisions, being suspicious and delaying talking issues out, it would be an added benefit to their overall compatibility. The Taurus energy connects itself to what it owns, its possessions and its money. Therefore they should not let what they own together as a couple come between their affection for each other.

It might help both these lovers to figure out what type of Aries energy they're dealing with. People with Aries as their Moon sign will be either aggressive (the *ram type* Aries personality), or soft-spoken and more passive (the *lamb type* Aries personality) or a balanced blend of both (the *ram/lamb* Aries personality). The Taurus type lover will get along better with the lamb type Aries personality because they are gentle and equally thoughtful, mirroring the Taurus essence.

Romance-seeking Aries Moon lovers and Taurus types make a good pair because the earthy Taurus energy slows their lovable but impetuous Aries Moon partner down, and makes them pay attention to practicality, while Aries Moon companions energize Taurus type partners into fearlessly embracing life, relaxing some of their more rigid views, actively searching for fun and taking some risks once in a while. The Taurus type partner won't take too many risks, but may take some carefully calculated ones in order to make their Aries Moon lover happy. This duo can create a formidable emotional support system for one another as the years go by.

What the Aries Moon lover imagines, the Taurus essence *actualizes,* and will help create a firm foundation, usually financial, for their Aries Moon lover and in return, expect their full loyalty and trust. The Aries Moon lover can help their Taurus type lover be more open and trusting emotionally, and try to relax when things are not perfect. If things get out of hand during a little romantic clash of wills, patient and stable Taurus types will sit tight and wait for their openhearted Aries Moon sweetheart to offer an olive branch, which they invariably will. This strengthens their love more than anything else can. If the olive branch scenario doesn't happen quickly, the earthy Taurus type mate could feel dejected and begin questioning everything.

Neither of them should wait too long to say they're sorry. Doubt has no place in the Aries Moon/Taurus Sun, Moon or Rising sign relationship and both partners should make every effort to talk through their differences the *same* day they occur. Waiting too long might cause fear to set in, which can be hard to remove. Aries Moon lovers may become quite attached to their earthy partner's sense of romance and an easily expressed style of passion. The Aries Moon lover can learn what true sensuality is from their Taurus type partners. While the Taurus type partner will learn what blind trust is from their sometimes endearingly childlike (but never childish) Aries Moon lover.

This romantic pairing can last if the Aries Moon lover watches what they say around their life-mate, who may be as sensitive to rejection as they are to genuine appreciation. This pair of lovers can make their love story last if they are open to adopting even the slightest of changes in their personalities, because it will pay off in a big way. Aries Moon soul mates can teach their lovers that love is a freely given trust, while the Taurus type lover can show their soul mate that love is unshakeable dedication.

Aries Moon vs. Gemini Sun, Moon or Rising Sign
The Fire and Air Relationship

Fire: "I need romance and passion to really enjoy my relationship. Will my boyfriend be a faithful mate for life?" the fiery female partner wonders. "I want an active and freedom-loving partner. Will my girlfriend understand my need for true freedom in life or be too controlling?" the fiery male lover thinks to himself.

Air: "Is my boyfriend open-minded enough and will he appreciate my outspoken side? I need a life mate who will talk to me, communicate with me about everything and not clam up and brood." the airy female partner muses. "Will my girlfriend allow me to do the things I love or will she try to restrict me from expressing myself?" the airy male lover wonders.

Aries Moon lovers usually get along famously with lovers who have their Sun, Moon or Rising sign in the wonderfully expressive air sign of Gemini. Air feeds fire and makes it burn brightly. But air can also make a fire burn out of control and cause destruction, so care should be taken that airy and changeable Gemini types don't initiate a relationship they have no intention of pursuing. Each partner symbolizes an element. Understanding that element helps us delve deeper into the real personality of that partner. Fire represents a burning passion, a sense of invincibility and a soaring inspiration. Air represents an incredible intellectualism, an ability to communicate through any medium creatively. Elementally, fire and air can co-exist remarkably well. Fire needs the oxygen in the air to burn its brightest, while the air or the atmosphere needs the heat of fire to combat the frozen, motionless energy of a merciless winter.

Be that as it may, if the air in the form of wild winds blows too forcefully, it can extinguish a small fledgling flame that is trying desperately to become a productive fire, while fire, if it burns too hot, can rob the air of all its oxygen and change its nature completely. Balancing the attributes of each element is key. The Gemini energy tends to vacillate and change their minds a lot, and this may annoy the slightly impatient but romantic Aries Moon lover who wants to know if they are a couple with a future or not. Gemini types should be more honest and forthright when stating their plans for their joint future, while Aries Moon lovers shouldn't press the issue if they can plainly see that their affections are not being properly returned.

Sometimes it is good to stop pushing if the time is not ripe for questions, decisions and finalities. If this fire and air pairing does begin a relationship, it will be a good one due to the basic compatibility between these elements, as each needs the other to be productive. As a precaution, this impulsive pair of lovers should begin their connection as fast friends and confidants, before rushing the sexual part of the relationship. If a friendship is built on solid ground, and if it grows in depth and intensity, then they will know that they are progressing along the right path. Fiery and energetic Aries Moon companions may adapt very well to the active, intellectually sharp energy of Gemini types. As for the Gemini type lover, their ultimate choice will be someone who is emotionally flexible and does not take things too seriously. They love partners who are wise but also funny and can be their best friend *first* and lover second.

It might help the Gemini type lover to find out what kind of Aries Moon partner they have fallen in love with. People with Aries as their Moon sign will be either aggressive (the *ram type* Aries personality), or soft-spoken and more passive (the *lamb type* Aries personality) or a balanced blend of both (the *ram/lamb* Aries personality). Gemini types may get along best with the last category, because it will be able to provide the gentility needed to deal with the Gemini type mate, as well as refuse to be pushed around if their mate is dominant by nature.

The Mercurial Gemini energy may inadvertently make their Aries Moon sweetheart more restless than they already are, while adventurous Aries Moon mates might cause their Gemini type mates to be more reckless and lean toward expressing true emotion on the spur of the moment, with its expression as their *sole* focus. The Aries Moon energy creates a sweet sentimentality in Gemini types, and the Gemini essence makes their Aries Moon partners more gregarious and opinionated. Both the friendship vibration as well as a relationship may work out well between them as long as Aries Moon lovers can control the double dose of restlessness running through their systems, and the Gemini essence can learn to be more intense about love, take their partner more seriously and show an equal desire for merging destinies together when the time is perfect.

Gemini types may admire their Aries Moon lover's undeniable charisma and appeal, and help their fiery lover feel more free and comfortable in bringing any cause or concept to the world's attention. The Aries Moon soul mate awakens in their Gemini type lover a sense of passion and a red hot Mars-type of sensuality. Gemini types become more driven and idealistic around their Aries Moon lovers. If they keep the lines of *tactful* communication always open, they can last a lifetime.

Aries Moon vs. Cancer Sun, Moon or Rising Sign
The Fire and Water Relationship

Fire: "I need romance and passion to really enjoy my relationship. Will my boyfriend be a faithful mate for life?" the fiery female partner wonders. "I want an active and freedom-loving partner. Will my girlfriend understand my need for true freedom in life or be too controlling?" the fiery male lover thinks to himself.

Water: "Is my boyfriend emotionally stable and wise about our joint finances? Or will debts pile up in the first year of marriage? I need a supportive, life-long lover as well as a loving one." the watery female lover thinks to herself. "Will my future spouse conserve our financial resources or spend unwisely without thought for the future? I can connect better romantically if I know that my chosen life-mate is passionate as well as mature and pragmatic." the watery male lover wonders.

Aries Moon lovers can enjoy a highly intense and security-centered relationship with a lover who has their Sun, Moon or Rising sign in watery Cancer, if each does the following things: the Aries Moon lover has to learn to handle the moods of their Cancer type lover with delicacy and sensitivity, while the Cancer type partner should learn how to handle the active, restless and intense Aries Moon personality with more diplomacy. Each partner symbolizes an element. Understanding that element helps us delve deeper into the real personality of that partner. Fire represents a burning passion and a soaring inspiration. Water represents an emotional purity, an ability to intuit, as well as a soft and inviting sensuality.

Elementally, water and fire are compatible, but adjustments have to be made for a full chance at success. Water needs fire to create an atmosphere of warmth and security, allow food to be cooked, as well as afford us those relaxing hot showers. While fire needs water to cool itself off if it is beginning to burn dangerously bright. Water must be careful around fire and not completely extinguish its hopeful energy, and fire must be used carefully around water because hot water can scald. Balance between the elements is key.

The sign of Cancer is ruled by the Moon while the Aries Moon lover functions under the influence of Mars. Mars and the Moon project very different energies in the planetary family, and these energies will work themselves out within the Aries Moon/Cancer relationship. The Moon's essence is perceptive and soft-spoken, while Mars is outspoken and full of opinions, aggression and force. Also, both signs (Aries and Cancer) are cardinal in quality; so each leads in their own way; one with energy and the other with patience and tenacity. Mars-ruled, Aries Moon lovers use a commanding sense of authority to get their way while the Moon-ruled, Cancer type mate uses gentle passivity and persuades to get their way.

It might help the Cancer type lover to find out what kind of Aries Moon partner they have fallen in love with. People with Aries as their Moon sign will be either aggressive (the *ram type* Aries personality), or soft-spoken and more passive (the *lamb type* Aries personality) or a balanced blend of both (the *ram/lamb* Aries personality). They may find maximum compatibility with the last category; it will help them find both sensitivity and strength in their lover.

Cancer type partners have a cooling effect on their hot-tempered and excitable Aries Moon partner, and the Aries Moon partner can energize the watery Cancer persona into being more fearlessly expressive, and tap into the Aries Moon lover's high energy to initiate projects and toss ideas around. Aries Moon partners love to be noticed and the Cancer essence loves to nurture, provide that attention and create the best conditions for emotional 'nesting'. Cancer symbolizes the home sector to Aries, so there will be a desire in each to bond on a very emotionally charged level. The Aries Moon energy focuses out of the home sector, while the watery Cancer type lover focuses *specifically* on the home front.

Both are sensitive to being rebuffed, so the slightest rejection will take a long time to heal and both have to be cautious about what messages they are putting out there. The Cancer essence must be careful to not show the least sign of possessiveness toward their impulsive Aries Moon lover (who needs lots of freedom and likes to pick their own friends and social schedule), and the Aries Moon person must never abandon observing those little sentimental courtesies that can keep this relationship going, like remembering birthdays, anniversaries, Valentine's Day (Cancer types need regular assurances of love). The Cancer essence is as easily moved as their Aries Moon lover, so neither should deliberately push each other's emotional triggers on a bad day.

Aries Moon lovers are romantic and very ardent when in love. Cancer types need to make sure that what they feel is true and what they're experiencing is the real thing, because they could experience an emotional dislocation at the slightest betrayal. As long as the Aries Moon lover doesn't rush the normal pace of their love and lets it blossom on its own timetable, and as long as the Cancer type lover can learn to give their Aries Moon lover lots of trust, this love will not just bloom, it will flourish. The sensitive and caring Cancer type lover brings out the protector in their Aries Moon partner, while the fiery Aries Moon energy brings out their tenderhearted Cancer type soul mate's pronounced maternal side. An unwavering and unshakable trust will be the strongest tie between them and both lovers should go out of their way to modify their personalities to accommodate their sweethearts. This romantic pairing has an excellent chance of turning their relationship into their own, very special love story.

Aries Moon vs. Leo Sun, Moon or Rising Sign
The Fire and Fire Relationship

Fire: "I need romance and passion to really enjoy my relationship. Will my boyfriend be a faithful mate for life?" this fiery female partner wonders. "I want an active and freedom-loving partner. Will my girlfriend understand my need for true freedom in life or be too controlling?" the fiery male lover thinks to himself.

Aries Moon lovers get along particularly well with lovers who have their Sun, Moon or Rising sign in fiery Leo, because fire feeds fire and can understand typical fire sign life-goals. Each partner symbolizes an element. Understanding that element helps us delve deeper into the real personality of that partner. Fire represents a need for true passion, a sense of undying optimism and a soaring inspiration. Elementally, fire supports fire beautifully. A good example of this would be the magnificent, glittering fireworks that light up the night sky at New Year's Eve.

The double fire relationship makes each lover want to reach out to each other, be more fearless about facing life and seek out passion by building trust. Fire is one of the most important elements because without it, the world would freeze and become useless. With the gift of heat, the great oceans move, frozen icebergs melt and create more water and frozen hearts begin to feel the depth of human emotion once again. Emotions, if well appealed to, can rebuild long broken relationships. Fire energy must also be maturely handled to bring forth its best attributes. A fire that burns too hot dies away just as quickly. Therefore, the key is to let it burn *slowly and longer*, changing it from a destructive fire to a productive fire. Too much fire can cause destruction, but if its power is controlled and tempered, it can turn into the comforting heat of the fireplace that keeps our homes so warm and cozy when the harshness of winter comes upon us. Balancing the attributes of this important element is key.

While sexual compatibility will never be a problem between two loving fire signs, and both will be very emotionally attached, occasionally tempers may flare and cause a strange confusion in both these lover's hearts. But this tension quickly passes because both the Aries Moon lover and their generous Leo type mate forgive easily and happily. There may also be a subconscious desire to start a family. Fire signs are quite dominant by temperament and two willful lovers might clash once in a while. But both will be eager to meet each other half way, if the lines of *tactful* communication can be kept open, and sharply worded accusations are curtailed in the heat of the moment.

Aries Moon lovers are ruled by the planet Mars and their Leo type partner functions under the energy of the mighty Sun. The Sun and Mars are similar in some ways and yet in some ways, stand in stark contrast to each other. The Sun illuminates everything it touches and is the source of life on earth. It brings clarity and shares its warmth with the world. It will therefore cause a great deal of changes to occur in the life of the Aries Moon lover in the sense that it may make a hot energy, hotter or more potent. Muscle bound Mars, on the other hand, rules pure warrior-like aggression and lives to protect the weak and defenseless of this world. Both these planetary forces are impulsive, powerful and therefore must be handled extremely carefully because their essence will change on the field of love and intimacy. The Sun is hot and so is Mars. Mars is a dominant force and so is the Sun. Two dominant people cannot exist peacefully in a love relationship unless one of them learns the subtle and often secret art of compromise and balance. The partner who loves the most will learn this subtlety more quickly and willingly.

Aries Moon partners are assertive and so is the Leo essence. If they can reach an agreement as to who directs and who follows, provided the partner leading has only the best interests of the relationship at heart, goodwill will surely flow. The Leo type lover needs to make sure that their Aries Moon lover is never neglected, while the Aries Moon lover should ensure that patience and diplomacy are used in every situation. Both are fiercely loyal and acutely sensitive to rejection. This is a good marriage match, particularly if both lovers are fiery without being impatient and can be mature about forgiveness within human relationships.

If they can forget and forgive the smaller, inconsequential transgressions, they can last together for a lifetime. Both need a lot of *regular, verbal and physical appreciation* from each other. This type of reinforcement will work magic. Leo types are fixed in habit and temperament and the Aries Moon essence likes to instigate change due to a fondness for excitement. If impetuous Aries Moon partners can learn to slow down and observe the signals their mates give off, their compatibility level will rise. Also, Leo types need to be genuinely respected, so the Aries Moon lover shouldn't poke and prod their sensitive Leo type lover's ego too much.

It might help the Leo type lover to find out what kind of Aries Moon partner they have fallen in love with. People with Aries as their Moon sign will be either aggressive (the *ram type* Aries personality), or soft-spoken and more passive (the *lamb type* Aries personality) or a balanced blend of both (the *ram/lamb* Aries personality). The second last category will suit them best if they're the dominant kind.

When both lovers share the energy of the same element, there could be an overwhelming of sorts where there is nothing to contrast their love and balance it out. One of them will have to be the rock of the relationship, the partner who will be vigilant and make sure that the relationship is not in any danger of collapsing, that money is not being spent without regard for the future (money issues sadly lie at the heart of many lovers separating) and that a regular income keeps coming in. Both Aries Moon partners and their Leo soul mates are diehard romantics, and this could be the single best secret to keeping them together, year after year. If they can remember those special days, like birthdays, Valentine's Day, the-first-time-we-met anniversaries and other memorable occasions, it can bring them closer. This fiery couple can experience the purest and most devoted love of all; they will be eager to create and star in their own special love story.

Aries Moon vs. Virgo Sun, Moon or Rising Sign
The Fire and Earth Relationship

Fire: "I need romance and passion to really enjoy my relationship. Will my boyfriend be a faithful mate for life?" the fiery female partner wonders. "I want an active and freedom-loving partner. Will my girlfriend understand my need for true freedom in life or be too controlling?" the fiery male lover thinks to himself.

Earth: "Does my boyfriend manage his finances maturely or will I end up paying his bills and supporting him? I need stability and true commitment before I can enjoy the romance between us." the earthy female thinks to herself. "Will my future wife spend my hard earned cash on frivolous items at the mall or be wise enough to save up for our retirement?" the earthy male lover wonders.

Aries Moon lovers can enjoy a productive and successful relationship with a lover who has their Sun, Moon or Rising sign in Virgo, if the Virgo essence is properly understood the *first time* by the Aries Moon lover, as both signs have vividly different life agendas. Fire and earth can exist well if the relationship is carefully nurtured according to the temperament of the elements. Each partner symbolizes an element. Understanding that element helps us delve deeper into the real personality of that partner. Fire represents a need for constant action, fairness and a trust that is easily given. Earth represents an unmatched stability and reliability: earth is a faith in love and an undying dedication to a relationship, even when faced with seemingly insurmountable problems.

Elementally, fire and earth can support each other wonderfully. Fire needs the earth so that it has support to burn on, while the earth needs fire to give it warmth, so that the winter's last vestiges are melted away. Fire, however, must be handled in a mature way, because it can cause destruction if not controlled, while the earth can cause a landslide to occur and rearrange the map in one stroke. When these energies mingle in appropriate amounts, the fire element warms our feet through the fireplaces in our homes, helps cook our food and the earth element provides a stable base and foundation for us to build our homes and lives on. Balancing the attributes of each element is key.

The Aries Moon lover is ruled by the planet Mars and their Virgo type partner functions under the energy of the messenger planet Mercury. Mercury and Mars are similar in some ways (both get excited about the new and untried) and yet in some ways, stand in stark contrast to each other (Mars acts first and usually never thinks, while quick-witted Mercury thinks and talks enough for both of them). Mercury is mentally restless and very analytical, and sees people through reason's cold eyes rather than emotion's easily swayed vision. It will therefore cause a great deal of changes to occur in the life of the dynamic Aries Moon lover by making them more practical and observant. Muscle bound Mars, on the other hand, rules pure warrior-like aggression and lives to protect the weak and help the defenseless set the record straight.

Both these planetary forces are powerful and therefore must be handled extremely carefully because their essence will change on the field of love and intimacy. Mercury is outspoken and so is Mars. Mars likes to push forth and do things quickly and Mercury likes to analyze everything first. Two dominant people cannot exist peacefully in a love relationship unless one of them learns the subtle and often secret art of compromise and balance. One of them will have to hold their tongue when sharp words are about to pop out.

It might help the Virgo type lover to find out what kind of Aries Moon partner they have fallen in love with. People with Aries as their Moon sign will be either aggressive (the *ram type* Aries personality), or soft-spoken and more passive (the *lamb type* Aries personality) or a balanced blend of both (the *ram/lamb* Aries personality). They may find more compatibility with the lamb type Aries personality who may prove to be more patient than the more aggressive Aries Moon mate.

Virgo types love to bring order and purpose to any relationship (at work or at home) while Aries Moon partners are fast-moving, action-packed creatures who may sometimes lack the tact that witty Virgo types look for in a life-companion. Aries Moon lovers are casual and ambitious by turns, while the Virgo essence is specifically goal-oriented and hardworking. Love between these two differing energies can survive if the Virgo type partner can teach the Aries Moon lover to slow down and be more practical, and if the Aries Moon lover can teach their Virgo type soul mate to relax, mellow out, control their critical side and chase pleasure and happiness instead of chasing the mailman to pay a late bill.

The Aries Moon partner will tell the Virgo type partner that it is okay to be a little self-indulgent once in a while, and to not feel guilty if they do. The astute Virgo energy streamlines their relationship, creates an unshakable and reliable structure for Aries Moon mates to base their life on, and teaches them the invaluable art of observing details, while the Aries Moon lover brings workaholic Virgo's blood pressure down by making them laugh and engaging Virgo's brainy and literary side. The earthy Virgo type partner will have to watch out for one small detail that may have a big influence on how this couple gets along in the daily scheme of things: Virgo types must try not to complain about everything little thing that goes wrong, and never criticize or correct their fiery Aries Moon lover more than once a day. If at all possible, they should make it look more like an obiter dictum or a comment in passing than a criticism. Virgo types may tend to instinctively 'disinfect' the relationship or interfere with the natural pace of the relationship a bit too often, which could cloud the real path of the relationship.

When the sensitive and active Virgo mind is stressed, it reacts by trying to fix anything in sight and this could begin with a comment. They should watch how they address their Aries Moon lover (and do so tactfully) and they could save themselves a lot of unnecessary aggravation. The Aries Moon lover should also take care and treat their Virgo type partner with the utmost respect and dignity because this show of respect will go further than romance or passion in solidifying their bond for years to come.

The Virgo type life-companion is completely devoted and committed when their love has been pledged (and it won't be pledged very often), while their Aries Moon partner finds it hard going to make changes in their life to fit in another person unless they are head over heels in love with them. The Aries Moon mate must be honest and loyal while their lovers must give them a little more freedom to be able to fully enjoy the magic that comes with being a lunar Aries lover. If they can achieve this, even to a little extent, this extra effort will pay off in a big way.

Aries Moon vs. Libra Sun, Moon or Rising Sign
The Fire and Air Relationship

Fire: "I need romance and passion to really enjoy my relationship. Will my boyfriend be a faithful mate for life?" the fiery female partner wonders. "I want an active and freedom-loving partner. Will my girlfriend understand my need for true freedom in life or be too controlling?" the fiery male lover thinks to himself.

Air: "Is my boyfriend open-minded enough and will he appreciate my outspoken side? I need a life mate who will talk to me, communicate with me about everything and not clam up and brood." the airy female partner muses. "Will my girlfriend allow me to do the things I love or will she try to restrict me from expressing myself?" the airy male lover wonders.

Aries Moon lovers will attract any person who has their Sun, Moon or Rising sign in airy Libra, because Libra represents matrimony and love to the Aries energy. The pull here will be one of marriage. The signs are polarized here, but adjustments can be made with great success. Elementally, the air element has to be careful not to fan the flames of their fiery partner too brightly if they plan to have no future together. While the fire element must take care and not let the conversations between them go round and round and turn into just a lot of hot air. These two will get along quite nicely if the Aries Moon lover keeps in mind that the Libra essence thrives when they are regularly appreciated, both physically and intellectually.

Aries Moon partners can be hasty and prone to losing that famous Martian temper and Libra type personalities are very sensitive to any raising of the voice or even the slightest discordant tone in their lover's voice. Libra type partners should keep in mind that Aries Moon mates need to be handled tactfully and with tenderness every time. If the Aries Moon lover can keep the romance alive (remember special anniversaries, birthdays, Valentine's Day, write love notes, share poetry) and be generally more affectionate with Libra, and if the Libra essence can give the Aries Moon lover a good degree of freedom (to spend time with friends, to pursue personal goals not related to their relationship), this match will work out and last decades.

It might help the Libra type lover to find out what kind of Aries Moon partner they have fallen in love with. People with Aries as their Moon sign will be either aggressive (the *ram type* Aries personality), or soft-spoken and more passive (the *lamb type* Aries personality) or a balanced blend of both (the *ram/lamb* Aries personality). They may find more compatibility with the ram/lamb type Aries personality, which is strong, like Mars and tender, like Venus by turns.

Aries Moon partners stimulate Libra type lovers into being more outspoken, fearless and independent, while the Libra energy brings out the Romeo (or Juliet, as the case may be) in their Aries Moon lover. These two share the soul mate energy. Both Aries Moon partners and Libra types are strong intellectuals and frequent and earnest communication is very important to both. While they can mingle interests easily, it should be noted that the only situation in which Libra types begin to lose patience with their Aries Moon lovers, is when they refuse to commit to a future together but won't terminate the relationship either, thereby sending out mixed signals. Leaving Libra in limbo? Not a good idea. Usually, Libra types are known for being the best fence sitters of the zodiac, but when their hearts are involved, another's indecision may cause a lot of emotions to well up.

This could also work the other way, with the indecisive Libra type lover refusing to make up their mind, while an impatient Aries Moon lover stares at their wristwatch waiting for a yes or a no to marriage. There is a good chance that both of them may be impulse shoppers (Venus loves to shop and restless Mars is no coupon clipper), so one of them will have to be the financial watchdog and make sure that the money aspect of their relationship doesn't cause problems that might spill into other areas (money issues sadly lie at the heart of many lovers separating). Libra is a marriage sign, while the typical Aries Moon lover thrives in an unfettered friendship first.

Libra types want to see their partner in their future and may need some tangible proof (a ring, an engagement party) that marriage is on the cards. Aries

Moons positively recoil from being pressured. One way to combat this would be for both of them, the romantic Libra type lover, as well as the fun-loving Aries Moon lover, to begin their courtship *slowly* and keep it from burning too hot too fast. Gradually getting to know one another would help immensely. The only way for this relationship to survive is for the Libra type partner to allow their Aries Moon lover the chance to decide on their own timetable, as to what shape they want their love to take, while the Aries Moon lover could try to understand their deeply partnership-oriented and attractive Libra partner's heart. Neither should hold back how they feel (but do so with tact) and they should be able to get to the heart of any differences and resolve them quickly.

Aries Moon lovers are ruled by Mars, the planet that rules aggression and war, but most importantly, Mars likes to draw our attention to the truth hidden behind problems that may have been lurking beneath the surface of a relationship but have not been dealt with over many years. Unafraid of confrontation, Mars makes the Aries Moon lover come out and confront the pesky problem and be done with it forever. This brings the relationship up to the highest level of truth and honesty, which is always good for the overall health of the relationship in the long run. If disagreements arise, neither of them should wait too long to say they're sorry. Doubt has no place in the Aries Moon/Libra Sun, Moon and Rising sign relationship, and both partners should make every effort to talk out differences the *same* day they occur. Waiting too long might cause fear or suspicion to set in, which can be hard to remove in the long run.

This love story can be a glorious experience for both of these star crossed lovers, mainly because Mars-ruled, Aries Moon partners represent the passion in the relationship, while Venus-ruled, Libra type lovers are associated with love and commitment. Mars and Venus are eternal soul mates and have danced in the heavens for eons, creating their own magical romance in the skies. When this magic makes its presence felt in this relationship, Mars and Venus will get a chance to meet and love once more through the Aries Moon and Libra Sun, Moon, and Rising sign partnership. What better reason than that to give it their best shot?

Aries Moon vs. Scorpio Sun, Moon or Rising Sign
The Fire and Water Relationship

Fire: "I need romance and passion to really enjoy my relationship. Will my boyfriend be a faithful mate for life?" the fiery female partner wonders. "I want an active and freedom-loving partner. Will my girlfriend understand my need for true freedom in life or be too controlling?" the fiery male lover thinks to himself.

Water: "Is my boyfriend emotionally stable and wise about our joint finances? Or will debts pile up in the first year of marriage? I need a supportive, life-long lover as well as a loving one." the watery female lover thinks to herself. "Will my future spouse conserve our financial resources or spend unwisely without thought for the future? I can connect better romantically if I know that my chosen life-mate is passionate as well as mature and pragmatic." the watery male lover wonders.

Aries Moon lovers can enjoy an intense and emotionally rewarding relationship with any person who has their Sun, Moon or Rising sign in the sensitive and wise water sign of Scorpio, if certain adjustments are made in both personalities. The fire and water relationship, elementally, contains differing attributes. Each partner symbolizes an element. Understanding that element helps us delve deeper into the real personality of that partner. Fire represents a passion for life, an endearing innocence and a sense of openness and trust. Water represents an emotional purity, an ability to sympathize as well as a soft and inviting sensuality. Elementally, water and fire are compatible, but some compromises have to be made for a full chance at success.

Water needs fire to create an atmosphere of warmth and security in our homes, as well as afford us those relaxing hot showers. While fire needs water to cool itself off if it is beginning to burn dangerously bright. Water must be careful around fire and not completely extinguish its hopeful energy, and fire must be used carefully around water because hot water can scald. Balance between the elements is key. Scorpio is deep, emotional and thrives on stability while Aries Moon lovers need a regular dosage of excitement and stimulation to feel like they're really living and enjoying their life to the fullest. Both are capable of great and lasting love, and sexual compatibility will never be a problem as both of them are incredibly passionate.

Aries Moon lovers are ruled by the planet Mars and their Scorpio type partner functions under the energy of Pluto. Pluto and Mars are similar in some ways and yet in some ways, couldn't be more different. Mysterious Pluto is a somber, serious and wise planet that will not stand by and watch an injustice continue even for a minute. It transforms whatever it touches by changing it from the inside out and from the ground up, and will therefore cause a great deal of changes to occur in the life of the rough-and-tumble Aries Moon lover.

Muscleman Mars, on the other hand, rules pure warrior-like aggression and lives to protect the weak and voiceless victims of this world. Both these planetary forces are powerful but volatile and therefore must be handled extremely carefully because their essence will change on the field of love and intimacy. Pluto is fearless and so is Mars. Mars is a dominant force and so is Pluto. Neither will give up the chance to win if threatened. Two dominant people cannot exist peacefully in a love relationship unless one of them learns the subtle and often secret art of compromise and balance. The partner who loves more or gets more out of the relationship will learn this art quickly and willingly.

The protective Scorpio essence brings out a great tenderness in their Aries Moon mates, while the happy-go-lucky Aries Moon partner causes the usually suspicious and careful Scorpio type lover to lay down that ever present guard and be more joyful and stress-free. The fiery energy of Aries Moon partners can also draw out their Scorpio lover's danger-loving side and bring out the risk taker in them. To the slightly child-like Aries Moon lover, danger symbolizes fun, but to the more serious Scorpio type lover, danger is *thrilling* on many levels. The Scorpio essence is intense and focused, demanding total loyalty (even from friends), which Aries Moon partners can supply if appealed to in the right way – with love, sensitivity and zero demands.

When the chips are down, Aries Moon lovers will protect their Scorpio type mate with every ounce of strength they have, while Scorpio type partners will lay down their life to protect their Aries Moon soul mate. The only weak spot is that both can occasionally lose their tempers and say the wrong thing to each other, without meaning it. Aries Moon lovers can forgive small transgressions easily, but the intense Scorpio type lover may have trouble offering the olive branch, at least for some time. They will have to be soothed and appealed to all over again. This relationship can last if Scorpio type mates can be less controlling of situations and more trusting of their sweetheart's behavior and themselves.

It might help the Scorpio type lover to find out what kind of Aries Moon partner they have fallen in love with. People with Aries as their Moon sign will be either aggressive (the *ram type* Aries personality), or soft-spoken and more passive (the *lamb type* Aries personality) or a balanced blend of both (the *ram/lamb* Aries personality). If the Scorpio type mate is dominant, they will get along with the passive Aries Moon mate, but if they are also passive, they will be attracted to the super-charged, ram type Aries Moon personality.

Also, the watery Scorpio essence is financially pragmatic and very focused on the correct management of resources, especially if they have become joined through matrimony. The Aries Moon partner may not, at least initially, be too interested in the money factor, especially if their lover handles everything efficiently and makes all the decisions. It would help a lot if the impulsive Aries Moon companion applies a little discretion as to their spending habits so that their tense lover can relax when they walk out of the house with *their* credit card and a three page list of things to buy. This relationship can work out beautifully if the Aries Moon lover is more tactful around their sensitive Scorpio type partner, and if the Scorpio type soul mate can grant their Aries Moon companion a little more freedom and learn to be more forgiving of them; this pair has success written all over it.

Aries Moon vs. Sagittarius Sun, Moon or Rising Sign
The Fire and Fire Relationship

Fire: "I need romance and passion to really enjoy my relationship. Will my boyfriend be a faithful mate for life?" the fiery female partner wonders. "I want an active and freedom-loving partner. Will my girlfriend understand my need for true freedom in life or be too controlling?" the fiery male lover thinks to himself.

Aries Moon lovers get along remarkably well with any person who has their Sun sign, Moon sign and Rising sign in the wisdom-seeking and fiery sign of Sagittarius. Each partner symbolizes an element. Understanding that element helps us delve deeper into the real personality of that partner. Fire represents a burning passion, a hunger for adventure and a soaring inspiration. Elementally, fire supports fire beautifully. A good example of this would be the magnificent fireworks that light up the night sky at New Year's Eve. The double fire relationship illuminates the worlds of two trusting soul mates who revel in being their best, living their best and loving their best.

Fire is one of the most important elements because without it, the world would freeze and become useless. With the gift of heat, the great oceans move, frozen icebergs melt and create more water and frozen hearts begin to feel the depth of human emotion once again. Fire energy must also be maturely handled to bring forth its best attributes. A fire that burns too hot dies away just as quickly. Therefore, the key is to let it burn *slowly* and longer, changing it from a destructive fire to a productive fire. Too much fire can cause destruction, but if its power is controlled and tempered, it can turn into the comforting fireplace that keeps our homes so warm and cozy when the bitterness of a motionless winter descends over the land. Balancing the attributes of this exciting element is key.

The Sagittarius essence is very similar to the Aries Moon personality, both need great gobs of freedom and a happily given trust to fully *live* the relationship. The only problem they might encounter is when both feel the other is not invested enough for the love to survive due to other, usually temporary interferences. Fire signs also have fiery tempers but traditionally, they cool quickly and the thought of reaching for that olive branch is never far from their hearts. Aries Moon lovers encourage the Sagittarius essence into blooming, becoming more expansive and reaching the greatest heights possible, while the Sagittarius type energy helps the Aries Moon lover in realizing their most cherished dreams, while encouraging their risk-loving side even more.

It might help the Sagittarius type lover to find out what kind of Aries Moon partner they have fallen in love with. People with Aries as their Moon sign will be either aggressive (the *ram type* Aries personality), or soft-spoken and more passive (the *lamb type* Aries personality) or a balanced blend of both (the *ram/lamb* Aries personality). The more forceful and dominant Sagittarius mate will get along best with the non-confrontational and mellow ram/lamb Aries Moon personality, because they prefer partners who are strong when the situation demands it as well as passive enough to not challenge their authority.

Aries Moon partners are ruled by Mars, the planet that governs aggression and war, but most importantly, Mars like to draw our attention to the truth hidden behind problems that may have been lurking beneath the surface of a relationship, but have not been dealt with over many years. Unafraid of confrontation, Mars makes the Aries Moon lover come out and confront the pesky problem and be done with it forever. This brings the relationship up to the highest level of truth and honesty, which is always good for the overall health of the relationship in the long run.

Mars controls the Aries Moon lover, and their Sagittarius type partner functions under the energy of Jupiter. Jupiter and Mars are similar in some ways and yet in some ways, stand in stark contrast to each other. They both have the very same sense of fun and upbeat, life-loving energy. Philosophical Jupiter is a giant, jovial planet that is eager to jump into life, experience it from every angle and seek out precious life-knowledge from every person they meet. Through their Sagittarius lover, Jupiter causes the Aries Moon lover to take more risks, be more daring and take great, big Jupiter-style leaps into the unknown. No guts, no glory! No glory, no fun.

Muscleman Mars, on the other hand, rules the pure warrior-instinct and lives to protect the weak and victimized of this world. Mars, through the Aries Moon lover, causes the Sagittarius type lover to be even more fun-loving and aggressive. Both these planetary forces are powerful and volatile and therefore must be understood carefully because their essence will change on the field of love and intimacy. Jupiter loves adventure and diversity and so does Mars. Mars is a pioneer and trail blazer and so is Jupiter. Two dominant people cannot exist peacefully in a love relationship unless one of them learns the subtle and often secret art of compromise and balance. The partner who loves more or gets more out of the relationship will learn this art quickly and willingly.

When it comes to success, both the Sagittarius type lover and the Aries Moon partner will not display the slightest jealously toward each other and will actually encourage each other and feel proud of their various achievements. Each openheartedly exults in the other's success. Bonded through a compatible aspect, they will be each other's strongest champions no matter how much time passes by.

Often the most miniscule of reasons get blown out of proportion between them, which can be avoided if they both were more observant of each other's changing moods. Intellectually well-matched and protective of one another, their friendship will never perish, and if both are mature souls and can easily and frequently forgive, their relationship can survive the greatest storms and reach the safety of the shore of old age. This relationship has a good chance of success if the relationship begins as a long-term friendship, giving each time to acclimatize themselves to each other according to their own emotional timetables.

Sagittarius type lovers help Aries Moon partners to be more emotionally flexible and infuse them with a Jupiter style live-and-let-live ideology, while the Aries Moon essence introduces the fiery Sagittarius type love to the idealistic Mars style, *"Let's go do stuff!"* energy, and a desire to leave an impressive legacy behind. The generally happy Sagittarius energy needs a lover who is passionate but also *temperamentally large* or accommodating enough to fit into the 'wide angle' or emotionally all-encompassing Sagittarius life theme. And the Aries Moon lover just might fit the bill.

The fiery Sagittarius partner may, at least sometimes, not want some of the same things that an Aries Moon lover absolutely requires to enjoy life, but the friendship aspect of a relationship with a lover with an Aries Moon sign should not be underestimated. A gradual and regular interaction can bring both partners face to face with each other as confidants before they become lovers too soon. Honor and respect is of great value to Aries Moon lovers and it must be stressed that a relationship built on mutual respect instead of only passion will usually outlast a one-dimensional physical relationship that could die out remarkably quickly.

Sagittarius types are sweetly romantic and will enjoy not having to wonder if their jumpy but devoted Aries Moon lover will be faithful or not: philosophical Sagittarius can help preserve the newness and the truth of a relationship if they are truly in love, or have been burned many times by partners who repeatedly failed to understand them.

Aries Moon vs. Capricorn Sun, Moon or Rising Sign
The Fire and Earth Relationship

Fire: "I need romance and passion to really enjoy my relationship. Will my boyfriend be a faithful mate for life?" the fiery female partner wonders. "I want an active and freedom-loving partner. Will my girlfriend understand my need for true freedom in life or be too controlling?" the fiery male lover thinks to himself.

Earth: "Does my boyfriend manage his finances maturely or will I end up paying his bills and supporting him? I need stability and true commitment before I can enjoy the romance between us." the earthy female thinks to herself. "Will my future wife spend my hard earned cash on frivolous items at the mall or be wise enough to save up for our retirement?" the earthy male lover wonders.

Aries Moon lovers can enjoy a remarkably rewarding and successful relationship with lovers who have their Sun, Moon or Rising sign in the earthy and commitment-minded sign of Capricorn. Each partner symbolizes an element. Understanding that element helps us delve deeper into the real personality of that partner. Fire represents a burning passion and a soaring inspiration. Earth represents an unmatched stability and reliability: earth is a faith in love and an undying dedication to a relationship. Elementally, fire and earth can support each other wonderfully. Fire needs the earth so that it has support to burn on, while the earth needs fire to give it warmth, so that the winter's last frozen touch is melted away.

Fire, however, must be handled in a mature way, because it can cause destruction if not controlled, while the earth can cause a landslide to occur and rearrange the map in one stroke. When these energies mingle in appropriate amounts, the fire element warms our homes, and the earth provides a stable base and foundation for us to build our homes and lives on. Balancing the attributes of each element is key. Aries Moon partners have great lessons to learn from the stable Capricorn energy. Capricorn type partners can help actualize the most impossible dreams that an ambitious Aries Moon lover can envision. And what the Aries Moon lover envisions, their earthy mate *stabilizes*.

Aries Moon lovers are ruled by the planet Mars and their Capricorn type partner functions under the energy of Saturn. Saturn and Mars are similar in some ways and yet in some ways, stand in stark contrast to each other. Both are focused and passionate about a goal. Saturn is a somber, serious and wise planet that has been placed in charge of human karma and the accountability between human beings. Ancient, disciplined and concerned with duty and responsibility, Saturn causes relationships to enjoy longevity and stability if both partners are mature and faithful.

The Saturn energy therefore causes a great deal of changes to occur in the life of the sometimes reckless, Aries Moon lover through their Capricorn partner. Muscle bound Mars, on the other hand, rules pure warrior-like aggression and lives to protect the weak and helpless of this world. Mars governs the Aries Moon lover. Both these planetary forces are powerful and therefore must be handled extremely carefully because their essence will change on the field of love and intimacy. Saturn is cautious and double checks everything before committing, while Mars is fearless and never thinks twice if their heart has been captured. Mars is a dominant force and so is Saturn. Two dominant people cannot exist peacefully in a love relationship unless one of them learns the subtle and often secret art of compromise and balance. The partner who loves more will spend more time balancing the relationship.

Primarily supportive and protective, Capricorn types can teach their Aries Moon lover how to create a legacy and leave something tangible and powerful behind, while bringing to their attention the fact that planning ahead for that rainy day is an incredibly good thing for a risk-loving Aries Moon partner to do. Impetuous Mars causes the Aries Moon mate to blurt out *"Let's dive head-long into a new romance! I don't know you too well but you have the most beautiful eyes I've ever seen and I may already be in love with you."* The Saturn influence causes the Capricorn partner to reply, *"I think I like you, you're kinda cute, but I'll see if you're still in my life a month from now. If you are, I'll think about falling in love with you."*

Aries Moon partners become more frugal, driven and success-oriented around the Capricorn essence. They also learn to finish those projects that they usually leave half done. Capricorn type partners become more vocal and expressive around the fiery energy of their Aries Moon lover, while Aries Moon mates should learn to listen more carefully when the wise Saturn energy speaks through their mate. Capricorn types receive from their Aries Moon lovers a new perspective on life, where they can be more optimistic, light-hearted and feel more confident about themselves (Aries Moon lovers can help alleviate their Capricorn type partner's occasional depression or melancholia).

The Capricorn essence slows down the fast-paced, sometimes scattered, fiery Aries Moon energy and causes it to look before it takes those giant leaps into nowhere in particular. Capricorn type partners will make sure that the 'nowhere in particular' becomes *somewhere very important*. The Aries Moon lover will learn to ration their time, and want to successfully attempt bigger and better things with the aid of the guidance of Capricorn type lovers. With the earthy Capricorn energy to support happy-go-lucky Aries Moon lovers, they can change their outlook on life and become drawn to their ambitious side more than their purely experimental, fun-loving side. The only problem that could crop up could be their Capricorn type lover's tendency to put too much pressure on their Aries Moon partner (and themselves) to achieve a certain goal. Capricorn types can get very serious about the smallest things, which could hurt their relationship or even their health.

As for managing finances, it should be kept in mind that the Capricorn energy is more frugal than careless, especially when it comes to a precious resource like income. Impulsive Aries Moon lovers should take to spending within reason and always consult their earthy partners before big purchases are made. This courtesy alone will help smooth out a majority of their problems. Another important tip revolves around the Saturn-induced spells of sadness that sometimes come over the typical Capricorn type lover; at times like that the impetuous Aries Moon lover should step back, try not to overwhelm their mate with a hundred and one questions, and give their partner lots of space and a steady supply of TLC *but only when it is asked for.*

Capricorn types are very self-sufficient, so the signals they give out will have to be carefully interpreted. Together, both these cardinal energies can create a formidable empire that will stand the test of time, with the dependable Capricorn type partner supplying the stability and direction, and the Aries Moon lover supplying the joy of closeness and intimacy, with lots of fun and happiness thrown in!

Aries Moon vs. Aquarius Sun, Moon or Rising Sign
The Fire and Air Relationship

Fire: "I need romance and passion to really enjoy my relationship. Will my boyfriend be a faithful mate for life?" the fiery female partner wonders. "I want an active and freedom-loving partner. Will my girlfriend understand my need for true freedom in life or be too controlling?" the fiery male lover thinks to himself.

Air: "Is my boyfriend open-minded enough and will he appreciate my outspoken side? I need a life mate who will talk to me, communicate with me about everything and not clam up and brood." the airy female partner muses. "Will my girlfriend allow me to do the things I love or will she try to restrict me from expressing myself?" the airy male lover wonders.

Aries Moon lovers can get along wonderfully with lovers who have their Sun, Moon or Rising sign in the open-minded and friendly air sign of Aquarius. Each partner symbolizes an element. Understanding that element helps us delve deeper into the real personality of that partner. Fire represents a burning passion and an eager, optimistic and active temperament. Air represents an incredible intellectualism and creative genius. Elementally, fire and air can co-exist remarkably well. Fire needs the oxygen in the air to burn its brightest, while the air or the atmosphere needs the heat of fire to combat the frozen energy of a bone-chilling winter.

Be that as it may, if the air in the form of wild winds blows too forcefully, it can extinguish a small fledgling flame that is trying desperately to become a productive fire, while fire, if it burns too hot, can rob the air of all its oxygen and change its nature completely. Balancing the attributes of each element is key. Care should be taken that fixed and airy Aquarian types give the relationship some breathing space and let it emerge in its own, distinctive mold instead of hastening it along.

The first desire between these two energies will be one of creating a life-long friendship. Aquarius types are unique, one-in-a-million personalities and Aries Moon partners like their lovers to be different and rare; this creates an attraction between them. Both these signs are terrified of ending up with a humdrum lover who seems like a clone of their friend's partners: they want their lover to stand out and look strikingly original. Aquarius types bring out in their Aries Moon lovers a need to look at life through the ideal of equality and fairness for all people. There will always be some lost cause that the typical, socially conscious Aquarian will be drawn towards. The average Aquarian type person will shudder at the thought of living a nine-to-five existence for the rest of their lives, which is a fear they share with their Aries Moon mate.

It would help the Aquarian type lover to figure out what type of Aries energy they have fallen in love with. People with Aries as their Moon sign will be either aggressive (the *ram type* Aries personality), or soft-spoken and more passive (the *lamb type* Aries personality) or a balanced blend of both (the *ram/lamb* Aries personality). They may find greater compatibility with the ram/lamb type Aries Moon personality which may be able to supply just the right amount of romance and independence.

Desire spreads easily to the quickly inspired and active Aries Moon energy, creating a stalwart and readymade supporter for Aquarius. Aquarius types have the vision and an Aries Moon lover will blindly follow that pioneer spirit to the end of the earth and back. This air sign gifts their Aries Moon lover a sharp and expansive focus, be that the home sector or the career sector. The downside of this combination is that sometimes the airy Aquarian can get distracted and cause their Aries Moon companion to lose the initial fervor that fired their soul. Losing interest mid-stream could leave Aries Moon partners confused and bewildered, running off to find a new soul mate without having gotten a fair chance to experience the first one adequately.

A clash of timetables could cost both these good souls a life-long friendship. The plus side (and there are many) of this combination is an Aries Moon lover's ability to breathe life into Aquarius' stagnant projects and help toss them back on the front burner. The Aries energy says *"Go, go, go!"* and this gives Aquarius types the fighting spirit that may have been previously lacking. The fiery energy of the Aries Moon partner can understand remarkably well, their Aquarian type partner's unutterable inner yearning for freedom within close relationships, mainly because the Aries Moon lover needs an incredible amount of freedom within primary relationships themselves; they're both wired with the same mental circuitry.

Aries Moon lovers should be more patient around the Aquarian energy and the Aquarian type partners should follow through on any promises made. Honor is a key link between them, as is a genuine respect for each other's personal space. When in love, both these signs revel in mingling freedom with passion, and these lovers are advised to *slow down* the initial, frenetic pace of their love relationship so that it doesn't burn too hot, too quickly and die out. If a candle has been carefully lit, why leave it near an open window on a stormy, windy day?

Airy Aquarius types will want to speed up (air signs work fast, like the winds) various aspects of the connection due to an irrepressible curiosity, while their trusting Aries Moon partners will join in with wild abandon. A steady, smoldering fire is preferable to something that is initially exciting but does not last and leaves no trace. Together, both these energies support each other, fill each other with excitement and stand up for each other when the world begins it age-old rants on conformity.

Aries Moon vs. Pisces Sun, Moon or Rising Sign
The Fire and Water Relationship

Fire: "I need romance and passion to really enjoy my relationship. Will my boyfriend be a faithful mate for life?" the fiery female partner wonders. "I want an active and freedom-loving partner. Will my girlfriend understand my need for true freedom in life or be too controlling?" the fiery male lover thinks to himself.

Water: "Is my boyfriend emotionally stable and wise about our joint finances? Or will debts pile up in the first year of marriage? I need a supportive life-long lover as well as a loving one." the watery female lover thinks to herself. "Will my future spouse conserve our financial resources or spend unwisely without thought for the future? I can connect better romantically if I know that my chosen life-mate is passionate as well as mature and pragmatic." the watery male lover wonders.

Aries Moon lovers can blend energies nicely with lovers who have their Sun, Moon or Rising sign in the watery and poetic sign of Pisces. Each partner symbolizes an element. Understanding that element helps us delve deeper into the real personality of that partner. Fire represents a burning passion and a soaring inspiration. Water represents an emotional purity as well as a soft and inviting sensuality.

Elementally, water and fire are compatible, but adjustments have to be made for a full chance at compatibility. Water needs fire to create an atmosphere of warmth and security in our homes, as well as afford us those relaxing hot showers. While fire needs water to cool itself off if it is beginning to burn dangerously bright. Water must be careful around fire and not completely extinguish its hopeful energy, and fire must be used carefully around water because hot water can scald. Balance between the elements is key.

The Piscean essence is soft, alluring and is drawn to the hypnotism of fantasy rather than the boredom of practicality. Neptune, the ruler of Pisces, is the fantasy weaver planet and has been placed in charge of dreams and beautiful illusions in order to tempt us from our dreary lives. Being around an Aries Moon lover pushes Pisces type partners into becoming more focused on projects and begin to tap into their own latent fighting spirit, which proves very therapeutic. The Pisces type mate helps the Aries Moon lover into getting back in touch with their sympathetic, sensitive and creative side.

It would help the Pisces type lover to figure out what type of Aries energy they have fallen in love with. People with Aries as their Moon sign will be either aggressive (the *ram type* Aries personality), or soft-spoken and more passive (the *lamb type* Aries personality) or a balanced blend of both (the *ram/lamb* Aries personality). The sensitive Pisces type lover will find a special ease with the lamb type Aries Moon personality, because this type of Aries Moon mate will be just as soft-natured and sensitive as them.

Both partners would do well to remind each other that they must build a solid foundation first: one of friendship and most importantly, of raw honesty. Communication glitches could cause hurt feelings between these two earnest lovers who may feel that they are true soul mates. The typical Pisces energy sometimes forgets and unknowingly omits mentioning the details, while Aries Moon partners may be too trusting and never think to ask. Both should speak clearly to each other and encourage one another to communicate their feelings frequently. The key to doing this is in short, clear sentences that are a perfect picture of the emotions in their heart at that time. Pisces types like their lovers to show that they are in tune with them by being as intuitive as they are, but most people are not as gifted as they are. Which means that direct, straight talk is in order to avoid confusion.

Aries Moon lovers need to be very patient with their Pisces type lover and handle them with tenderness, as their feelings could be easily offended. The Aries Moon lover is ruled by Mars, the planet of raw, uncontrolled energy and drive, while Neptune rules the Pisces type partner. Mars (fire) and Neptune (water) are opposites; Mars is strong and assertive while Neptune is passive and prone to accepting illusion for reality. The Pisces energy brings out their Aries Moon partner's artistic side, while the Aries Moon energy causes the watery Pisces type person to be more in-tune with facing life's troubles with optimism and courage. No one mood will be constant with the mutable, slightly changeable, Pisces lover and no one emotion will last forever, which is good because it gives them a chance to get over problems easily without brooding about them. The Pisces type partner must watch out for a tendency toward obsession, which could be unhealthy for them if it brings them closer to a toxic personality who may be capable of deceiving them by using attention, flattery or love.

The Pisces type lover is emotional and susceptible to being the center of needless misunderstandings, so once again, the most energetic and impatient Moon sign in the entire zodiac family will have to use greater clarity and tact when approaching their soft-hearted Pisces type lover. Some people with Pisces placed prominently in their natal charts will sometimes suffer from low self-esteem due to the influence of Neptune. Neptune causes doubt to surface in the delicate and impressionable Pisces psyche, making it difficult for them to figure out who they really are and causing them to undervalue themselves and feel neglected over the slightest inattention.

Therefore, the Aries Moon partner will have to help bolster their water sign lover's self-confidence, but in a subtle way. Mars-influenced Aries Moon mates can also have a big effect on how their water sign lover makes important decisions (Pisces types desire approval from emotionally stronger partners), so words should be carefully chosen. The Pisces energy softens up their Aries Moon sweetheart considerably. Each supports the other selflessly, and if good communication skills are learnt and effectuated early on, this could be a great relationship.

Chapter 14
The Taurus Moon Sign Lover

Taurus Moon vs. Aries Sun, Moon or Rising Sign
The Earth and Fire Relationship

Earth: "Does my boyfriend manage his finances maturely or will I end up paying his bills and supporting him? I need stability and true commitment before I can enjoy the romance between us." the earthy female thinks to herself. "Will my future wife spend my hard earned cash on frivolous items at the mall or be wise enough to save up for our retirement?" the earthy male lover wonders.

Fire: "I need romance and passion to really enjoy my relationship. Will my boyfriend be a faithful mate for life?" the fiery female partner wonders. "I want an active and freedom-loving partner. Will my girlfriend understand my need for true freedom in life or be too controlling?" the fiery male lover thinks to himself.

Taurus Moon lovers can exist remarkably well with lovers who have their Sun, Moon or Rising sign in the fiery sign of Aries. Each partner symbolizes an element. Understanding that element helps us delve deeper into the real personality of that partner. Fire represents a burning passion and a soaring inspiration. Earth represents an unmatched stability and reliability: earth is a faith in love and an undying dedication to a relationship. Elementally, fire and earth can support each other effectively. Fire needs the earth so that it has support to burn on, while the earth needs fire to give it warmth and light, so that winter's last frozen touch is melted away to make way for the approaching spring of hope.

Fire, however, must be handled in a mature way, because it can cause destruction if not controlled, while the earth element can cause a landslide to occur and rearrange the map in one stroke. When these energies mingle in appropriate amounts, the fire element warms our homes and helps cook our food, and the earth element provides a stable base and foundation for us to build our homes and lives on. Balancing the attributes of each element is key. The Taurus Moon lover can soften up their Aries type partner's jumpy persona, and bring out in them a patient, sensual and more sympathetic side. They can also help the impatient Aries type lover to be more careful about finances and take better care of their money because Taurus is a strong money sign.

The Taurus Moon sign is made up of two, distinct personality types, and knowing which personality type we're dealing with in our lover will aid with long-term, day-to-day compatibility. The first type is the *builder type* of Taurus Moon lover and the second type is the *stabilizer type*. The builder type is ambitious, industrious and set in their ways, while the stabilizer type is less career-driven and more comfortable in love relationships and in the family atmosphere. The builder type is dominant and may clash with the equally dominant Aries energy, therefore the Aries type lover would do well if they paired up with the stabilizer type of Taurus Moon personality, in order to reduce power struggles that could cause their relationship to weaken due to tension.

Aries type lovers are ruled by the planet Mars and their Taurus Moon partner functions under the energy of Venus. Venus and Mars are similar in some ways (they are both eager for each other's companionship and true intimacy) and yet in some ways, are near perfect opposites of each other (Mars is pure male energy and Venus represents the female essence). Beauty-loving Venus, the Goddess of love and relationships, is a harmony-seeking planet and enjoys the company of her lover Mars more than anyone else in the planetary family. Aesthetic Venus harmonizes and helps relieve and release tension. Mars enjoys a special place in Venus' heart; these cosmic lovers are the original Romeo and Juliet of the solar system, but with a much happier ending, of course.

Venus transforms whatever it touches by creating desire and sensuality, and will therefore cause a great deal of positive changes to occur in the life of the Aries type lover through their mate. Muscle bound hunk Mars, on the other hand, rules pure warrior-like aggression and lives to protect the weak and defenseless of this world. Both these planetary forces are compatible in the world of love and intimacy. Venus loves to be in love and so does Mars. Mars is a dominant force and Venus is receptive and feminine. This makes the Taurus Moon and Aries type lovers a perfect match, don't you think?

When it comes to real life couples, merging bank accounts will come up at some point in time, because Taurus Moon lovers secretly judge people by the way they handle their financial assets and manage their income. Their Aries type lover brings to this fire and earth relationship, an irrepressible sense of fun and happiness, which is something careful and prudent Taurus Moon partners always save for last. Taurus Moon partners usually are more tradition-minded about most things. Aries types will infuse their Taurus Moon lover's life with excitement and super-charge it with energy! The Aries type lover will show their Taurus Moon partner that it is more fun to eat dessert first and dinner later, and this helps bring their earthy partner's guard down considerably. *"Let's do something forbidden, sweetheart!"* the impetuous Aries type mate suggests. The Taurus Moon lover will roll their eyes but rarely be able to say no to their endearing Aries type partner.

Taurus Moon lovers will help their Aries type partner streamline their life, make better business decisions and get back in touch with their calm and patient side. No one is more patient than a Taurus Moon lover and the Aries energy can gain a lot by learning from this Moon sign. Both will effectively train one another into picking up traits that make their overall personalities well rounded and wholesome. The Taurus Moon partner must keep in mind that their fiery lover responds more quickly to kindness and regular attention than to being aloof or stern, while the Aries type companion must never try to push their outwardly strong but inwardly sensitive Taurus Moon lover into making a decision that they are not ready to make.

Box a Taurus Moon partner into a corner and things will come to a total stand-still, which benefits no one. One more tip for the Aries type partner who is totally in love with their earthy Taurus Moon lover, is to remember that Taurus rules the throat, and if they use a soft, non-threatening voice when communicating with them, their point will register quicker. Taurus responds to music and recognizes the magic hidden in sound. This is a good, stable marriage connection if both partners learn to be less intense during the day, and save that intensity for when the skies begin to turn violet and evening draws down its shade for the night, helping these two lovers step into a world all their own.

Taurus Moon vs. Taurus Sun, Moon or Rising Sign
The Earth and Earth Relationship

Earth: "Does my boyfriend manage his finances maturely or will I end up paying his bills and supporting him? I need stability and true commitment before I can enjoy the romance between us." the earthy female thinks to herself. "Will my future wife spend my hard earned cash on frivolous items at the mall or be wise enough to save up for our retirement?" the earthy male lover wonders.

Taurus Moon lovers can get along nicely with lovers who have their Sun, Moon or Rising sign in their own earthy sign of Taurus. Elementally, earth can make earth even stronger, so that enormous edifices can be built, brick by brick, without the slightest fear of their collapsing. Imagine an ancient house: each brick symbolizes the solid, immovable and protective energy of the earthy Moon sign of Taurus. On the other hand, if a relationship is inundated by the effects of an immovable energy, no progress will be made, causing stagnation and later, estrangement to occur in the hearts of true lovers.

Each partner symbolizes an element. Understanding that element helps us delve deeper into the real personality of that partner. Earth represents an unmatched stability and reliability: earth is a faith in love and an undying dedication to a relationship. Elementally, the double earth vibration is very supportive. The first function of the earth element is to help other structures stand tall while carrying their load on itself. Earth is one of the strongest elements and is also the most modest when seen through the essence of earthy Moon signs (Taurus, Virgo, Capricorn). When nourished, the earth yields great bounties of food and nutrition, but when it is neglected, it hardens, becomes useless, dry and parched. When the earth is in a stable mood, everything is safe and life continues without a glitch. But if that ever-dependable earth decides to move, we will see earthquakes, both physically, and in our emotional lives.

The Taurus Moon sign is made up of two, distinct personality types, and knowing which of the two types we're dealing with will aid with getting along on a daily basis. The first type is the *builder type* and the second type is the *stabilizer type*. The builder type is ambitious, smart, dominant and has difficulty adapting to sudden change, while the stabilizer type of Taurus Moon lover is romantic, less career-driven and more comfortable in a stable marriage or while nurturing their family. The builder type, being dominant by nature, may clash with an equally assertive lover, therefore the Taurus type lover would do well if they paired up with the stabilizer type of Taurus Moon lover, in order to make sure that one lover can handle the other's tendency to take control and lead.

When an earth sign partner withdraws due to neglect or betrayal from a lover, it will be very difficult indeed to get them to open their hearts again. Which is why it is best to manage everything perfectly from the start. When threatened, the earth element vibration sits still and refuses to move or take any action. This is when they must be given time to assess the situation, heal and then be approached again in a sincere manner. Earthy Moon signs must be respected before they are loved. Balancing the attributes of this fascinating element is key.

The double Venus energy that surges through this earthy relationship will help this couple feel an incredible empathy for each other, as well as a deep understanding of one another's basic life goals. The only problem that might cause a stirring of negative emotions is when one of them is ready to commit to a marriage or long-term relationship and the other still harbors doubts. When this occurs, both partners need to handle the situation with extreme caution. If one of them is sure they've found the love of their life, the battle is half won already. The best thing to do is to give the partner who is still making up their mind, some space and freedom. The stable Taurus Moon energy reacts negatively if it feels like it is being pressured, which they translate as a threat. If their lover is patient, they will probably decide to be with them after all, because they were able to respectfully wait (while others didn't) while they made the most important decision of their life.

This couple must never let the respect and honor between them as friends ever change, no matter how many years they remain married. The desire for a strong union that can last for decades will be evident in both partners. Taurus is the most sensitive of all the Moon signs, and is known for its patience and ability to tolerate almost anything (sometimes even an excruciatingly bad marriage). But when both partners have the same Taurus energy in them, neither may want to make the first move when there are differences of opinion. Frequent communication, even if both of them want to run to their rooms and brood, will help carry this relationship out of the dangerous waters of misunderstandings that often take too long to sort out.

No matter who is wrong or right, quickly and genuinely offering the olive branch can mean the difference between a relationship between strangers who are simply attracted to each other physically, and soul companions who will never tolerate seeing a relationship they so tenderly built, dying away due to pride or neglect. Taurus is ruled by Venus, and the one thing that Venus will not tolerate in a relationship is detachment from a lover.

Venus carefully creates an avenue for two people to discover intimacy and trust between them (and then build on that trust gradually) and if anything threatens that creation, and if their lover stands by and lets it happen, Venus will be too hurt for words and will turn around and walk away forever. The Taurus Moon energy enjoys being around their family, being surrounded by lots of little kids and having their cherished elders near them. This family-oriented and tradition-loving sign thrives in long-term marriages where neither partner has any doubt about the other's loyalty. And even though both partners will be sharing a double dose of compatible Venus power, both must still test each other out, at least in the initial, critical phases of their courtship.

Harmonious Venus, the ruler of Taurus, thrills to see people falling in love all over the world. These lovers would do well to bring their relationship out of the Venus fantasy world and back into their daily life where toast does get burned, bills do get paid late and laundry may not arrive on time occasionally. Their best bet is to be infallibly honest with each other when dealing with finances and expenses (Taurus is an astute money sign), encourage each other in pursuing their most cherished goals, and keep the marriage from becoming so boring that there is no excitement left to enjoy. Both partners should keep from getting on each other's nerves by bringing forth each other's carefree and fun-loving side more. With the solid support system they have in each other, they needn't worry. Children will bring this pair closer, but *both* must be ready for that big step.

Taurus Moon vs. Gemini Sun, Moon or Rising Sign
The Earth and Air Relationship

Earth: "Does my boyfriend manage his finances maturely or will I end up paying his bills and supporting him? I need stability and true commitment before I can enjoy the romance between us." the earthy female thinks to herself. "Will my future wife spend my hard earned cash on frivolous items at the mall or be wise enough to save up for our retirement?" the earthy male lover wonders.

Air: "Is my boyfriend open-minded enough and will he appreciate my outspoken side? I need a life mate who will talk to me, communicate with me about every-thing and not clam up and brood." the airy female partner muses. "Will my girlfriend allow me to do the things I love or will she try to restrict me from freely expressing myself?" the airy male lover wonders.

Taurus Moon lovers can get along quite well with lovers who have their Sun, Moon or Rising sign in the communicative air sign of Gemini. Each partner symbolizes an element. Understanding that element helps us delve deeper into the real personality of that partner. Earth represents an unmatched stability and reliability: earth is a faith in love and an undying dedication to a relationship no matter how bad things get. Air represents an incredible intel-lectualism and a desire to communicate without restrictions.

Elementally, earth and air are quite compatible. The earth needs the oxygen in the air so that fields can be cultivated and made arable, while the air always has millions of particles of the earth flying around within it. Each element can exist within the other. But if the air mixes with the earth in inappropriate amounts, it can create a sandstorm, blinding everyone. By the same token, if the earth has too much air in it, it ceases to be solid and stable, and unable to allow structures to stand on it. Balancing the attributes of each element is key.

The Taurus Moon sign is made up of two, different personality types, and learning to tell them apart will aid with deciphering each type's approach to love. The first type is the *builder type* and the second type is the *stabilizer type*. The builder type is ambitious, self-sufficient and rejects sudden change, while the stabilizer type is romantic, accommodating and more family-oriented. The builder type of Taurus Moon lover is dominant and may clash with the equally dominant Gemini energy, therefore the Gemini type lover would do well if they paired up with the stabilizer type of Taurus Moon personality, in order to eliminate future power struggles.

As with every relationship, some adjustments will have to be made, but they will benefit both partners in the long run. Taurus Moon lovers are creatures of fixity and feel comfortable when things don't change too much. The security of pre-dictability is something they count on. The Gemini type partner's desires thrive on the energy of change and they seek it out with great delight. How are these two vividly disparate energies to find joy together? They could start by working with the information they have: Taurus Moon lovers should allow their Gemini type partners a little more leeway in life, and try to comprehend their need for stimulation and activity, and their Gemini type partner can make sure to never force their lover into moving at a faster pace than they feel comfortable with.

Taurus Moon partners enjoy relationships where they can take their time and get to know their lover on a variety of levels, without being pushed or prod-ded into committing before they are emotionally ready. Also, when the Tau-rus Moon lover is ready to be part of a life long relationship, they may still *wait* to hear the views of their gregarious partner first before they make their own views known. There may always be a fear of being rejected in the earthy Taurus Moon lover, especially by their adoring air sign mate. The Gemini type partner must also keep one thing in mind at all times: if they pledge their love to their Taurus Moon soul mate, or if they make a promise, they must make sure that they honor their word, come what may.

The occasionally suspicious Taurus Moon lover will find ways of testing their partner for long-term reliability. They want to make sure they're getting the real deal, and not someone who takes love and commitment lightly. Speed daters need not apply. Both lovers will have to show tolerance and try not to judge their partner, but affirm that their love will be strong enough to weather any storm together. Taurus Moon mates need a partner who will be dependable with finances and can be trusted with making the right financial decisions. They need to have some tangible proof from their restless Gemini type partner that they intend to stick around for a long time. The Gemini essence refrains from making promises because they know that they are very likely to change their mind come the morning. If, however, they are positive of how they feel about their attractive Venus-ruled mate, then they can go ahead and jump in with both feet.

Gemini awakens in their Taurus Moon lover a desire for original self-expression, and the Taurus Moon mate awakens in the Gemini type partner, a need to put down roots and settle down comfortably. Gemini types may struggle a bit with the decision to marry, because while part of them will want to be free of responsibilities, the other will want a taste of what it is to enjoy life's many inevitable stages with their lover, whose loyalty they will never have cause to doubt. Taurus Moon lovers will provide the foundation and their Gemini type lover will provide the spontaneity and fun to preserve the buoyancy in this relationship.

Taurus Moon vs. Cancer Sun, Moon or Rising Sign
The Earth and Water Relationship

Earth: "Does my boyfriend manage his finances maturely or will I end up paying his bills and supporting him? I need stability and true commitment before I can enjoy the romance between us." the earthy female thinks to herself. "Will my future wife spend my hard earned cash on frivolous items at the mall or be wise enough to save up for our retirement?" the earthy male lover wonders.

Water: "Is my boyfriend emotionally stable and wise about our joint finances? Or will debts pile up in the first year of marriage? I need a supportive life-long lover as well as a loving one." the watery female lover thinks to herself. "Will my future spouse conserve our financial resources or spend unwisely without thought for the future? I can connect better romantically if I know that my chosen life-mate is passionate as well as mature and pragmatic." the watery male lover wonders.

Taurus Moon lovers can get along famously with lovers who have their Sun, Moon or Rising sign in the emotive water sign of Cancer. Earth and water have a symbiotic relationship and both nurture and strengthen one another. Water needs the support of the structure of the land in order to flow where it wants, while the earth needs water to feel the full effects of true and nourishing fertility. Be that as it may, if the earth overwhelms water, the water could become undrinkable. And if water overwhelms the earth, for example in the form or a hurricane, the earth could easily be obliterated. Balance is key, as is a good knowledge of how each can help or hinder each other over the long term.

The Taurus Moon sign is made up of two, different personality types, and learning about each one's approach to intimacy will aid with long-term compatibility. The first type is the *builder type* and the second type is the *stabilizer type*. The builder type is result-oriented, ambitious and fears change, while the stabilizer type is romantic and thrives in close relationships and a loving, family environment. The builder type of Taurus Moon lover is dominant and may do well if they paired up with a non-confrontational lover in order to reduce problems with control issues within the relationship.

Taurus Moon lovers will thrive with a partner who appreciates their seriousness about love and settling down, while the Cancer type lover will appreciate a partner who won't run from an emotionally expressive soul mate. The Taurus Moon mate is also emotional like their Cancer type lover, but as is the nature of the earth element, they may tend to internalize emotions for years. Both these signs like to collect and preserve things and both are tradition loving, family-friendly signs. Cancer type lovers want to establish roots with their lover, and expect proper commitment and long-term loyalty, while Taurus Moon lovers expect the same, and will show less of their inner feelings until the time is right and the conditions are perfect. They're patient, and yes, they'll wait.

The Taurus Moon lover is ruled by romantic Venus, while the Cancer type partner responds to the imaginative energy of the Moon. The Moon and Venus are similar in quality: both are harmony-seeking, peace-loving and will avoid a direct confrontation if possible. Be that is it may, both the Taurus Moon mate and their Cancer type lover must engage in honest communication and never let things fester inside for too long. Otherwise, their emotional walls may go up and neither may be willing to trust the other with regard to resolving any issue.

Both appreciate a careful, modest and frugal lover who can be depended on to not empty their bank account every time a birthday or special occasion rolls around. The Cancer type lover must be sure to never overwhelm their Taurus Moon lover with too intense a show of feelings, because this might cause their earthy lover to become confused and try to withdraw from the situation, at least for a while. A little bit of emotion is good and healthy, but creating or inflating an issue to attract their lover's attention may not be right for the long haul. The Taurus Moon lover must also face difficult issues when the time is right and not expect them to disappear on their own because it may be a touchy subject. Some Cancer type partners have a fear of abandonment, which may creep into their closest relationship. The earthy Taurus Moon lover enjoys being with a partner who is emotionally balanced, takes most difficulties things in their stride and does not constantly complain about the smallest occurrences that can be better handled in a calm, relaxed manner.

A temperamentally flexible lover will maintain a practical view of things and remain in control in even the most volatile of situations. The Cancer type mate is capable of bringing great gifts to their relationship, by creating a nurturing and comfortable environment in a way that only they can. The 'nester' Cancer energy brings emotional security to their partner and brings out their trusting and patient side. This is a good, stable combination, especially if having a family is part of their plans for the future. This combination can last forever, because these two share the soul mate energy.

Taurus Moon vs. Leo Sun, Moon or Rising Sign
The Earth and Fire Relationship

Earth: "Does my boyfriend manage his finances maturely or will I end up paying his bills and supporting him? I need stability and true commitment before I can enjoy the romance between us." the earthy female thinks to herself. "Will my future wife spend my hard earned cash on frivolous items at the mall or be wise enough to save up for our retirement?" the earthy male lover wonders.

Fire: "I need romance and passion to really enjoy my relationship. Will my boyfriend be a faithful mate for life?" the fiery female partner wonders. "I want an active and freedom-loving partner. Will my girlfriend understand my need for true freedom in life or be too controlling?" the fiery male lover thinks to himself.

Taurus Moon lovers can enjoy a good and emotionally fulfilling relationship with partners who have their Sun, Moon or Rising sign in the cheerful and generous fire sign of Leo. Each partner symbolizes an element. Understanding that element helps us delve deeper into the real personality of that partner. Fire represents an undying optimism, a burning passion and a desire to enjoy the best that life can offer. Earth represents an unmatched stability and reliability: earth is a faith in love and an undying dedication to a relationship. Elementally, fire and earth can support each other wonderfully.

Fire needs the earth so that it has support to burn on, while the earth needs fire to give it warmth, so that the winter's frozen spells can be broken and melted away. Fire, however, must be handled in a mature way, because it can cause destruction if not controlled, while the earth can cause a landslide to occur and rearrange the map in one stroke. When these energies mingle in appropriate amounts, the fire element warms our homes, heats our food and the earth element provides a stable base and foundation for us to build our lives on. Balancing the attributes of each element is key.

The Taurus Moon sign is separated into two, different personality types, and knowing which one your lover fits into will be helpful in creating a closer bond with them. The first type is the *builder type* and the second type is the *stabilizer type*. The builder type is result-oriented, highly ambitious, assertive and sees change as a negative thing, while the stabilizer type will finding greater meaning in intimate relationships than in pushing their career goals forward. Love will always take precedence over a job or career success for the stabilizer type of Taurus Moon lover. The builder type of Taurus Moon partner is dominant and may clash with the equally dominant Leo energy, therefore the Leo type lover would do well if they paired up with the stabilizer type of Taurus Moon personality, in order to lessen disruptive control issues between them.

In many ways, both these fixed signs are alike: Leo type partners enjoy being in a relationship and prefer it to being single, and Taurus Moon lovers work hard at keeping a good relationship that is producing the results they want, afloat, especially if their lover has the *most* of the important qualities they seek in a life-mate. Taurus Moon mates are usually careful about who they fall in love with. Ruled by Venus, the Goddess of love and relationships, Taurus Moon partners usually have a good idea as to who will be a good life companion, and who might not comprehend their view of what a relationship or committed marriage should be. They may feel that it is better to know ahead of time, if their requirements match their partner's, instead of finding out much later, when they might be standing on the doorstep of disappointment.

Taurus Moon partners think long term. The only thing they may have to watch out for is their fiery Leo mate's desire for appreciation and admiration:

Leos need to be heard! Leo type lovers like to hear their partner *verbalize* appreciation, and sometimes their Taurus Moon partner may become complacent with the relationship and forget to do this. Both are undoubtedly very loving and the passion they experience will be rare and unforgettable for both. Marriage is also a fine idea if both of them keep a few points in mind. Leo type partners should never force their hard working and faithful Taurus Moon partner to enter into any phase in life before they are ready. These decisions may include topics such as when to start a family, where to buy a house and where to move.

Taurus Moon lovers won't mind a long courtship: they like to test out their partner and feel that time is always on their side. But impulsive Leo type lovers may not be so patient and may take off in search of another lover who is eager to be with them, without fully understanding their earthy lover or giving them time to understand them. Also, Taurus Moon lovers need financial stability before fully committing their heart to one person, and the Leo energy could certainly provide that. Taurus is a financial sign and they often judge their lovers by trying to find out how they handle money as well as save and invest it. Better balance that checkbook, dear Leo!

If the fire sign Leo partner can watch how much they spend, and if pragmatic Taurus Moon mates can curtail how much they worry about finances, this could be a solid partnership. The Leo energy brings out the carefree romantic in their Taurus Moon soul mate, and the Taurus Moon lover brings out their Leo type partner's sensitive and cautious side. The Sun rules the Leo type mate, and Taurus Moon partners are governed by Venus. Venus will look for a dominant, confident lover to merge destinies with and the Sun can provide the security Venus needs. The Sun is powerful and brilliant and beautiful Venus is usually passive but sometimes outspoken. The Sun likes to be looked up to for protection and Venus likes the attention she gets from the Sun-ruled Leo type lover. Over all, this could be a good match if the Sun-ruled Leo lover curtails their tendency to take over the decision making process and forget to ask their mate's opinion, and if the Venus-ruled Taurus Moon partner learns to speak up if the balance tips too much in their mate's favor.

Taurus Moon vs. Virgo Sun, Moon or Rising Sign
The Earth and Earth Relationship

Earth: "Does my boyfriend manage his finances maturely or will I end up paying his bills and supporting him? I need stability and true commitment before I can

enjoy the romance between us." the earthy female thinks to herself. "Will my future wife spend my hard earned cash on frivolous items at the mall or be wise enough to save up for our retirement?" the earthy male lover wonders.

Taurus Moon lovers can get along quite well with partners who have their Sun, Moon or Rising sign in the reliable earth sign of Virgo. Similar earthy energies blend well and can support each other over the long haul. Earth signs usually take relationships quite seriously and worry a great deal about whether or not their chosen partner will stand the test of time with them. Each partner symbolizes an element. Understanding that element helps us delve deeper into the real personality of that partner. Earth represents an unmatched stability and reliability: earth is a faith in love and an undying dedication to a relationship despite problems or incompatibility.

Elementally, the double earth vibration is very supportive. The first function of the earth element is to help other structures stand tall while carrying their load on itself. Earth is one of the strongest elements and is also the most modest when seen through the essence of earthy Moon signs (Taurus, Virgo, Capricorn). When nourished, the earth yields great bounties of food and nutrition, but when it is neglected, it hardens, becomes useless, dry and parched. When earth is in stable abundance, everything is stable and life continues without a problem. But if that ever-dependable earth decides to move, we will see earthquakes, both physically, and in our emotional lives.

The Taurus Moon sign is separated into two, varying personality types, and your compatibility level will depend on which type of personality your lover predominantly expresses. The first type is the *builder type* and the second type is the *stabilizer type*. The builder type is exactly that, a strong builder of a foundation of success, and their interests will be rooted in rising up in the professional world, while the stabilizer type will strive to stabilize and fortify their closest love bonds while placing their jobs, vocations and professional dreams *below* their heart's truest desires. The builder type is dominant and would do well if they paired up with a non-combative lover, in order to reduce power struggles between two assertive lovers.

When an earth sign partner withdraws due to neglect or betrayal from a partner, it will be very difficult indeed to get them to open their hearts again. Which is why it is best to effectively win their trust from the start. When threatened, the earth element sits still and refuses to move or take any action. This is when they must be given time to heal and then be approached again in a sincere manner. This is the one element on which stands our whole world, which is why earth signs must be offered respect before they are loved. Balancing the attributes of this stable element is key.

Virgo type partners bring their detail-loving and practical natures to this relationship, and their Taurus Moon lover will appreciate how hard working and singularly dedicated they are. The Taurus Moon partner adds romance and sensitivity to the union, which helps their worrywart Virgo type lover express their sensual side more often instead of keeping it under wraps all the time. The Taurus Moon partner will encourage their Virgo type soul mate to use the paintbrush and canvas more often than they use the vacuum cleaner (or the PC at work).

The Venus-ruled Taurus Moon lover is creative, loves music and this will bring out their Virgo type lover's literary and expressive side, which is excellent for their Virgo type partner's health. One point that should be kept in mind is that Taurus Moon lovers are sensitive, and Virgo type partners must watch how they approach the strong and steady Taurus Moon energy, because Taurus doesn't take criticism very well and might take it too seriously or personally. The helpful Virgo type partner may only be trying to assist but they must be careful about *how* they say things. Taurus Moon lovers are susceptible to kindness, and respond better to soft-spoken partners who won't approach aggressively and demand things to be done *now*. Virgo's criticisms must be presented as suggestions.

Virgo types usually make excellent partners and the Taurus Moon lover may be the perfect addition to their lives. Taurus Moon partners are creatures of habit and their Virgo energy mates could bring with them a solid system of regularity in daily living that they will find comfortable to adapt to. Taurus Moon mates feel secure within routines and tradition. Financially cautious, neither will have to worry about the other over charging credit cards before the first of the month or forgetting to pay the gas bill (as money issues lie at the heart of many lovers separating). This is a stable and harmonious combination if having children is on the cards at some point, as both make devoted parents.

Taurus Moon vs. Libra Sun, Moon or Rising Sign
The Earth and Air Relationship

Earth: "Does my boyfriend manage his finances maturely or will I end up paying his bills and supporting him? I need stability and true commitment before I can enjoy the romance between us." the earthy female thinks to herself. "Will my

*future wife spend my hard earned cash on frivolous items at the mall or be wise
enough to save up for our retirement?" the earthy male lover wonders.*

*Air: "Is my boyfriend open-minded enough and will he appreciate my outspoken
side? I need a life mate who will talk to me, communicate with me about everything and not clam up and brood." the airy female partner muses. "Will my
girlfriend allow me to do the things I love or will she try to restrict me from
openly expressing myself?" the airy male lover wonders.*

Taurus Moon lovers can get along rather well with partners who have their
Sun, Moon or Rising sign in the romantic air sign of Libra. Earth and air
can be quite compatible under the right circumstances. Each partner symbolizes an element. Understanding that element helps us delve deeper into the
real personality of that partner. Earth represents a desire to build and secure
using an unmatched stability and reliability: earth is a faith in love and an
undying dedication to a relationship. Air represents a desire to express, an
incredible intellectualism and creative genius. Their passion is to communicate
millions of ideas to the world in an original and memorable format.

The Taurus Moon sign is divided into two, specific personality types, and your
compatibility with them will depend on how well you adjust to each. The first
type is the *builder type* and the second type is the *stabilizer type*. The builder
type is usually strongly focused on creating an unshakeable foundation of success, and their interests will be in rising up in the professional world, while the
stabilizer type will strive to stabilize their love relationships, family connection
with children and parents and help them achieve their dreams with great dedication. The builder type is dominant and may do well if they paired up with
a patient, passive or non-confrontational lover, in order to make sure that
clashes between two dominant lovers are avoided and harmony is easily maintained.

Both the Taurus Moon lover and the Libra type mate are ruled by Venus, the
Goddess of relationships and love. That alone shows that they've been green-
lighted by Astrology. With a double dose of Venus power surging through this
relationship, romance will never be lacking. Both Taurus Moon lovers and
anyone with Libra prominently placed in their natal charts will respond
quickly to companionship-oriented Venus energy. Tradition-loving and routine-oriented, Taurus Moon partners make faithful and capable partners and
will usually want to create a firm structure within which a family (or a project)

can be raised. Libra types are *very* sensitive to beauty in a woman and attractiveness in a man, and will be drawn to their Taurus Moon partner's patience, pragmatism and tenderness. Libra type partners can energize the earthy Taurus Moon lover by infusing in them an excitement for life and new, intellectually stimulating experiences.

Movies, books, art, good conversation and music will be a favorite of this double Venus power couple. The only problem they might like to watch out for is the Libra type mate's indecisiveness, or worse, a tendency to make up their mind and then suddenly change it. Stable Taurus Moon partners need a definite answer, preferably written in stone so that there is a surety they can depend on. *"So, what's it going to be, honey? Is it a yes or a no? Are you on board with me or should I walk away?"* the Taurus Moon lover questions.

When it comes to commitment, the Libra type mate will commit but perhaps take too long to decide. The Taurus Moon lover, on the other hand could also take too long to decide if their Libra type partner is best for their lifestyle, because earthy Taurus Moon mates like to be very sure of what kind of long term deal they are getting into. They both need to give each other the gift of space to decide without undue pressure. This alone will bring them closer because other lovers will get impatient, get angry and stomp out of the house, vowing never to return. Caution might tip the balance in the most patient lover's favor.

The Libra essence is very marriage minded, which suits their Taurus Moon partners just fine, if they are ready for matrimony themselves. This could be a successful pairing, where the Taurus Moon soul mate provides the comfort and stability and the Libra type companion provides the spontaneity and excitement. Libra is elegant, while Taurus Moon lovers are sensual, therefore this doubly attractive, *amor*iented couple could learn many things from each other.

Taurus Moon vs. Scorpio Sun, Moon or Rising Sign
The Earth and Water Relationship

Earth: "Does my boyfriend manage his finances maturely or will I end up paying his bills and supporting him? I need stability and true commitment before I can enjoy the romance between us." the earthy female thinks to herself. "Will my future wife spend my hard earned cash on frivolous items at the mall or be wise enough to save up for our retirement?" the earthy male lover wonders.

Water: "Is my boyfriend emotionally stable and wise about our joint finances? Or will debts pile up in the first year of marriage? I need a supportive, life-long lover as well as a loving one." the watery female lover thinks to herself. "Will my future spouse conserve our financial resources or spend unwisely without thought for the future? I can connect better romantically if I know that my chosen life-mate is passionate as well as mature and pragmatic." the watery male lover wonders.

Taurus Moon lovers can experience a highly fulfilling relationship with partners who have their Sun, Moon or Rising sign in the intense, water sign of Scorpio. The pull here will be one of marriage as these signs are polarized or opposite each other on the zodiac family wheel. Elementally, earth and water can sustain each other beautifully. The earth needs the refreshing nourishment of the element of water to feed its fields and farms, making our world green and lush, while water needs the support of earth in order to form its boundaries and give it direction. Both signs are alike but also dissimilar in their own way. When the seventh sector comes into play, there will be, at some point or the other, a desire to merge destinies on a legal level.

It would help the Scorpio type lover if they knew exactly which of the two, specific Taurus Moon personality types belongs to their lover. The first type is the *builder type* and the second type is the *stabilizer type*. The builder type is a strong builder of a support system for others, and their interests will include creating a name for themselves in the professional world, while the stabilizer type will strive to stabilize their closest love bonds while placing their jobs, vocations and professional dreams below their heart's ambitions, which will include long-term domestic harmony. The builder type is dominant and may clash with equally dominant lovers, therefore the Scorpio type lover would do well if they paired up with the stabilizer type of Taurus Moon personality, in order to make sure that two assertive types don't end up matching wits all the time.

Taurus Moon partners are stable and emotionally vibrant, but only with the right person. Scorpio type mates look for a lover who is intensely perceptive like them, or at least understands why they take certain aspects of life to heart: Scorpio abhors pointless social mingling and searches for value and quality in a mate. They like to experience life at a deep intrinsic level, which may be too deep for the average human being to comprehend, hence the search for a lover who has some of the rare qualities they seek. But Taurus Moon lovers will know exactly how that enigmatic Scorpio heart works and what it needs to feel secure. Both are financial signs and their financial views will either bring them closer or create unwanted tension between them, usually over the smallest expenditures.

Be that as it may, they should never let the respect and honor between them as friends ever change, no matter how many years they remain together. The desire for a strong union that can last for decades will be evident in both partners. Taurus is the most sensitive of all the earthy Moon signs, and is known for its patience and ability to tolerate almost anything (sometimes even an excruciatingly bad relationship). But when one of the partners has the Taurus Moon energy in them and the other is watery by essence, neither may want to make the first move when there are differences of opinion. Frequent communication, even if both of them want to run to their rooms and brood, will help carry this relationship out of the dangerous waters of suspicions and misunderstandings that often take too long to sort out.

This union between the Taurus Moon lover and their Scorpio type partner will be, on many levels, a merging of the power of the planets Venus and Pluto. Mysterious Pluto is a somber, serious and wise planet that demands the best and will not stand by and watch an injustice continue even for a minute. It transforms whatever it touches by changing it from the inside out and from the ground up, and will therefore cause a great deal of changes to occur in the life of the Taurus Moon lover. Venus is a passive and receptive planet and looks for stronger, more dominant lovers with whom to interact.

Falling in love with a Scorpio type partner is easy; getting them to fall in love with you may be a little difficult. As one of the most charismatic but stoic signs in the zodiac family, trying to figure out how they feel about you may be challenging. The Scorpio type mate will be either mature about using control and power in their relationships, or perhaps not quite as wise as others think they are. It depends on what kind of Scorpio they are. Scorpio type lovers are sometimes incredibly possessive in love relationships as well as about their children/money. And even though this sign has been erroneously labeled the most sexual of all the signs in the zodiac family, not all people with Scorpio as their Moon, Sun or Rising sign may deserve that title. The Taurus Moon sign can be equally passionate. But a natural trust must come before passion can be awakened in the Taurus Moon heart.

When problems occur, no matter who is wrong or right, quickly and genuinely offering the olive branch can mean the difference between a relationship between strangers who are simply attracted to each other physically, and soul companions who will never tolerate seeing something they so tenderly built, dying away due to pride or inconsideration. The Taurus Moon energy enjoys being around their family, being surrounded by lots of little kids and having their cherished elders near them and the Scorpio energy does as well. These family-oriented and tradition-loving signs thrive in long-term marriages where neither partner has any doubt about the other's fidelity. And even though both partners may be indubitably in love, both must still test each other out, at least in the initial phases of their courtship.

Both the Scorpio type mate and the Taurus Moon lover worry about the proper management and use of money and resources, so if they're both on the same page about that, ninety percent of their problems will disappear. Taurus Moon partners love spending time in nature and their Scorpio type partner will know exactly why this form of rejuvenation is needed. This will be a close and long term union because neither will carelessly destroy something that takes so much out of them emotionally to create. The only problems between them may circle around the Taurus Moon lover's slowness or reluctance in giving the go ahead for certain projects and the Scorpio type lover's tendency to worry and become a tad too intense about simple matters.

Both signs are also incredibly possessive of each other and the time they spend with one another. This relationship will benefit if Scorpio type mates can be less concerned by and more trusting of their sweetheart's behavior. No matter what their daily occupations may be, they would do well to schedule some alone time regularly so that their connection remains fresh and potent. This combination can last forever, because both lovers will try to be patient with each other and lend each other the balance they need from time to time, verbally and non-verbally. These two share the soul mate energy.

Taurus Moon vs. Sagittarius Sun, Moon or Rising Sign
The Earth and Fire Relationship

Earth: "Does my boyfriend manage his finances maturely or will I end up paying his bills and supporting him? I need stability and true commitment before I can enjoy the romance between us." the earthy female thinks to herself. "Will my future wife spend my hard earned cash on frivolous items at the mall or be wise enough to save up for our retirement?" the earthy male lover wonders.

Fire: "I need a stable romance and fiery passion to really enjoy my relationship. Will my boyfriend be a faithful mate for life?" the fiery female partner wonders. "I want an active and freedom-loving partner. Will my girlfriend understand my

need for true freedom in life or be too controlling of what I want to do?" the fiery
male lover thinks to himself.

Taurus Moon lovers can enjoy a good and uplifting relationship with partners who have their Sun, Moon or Rising sign in the fiery, wisdom-lov-
ing sign of Sagittarius. But adjustments may have to be made due to how
differently each sign looks at love and bonding. Each partner symbolizes an
element. Understanding that element helps us delve deeper into the real personality of that partner. Fire represents a burning passion and a soaring inspiration. Earth represents an unmatched stability and reliability: earth is a faith
in love and an undying dedication to a relationship. Elementally, fire and earth
can support each other wonderfully.

Fire needs the earth so that it has support to burn on, while the earth needs fire
to give it warmth, so that the winter's last traces are melted away. Fire, however, must be handled in a mature way, because it can cause destruction if not
controlled, while the earth can cause a landslide to occur and rearrange the
map in one stroke. When these energies mingle in appropriate amounts, the
fire element warms our homes, heats our food and the earth element provides
a stable base and foundation for us to create our lives on. Balancing the attributes of each element is key.

Any one in love with a Taurus Moon person should know which of the two,
well-defined Taurus Moon personalities they are likely to exhibit. The first
type of Taurus Moon personality is the *builder type* and the second type is the
stabilizer type. The builder type feels most fulfilled when they are able to build
a strong foundation in life, the kind that can support their professional dreams
as well their private ones, while the stabilizer type will strive to stabilize their
most important love relationships in life. Their heart will draw them toward
creating a harmony-oriented marriage or relationship; a peaceful family atmosphere after marriage will be key to their happiness. The builder type is dominant and may clash with the equally dominant Sagittarius type lover, therefore
the Sagittarius type lover would do well if they paired up with the stabilizer
type of Taurus Moon personality, in order to eliminate daily power struggles.

Taurus Moon lovers will look for a partner who is passionate and thrives with
one partner, which quickly removes the tension and guesswork out of a new
relationship that is usually built on shaky ground. The expansive Sagittarius
energy needs a lover who is passionate but *temperamentally large* or emotionally accommodating in many aspects of life. In other words, if problems arise,
they need someone who doesn't make an already serious situation more fright-

ening by becoming emotional about it, but instead, looks calmly for ways to efficiently resolve it in the smallest amount of time possible. The Taurus Moon partner expects that changes be kept to a minimum so that adjustments will never be needed, while the Sagittarius type mate feels that life can be enjoyed no matter how many changes come into their lives as a couple. Taurus Moon mates think that life changes are a chore, while the Sagittarius energy perceives change as exhilarating and refreshing.

One sign fears change while the other is revitalized by it. The dynamic Sagittarius partner may, at least sometimes, not want some of the same things that a Taurus Moon lover absolutely requires to feel secure in life. They could achieve success despite these two rather disparate planetary energies, because they could start out as good friends (Taurus Moon mates make the most reliable confidants) and remain so, until they are both sure that they are on the same page regarding long term expectations.

Sagittarius types are sweetly romantic and will enjoy not having to wonder if their Taurus Moon lover will be faithful or not: philosophical Sagittarius can preserve the truth of a relationship if they are truly in love, or have learned the hard way by being burned many times by partners who repeatedly failed to understand them, manipulated them and cost them their sense of trust. Sagittarius types can infuse their earthy Taurus Moon lover's life with excitement, a love of adventure, travel and lots of fun experiences where both can let their guards come down and relax. The Taurus Moon lover should give their Sagittarius type lover lots of space, emotional and physical, if they really want them in their life.

Sagittarius is mutable and flexible, and will make *some* changes to accommodate their Taurus Moon partner, but they must be truly in love to go through the effort needed. The Sagittarius type lover says *"I love you so much, I want you to run with me, travel with me, seek wisdom with me and be my soul mate!"* The cautious Taurus Moon lover answers *"I'd love to, but I need you to stabilize what we have first and put some roots down, and then, when we retire, if we have enough funds, we'll go traveling."* Even an adventurous Taurus Moon mate will look before they leap.

Things will work out if the relationship begins as a long-term friendship, giving each enough time to acclimatize themselves to their relationship at their own emotional timetables. Taurus Moon soul mates can introduce their fiery lovers to true sensuality mingled with a genuine affection that never wavers, while their Sagittarius type sweetheart introduces them to being more relaxed in the face of risk and invite more fun into their lives. Both will effectively train one another into picking up traits that make their overall personalities well rounded and more wholesome.

Taurus Moon vs. Capricorn Sun, Moon or Rising Sign
The Earth and Earth Relationship

Earth: "Does my boyfriend manage his finances maturely or will I end up paying his bills and supporting him? I need stability and true commitment before I can enjoy the romance between us." the earthy female thinks to herself. "Will my future wife spend my hard earned cash on frivolous items at the mall or be wise enough to save up for our retirement?" the earthy male lover wonders.

Taurus Moon lovers can enjoy an excellent relationship with partners who have their Sun, Moon or Rising sign in the earthy and ambitious sign of Capricorn. With both partners operating under the stability of the earth energy, this could be a successful relationship in the making if they both apply themselves. Each partner symbolizes an element. Understanding that element helps us delve deeper into the real personality of that partner. Earth represents an unmatched stability and reliability: earth is a faith in love and an undying dedication to a relationship no matter how many roadblocks they have to face. Elementally, the double earth vibration is very supportive. The first function of the earth element is to help other structures stand tall while carrying their load on itself.

Earth is one of the strongest elements and is also the most modest when seen through the essence of earthy Moon signs (Taurus, Virgo, Capricorn). When nourished, the earth yields great bounties of food and nutrition, but when it is neglected, it hardens, becomes useless, dry and parched. When the earth element is stable, life continues without a glitch. But if that ever-dependable earth decides to move, we will see earthquakes, both physically, and in our emotional lives. When an earth sign partner withdraws due to neglect or betrayal from a partner, it will be very difficult indeed to get them to open their hearts again. Which is why it is best to manage everything perfectly from the start.

When threatened, the earth element vibration sits still and refuses to move or take any action. This is when they must be given time to heal, assess what happened and then be approached again in a sincere manner. This is the one element on which stands our whole world, which is why earthy Moon signs must be respected before they are loved. Most Capricorn type partners are driven careerists, and need a partner who is emotionally sensitive but also careful about managing money and securing it. Taurus Moon partners are closely associated with the money factor, because Taurus is a financial sign. Ambitious Capricorn type lovers usually tend toward building something that they can refer to as their personal legacy. This is important to grasp because they will look for a lover who won't interfere with this desire.

The Taurus Moon personality comes in two shades, and familiarizing ourselves with each one can help us in understanding their deeper motivations. The first type is the *builder type* and the second type is the *stabilizer type*. The builder type is exactly that, a strong builder of a foundation of success, and their interests will be in rising up in the professional world, while the stabilizer type will strive to stabilize their closest love bonds while placing their jobs, vocations and professional dreams below their heart's truest desires. The builder type is dominant and may clash with the equally dominant Capricorn energy, therefore the Capricorn type lover would do well if they paired up with the stabilizer type of Taurus Moon personality, in order to make sure that daily power struggles don't threaten to shake the peace of their relationship.

The Capricorn type mate has a deep and emotional need to leave a mark on the world so that respect and prestige are theirs forever. Capricorn type partners work really hard and they need a partner who can genuinely appreciate that dedication to success. Both Taurus Moon lovers and their Capricorn type partners take life seriously, as well as love. Commitment is not a word their lover should be scared of, because these earth signs have no patience for such fear and lack of maturity. *"If you're going to do something, do a fantastic job the first time, mistakes cost time and money"*, they believe. Elementally, the double earth vibration supports and protects. Earth needs more earth underneath it and on top of it to create an edifice of strength and stability.

But too excessive an influence of any element can overwhelm a relationship, which may thrive better when presented with a contrast of temperaments. When they feel they're under threat or under pressure, earthy Moon signs refuse to take any action. The only thing the Taurus Moon partner and their Capricorn type soul mate need to bear in mind is that if there is ever a breakdown in communication, both of them will wait for *the other* to offer the all important olive branch. It is crucial that neither of these earthy lovers wait too long to communicate quickly and rebuild their connection. The longer they wait, the more disillusionment they may feel.

No matter who is wrong or right, quickly and genuinely offering the olive branch can mean the difference between a relationship between strangers who are simply attracted to each other physically, and soul companions who will never tolerate seeing something they so tenderly built, dying away due to pride. Both these earthy lovers need to feel special to their life-partner and both need to be treated with the utmost care and tenderness. Harsh words spoken in haste are not easily forgotten by either.

They must never let the respect and honor between them as friends ever change, no matter how many years they remain together. The desire for a strong union that can last for decades will be evident in both partners. They will want their marriage to be a success story the whole world can envy. Taurus is the most sensitive of all the earthy Moon signs, and is known for its patience and ability to tolerate almost anything (sometimes even an obviously unsuitable marriage partner). Frequent communication, even if both of them want to run to their rooms and brood, will help carry this relationship out of the darkness of misunderstandings that often take too long to sort out.

The Taurus Moon energy as well as the Capricorn type partner enjoys being around their family, being surrounded by lots of little kids and having their cherished elders near them. These family-oriented and tradition-loving signs thrive in long-term marriages where neither partner has any doubt about the other's loyalty. This will be a stable union if emotions are kept in check and neither partner puts too much pressure on the other, but learns to read the signals they send out first.

The Taurus Moon lover is ruled by Venus, the planet of relationships and love, while the Capricorn type lover functions under the energy of Saturn. Saturn rules commitment, longevity and discipline and will demand a serious effort from the Capricorn type lover in order to create a strong marriage. Venus craves intimacy and companionship and lacks Saturn's karmic wisdom, but will tend to follow and emulate the more take-charge and dominant Saturn energy in the form of the Capricorn type partner.

Taurus Moon vs. Aquarius Sun, Moon or Rising Sign
The Earth and Air Relationship

Earth: "Does my boyfriend manage his finances maturely or will I end up paying his bills and supporting him? I need stability and true commitment before I can enjoy the romance between us." the earthy female thinks to herself. "Will my future wife spend my hard earned cash on frivolous items at the mall or be wise enough to save up for our retirement?" the earthy male lover wonders.

Air: "Is my boyfriend open-minded enough and will he appreciate my outspoken side? I need a life mate who will talk to me, communicate with me about every-thing and not clam up and brood." the airy female partner muses. "Will my girlfriend allow me to do the things I love or will she try to restrict me from freely expressing myself?" the airy male lover wonders.

Taurus Moon lovers can enjoy a memorable relationship with partners who have their Sun, Moon or Rising sign in the broad-minded sign of Aquarius. This earth and air combination can survive if both partners can understand what separates them and what brings them together. Elementally, earth and air can exist symbiotically. The air or our atmosphere, needs the earth to cling to, and the earth needs the air to blow away the smog and pol-lution so that plants, trees and gardens can flourish and grow green.

The Taurus Moon sign is separated into two, varying personality types, and your compatibility level with them will depend on which type of personality your lover predominantly expresses. The first type is the *builder type* and the second type is the *stabilizer type*. The builder type works hard and is diligent in creating a foundation on which to base their life and ambitions, while the stabilizer type will strive to create a stable environment in which key relation-ships, especially family and marital ones, can evolve and experience security.

Taurus Moon partners are tradition-minded and like to follow a set pattern in life, because they find that routine brings with it a sense of security. This is a family-friendly Moon sign and feels, if family relationships have been gener-ally healthy in their past, close to their parents and siblings. Aquarius type partners, on the other hand, are broad-minded enough to consider their *friends* their family and their family their friends. They need to be with a very emotionally flexible partner who forgives easily and can grasp the unusual Aquarian life philosophy.

Aquarian type partners are loving but not the most traditional of mates, and their idea of love and marriage may clash with what the Taurus Moon lover has in mind for them as a couple. Taurus Moon lovers will test out their mates to see if they will be trustworthy and dependable in the long run, while Aquar-ian type lovers will also test their potential partners to check if they can ade-quately provide the *consistent level of personal freedom* they need to feel truly fulfilled in life. Aquarian type partners have a very unique idea of what the per-fect love relationship should be: they want a lover with whom they can bond intellectually first and romantically second. Passion or mushy romance is not something they feel drawn to, and they need to know that their partner is a best friend first and a compatible lover second.

Uranus, the erratic and unpredictable renegade planet rules Aquarius, and romantic Venus rules the Taurus Moon partner. When these two lovers meet on the field of love, they will invoke the power of the planets Venus and Uranus in their midst. Venus is partnership-oriented and thrives in loving and highly interactive relationships. Taurus Moon mates love doing everything with their partner: going to the movies, going for a hike, or reading poetry together, for example. The Uranus-ruled Aquarian lover also enjoys romance but will need to spend time with their friends too and will not allow another person to direct their social calendar. In their minds, their lover and their friends share the same high pedestal.

Venus-ruled, Taurus Moon partners can fall victim to neglect from a lover rather quickly and may want to know if their lover also places them first, like they place them above all else in their heart. This is where understanding, and lots of it, will be needed. The fixed Aquarius type lover cannot, and *will not* change or abandon their friendships for their lover (but should watch out for betrayal by a close friend). The Venus-ruled Taurus Moon mate will have to make the compromises and adjustments, as well as stay ready for any unplanned surprises their Aquarian lover may decide to toss their way.

A partner who causes an emotional overload in an Aquarius type lover will soon find that they stop communicating with them. Emotional gridlock can be avoided if both of them keep talking out grievances instead of hoping they will disappear on their own. The Taurus Moon mate may lean more toward keeping a lot of their feelings inside, sometimes for years at a time, which could seriously hurt their relationship. Their airy Aquarian type mate, on the other hand, may tend to share too much at the wrong time, when that information cannot be properly interpreted and grasped. Timing is everything in the game of love.

Taurus Moon lovers place a high degree of emphasis on passion in a relationship, but it can only fully be expressed if their partner has already truthfully committed to them. Taurus is a financial sign, so this couple will have to make sure that one partner's spending habits don't steadily drive the other one crazy (money issues sadly lie at the heart of many lovers separating). Frugal and usually adept at the careful investing of money, Taurus Moon mates will expect the same kind of attention to financial management from their intellectual, idealistic Aquarian type lovers, who are very experimental and usually less involved with the practical aspects of life.

It is essential that both partners learn to frequently communicate the musings of their heart. Most lovers are not mind readers and shouldn't have to be. Keeping their true feelings from each other may create unnecessary pressure on their relationship. This combination of fixed signs can work if Taurus Moon lovers will allow their Aquarian type partners to express their love in *their own way*, and if the Aquarius type partner can learn to be *consistently* more attentive and sensitive to the Taurus Moon psyche and honor the promises they make to them.

Taurus Moon vs. Pisces Sun, Moon or Rising Sign
The Earth and Water Relationship

Earth: "Does my boyfriend manage his finances maturely or will I end up paying his bills and supporting him? I need stability and true commitment before I can enjoy the romance between us." the earthy female thinks to herself. "Will my future wife spend my hard earned cash on frivolous items at the mall or be wise enough to save up for our retirement?" the earthy male lover wonders.

Water: "Is my boyfriend emotionally stable and wise about our joint finances? Or will debts pile up in the first year of marriage? I need a supportive life-long lover as well as a loving one." the watery female lover thinks to herself. "Will my future spouse conserve our financial resources or spend unwisely without thought for the future? I can connect better romantically if I know that my chosen life-mate is passionate as well as mature and pragmatic." the watery male lover wonders.

Taurus Moon lovers can enjoy an incredibly successful relationship with partners who have their Sun, Moon or Rising sign in the watery and intuitive sign of Pisces. Each partner symbolizes an element. Understanding that element helps us delve deeper into the real personality of that partner. Earth represents a desire to build and secure, to stabilize and safeguard. Water represents a desire to feel, empathize and symbolizes an emotional purity as well as a soft and inviting sensuality.

Elementally, water and earth are quite compatible. Water needs the earth to give it direction and arrange the boundaries and flow of its bodies of water, while the earth needs water so that fruitful farms that feed millions, and gardens and trees grow tall and green. The earth receives true nourishment in the form of rain from the water bearing clouds in the sky. Each element supports the other beautifully. But care must be taken so that one element doesn't overwhelm the other. If there is too much earth in water, it would be impossible to drink it. If there is not enough water in the earth, nothing grows anywhere. Balancing the attributes of each element is key.

The Taurus Moon sign is divided into two, distinct personality types. The first type of Taurus Moon personality is the *builder type* and the second is the *stabilizer type*. The strong, dependable builder type does exactly what its title suggests; it builds a solid foundation in life and creates it with a hope that what they choose to pour their energies into will last a lifetime, be it a career, business, marriage or family. This type can be ambitious, dominant and driven, and may take failure, criticism or opposition very hard. The stabilizer type is more easy-going, romantic, poetic and will feel at total ease in the relationship, marriage or family setting, while handling career changes with grace. They will prefer to devote their energies toward more emotional and private avenues of self-expression, such as interpersonal relationships. The builder type of Taurus Moon lover is dominant and may do well if they paired up with the accommodating Pisces type of lover, so that their love can grow in a non-combative and peaceful environment.

The Pisces energy is very compatible with the earthy Taurus Moon essence because water and earth signs have more life goals in common than other signs. Taurus Moon partners require emotional commitment before they will let their heart immerse itself into the great and deep Piscean waters of emotion and intuition. Pisces type lovers are deeply emotional by temperament themselves, and need a partner, an anchor who will provide a rock-solid foundation on which they can rely. The Pisces energy brings sensitivity and faith to a sometimes, skeptical Taurus Moon lover, while the Taurus Moon lover aids their watery lover in finding their voice and feeling more confident about their more difficult life choices.

Artistic and imaginative Pisces type partners, more than their Taurus Moon mates, need to be able to think clearly and require a lover who can bring them out of any self-doubt, which may plague them during certain times in their lives. Neptune rules the sign of Pisces, and while it can inspire and create the most beautifully haunting fantasies man can dream of, it can also cause a great deal of confusion and self-deception in the tender Pisces heart. Which is why frequent and clear communication should be a rule of this relationship. The Pisces type partner must watch out for a tendency toward obsession, which could be unhealthy for them if it brings them closer to a toxic personality who may be capable of deceiving them. They must learn to read those red flags on time.

Taurus Moon partners are emotional, but find it hard to have to deal with a lover who is twice as emotional and sensitive as they are. An emotional overload could cause the usually stable Taurus Moon partner to lash out verbally or completely withdraw from discussing the problem at hand. Financially, the Pisces type mate may be more impulsive when spending cash, and this may pose a problem because Taurus is a financial sign and most Taurus Moon folks are very prudent about managing their resources properly, at the right time and in the right way.

This is a good match provided the Pisces type lover learns not to push their earthy Taurus Moon lover into making any decision before they are ready. Taurus Moon mates should help their sensitive, watery partner express their practical side more than their trusting side and help to regularly bolster their delicate self-esteem. Pisces type partners must also remember never to withhold any information, no matter how inconsequential it may seem to *them*, from their Taurus Moon lover. If Taurus Moon lovers begin to doubt their partner even a little, that little doubt could spread into a full fledge suspicion and wreck the relationship.

This is a good combination if a family is planned. The Taurus Moon energy supports and grounds the watery Pisces type partner, while the beautifully fluidic Pisces energy lifts their Taurus Moon sweetheart out of the boring world of checkbooks, chores and financial planning and puts them down into the sensual world of romance, poetry and heartfelt promises.

Chapter 15

The Gemini Moon Sign Lover

Gemini Moon vs. Aries Sun, Moon or Rising Sign
The Air and Fire Relationship

Air: "Is my boyfriend open-minded enough and will he appreciate my outspoken side? I need a life mate who will talk to me, communicate with me about everything and not clam up and brood." the airy female partner muses. "Will my girlfriend allow me to do the things I love or will she try to restrict me from freely expressing myself?" the airy male lover wonders.

Fire: "I need romance and passion to really enjoy my relationship. Will my boyfriend be a faithful mate for life?" the fiery female partner wonders. "I want an active and freedom-loving partner. Will my girlfriend understand my need for true freedom in life or be too controlling of my daily life?" the fiery male lover thinks to himself.

Gemini Moon lovers can have a very compatible relationship with partners who have their Sun, Moon or Rising sign in the active and happy-go-lucky fire sign of Aries. Each partner symbolizes an element. Understanding that element helps us delve deeper into the real personality of that partner. Fire represents an active, joyous and restless temperament and a need to experience life from every angle. Air represents a need to express oneself and assimilate information in a myriad different formats.

Elementally, fire and air can co-exist remarkably well. Fire needs the oxygen in air to burn its brightest, while the air or the atmosphere needs the heat of fire to remove the last traces of a merciless winter. Be that as it may, if the air in the form of wild winds blows too forcefully, it can extinguish a small fledgling flame that is trying desperately to become a productive fire, while fire, if it burns too hot, can rob the air of all its oxygen and change its nature completely. Balancing the attributes of each element is key.

The fascinating Gemini Moon personality is divided into two separate, versions. The first type of Gemini Moon personality is the *serious type* and the second is the *fun-loving type*. The serious type is mature, ambitious, organized, yearns to reach the top of their profession and will express dominant leadership characteristics in love relationships. The second type of Gemini Moon personality is the fun-loving type; mental stimulation is crucial to them (boredom makes them irritable), this type is not as methodical as the serious type of Gemini Moon person, and may tend to scatter their energies easily. While they may lack the goal-oriented temperament of the serious type of Gemini Moon type, they may be just as assertive and dominant in relationships or friendships.

Gemini Moon lovers are mentally restless and active partners who need a mate who won't ask them to slow down in life, but actually join them in enjoying it more by doing things their way and having fun. There is an intellectual bonding here that helps the relationship progress along the lines of original and truthful communication, something that should exist between all lovers. Gemini Moon lovers are interesting conversationalists and need lovers who can keep up with them as well as challenge them to better themselves. Aries type partners may fit the bill nicely because Aries is a very self-motivated, energetic sign that thrives when their lover understands their emotionally vibrant persona without trying to change their impulsive nature.

Aries brings out the innovative teacher, skilled writer and speaker in their Gemini Moon lover, while Gemini Moon mates aid Aries types in fearlessly expressing themselves and coming up with brilliant ideas that are always percolating inside the Aries mind. In a love relationship, both are curious and will want to speed up their relationship, wanting to experience all the passion there is within the first few months of meeting each other. They are advised to wait and *actively* slow down the pace of their courtship to a more manageable speed, so that they can attach themselves emotionally to each other's non-sexual personalities first.

This over-active relationship could burn out too soon and that would be a shame because together, they could be each other's strongest champions and inspiration. The Gemini Moon lover is ruled by Mercury, the communication planet; and the Aries type mate is ruled by Mars, the most energetic and passionate planet in the solar system family. Mars makes this relationship achievement-oriented and filled with optimism, while Mercury causes it to be extremely interactive and exciting. Both are eager and opinionated, and will have to work to keep those conversations from morphing into arguments.

The clever Gemini Moon mate can talk circles around the Aries type lover, but should refrain from doing so. While the Aries type mate may get impatient if their viewpoint is not grasped instantly, causing them to explain themselves again and again. Both could get irritable easily. The literary and expressive Gemini Moon lover brings out their Aries type lover's best intellectual qualities, while the Aries type mate may bring out the Gemini Moon lover's desire to ponder love, intimacy and romance. This relationship can last if it begins as a truthful, stable friendship for a prolonged period of time, where the focus is less on winning arguments and more on developing a genuinely caring attitude toward each other by giving up that which we love in order to make our mate more comfortable. Both these lovers need to concentrate on how *they* affect their mate, instead of only focusing on how their lover makes them feel.

Gemini Moon vs. Taurus Sun, Moon or Rising Sign
The Air and Earth Relationship

Air: "Is my boyfriend open-minded enough and will he appreciate my outspoken side? I need a life mate who will talk to me, communicate with me about everything and not clam up and brood." the airy female partner muses. "Will my girlfriend allow me to do the things I love or will she try to restrict me from freely expressing myself?" the airy male lover wonders.

Earth: "Does my boyfriend manage his finances maturely or will I end up paying his bills and supporting him? I need stability and true commitment before I can enjoy the romance between us." the earthy female thinks to herself. "Will my future wife spend my hard earned cash on frivolous items at the mall or be wise enough to save up for our retirement?" the earthy male lover wonders.

Gemini Moon lovers can have a good relationship with partners who have their Sun, Moon or Rising sign in the dependable earth sign of Taurus. Each partner symbolizes an element. Understanding that element helps us delve deeper into the real personality of that partner. Earth represents an unmatched stability and reliability: earth is a faith in love and an undying dedication to a relationship. Air represents an incredible intellectualism and creative genius that can take communication to a whole new level, and bring millions of messages and information to the world in an eloquent and original format.

Elementally, earth and air are quite compatible. The earth needs the oxygen in the air so that fields can be cultivated and made arable, while the air always has particles of the earth flying around within it. Both elements dwell within one another. But if the air mixes with the earth in inappropriate amounts, it can create a sandstorm, blinding everyone. By the same token, if the earth has too much air in it, it ceases to be solid and stable, and unable to allow any structure to stand on it. Balancing the attributes of each element is key.

The Gemini Moon personality is divided into two separate, versions. The first type of Gemini Moon personality is the *serious type* and the second is the *fun-loving type*. The serious type is self-controlled, ambitious, drawn to the world of academia and will express dominant leadership characteristics in love relationships quite readily. The second type of Gemini Moon personality is the fun-loving type; this type is not as organized or ambitious as the serious type of Gemini Moon person, and may find it hard to structure their lives, as routine may make them feel restricted and restless. This type may be just as assertive and dominant in relationships however.

The earthy Taurus energy may be difficult for the airy Gemini Moon lover to initially adapt to, but being quick and observant, they will certainly get into the flow of things and learn to anticipate their lover's likes and dislikes as time wears on. Gemini Moon mates have the gift of being able to get along with a variety of people, and it won't be difficult for them to charm their Taurus type lover. Taurus type partners are very grounded emotionally and make passionate lovers, while Gemini Moon lovers, who may enjoy passion, may sometimes put intellectualism ahead of passion. The Gemini Moon person's search in life is one of finding the best, truly free medium of expressing their considerable intellectual capabilities.

A partner who understands this and encourages their expressive side will bond quickly with them. Taurus type lovers need tangible forms of confirmation (rings, an engagement party in front of close friends and relatives) from their mates so that they can rest assured that they are properly invested in creating a future together. And when it comes to picking one person to settle down with, the Gemini Moon lover might need a little extra time to confidently make the right decision. Gemini Moon partners want to know for sure that their lover won't restrict their unique style of living their life, spending time with various friends and their desire to be as unrestricted as possible.

Also worth nothing is that the Taurus type mate may lean more toward keeping a lot of their feelings inside, sometimes for years at a time, which could seriously hurt their relationship. Their gregarious and magnetic Gemini Moon mate, on the other hand, may tend to share *too much at the wrong time*, when that information cannot be properly interpreted and grasped. An emotional overload could cause the usually stable Taurus type partner to lash out verbally or completely withdraw from discussing the problem. Timing is everything and socially adept Gemini Moon partners can be the masters of perfect timing if they wish.

Taurus type mates may feel confused and threatened if a promise is not realized at the right time and may walk away, thinking that their Gemini Moon partner is too self-absorbed to notice them. This would be a shame because both these lovers really can make each other quite happy. The Gemini Moon essence brings out in their Taurus type lover a sense of freedom, and an open-hearted appreciation for self-expression, while the Taurus type lover introduces the Gemini Moon partner to sensuality, trust and real, reassuring stability, something the Gemini Moon lover will search for more and more as they begin to age and the nester in them emerges.

Gemini Moon vs. Gemini Sun, Moon or Rising Sign
The Air and Air Relationship

Air: "Is my boyfriend open-minded enough and will he appreciate my outspoken side? I need a life mate who will talk to me, communicate with me about everything and not clam up and brood." the airy female partner muses. "Will my girlfriend allow me to do the things I love or will she try to restrict me from expressing myself in the way I want to?" the airy male lover wonders.

Gemini Moon lovers can have a compatible relationship with partners who have their Sun, Moon or Rising sign in their own air sign of Gemini. Each partner symbolizes an element. Understanding that element helps us delve deeper into the real personality of that partner. Air represents a need to absorb, teach, learn and excel in using a sense of creativity that can take communication to a whole new level, and bring millions of messages and information to the world in an eloquent and original format.

Elementally, the double air vibration can mix energies beautifully. Air supports air and blends with it seamlessly. But it should be noted that a whole lot of air going around without aim only becomes a destructive typhoon. While, when it is controlled and properly tempered, it becomes the clean, fresh breeze that we expect when we open the windows of our homes in the springtime.

The intriguing Gemini Moon personality is divided into two separate, versions. The first type of Gemini Moon personality is the *serious type* and the second is the *fun-loving type*. The serious type is intellectual by temperament, can control their impulsiveness well and strives to rise up in the world and experience true, often hard won professional success. The second type of Gemini Moon personality is the fun-loving type; this type may need help getting organized and adhere to a proper routine. Both types are assertive and dominant in relationships or friendships.

Gemini is ruled by Mercury; the planet of speech. With a double shot of talkative Mercury surging through the veins of this relationship, communication will never be lacking. In fact, it would be conducive to the health of the relationship if once in a while, both partners spent time together without expressing anything, but just drinking in the atmosphere of being close to each other. They must learn that not everything can and should be expressed through words, but that letting the interplay between feelings and emotions enter the picture would bring them closer to each other than they ever imagined. Gemini Moon partners need a great deal of freedom in their lives: the freedom to think, to believe and to say whatever they want without fear of reprisals from their life-mate. This is something that only another Gemini type person can comprehend.

Be that as it may, too much similarity is as hurtful to a love connection as are too many differences. When two strongly Mercurial lovers get together in the game of love, invariably there will be times when one says something to the other without thinking or processing it first, creating in them a confusion that is unbearable. One partner has to provide the contrast of personalities without which the relationship might begin to atrophy. For example, one of these two Gemini lovers will have to be prudent about expenditures or be more invested in creating a regular income. If one of them agrees to take on the responsibility of being the stabilizer in the union, it will take a considerable amount of pressure off the relationship.

Two airy personalities may need some serious grounding if this relationship is to stand the test of time. Their eloquent words have to mean something and that can only happen if one of them becomes the security watchdog of the relationship. When things seem to go wrong, when misunderstandings occur over the smallest things and when two people who deeply love each other, cannot seem to find a reliable way to express their feelings, one of them will have to slow down and take charge. It is very difficult indeed to take charge of or control the element of air. But this can be done if these two airy lovers speak more with their hearts and eyes and less with their voices.

Sometimes, a relationship with two expressive Gemini lovers may generate a lot of communication, but find that what they really wanted to say, remained sadly unsaid. That is when the power of true love enters the picture. These two lovers should support each other, but not forget to be their original, enigmatic selves as well. The beautiful mutability (or emotional flexibility) of this sign can ensure that this will be a love story that is truly memorable.

Gemini Moon vs. Cancer Sun, Moon or Rising Sign
The Air and Water Relationship

Air: "Is my boyfriend open-minded enough and will he appreciate my outspoken side? I need a life mate who will talk to me, communicate with me about every-thing and not clam up and brood." the airy female partner muses. "Will my girlfriend allow me to do the things I love or will she try to restrict me from openly expressing myself?" the airy male lover wonders.

Water: "Is my boyfriend emotionally stable and wise about our joint finances? Or will debts pile up in the first year of marriage? I need a supportive life-long lover as well as a loving one." the watery female lover thinks to herself. "Will my future spouse conserve our financial resources or spend unwisely without thought for the future? I can connect better romantically if I know that my chosen life-mate is passionate as well as mature and pragmatic." the watery male lover wonders.

Gemini Moon lovers can have a loving relationship with partners who have their Sun, Moon or Rising sign in the intuitive water sign of Cancer. Some personality adjustments may have to be made, but then which relationship doesn't require adjustments? Each partner symbolizes an element. Understanding that element helps us delve deeper into the real personality of that partner. Air desires to express and represents an incredible intellectualism and creative genius. Water desires to feel and empathize and represents an emotional purity as well as a soft and inviting sensuality. Elementally, air and water are quite compatible and can have a symbiotic relationship. Water contains elements of the air in the form of millions of microscopic bubbles, while the air contains water in the form of moisture. Each supports the other but the balance can be tipped if care is not taken in handling each element in the proper way.

The Gemini Moon personality is divided into two separate, versions. The first type of Gemini Moon personality is the *serious type* and the second is the *fun-*

loving type. The serious type is studious, ambitious, focused and looks to their career accomplishments for true fulfillment in addition to other things in life. The second type of Gemini Moon personality is the fun-loving type; they are seekers of merriment, friendly and devote most of their energies to non-professional matters. The fun-loving type of Gemini Moon lover may be just as assertive and dominant in relationships or friendships.

The Cancer type lover is one of the most emotional and sensitive of all the signs, and when they look for a life-companion, they will look for someone who is wise as well as supportive. They need a lover who is able to understand their moods and fluctuating emotional rhythms without judging them negatively or jumping to conclusions about what is really bothering them.

The Gemini Moon partner also has a set of important requirements in a relationship without the fulfillment of which they cannot relax and enjoy their partner. As an air sign, gregarious Gemini Moon partners revel in a relationship where any problems can be talked out quickly and resolved efficiently. *"Let's get this issue behind us and get on with life!"* the Gemini Moon partner says. Cancer types are so sensitive that they may be too busy being upset over what happened and may not want to dive head long into a discussion about who did what. Part of the Cancer persona wants to be understood without any excessive words being exchanged. Intuitionist Cancer types will wonder if their Gemini Moon is lover is even listening to their grievances and feel terribly ignored, which sends them deeper and deeper into their protective, emotional shell, causing them to brood for a little longer.

Initially, there may be some confusion in the heart of the Cancer type partner as to how they can successfully comprehend their carefree and easygoing partner. They may try to imitate them and try to think like them. The watery Cancer type partner may be trying very hard indeed to understand their airy partner but may not be able to properly interpret the emotional language of the Gemini Moon lover. The Gemini Moon lover, on the other hand may think that they have their sensitive lover all figured out, but that may not be true. It would take the restless Gemini Moon mate a very long time indeed to fully grasp the incredibly deep character of the Cancer type persona.

Come what may, this pair should never let the respect and honor between them as friends ever change, no matter how many years they remain together. Cancer is the more sensitive of the two, and is known for its patience and ability to tolerate almost anything (sometimes even an excruciatingly bad marriage). No matter who is wrong or right, quickly and genuinely offering the olive branch can mean the difference between a relationship between strangers who are simply attracted to each other physically, and soul companions who will never tolerate seeing something that they so tenderly built, dying away due to pride or neglect. The maternal Cancer energy enjoys being around their family, being surrounded by lots of little kids and having their cherished elders near them. This family-oriented and tradition-loving sign thrives in long-term marriages where neither partner has any doubt about the other's loyalty. The Gemini Moon lover also enjoys this, but may also need to be around casual friends in a social setting. The Cancer type mate is usually home-centered, while their mate will focus outside of the home sector for more satisfaction and appreciation.

They could both keep in mind the following points: the Cancer type lover functions on purely emotional energy and finds excessive logic and rational-ization a serious roadblock to enjoying life, while the airy Gemini Moon lover may consider too much emotionality in a lover a perplexing problem which they cannot circumvent, causing them to get irritable and impatient. Logic and emotion can co-exist if both lovers can learn to tone down the dosage of each according to the time and situation. The Cancer type lover could learn to not take the smallest problems quite so seriously, while their Gemini Moon lover could learn to take certain issues *more* seriously, so that both of them can reach a level playing field of daily interaction.

This couple's best bet is to handle each other tactfully and learn each other's triggers and fears so that any possible emotional gridlock can be eliminated before it gets out of hand. The Cancer type partner fears never being under-stood; but they shouldn't push too hard *nor* totally withdraw from the scene when disagreements arise and cause them to feel disheartened. The Gemini Moon lover fears being dominated or controlled and may feel boxed in over miniscule issues. Both need to refrain from either emotionalizing issues too much, or ignoring them point blank. The Cancer type partner might like to be more expressive and actually share how they feel when their lover asks for their input, instead of expecting them to automatically know their emotional status.

This will be a union of the energies of Mercury, the ruler of the Gemini Moon lover, and the Moon, the ruler of the Cancer type lover. Mercury is brilliant, quick and restless, while the Moon is maternal, calm and security-seeking. Clever Mercury may sometimes not understand the dreams of the Cancer type partner but over time, they can learn to blend their dreams into one. Gemini is nothing if not emotionally flexible, which is a great and useful quality to have when dealing with their one-in-a-million Moon-ruled lover.

Gemini Moon vs. Leo Sun, Moon or Rising Sign
The Air and Fire Relationship

Air: "Is my boyfriend open-minded enough and will he appreciate my outspoken side? I need a life mate who will talk to me, communicate with me about every-thing and not clam up and brood." the airy female partner muses. "Will my girlfriend allow me to do the things I love or will she try to restrict me from expressing myself?" the airy male lover wonders.

Fire: "I need romance and passion to really enjoy my relationship. Will my boyfriend be a faithful mate for life?" the fiery female partner wonders. "I want an active and freedom-loving partner. Will my girlfriend understand my need for true freedom in life or be too controlling?" the fiery male lover thinks to himself.

Gemini Moon lovers can have a highly expressive relationship with part-ners who have their Sun, Moon or Rising sign in the open-hearted fire sign of Leo. Each partner symbolizes an element. Understanding that element helps us delve deeper into the real personality of that partner. Fire represents a desire to experience the rawness of life and a hunger for adventure, romance and spontaneity. Air represents a desire to express, using an incredible intel-lectualism and creative genius. Elementally, fire and air can co-exist remark-ably well. Fire needs the oxygen in the air to burn its brightest, while the air or the atmosphere needs the heat of fire to combat a frozen winter. Be that as it may, if the air in the form of winds blows too forcefully, it can extinguish a small fledgling flame that is trying desperately to become a productive fire, while fire, if it burns too hot, can rob the air of all its oxygen and change its nature completely. Balancing the attributes of each element is key.

The fascinating Gemini Moon personality is divided into two separate, ver-sions. The first type of Gemini Moon personality is the *serious type* and the sec-ond is the *fun-loving type*. The serious type takes ambition more seriously than relationships; hard won professional accolades seem to emotionally uplift them to a greater degree than anything else. The second type of Gemini Moon per-sonality is the fun-loving type; this type is merry, jovial and lacks the single-mindedness of the serious type of Gemini Moon lover. The one thing they both share in common is that when it comes to marriage, they are both assertive and dominant. Their best bet is to find a partner who will not compete with them or challenge their direct way of handling issues within the relationship.

Fiery Leo type partners will feel energized by a Gemini Moon lover, because the Gemini Moon mate can inspire a rare expressiveness in their Leo type partner. The Gemini Moon lover needs a partner who understands their need to be free in everything that they do. Freedom of expression is extremely important to the gregarious and mentally restless Gemini Moon persona. One thing that should be kept in mind with this pairing is the Leo type partner's tendency to take control of the relationship and forget to ask their Gemini Moon partner how they feel about it. Leo types mean well and remember little when they're in love! But Gemini Moon lovers do need to be consulted when *any* decision is taken and will value this courtesy in a lover.

Leo type mates may also exhibit that fire sign temper once in a while, but if they receive some time and space in which to process how they feel, they will soon walk up to their lover and offer an olive branch. What might cause them to lose their temper? It might have something to do with the Gemini Moon lover's tendency to speak first and think later. Such spontaneity of expression is good in some situations but not in all. Sometimes the wrong words tumble out at the wrong time and cause some serious damage, because the fire sign of Leo is sensitive but will not show it if their pride has been deeply hurt. But this can be easily sorted out, if a little diplomacy is used by both of them. As an air sign, gregarious Gemini Moon partners revel in a relationship where any problems can be talked out quickly and resolved efficiently.

The Leo type lover brings forth in the Gemini Moon lover a sense of romance and makes them feel good about themselves physically. When a Leo type mate decides to romance their chosen beloved, they're in for quite a memorable time, because Leo type lovers are romantic traditionalists. Whether male or female, the Leo type mate will woo their lover with flowers, compliments and fine dining. The Gemini Moon lover helps the Leo essence feel free in truly expressing who they are to the world without restrictions and doubt. Like some of the romantic pairings mention above, this relationship will benefit from starting off as a solid, long-term friendship and then gradually progressing into a deeper, more emotionally significant bond.

Gemini Moon vs. Virgo Sun, Moon or Rising Sign
The Air and Earth Relationship

Air: "Is my boyfriend open-minded enough and will he appreciate my outspoken side? I need a life mate who will talk to me, communicate with me about everything and not clam up and brood." the airy female partner muses. "Will my girlfriend allow me to do the things I love or will she try to restrict me from openly and truthfully expressing myself?" the airy male lover wonders.

Earth: "Does my boyfriend manage his finances maturely or will I end up paying his bills and supporting him? I need stability and true commitment before I can enjoy the romance between us." the earthy female thinks to herself. "Will my future wife spend my hard earned cash on frivolous items at the mall or be wise enough to save up for our retirement?" the earthy male lover wonders.

Gemini Moon lovers can have an expressive and meaningful relationship with partners who have their Sun, Moon or Rising sign in the duty-oriented earth sign of Virgo. Each partner symbolizes an element. Understanding that element helps us delve deeper into the real personality of that partner. Earth represents an unmatched stability and reliability: earth is a faith in love and an undying dedication to a relationship despite any problems along the way. Air represents an incredible intellectualism and creative genius that can take communication to a whole new level, and bring millions of messages and information to the world in an eloquent and original format. Elementally, earth and air are quite compatible.

The amazing Gemini Moon personality is divided into two separate, versions. The first type of Gemini Moon personality is the *serious type* and the second is the *fun-loving type*. The serious type is dominant by temperament, intellectually vibrant, determined and feels most comfortable when achieving career success than being cocooned in the family environment. The second type of Gemini Moon personality is the fun-loving type; this type is equally dominant in love relationships, is easy-going, has a great sense of humor, can get along with a variety of people and seeks excitement.

This Gemini Moon/Virgo Sun, Moon or Rising sign relationship will function under a double dose of inquisitive Mercury running through its core. Super-fast Mercury rules both these lovers and will affect both of them in its own inimitable style. Mercury will bring out this couple's creative or entrepreneurial side, causing them to start or invest in a business together. Gemini Moon lovers are expressive and energetic partners who thrive in openhearted and open-minded unions, where their lovers won't take what they do wrong too seriously, but will join them in making the most of life. The Virgo type partner is usually a good choice for any person looking for a structured relationship; their emotionally flexible style is one of their strongest and most coveted traits.

The one thing that a Gemini Moon partner will delight in most with a typical Virgo partner, is that this sign vibration almost never resorts to hysteria or drama when things go wrong and wires get crossed between lovers. Problem solver extraordinaire, the Virgo type mate will calmly bring up what is wrong and in their cool and calm style, proceed to sort out misunderstandings. As an air sign, gregarious Gemini Moon partners revel in a relationship where any problems can be talked out quickly and resolved efficiently. *"Let's figure out what went wrong and be done with it!"* the Gemini Moon partner says. The Gemini Moon person loves to communicate on many different levels and the Virgo type partner will also enjoy the communication aspect of this union; Mercury *has* to discuss everything! The Virgo essence lends a solid foundation to the sometimes disorganized but brilliant Gemini Moon energy.

The Virgo partner, after marriage, will make sure that their home is well stocked with nutritious and healthy foods: for example, wheat instead of white bread, sweet baby carrots instead of candy, and freshly squeezed orange juice instead of sodas and alcohol. They will take a special interest in what their lover eats and will try to instill in them good dietary habits, something that will allow both of them to age together and be young and agile even when they are in their golden years. The health-conscious Virgo lover will invest in a membership to the health gym, or get a treadmill for their home; all of this benefits the Gemini Moon lover in the long run.

One thing that this couple should watch out for is the Virgo type partner's habit of correcting (which, when done to an extreme could be construed as criticizing) their lover over small things and their occasional irritability. The Gemini Moon partner's tendency to sometimes gloss over details or omit them totally, thinking that sharing them will not serve any purpose but cause more communication glitches, could also cause problems. Things could get complicated in the arena of joint bank accounts and credit cards that are used without the other partner knowing about big purchases. The Virgo energy is frugal and conservative and hopes that their lover will accept and respect this bent of mind.

The Virgo type partner is very helpful and attentive and will expect total honesty from their partner. They will lend their earthiness to balance the occasionally agitated Gemini Moon energy from time to time. There's a lot the Gemini Moon partner can learn from their Virgo type lover. The Gemini Moon soul mate can bring their devoted but intellectually hungry love mate out of their duty-bound shell and help them be less anxious. The worrywart Virgo type soul needs to be with a partner who can bring out their fun-loving side more often, and show them that life is not all responsibility and work. The loving Gemini Moon mate just might do the trick.

Gemini Moon vs. Libra Sun, Moon or Rising Sign
The Air and Air Relationship

Air: "Is my boyfriend open-minded enough and will he appreciate my outspoken side? I need a life mate who will talk to me, communicate with me about everything and not clam up and brood." the airy female partner muses. "Will my girlfriend allow me to do the things I love or will she try to restrict me from truthfully expressing myself?" the airy male lover wonders.

Gemini Moon lovers can have a quality relationship with partners who have their Sun, Moon or Rising sign in the romantic air sign of Libra. Each partner symbolizes an element. Understanding that element helps us delve deeper into the real personality of that partner. Air represents an incredible intellectualism and creative genius and it desires to *express* itself. Elementally, the double air (Gemini Moon/Libra) vibration can mix energies beautifully. Air supports air and blends with it seamlessly. But it should be noted that a whole lot of air going around without aim only becomes a destructive typhoon. While, when it is controlled and properly tempered, it becomes the fresh spring breeze that we expect when we open the windows of our homes in the early springtime.

The interesting Gemini Moon personality is divided into two separate, versions. The first type of Gemini Moon personality is the *serious type* and the second is the *fun-loving type*. The serious type performs best in the academic, business or political setting; their goals in life may involve creating a niche for themselves in society and shining in their chosen profession. The second type of Gemini Moon personality is the fun-loving type; this type enjoys relationships and friendships but lacks the sheer determinism of the serious type of the Gemini Moon personality type. Romance and fun may be more important to them than career success. Both these Gemini Moon types are assertive and outspoken in relationships, therefore lovers who will never compete with them and can understand their tendency to take charge of a relationship will fare best with them.

When two multi-tasking air sign energies combine in the game of romance, there will be a lot of banter as well as a lot of chances for sending out the wrong message to each other. They key in this double air relationship is to find the real purpose of the coming together of these two vibrant souls. Of the two, the Gemini Moon lover is sometimes more impulsive in saying the wrong thing at the wrong time. This may occur innocently but the repercussions will be real. Marriage-minded Libra type lovers are very sensitive, especially when dealing with a love partner. Both are strong intellectuals and frequent communication is very important to both. The Gemini Moon partner has a set of important requirements in a relationship, without the fulfillment of which they cannot relax and enjoy their partner. As an air sign, gregarious and loving Gemini Moon partners revel in a relationship where any problems can be talked out quickly and resolved efficiently. *"Let's sort out this problem and get on with our lives! There's so much to do, so much to see!"* the Gemini Moon partner says.

While they can mingle interests easily, it should be noted that the only situation in which Libra types begin to lose patience with their Gemini Moon lovers is when they refuse to commit to a future together but won't terminate the relationship either, or perhaps end up sending mixed messages without meaning to in any way. Usually, Libra types are known for being the best fence sitters of the zodiac, but when their hearts are involved, another's indecision may cause a lot of emotions to well up. *"If he loved me, he'd have agreed to get married by now!"* the Libra type female reasons. *"If she really loved me, she'd have no trouble giving me the time I need to make the most important decision of my life."* the Gemini Moon male answers.

There is a good chance that both partners are impulse spenders (Mercury sees, Mercury likes, Mercury buys and Venus invented the shopping mall), so one of them will have to be the financial watchdog and make sure that the money aspect of their relationship doesn't cause trouble in other areas. Libra is a strongly marriage-oriented sign, while the typical freedom-loving Gemini Moon lover thrives on an unfettered friendship first so that it can serve as a potential testing ground.

Gemini Moon lovers guard their autonomy jealously, and Libra type lovers may need some tangible proof (a ring or an engagement party with all their mutual close friends invited) that marriage is on the cards. One way to manage this would be for both of them, the romantic Libra type lover, as well as the restless but endearing Gemini Moon lover, to begin their courtship slowly and keep it from burning too hot, too fast. Even though two fast and furious air signs may not see the judgment in this piece of advice, gradually getting to know one another would help cast clarity over the situation and balance out expectations from the beginning.

One way for this relationship to survive is for the Libra type partner to allow their Gemini Moon lover the chance to decide on their own timetable, as to what shape they want their love to take, while the Gemini Moon lover could try to understand their deeply partnership-oriented and attractive Libra partner's heart. Libra seeks harmony outside of themselves so that they can feel it take root inside of themselves. A fear of conflict and a tendency to postpone discussions that may cause tension are not recommended; Libra types should learn to express themselves like their mates do. Neither should hold back how they feel and they should be able to get to the heart of any differences quickly. If they can keep their friendship alive, their love won't be far behind, no matter what differences of opinion they may have once had.

For a good level of daily compatibility, they could both keep in mind the following points: the Libra type lover functions on purely relational energy (emphasizing one-on-one interactions with a lover) and finds excessive detachment from a lover a serious roadblock to enjoying life, while the airy Gemini Moon lover may consider too much emotionality in a lover a perplexing problem which they cannot tolerate. Logic and emotion can co-exist if both lovers can learn to tone down the dosage of each according to the time and situation. The Libra type lover could learn to not take the smallest problems in their relationship quite so seriously, while their Gemini Moon lover could learn to take certain issues a little more seriously, so that both of them can reach a level playing field of personal interaction.

This couple's best bet is to handle each other tactfully and learn each other's triggers and fears so that any possible emotional gridlock can be eliminated before it gets out of hand. The Libra type partner typically fears the destruction of their primary love relationship. They might want to try not to push too hard for reconciliation (and maybe let it happen gradually) nor totally withdraw from the scene feeling defeated. Their Gemini Moon lover fears being controlled by a lover and also fears being made to carry too heavy a burden of responsibilities that don't gel with their core beliefs in life. Given a bit of adjustment and a careful matching of life goals ahead of time, this will be a romantic and exciting relationship.

Gemini Moon vs. Scorpio Sun, Moon or Rising Sign
The Air and Water Relationship

Air: "Is my boyfriend open-minded enough and will he appreciate my outspoken side? I need a life mate who will talk to me, communicate with me about every-

thing and not clam up and brood." the airy female partner muses. "Will my girlfriend allow me to do the things I love or will she try to restrict me from truly expressing myself?" the airy male lover wonders.

Water: "Is my boyfriend emotionally stable and wise about our joint finances? Or will debts pile up in the first year of marriage? I need a supportive life-long lover as well as a loving one." the watery female lover thinks to herself. "Will my future spouse conserve our financial resources or spend unwisely without thought for the future? I can connect better romantically if I know that my chosen life-mate is passionate as well as mature and pragmatic." the watery male lover wonders.

Gemini Moon lovers can enjoy a deeply fulfilling relationship with partners who have their Sun, Moon or Rising sign in the emotional water sign of Scorpio. Each partner symbolizes an element. Understanding that element helps us delve deeper into the real personality of that partner. Air represents an incredible intellectualism and creative genius that can take communication to a whole new level, and bring millions of messages and information to the world in an eloquent and original format.

Water represents a desire to invoke raw, purifying emotion so that life is charged with authenticity instead of superficiality. Elementally, air and water are quite compatible and can enjoy a symbiotic relationship. Water contains elements of the air in the form of millions of microscopic bubbles, while the air contains water in the form of moisture. Each supports the other but the balance can be tipped if care is not taken in handling each element in the proper way.

If air and water mix in inappropriate amounts, we could have a hurricane on our hands. When the element of water is mishandled, it could cause drowning, while the mishandling of the element of air could cause a tornado. Balancing the attributes of each element is key. Scorpio type lovers are intense and take relationships and love very seriously while Gemini Moon lovers inevitably need an enormous degree of freedom in their relationships. The emotional Scorpio lover will hold their carefree Gemini Moon lover to *every* promise they make, and carefully test them to see if they are really as involved in their love relationship as they say they are.

The fascinating Gemini Moon personality is divided into two separate, versions. The first type of Gemini Moon personality is the *serious type* and the second is the *fun-loving type*. The serious type has much in common with the Scorpio type persona. They are equally ambitious, focused and will find great fulfillment in receiving professional acclaim and appreciation from peers. The second type of Gemini Moon personality is the fun-loving type; this type is happy and easy to get along with most of the time, and may need to adapt to the mature approach of the Scorpio type lover for maximum compatibility. Scorpio types will help the fun-loving type of Gemini Moon lover become more serious and focused on projects as well as help them soak in some of their legendary Plutonic intensity and magnetism. Neither partner should try to dominate the other, as they're both assertive lovers.

Gemini Moon lovers are changeable but highly motivating personalities. It is that changeable part that their water sign lover may have a problem with. The Scorpio essence wants a stalwart and powerful partner who will stand beside them no matter how many difficult situations life throws at them. *"You're in it with me for the long haul, or you're out for life."* warns the all-or-nothing Scorpio type lover. *"Lighten up, will ya? It's only a bit of fun!"* thinks the happy-go-lucky Gemini Moon mate, at least initially in the relationship. And while Gemini Moon mates understand that intensity, they may have a very unusual way of expressing their love. Scorpio type lovers function on purely emotional energy; it is their daily fuel and they are unable to view life in a casual, disinterested or flippant manner. Gemini Moon lovers find people who take life too seriously very stifling, and usually this difference will rear its ugly head when the management of finances is being discussed (money issues sadly lie at the heart of many lovers separating).

While sexual compatibility will never be in question, how each partner spends money (especially each other's money) will be a topic of discussion. The Gemini Moon energy is not too focused, in most cases, on preparing for that rainy day, which they think might never even come. So, why spoil the countless blessings of today by worrying about tomorrow? Watery Scorpio types, on the other hand, cannot rest knowing that they have just given their credit card to a possibly spendthrift and careless lover. Scorpio is a financial sign, and this sign judges partners not only on how they look and how they manage emotions, but also on *how careful they are with their cash.*

"Don't hold your feelings back when I'm around, sweetheart! Don't be so quiet. Tell me what's really going on in your heart!" implores the Gemini Moon lover. Their water sign lover may hear this but still ponder about the right time to open their heart in front of their charismatic lover. Scorpio type lovers are also easily hurt when words are used rashly, and can carry bitter memories for a very

long time whether any real harm was meant or not, while Gemini Moon lovers *need* to express everything very clearly and frequently. In many ways, they feel a sense of rejuvenation through communicating (not by hearing others but by talking themselves) and a sense of well being that they cannot derive from any other act.

For maximum compatibility, they could both keep in mind the following points: the Scorpio type lover functions on purely emotional energy and finds excessive logic and verbosity a serious roadblock to enjoying life, while the airy Gemini Moon lover may consider too much sentimentality in a lover a perplexing problem which they cannot get around. Logic and emotion can coexist if both lovers can learn to tone down the dosage of each according to the time and situation. The Scorpio type lover could learn to not take the smallest problems quite so seriously, while their Gemini Moon lover could learn to pay special attention to certain issues, so that both of them can reach an equal playing field of communication.

In many ways, this love story is a mix of the energies of Pluto (the ruler of Scorpio) and Mercury (the ruler of Gemini). As the slower moving planet, mysterious and wise Pluto will always have precedence over the smaller, quicker planet Mercury. Therefore the Scorpio type lover must watch their tendency to control the relationship too strictly. If their Gemini Moon lover cannot function within a reasonable sphere of personal freedom, they are quite likely to abruptly walk out of this unfinished love story, tragically, never to return. And if the trust between them deteriorates instead of growing stronger, the Scorpio type lover may also walk out abruptly, offering no explanation.

This couple's best bet is to handle each other tactfully and learn each other's triggers and fears so that any possible emotional gridlock can be eliminated before it gets out of hand. The Scorpio type partner fears betrayal from a lover the most (despite having done their utmost to save their relationship) while the Gemini Moon lover fears being dominated by their mate and losing their freedom to someone else's agendas in life.

This relationship can last if Scorpio type mates can be a little less worried and more trusting of their sweetheart's behavior, and if Gemini Moon lovers can be open to being introduced to the deeper aspects of love and intimacy, something that they may have always wondered about but never actually experienced. Effervescent and vibrant, Gemini Moon lovers can build a wonderful life with their watery lover, if they can watch what they say and avoid causing any verbal offence to those sensitive Scorpio nerves. While Scorpio type partners can learn to tone down their possessiveness and allow their Gemini Moon lover enough freedom so that they can spread their wings and learn to fly with them in the same, wide-open, blue sky. There's lots of love between them, and they can access it with consistent tact and faithfulness.

Gemini Moon vs. Sagittarius Sun, Moon or Rising Sign
The Air and Fire Relationship

Air: "Is my boyfriend open-minded enough and will he appreciate my outspoken side? I need a life mate who will talk to me, communicate with me about every-thing and not clam up and brood." the airy female partner muses. "Will my girlfriend allow me to do the things I love or will she try to restrict me from expressing myself the way I want to?" the airy male lover wonders.

Fire: "I need romance and passion to really enjoy my relationship. Will my boyfriend be a faithful mate for life?" the fiery female partner wonders. "I want an active and freedom-loving partner. Will my girlfriend understand my need for true freedom in life or be too controlling of my behavior?" the fiery male lover thinks to himself.

Gemini Moon lovers can have a wonderful relationship with partners who have their Sun, Moon or Rising sign in the fire sign of Sagittarius. Each partner symbolizes an element. Understanding that element helps us delve deeper into the real personality of that partner. Fire represents a desire to take risks (and experience growth from it), experience passion and live life to the fullest. Air represents a need to express itself as well as absorb, learn and share what life can teach us in an interesting way so that all may learn those life lessons.

The fascinating Gemini Moon personality is divided into two separate, ver-sions. The first type of Gemini Moon personality is the *serious type* and the sec-ond is the *fun-loving type*. The serious type has a mature approach to life, they're more verbally controlled than the fun-loving type of Gemini Moon lover and may excel in their chosen profession while thriving in a challenging atmosphere at work. The second type of Gemini Moon personality is the fun-loving type; their focus may lie in spending time with friends, having fun and generally taking life a little less seriously than most people. Both these types of the Gemini Moon personality are outspoken and every passing thought will make its way to their lips in a millisecond. They must watch their tendency to dominate less vocal mates, and it is best if they were paired up with non-confrontational, tolerant lovers.

Gregarious by nature, and eager to share the latest information with others, neither Gemini Moon mates nor Sagittarius types can keep secrets for too long. Both have big hearts but are also dissimilar in their own way. Gemini Moon lovers love frank, successful partners who will not restrict them in life, and not place them under any emotional pressure to do things (or not do things). Sagittarius types revel in relationships that allow them the grace of *full and unrestricted self-expression* as well as release them from responsibilities that they feel do not fit in with their core values in life.

Energetic communication and lots of it will keep the relationship strong and exciting. Sagittarius is a fire sign, so their emotions always run close to the surface. Ruled by the speech planet Mercury, eloquent Gemini Moon lovers love to air their thoughts frequently and sometimes this may cause some complications. This is because Gemini Moon lovers want a partner who is so accommodating that they never have to mince words around them. *"What's the point of having a soul mate if I can't tell you every single thing that happened to me today?"* they ask. Which means that sometimes, Sagittarian type lovers may have to hear some quizzical but interesting words from their partner. Sagittarius is more passionate and emotional than the airy Moon sign Gemini (who will display occasional moodiness, depending on the emotional state of each Geminian twin that day) and if matrimony is ever discussed, both will have to make an extra effort to keep the union strong and viable.

Both of them are dominant and set in their ways (neither will tolerate being controlled); so one of them will have to bend and compromise. As an air sign, gregarious Gemini Moon partners revel in a relationship where any problems can be talked out quickly and resolved efficiently. The fiery Sagittarius type partner also concurs, thankfully. Sagittarius types will probably not want every miniscule issue dragged out and dissected, and may not always want to dive into a discussion about who did what (unless of course financial problems are being discussed, then get ready to bring out those ear plugs, because both will want some serious answers).

Any prolonged detachment could lead this loving, devoted but impulsive couple right into divorce court, which is something neither of them wants. Sagittarius types can help keep the relationship afloat by encouraging their Gemini Moon lovers to be more practical and sticking to their promises, and Gemini Moon lovers can help by reminding their fire sign lovers that they needn't take everything they say to heart (the Gemini Moon lover must always state all the facts and never keep information from their fire sign lover, no matter how inconsequential it may seem to them at that time, because Sagittarius keeps their eyes on the bigger picture and sometimes trustingly forgets to ask about the nitty-gritty). One of them will have to be the stabilizing factor for the love to survive. If this happens, all will proceed very smoothly and allow them maximum time to enjoy each other instead of questioning each other. This is a stellar couple!

Gemini Moon vs. Capricorn Sun, Moon or Rising Sign
The Air and Earth Relationship

Air: "Is my boyfriend open-minded enough and will he appreciate my outspoken side? I need a life mate who will talk to me, communicate with me about everything and not clam up and brood." the airy female partner muses. "Will my girlfriend allow me to do the things I love or will she try to restrict me from expressing myself?" the airy male lover wonders.

Earth: "Does my boyfriend manage his finances maturely or will I end up paying his bills and supporting him? I need stability and true commitment before I can enjoy the romance between us." the earthy female thinks to herself. "Will my future wife spend my hard earned cash on frivolous items at the mall or be wise enough to save up for our retirement?" the earthy male lover wonders.

Gemini Moon lovers can have a productive and meaningful relationship with partners who have their Sun, Moon or Rising sign in the success-oriented earth sign of Capricorn. Elementally, air and earth can interact with purpose. The element of air needs the earth to cling to, while the earth needs the air to help blow away smog and pollution. Each partner symbolizes an element. Understanding that element helps us delve deeper into the real personality of that partner.

Earth represents a desire to nurture and build on past successes. Air represents a desire to express itself and leave a solid, intellectual contribution behind in the world. The fascinating Gemini Moon personality is divided into two separate, versions. The first type of Gemini Moon personality is the *serious type* and the second is the *fun-loving type*. The serious type is mature, ambitious, organized, yearns to reach the top of their profession and will express dominant leadership characteristics in love relationships. The second type of Gemini Moon personality is the fun-loving type; mental stimulation is crucial to them (boredom makes them irritable), this type is not as methodical as the serious type of Gemini Moon person, and may tend to scatter their energies easily. While they may lack the goal-oriented temperament of the serious type, they may be just as assertive and dominant in relationships or friendships.

Earthy Capricorn types are very concerned with where they're going in life and need a partner who is comfortable with walking through life together with them, and finding a purpose for their union, as a unit. The Gemini Moon lover may have a problem with the word *unit* because it might symbolize to them a loss of personal freedom after a relationship begins. *"Love means keeping your responsibilities in mind, honey."* the duty-conscious Capricorn type lover reminds. *"Responsibilities? I thought love meant freedom to do whatever you felt like, and have fun with your lover without having to stick to any schedules!"* the Gemini Moon mate answers. This may or may not be true, but the differences between both signs must be noted and understood. Gemini Moon lovers want their life partner to be active, highly intelligent and have a burning desire to enjoy life together.

The Gemini Moon lover's entire focus in life usually lies *outside* of the home sector. Capricorn types can only relax in a relationship if promises are made and kept; they want their lover to be comfortable with spending the rest of their lives as *their mate*. Commitment-wise, the slightest hesitation in a lover will be quickly sensed by the Capricorn type lover, and this will make them want to back out of the relationship in a hurry, bringing to a rather hasty close quite a promising love connection. Capricorn type mates can introduce their Gemini Moon lover to a stable, steady kind of passion, while the Gemini Moon lover can aid their earthy lover in spreading their intellectual wings and learning to express how they really feel, instead of keeping it all bottled up inside.

This is a good romantic pairing as long as the Gemini Moon lover refrains from keeping secrets from their Capricorn type lover, and the Capricorn type lover can handle their lover's need for true freedom without taking it too personally. The freedom their lover needs may not necessarily mean freedom from them and their love. Capricorn types are also financially frugal while their Gemini Moon lover will not appreciate a lecture on what to spend money on. Gemini Moon lovers need to be more diplomatic around their privately sensitive Capricorn type sweethearts, while Capricorn type lovers can benefit from the fun-loving and merry Gemini Moon persona, which helps with their occasional tendency to melancholia or depression due to Saturn's "tester" influence on them (Saturn may test them from time to time, to see if they are as resilient as they say they are).

It should be remembered that if a Capricorn type lover seems like they are undergoing a characteristic blue spell, the gregarious Gemini Moon lover must not try to talk them out of it, which will be their natural inclination. These Saturn-influenced moods are deep and need to be weathered properly and gotten out of their systems. A lot of space, emotional and physical, would be beneficial to the Capricorn type mate. After they seem to be coming out of it, a lot of TLC would be ideal. Timing and sensitivity is everything in this relationship, and the loving Gemini Moon lover just might seal the deal.

Gemini Moon vs. Aquarius Sun, Moon or Rising Sign
The Air and Air Relationship

Air: "Is my boyfriend open-minded enough and will he appreciate my outspoken side? I need a life mate who will talk to me, communicate with me about everything and not clam up and brood." the airy female partner muses. "Will my girlfriend allow me to do the things I love or will she try to restrict me from openly expressing myself?" the airy male lover wonders.

Gemini Moon lovers can have a stimulating relationship with partners who have their Sun, Moon or Rising sign in the freedom-oriented air sign of Aquarius. Each partner symbolizes an element. Understanding that element helps us delve deeper into the real personality of that partner. Air represents a desire to express oneself using an incredible intellectualism and creative genius that can take communication to a whole new level, and bring millions of messages and information to the world in an eloquent and original format. Elementally, the double air vibration (Gemini Moon/Aquarius) can mix energies beautifully. Air supports air and blends with it seamlessly.

The fascinating Gemini Moon personality is divided into two separate, versions. The first type of Gemini Moon personality is the *serious type* and the second is the *fun-loving type*. The serious type comes into their own on the world stage, their interests will be drawn toward education, business, teaching, law, salesmanship and perhaps even politics. The second type of Gemini Moon personality is the fun-loving type; this type is less concerned with achieving professional acclaim as long as their relationships, friendships and acquaintanceships go well. This type of Gemini Moon personality is cheerful most of the time and may lack the will power or verbal control of the serious-type of Gemini Moon personality. Both the fun-loving type as well as the serious type of Gemini Moon personality tend to be dominant in love relationships and friendships, often without even noticing it themselves, but it is imperative that they do not overpower their lovers by using words, which they will be adept at utilizing, thanks to their ruler Mercury. Patience is a key lesson to learn for this Moon sign.

Gemini Moon lovers want their partners to be unique, *more intellectually sensitive* than emotionally sensitive, and as communicative as they are. The Gemini Moon partner also has a set of important requirements in a relationship without the fulfillment of which they cannot relax in their relationship. As an air sign, gregarious Gemini Moon partners revel in a relationship where any potential problems can be taken care of quickly and resolved efficiently. Brooding over events that occurred a long time ago may not interest the Gemini Moon mate who prefers to live in the here and now.

Aquarian type lovers are more in-tune with Gemini Moon partners than other signs because both typically never place a very high emphasis on the traditional aspects of marriage and raising a family: their life focus lies *outside* of the home sector and they share the same mental circuitry. The Aquarian type lover wants to be tempted more by the ageless ideas in their partner's mind than their physical allure; which they know can fade with time. Each lover will, whether married or not, at some point in their lives, want to expand their intellectual and personal horizons and try new things out (new careers, for example). Freedom in all that they do is crucial to the air sign lover's ability to enjoy life. A restrictive lover who is possessive, needy and temperamental will soon find that neither air sign (Gemini Moon/Aquarius type lover) will want to be around them.

Gemini Moon lovers may at some point however, want to enter into the world of partnership (if one twin roams, the other, in a contrary fashion, will demand to start nesting) and long-term matrimony, but before they are ready for that stage, they will want to be absolutely positive that they have picked the right partner. Aquarian types, as a general rule, are not too interested in having a family and being homebound, because their interests revolve more around their friends, favorite social causes and pet projects.

Emotional gridlock can be avoided if both of them keep talking out grievances instead of hoping they will disappear on their own. No matter who is wrong or right, quickly and genuinely offering the olive branch can mean the difference between a relationship between strangers who are simply attracted to each other physically, and soul companions who will never tolerate seeing something they so tenderly built, dying away due to pride or neglect. If this romantic pair plans to have children, then one of them will have to actively take on the role of playing the rock of the relationship. There will be a need for stability, because two airy energies only end up creating more air, and unless there is a direction or emotional grounding, that precious airy energy may get sadly scattered. Intellectually well mated, both partners will be supportive of each other when the chips are down.

Finances will have to be watched as neither of them is particularly drawn to saving up for that proverbial rainy day. Aquarian type lovers enjoy passion, but like their Gemini Moon lover, know that there are a lot of other experiences out there, that are *equally* as good, even if they are non-sexual. The thrill of fighting for a lost cause attracts the Aquarian type lover, and what better partner than the expressive Gemini Moon mate to help them along or be their erudite spokesperson? Aquarians are emotionally cool but get passionate about an idea in a millisecond.

If this relationship is begun on the footing of friendship and is allowed to blossom slowly, like a fine wine is allowed to age, it will prove wonderfully healing to both these air sign wonders as time wears on. Friends who become confidants first and lovers second, will have a longer, more emotionally comfortable and significant relationship than friends who proceed directly from the friend stage to the sexual stage. This is an inspiring pair indeed.

Gemini Moon vs. Pisces Sun, Moon or Rising Sign
The Air and Water Relationship

Air: "Is my boyfriend open-minded enough and will he appreciate my outspoken side? I need a life mate who will talk to me, communicate with me about everything and not clam up and brood." the airy female partner muses. "Will my girlfriend allow me to do the things I love or will she try to restrict me from expressing myself the way I want to?" the airy male lover wonders.

Water: "Is my boyfriend emotionally stable and wise about our joint finances? Or will debts pile up in the first year of marriage? I need a supportive life-long lover as well as a loving one." the watery female lover thinks to herself. "Will my future spouse conserve our financial resources or spend unwisely without thought for the future? I can connect better romantically if I know that my chosen life-mate is passionate as well as mature and pragmatic." the watery male lover wonders.

Gemini Moon lovers can have a fulfilling relationship with partners who have their Sun, Moon or Rising sign in the sensitive water sign of Pisces. But due to the vivid differences in both personalities, emotional adjustments will have to be made on both sides. Each partner symbolizes an element. Understanding that element helps us delve deeper into the real personality of that partner. Air represents the passion of the intellect and an inspiring creativity. Water represents a natural empathy, an emotional purity as well as a soft and inviting sensuality. Elementally, air and water are quite compatible and can enjoy a symbiotic relationship.

The fascinating Gemini Moon personality is divided into two separate, versions. The first type of Gemini Moon personality is the *serious type* and the second is the *fun-loving type*. The serious type may prove to be just the right combination of strength and success that the Pisces type lover may seek in a lover. This type is mature in outlook, focused and can verbally control themselves rather well (Mercury makes them quite chatty). The second type of Gemini Moon personality is the fun-loving type; this type is more interested in romances and having fun with friends; climbing the career ladder may hold little interest for them. Both types are assertive in love relationships and must take care to let gentler partners also have their say in how things are run at home on a daily basis.

Gemini Moon lovers look for a mate who is attractive, hard to define and very communicative. Pisces type lovers are gregarious when in a mood and can charm the Gemini Moon lover right off their four feet (think Gemini twins) with that well-timed compliment or intelligent comment. The emphasis in this relationship is on change as well as *changing moods*, which the Pisces type partner is deeply immersed in. Both are emotionally flexible, mutable signs and may not be as terrified of change as the other fixed signs. The Gemini Moon lover is also affected by moods; they will vacillate between being very chirpy one morning and want to be left alone by the afternoon, mainly due to the changeable influence of dual Mercury, the ruler of Gemini and the energy of the Moon, which is never constant. Adapting to these changes is the key to the success of this relationship.

The charismatic Gemini Moon partner has a set of important requirements in a relationship without the fulfillment of which they cannot enjoy their partner. As an air sign, gregarious Gemini Moon partners thrive in a relationship where any problems can be resolved efficiently. Pisces types are so sensitive that they may be too busy feeling offended by little comments and may not want to dive head long into a 'tis-was about who did what. Part of that Pisces persona wants to be understood without any excessive words being exchanged. Intuitionist Pisces types will wonder if their Gemini Moon is lover is aware of their reactions, and feel terribly ignored, which causes them to begin to cocoon.

No one mood will be constant with the Gemini Moon lover and no one emotion will last forever, which is good because it gives them a chance to get over problems easily without brooding about them and letting them fester. The Pisces type lover is emotional and very easily hurt, so once again, the most gregarious sign in the entire zodiac will have to use more tact and sensitivity when talking to their Pisces type lover. Some people with Pisces placed prominently in their natal charts will sometimes suffer from low self-esteem due to the influence of ethereal and illusory Neptune. Neptune causes doubt to surface in the delicate and impressionable Pisces psyche. Therefore, the Gemini Moon partner will have to periodically help bolster their water sign lover's self-confidence. The Pisces type partner must watch out for a tendency toward dangerous obsessions, which could be unhealthy for them if it brings them closer to a toxic personality who may be capable of deceiving them under the guise of love or protection.

This could be a good romantic pairing if the Pisces type lover learns not to be so sensitive and be more realistic about life, while the Gemini Moon partner will have to learn to handle the moods and emotions of their partner with greater diplomacy. If the Pisces type lover can give their Gemini Moon partner freedom in all things, this will be a truly successful relationship. The expressive Gemini Moon lover encourages their Pisces type mate's fearless side, while the alluring Pisces type lover awakens in their Gemini Moon lover a sense of romance and sensuality. When Neptune works its magic through the Pisces type lover, it will be hard to resist.

Usually, nothing slows down the quickest Moon sign of the zodiac family, but their love for their attractive Pisces partner will do the trick. Neptune rules the sign of Pisces, and while it can inspire and create the most beautifully haunting fantasies man can dream up, it can also cause a great deal of confusion and self-deception in the tender Pisces heart. Which is why frequent and clear communication should be a rule of this relationship. The Gemini Moon lover is an intriguing and restless little bundle of a myriad emotions, desires and feelings, and only their Pisces lover can lift them out of the frenetic world of tricks, mental gymnastics and word games and gently put them down into the sensual world of romance, poetry and heartfelt promises.

Chapter 16
The Cancer Moon Sign Lover

Cancer Moon vs. Aries Sun, Moon or Rising Sign
The Water and Fire Relationship

Water: "Is my boyfriend emotionally stable and wise about our joint finances? Or will debts pile up in the first year of marriage? I need a supportive life-long lover as well as a loving one." the watery female lover thinks to herself. "Will my future spouse conserve our financial resources or spend unwisely without thought for the future? I can connect better romantically if I know that my chosen life-mate is passionate as well as mature and pragmatic." the watery male lover wonders.

Fire: "I need romance and passion to really enjoy my relationship. Will my boyfriend be a faithful mate for life?" the fiery female partner wonders. "I want an active and freedom-loving partner. Will my girlfriend understand my need for true freedom in life or be too controlling?" the fiery male lover thinks to himself.

Cancer Moon lovers can have a wonderful relationship with partners who have their Sun, Moon or Rising sign in the passionate fire sign of Aries. Each partner symbolizes an element. Understanding that element helps us delve deeper into the real personality of that partner. Fire represents passion, optimism and an inspiring courage. Water represents an ability to feel raw emotion and secure and protect love; it symbolizes an emotional purity as well as a soft and inviting sensuality.

There are two, specific types of the Cancer Moon personality, learning to distinguish between them is crucial to daily compatibility with them. The first type of Cancer Moon personality is the *careerist type* and the second is the *nurturing type*. The careerist type of Cancer Moon lover lives and breathes their work or business, relationships and finding the right lover may sometimes take a back seat to profit margins and business meetings. The nurturing type of Cancer Moon lover feels most fulfilled when they can contribute to close family and romantic relationships in a positive way; love and bonding is paramount to them, jobs and careers can wait. For this type, if there's no love, there's no life.

Cancer Moon lovers are true intuitionists and need the consistent and careful attention of their loved ones. While Aries type lovers are sometimes careless and tactless in speech (as the irrepressible 'bad boy' of the solar system, Mars, the ruler of Aries, cares little about manners), once they are truly in love, they will apply themselves and try to learn how the intricate and magical Cancer Moon heart works. The Cancer Moon lover provides a comforting sense of security to the usually restless and antsy Aries type partner, who needs nurturing sometimes but is too afraid to express this need (some Aries types are warrior-like and aggressive, and showing a need may seem like admitting a weakness to them). Cancer Moon lovers symbolize a safe harbor to them and gradually, this fire sign may be coaxed into letting their emotional armor fall.

Initially, there may be some confusion in the heart of the Cancer Moon partner as to how they can successfully comprehend their happy-go-lucky and energetic partner. They may try to think like them or envision life through their eyes. The watery Cancer Moon partner may be trying very hard indeed to connect to their fiery partner but may not be able to properly interpret the emotional language of the Aries type lover. The Aries type mate, on the other hand may think that they have a fairly good idea about what their lover wants out of life, but that may not be true. It would take the restless Aries personality a very long time indeed to fully grasp the incredible depth of the Cancer Moon persona.

Aries types must watch their tendency toward speaking before thinking, because this watery Moon sign is hurt by the smallest insensitivity, intentional or not. A little diplomacy will go far in winning and keeping the love of the captivating Cancer Moon lover. Cancer Moon partners also need to realize that their emotions may sometimes blind them to achieving a proper balance in life. They must battle a sometimes, suspicious nature, as well as a nature that can *feel* more easily than it can analyze. Fear can creep up into the heart of a Cancer Moon lover, and the Aries type lover won't enter into the deeper waters of commitment unless they are trusted blindly. The best way to make this fire and water relationship work and stand the test of time is to make each partner understand what the other fears and loves the most.

Aries types *fear* people who try to control them or restrict their way of life, and *love* partners who give freedom openly and also can receive it freely. The Cancer Moon lover *loves* a partner who can sense when they are uneasy or upset without them having to spell it out, and *fears* a mate who cannot deal with human emotions in a mature adult manner. Their intuitionism must be adequately matched by a soul mate for the trust and love to grow. The Cancer Moon influence helps the sometimes hot tempered Aries type lover to cool off and relax, while the Aries energy causes their Cancer Moon sweetheart to shed some fears and inhibitions, and learn to look to the future with happy anticipation, instead of a dread of what may come.

The Cancer Moon partner is ruled by the Moon, and the Aries type lover is ruled by Mars. When these two forces merge energies, the result will be tangibly felt in the daily give and take of the Cancer Moon/Aries Sun, Moon or Rising sign relationship. The Moon is cool, maternal and focused on secure, emotional 'nesting' while Mars is aggressive, forceful and intent on taking action and being the protector. Mars is impulsive, while the Moon may fear making any false moves in case a mistake is made. Each planetary body's energy can soothe these lovers beautifully and add a more mature dimension to their personas. The Aries type mate becomes more patient around their Cancer Moon lover, and the Cancer Moon lover develops a tougher, more confident exterior with the help of their dominant mate. The Aries type lover protects them from emotional excess and the Cancer Moon mate supports and neutralizes any hard edges in the usually boisterous but well-meaning Aries personality.

This couple's best bet is to handle each other tactfully and learn each other's triggers so that any possible emotional gridlock can be eliminated before it gets out of hand. The Cancer Moon partner might want to try not to totally withdraw from the scene if disagreements occur between them. The Aries type lover may be the more talkative partner sometimes, therefore the Cancer type partner might like to be more expressive and not put their candid lover through the painful exercise of having to guess what they have on their minds. This could be a splendid relationship if these two lovers made the slightest efforts at adjusting their likes and dislikes.

Cancer Moon vs. Taurus Sun, Moon or Rising Sign
The Water and Earth Relationship

Water: "Is my boyfriend emotionally stable and wise about our joint finances? Or will debts pile up in the first year of marriage? I need a supportive life-long lover as well as a loving one." the watery female lover thinks to herself. "Will my future spouse conserve our financial resources or spend unwisely without thought for the

future? I can connect better romantically if I know that my chosen life-mate is
passionate as well as mature and pragmatic." the watery male lover wonders.

Earth: "Does my boyfriend manage his finances maturely or will I end up paying
his bills and supporting him? I need stability and true commitment before I can
enjoy the romance between us." the earthy female thinks to herself. "Will my
future wife spend my hard earned cash on frivolous items at the mall or be wise
enough to save up for our retirement?" the earthy male lover wonders.

Cancer Moon lovers can have a truly wonderful relationship with partners who have their Sun, Moon or Rising sign in the dependable earth sign of Taurus. Each partner symbolizes an element. Understanding that element helps us delve deeper into the real personality of that partner. Earth desires stability and reliability: earth is a faith in love and an undying dedication to a relationship, even though there may be temporary difficulties to sort through. Water desires security and represents an emotional purity as well as a soft and inviting sensuality.

There are two, specific types of the Cancer Moon personality, knowing which one you've given your heart to can help with streamlining your approach to them. The first type of Cancer Moon personality is the *careerist type* and the second is the *nurturing type*. The careerist type of Cancer Moon lover yearns to make a success of themselves at work; they feel most fulfilled when they can fall back on professional achievements and show their capable, managerial or administrative side. Love will enter the picture one day, but they won't rush it. The nurturing type of Cancer Moon lover feels happiest when their primary love relationship or family connections proceed without any problems or miscommunications. Ever eager to connect to people emotionally, a good marriage will be their main focus in life.

The sign of Taurus is ruled by Venus, while the sign of Cancer is governed by the Moon. The Moon in Cancer gives a person an even more pronounced Cancer-type personality, almost like a double shot of emotional lunar power. Fortunately, water and earth share a symbiotic relationship. The Cancer Moon and Taurus energy make a wonderful combination, especially if the couple in question is planning on having a family at some point. Taurus types are just as sensitive as the Cancer Moon personality but can provide a firm foundation on which the relationship can grow and become rock-solid. The Cancer Moon personality appreciates the tender side of the usually quiet and introverted

Taurus type lover because they feel secure around their strong, protective energy.

Venus and the Moon (like planetary sisters) are similar in nature and quality. Blending these qualities in a relationship may not be too hard for either partner. Both the Moon as well as Venus thrive in and search for relationships in which love is easily expressed and needless mind games are kept to a minimum. Long-term emotional security will be the paramount requirement of both these lovers. Taurus type lovers can build a firm footing on which their relationship can stand for decades and become the envy of all their friends. The Cancer Moon lover can open an emotional channel for their earthy partner through which they can find acceptance and express their hopes and dreams more accurately and effectively.

The only problem this stellar couple could face is when the Cancer Moon lover resorts to being excessively emotional in order to get their Taurus type lover's attention. Cancer Moon partners must never make the mistake of pushing their earthy Taurus type mate into any position that they are uncomfortable with. Taurus types are patient and prefer dependable, steady and emotionally healthy lovers who don't fall apart at the slightest dispute or argument. Cancer Moon partners need a lover who is willing to be open to authentic emotional expressions and not run away from commitment and long-term relationships that culminate in a loving marriage. The Taurus type mate must also try to stop ignoring certain problems, hoping they will just disappear, and bravely deal with them when the time is right.

Both signs do well in marriages and will find it easier than most signs to create something stable out of a budding romance. The Taurus type mate can stabilize the sometimes, volatile emotions of their Cancer Moon sweetheart, while the Cancer Moon lover offers support, closeness and an opportunity for 'nesting' to their earthy partner. In order to make this relationship last a lifetime, neither partner should push the other's buttons, at least not knowingly. If communication ever breaks down, both these lovers should make an extra effort to offer the olive branch, so that their relationship doesn't come close to crumbling due to issues of pride between them.

The Cancer Moon lover as well as their Taurus type mate do well with frequent communication and have the tendency to brood a little if their feelings get hurt. They should talk their problems out and keep the honor and respect alive in their relationship, more than even passion. As best friends, they'd never let each other down to avoid saying they're sorry. This romantic pairing has success written all over it, if the partners are willing to try even a little to mend fences.

Cancer Moon vs. Gemini Sun, Moon or Rising Sign
The Water and Air Relationship

Water: "Is my boyfriend emotionally stable and wise about our joint finances? Or will debts pile up in the first year of marriage? I need a supportive life-long lover as well as a loving one." the watery female lover thinks to herself. "Will my future spouse conserve our financial resources or spend unwisely without thought for the future? I can connect better romantically if I know that my chosen life-mate is passionate as well as mature and pragmatic." the watery male lover wonders.

Air: "Is my boyfriend open-minded enough and will he appreciate my outspoken side? I need a life mate who will talk to me, communicate with me about every-thing and not clam up and brood." the airy female partner muses. "Will my girlfriend allow me to do the things I love or will she try to restrict me from openly expressing myself?" the airy male lover wonders.

Cancer Moon lovers can have a wonderfully expressive relationship with partners who have their Sun, Moon or Rising sign in the gregarious air sign of Gemini. Each partner symbolizes an element. Understanding that element helps us delve deeper into the real personality of that partner. Air represents an incredible intellectualism and creative genius. Water represents a desire to feel and sympathize, as well as support and protect. Elementally, air and water are quite compatible and can enjoy a symbiotic relationship.

There are two, specific types of the Cancer Moon personality, knowing which one you've fallen for can help you build a closer bond with them. The first type of Cancer Moon personality is the *careerist type* and the second is the *nurturing type*. The careerist type of Cancer Moon lover revels in putting their talents on the world stage; they are smart and intellectual and can handle any professional challenges well. Romance may be on their mind, but they're most like to say, *"Sure, I'd like to fall in love someday, but I have to make something of myself first and stand on my own two feet."* The nurturing type of Cancer Moon lover needs to create and maintain primary love relationships before they can even think about professional accolades. Protective and ultra-caring, their lover will get the best of their love and attention. Children will be of great importance to the nurturing type of Cancer Moon lover.

While sexual compatibility may never be a problem, emotional compatibility will require some active effort from both the Cancer Moon lover as well as their Gemini type partner. The Cancer Moon lover is one of the most emotional and sensitive of all the signs, and when they look for a life-companion, they will look for someone who is wise, mature and adaptable.

Cancer Moon mates need a lover who is able to understand their moods and fluctuating emotional rhythms without judging them negatively. Their goal is to find stability and security through marriage and the family unit, and their entire life focus (usually) lies *inside* of the home sector. The Gemini type partner's focus in life usually lies *outside* of the home sector, and they also have a set of important requirements in a relationship without which they cannot feel fulfilled. As an air sign, energetic Gemini type partners revel in a relationship where any problems can be discussed quickly and resolved, and they are given full freedom to do what they wish, and express themselves however they deem fit, without excessive criticism or finger-pointing.

Outspoken Gemini type partners will not take kindly to being told what to do by their life mate, no matter how deep their love is and how long they've known each other. When pushed into a corner, the expressive and never shy Gemini type mate might say something that, while it eloquently expresses how they feel, may bulldoze right over their watery lover's sentiments. Cancer Moon lovers are so sensitive that they may be too emotionally bruised, and may not want to admit that their loved one had just cut them to the core with mere words. Part of that Cancer Moon persona wants to be understood without any excessive words being exchanged. *"You should know me by now, honey. You should know how it irritates me when you do that."* or *"You know how it hurts me when you mention so and so…"* the Cancer Moon lover advises.

Intuitionist Cancer Moon lovers will wonder if their Gemini type lover is even paying attention to their grievances and feel terribly ignored, which makes them want to withdraw and share less and less with them. This couple's best bet is to handle each other tactfully and learn about each other's emotional triggers and fears, so that any possible clash can be eliminated before it gets out of hand. The Cancer Moon *fears* having to lose their most trusted support system in the form of their life mate, while their Gemini type mate *fears* losing their sense of personal freedom in a relationship that may have become too close for proper individuation to exist within it.

The Gemini type lover urges their Cancer Moon soul mate to communicate with them by saying *"Let your words connect to my heart, darling"*, while the emotionally astute Cancer Moon soul mate urges their gregarious Gemini type lover by saying *"Let your heart connect to mine without words."* This pair could make their relationship easily work, and success is theirs for the asking. With a little adjustment, theirs would be a hauntingly beautiful love story to remember.

Cancer Moon vs. Cancer Sun, Moon or Rising Sign
The Water and Water Relationship

Water: "Is my boyfriend emotionally stable and wise about our joint finances? Or will debts pile up in the first year of marriage? I need a supportive life-long lover as well as a loving one." the watery female lover thinks to herself. "Will my future spouse conserve our financial resources or spend unwisely without thought for the future? I can connect better romantically if I know that my chosen life-mate is passionate as well as mature and pragmatic." the watery male lover wonders.

Cancer Moon lovers can have a healing relationship with partners who have their Sun, Moon or Rising sign in their own water sign of Cancer. Any relationship that has twice the energy of the mystical Moon, will be a one-in-a-million experience. Each partner symbolizes an element. Understanding that element helps us delve deeper into the real personality of that partner. Water represents an emotional purity, a desire to secure and protect that which is important as well as express a soft and inviting sensuality. Elementally, water supports water wonderfully. Pour two glasses of water into a pitcher and we will not be able to tell where one begins and the other ends; their energies will have mingled seamlessly.

There are two, specific types of the Cancer Moon personality, making a clear distinction between them can help with figuring out which one you are most likely to find greater compatibility with. The first type of Cancer Moon personality is the *careerist type* and the second is the *nurturing type*. The careerist type of Cancer Moon lover needs to shine on the world stage and can be a wise and intelligent leader in their community. Much of their life-focus will be on making a professional success of themselves or being a self-made person. Capable and bright, they can do well in any field and will get very attached to their chosen occupation; it may end up becoming a part of their personality. The nurturing type of Cancer Moon lover thrives best when their family and children are near them and particularly when their lover is understanding of them. Finding a soul companion for life will always have more meaning for them than will winning professional acclaim. Children will be a particular source of interest for the nurturing type of Cancer Moon lover.

Cancer Moon lovers bond well with Cancer types. While this sympathetic bonding is good, the element of water (the water sign person), when threatened, betrayed or hurt, will freeze up and become a solid block of ice. Such emotional withdrawal can seriously damage a double water relationship. The only way to change this is to heat (provide attention and end further neglect of their delicate psyche) that block of ice into slowly melting. The emphasis should be on the word slow. Water signs are generally suspicious about instantly made promises and no follow through to back up what was said. Gradually, the frozen energy of ice changes into the fluidic, forgiving quality of water, the most emotional element of them all. Balancing the attributes of this amazing element is key.

Cancer Moon lovers are softhearted and yet can face the worst tragedies alone and bravely. Their one secret need in life is to locate a life-companion who can prove to them that genuine, supportive love is worth waiting for, and can help them heal any part of their life. A double Cancer vibration relationship demands that both the Cancer Moon partner as well as the lover who has Cancer placed prominently in their chart, understand that theirs will indubitably be an emotionally charged love story.

While it is good to have similarities in natal charts, it is also true that too much similarity can pose some problems in the long run. Both partners will have to balance their emotions out in such a way that neither will clash with the other's lunar rhythms. When one Cancer type lover is feeling blue, the other should give them the gift of solitude and vice versa. Trying to talk them out of it or offering support prematurely would hinder more than help. Mother them a little, but never smother them. Space and distance coupled with carefully timed TLC, will create a better line of communication between two Cancer energy lovers.

The maternal essence of this sign is healing but can also create an emotional avalanche in their partner's heart. The best thing to do when faced with a double water Cancer energy is to alternate the different parts of their sensitive personality. When one of them is full of energy and the other isn't, it is best to go on with their life and let their partner come out of their mood alone. Cautious, home loving and focused on 'nesting', this romantic pairing could make devoted parents. They should watch for a desire to over-emotionalize simple situations that should be better handled rationally and logically, as well as a tendency to cocoon and withdraw from the world and refuse to come out and address weaknesses.

The Cancer Moon mate's need to nurture and protect is very valuable and should be respected because it shows their selfless side. They should be more fearless and open themselves up to happiness; it will find them when they least expect it. They would do well to bring their relationship out of the lunar world of imagination and fears and back into their daily life. Their best bet is to be infallibly honest with each other when dealing with finances and expenses, encourage each other in pursuing their most cherished goals, and keep the marriage from becoming so boring that there is no excitement left to enjoy. Both partners should keep from getting on each other's nerves by bringing forth each other's carefree and fun-loving side more. Children will bring this pair closer, but both must be ready for that big step.

Cancer Moon vs. Leo Sun, Moon or Rising Sign
The Water and Fire Relationship

Water: "Is my boyfriend emotionally stable and wise about our joint finances? Or will debts pile up in the first year of marriage? I need a supportive life-long lover as well as a loving one." the watery female lover thinks to herself. "Will my future spouse conserve our financial resources or spend unwisely without thought for the future? I can connect better romantically if I know that my chosen life-mate is passionate as well as mature and pragmatic." the watery male lover wonders.

Fire: "I need romance and passion to really enjoy my relationship. Will my boyfriend be a faithful mate for life?" the fiery female partner wonders. "I want an active and freedom-loving partner. Will my girlfriend understand my need for true freedom in life or be too controlling of my behavior?" the fiery male lover thinks to himself.

Cancer Moon lovers can have a loving and exciting relationship with partners who have their Sun, Moon or Rising sign in the friendly fire sign of Leo. There are two, specific types of the Cancer Moon personality, finding out how each responds to love can aid with drawing closer to them. The first type of Cancer Moon personality is the *careerist type* and the second is the *nurturing type*. The careerist type of Cancer Moon lover needs the support of a solid career behind them to feel like they have successfully made their contribution to life. Love and romance may interest them but these concerns will always play second fiddle to carving out their own niche in their professional life. The nurturing type of Cancer Moon lover enjoys life most when all their family relationships are trouble-free and when their primary love relationship is based on full trust and reciprocity.

Leo type lovers are openhearted and thrive in long-term relationships where they are sure of their partner's allegiance toward them. Cancer Moon lovers need to know that their partner is not a temporary item in their life, but actually respects them and wants to build a secure future together. This particular fire and water romantic pairing is very beneficial from a family standpoint, because Leo is Sun-ruled and brings the father (male) essence while the Cancer Moon lover is Moon-ruled (twice over) and brings the important maternal essence to the relationship. This is a good balance of yin and yang, passive and strong, and while arguments may arise, the desire to get over them and resolve them will also be strong.

The only thing to watch out for is the Leo type lover's inclination toward taking charge of the relationship and occasionally giving vent to that fire sign temper. While their temper cools quickly and they may not mean anything serious by it, it is very possible that such an outburst could seriously damage the relationship and cause the Cancer Moon partner to begin to keep secrets and withdraw from discussing important matters openly for fear of a similar outburst. Cancer Moon partners are strong but can feel disheartened over the slightest ill-timed and harsh utterance, however innocent from the point of view of the Leo type partner.

The Leo type partner also has a set of important requirements in a relationship without the fulfillment of which they cannot give a hundred percent of themselves. As a fire sign, charismatic Leo partners revel in a relationship where any problems can be resolved fairly and rapidly. *"Let's not let this tiny issue come between us darling, we have grand dreams to achieve!"* the Leo type partner says. Cancer Moon lovers are sensitive and may feel too hurt and may not want to dive head long into a discussion about who did what. Part of that Cancer Moon persona wants to be understood without words and lengthy explanations. Intuitionist Cancer Moon mates will wonder if their Leo type lover is open to hearing about their problems and fears and may feel terribly ignored, which sends them deeper and deeper into their protective, emotional shell, causing them to brood for a little longer. This self-imposed isolation should not be discouraged because this is how the Cancer Moon sign rehabilitates itself.

Initially, there may be some confusion in the heart of the Cancer Moon partner as to how they can successfully comprehend their enigmatic Leo type partner. They may try to emulate them and try to see situations from their point of view. The watery Cancer Moon partner may be trying very hard indeed to understand what makes their lover tick but may not be able to properly interpret the emotional language of their fiery Leo type lover.

The Cancer Moon mate needs a stalwart partner who can be depended on for financial assistance if ever deemed necessary, and will also appreciate it if *they* go out of their way to offer financial assistance to their Leo type lover. The water element thrives when there is easy and quality communication between them and their chosen partner. They should learn to use their astute intuition to read into their passionate Leo type lover's heart (which is usually like an open book) and be able to anticipate when things could get confusing. The Leo essence, on the other hand, needs a physically demonstrative lover, whom he or she can show off in public and adore in private. Genuine admiration from peers is crucial to this fire sign's self-esteem: Leos yearn to be heard! Cancer Moon lovers make understanding and highly supportive partners who can maternalize the world of their fiery lover better than anyone else and soothe their sensitive fire sign nerves when the world fails to recognize their true worth.

Cancer Moon vs. Virgo Sun, Moon or Rising Sign
The Water and Earth Relationship

Water: "Is my boyfriend emotionally stable and wise about our joint finances? Or will debts pile up in the first year of marriage? I need a supportive life-long lover as well as a loving one." the watery female lover thinks to herself. "Will my future spouse conserve our financial resources or spend unwisely without thought for the future? I can connect better romantically if I know that my chosen life-mate is passionate as well as mature and pragmatic." the watery male lover wonders.

Earth: "Does my boyfriend manage his finances maturely or will I end up paying his bills and supporting him? I need stability and true commitment before I can enjoy the romance between us." the earthy female thinks to herself. "Will my future wife spend my hard earned cash on frivolous items at the mall or be wise enough to save up for our retirement?" the earthy male lover wonders.

Cancer Moon lovers can have a stable and intimate relationship with partners who have their Sun, Moon or Rising sign in the devoted earth sign of Virgo. Elementally, water and earth are quite compatible. Water needs the earth to give it direction and arrange the flow of its bodies of water, while the earth needs water so that fruitful farms that feed millions, and gardens and trees grow tall and green. The earth receives true nourishment in the form of rain from the water bearing clouds in the sky. Each element supports the other beautifully.

There are two, specific types of the Cancer Moon personality, and each type reacts to love in its own way. Studying that reaction may help with getting to know your lover on a more intimate level. The first type of Cancer Moon personality is the *careerist type* and the second is the *nurturing type*. The careerist type of Cancer Moon lover is very interested in working hard and reaching some plateau of professional success early in life. Their chosen profession will be very close to their heart and may become an extension of their personality. Love and marriage will also draw interest from them, but not until they have made their greatest contributions to their professional success. The nurturing type of Cancer Moon lover feel just as intensely about gathering as many confidants around themselves as possible. This type feels secure and content when their family, lovers, friends and children are physically near them, particularly if they have had generally positive interactions with their family members over the years. Children, in particular, will have a great impact on the emotions of the nurturing type of Cancer Moon lover.

The earthy Virgo energy blends nicely with the watery, emotional and anchor-seeking Cancer Moon lover. Both thrive in truly committed relationships and marriage is something that both could get used to once trust has been firmly established between them *over time*. Virgo type partners are hardworking and need to be in a relationship where they know that they are being appreciated and needed. If their lovers can frequently and verbally appreciate them, so much the better, because sometimes self-deprecating Virgo type partners may not want to be vocal enough to ask for everything they need.

Virgo represents the sixth sector of service and health. Any trouble or misunderstandings with a lover could easily cause the Virgo type lover to develop digestive problems (Virgo rules the digestive tract), while the Cancer Moon lover could develop chest conditions, like asthma, allergies, coughing, shortness of breath or wheezing (Cancer rules the chest region). The Cancer Moon personality needs frequent and tangible assurances from their life-companion that they will be there when they need them in a time of serious crisis. There is no better combination than this for long-term compatibility where each lover desires to take the relationship into the more comfortable and often pleasantly predictable zone of marriage.

Cancer Moon lovers must understand that Virgo type lovers do not do very well with partners who are overly emotional and use ultimatums to get their way; they need peaceful and simple lovers who pay more attention to the health of the over all relationship instead of concentrating only what drives them apart. Virgo types should also keep in mind that their Cancer Moon lover may take their correcting or criticizing too hard and see it as being picked on, which may not have been their intention at all. Virgo types should carefully phrase what they want to say and Cancer Moon lovers should learn to develop a thicker skin.

The Virgo type partner is devoted but when their friendship progresses to the level of intimacy, they will gradually want a more committed relationship. This will be music to the ears of their mate, who also values the respectability factor in a partnership of the hearts. But each mate should keep in mind what the other fears to better gauge their motivations; the Virgo type mate fears losing control over their lives and ending up with a lover who doesn't have the skills to maintain a responsible, adult relationship. If they lack clean personal habits and are sloppy in dress or uncultured in language, that will also go against achieving full acceptance. The Cancer Moon lover fears being betrayed or abandoned by their lover when they need them the most, and walking away from a carefully created family or romantic structure, leaving the Cancer Moon lover with a ton of responsibilities and bills to take care of. Both signs will take years to fully recover from a deliberate and massive betrayal such as this, but they *will* recover.

Being over-sensitive may work against the Cancer Moon lover in the long run and they should try to find the real cause of their reactions and fears. This romantic pairing is good if they plan to have a family, because well blended Virgo and Cancer energies often make for dutiful and understanding parents. Cancer Moon lovers bring out in their Virgo type lovers, a romantic and tender side, which is indeed the sweetest thing to have to experience. Virgo types enjoy supporting their lovers, but also enjoy, for once in their lives, being supported and nurtured themselves. The Virgo type mate helps their Cancer Moon soul mate by being the rock, the supportive anchor they have waited for their whole life. This pair will actually enjoy being helpful to each other, thereby making their bond an emotionally significant one. Being selfless feels particularly wonderful if that selflessness is promptly reciprocated by a lover. This will be a close relationship.

Cancer Moon vs. Libra Sun, Moon or Rising Sign
The Water and Air Relationship

Water: "Is my boyfriend emotionally stable and wise about our joint finances? Or will debts pile up in the first year of marriage? I need a supportive life-long lover as well as a loving one." the watery female lover thinks to herself. "Will my future

spouse conserve our financial resources or spend unwisely without thought for the future? I can connect better romantically if I know that my chosen life-mate is passionate as well as mature and pragmatic." the watery male lover wonders.

Air: "Is my boyfriend open-minded enough and will he appreciate my outspoken side? I need a life mate who will talk to me, communicate with me about every-thing and not clam up and brood." the airy female partner muses. "Will my girlfriend allow me to do the things I love or will she try to restrict me from openly expressing myself?" the airy male lover wonders.

Cancer Moon lovers can enjoy a romantic relationship with partners who have their Sun, Moon or Rising sign in the romantic air sign of Libra. Each partner symbolizes an element. Understanding that element helps us delve deeper into the real personality of that partner. Air represents an incredible intellectualism and creative genius that can take communication to a whole new level, and bring millions of messages and information to the world in an eloquent and original format. Water represents an emotional purity, a desire to connect to and secure all that is important, as well as a soft and inviting sensuality.

There are two, specific types of the Cancer Moon personality, and each type approaches love and romance differently. Knowing what they find important and what they don't can help with smoothing out relationships in the long run. The first type of Cancer Moon personality is the *careerist type* and the second is the *nurturing type*. The careerist type of Cancer Moon lover is intellectually vibrant, determined, ambitious and industrious. They may enjoy romance but will usually place their relationships on the back burner of life until they have made a full success of themselves in the professional sphere. The nurturing type of Cancer Moon lover yearns to love and be loved; children will be an intense area of interest in their lives, as will building and re-building permanent emotional connections to lovers. Marriage will also draw them, due to its legendary aura of stability.

With the power of Venus and the hypnotic Moon surging through this relationship, romance and genuine affection will never be lacking. Both Cancer Moon lovers and anyone with Libra prominently placed in their natal charts will respond quickly to partners who are easy to talk to, and place the development of trust before the pursuit of fun.

Cancer Moon lovers make faithful and capable partners, and will usually want to create a structure within which a family can be raised. Their life focus, in most cases, lies *inside* the home sector and revolves around the protection and nurturing of a few key relationships in their lives. Libra types are *very* sensitive to beauty in a woman and attractiveness in a man, and will be drawn to their Cancer Moon partner's patience and tenderness. Socially active Libra types can energize their watery Cancer Moon lover by infusing in them an excitement for life and new, intellectually stimulating experiences. Movies, books, art, travel and music will be a favorite of this artistic and imaginative Venus/Moon couple.

The only problem they might like to watch out for is Libra's tendency to be indecisive, or worse, make up their mind and then abruptly change it. Cancer Moon lovers need a definite answer, preferably written in stone so that there is a surety they can depend on. When it comes to commitment, Libra will commit but perhaps take too long to decide. The Cancer Moon lover, on the other hand could also take too long to decide if their Libra type partner is best for their lifestyle, because Cancer Moon lovers like to be very sure of what kind of permanent situation they are getting into. Fear of making a big mistake will probably keep them from making a decision, at least for a while.

Initially, there may be some confusion in the heart of the Cancer Moon partner as to how they can successfully comprehend their romantic and easygoing partner. Libra is sensitive but not too emotional, and tries to see and create harmony *outside* of themselves in order to find harmony inside of themselves. Air signs lean more toward a good balance of detachment and genuine interest at various times in the relationship. Libra types are social butterflies who pride themselves in being able to get along and forge bonds with literally anyone. While the care-taker essence of a Cancer Moon mate prides itself in being able to form very deep, emotionally significant and long lasting bonds with friends and lovers, whom they will treat as family.

Libra is very marriage or relationship-minded, which suits emotional Cancer Moon lovers just fine, if they are ready for matrimony themselves. Patience is key to handling sensitive Cancer Moon mates and understanding is key to relating to romantic Libra lovers. Libra type partners will be enthralled by the genuine and heartfelt manner in which their Cancer Moon lover supports them and watches over them, while the Cancer Moon partner will enjoy being around a lover who gives off harmonious energy and actually likes to *actively sort out* their relationship problems together before they become a cause for concern, a trait they might prefer to the raucous and agitated energy of some of the more assertive fire signs. This is a compatible couple!

Cancer Moon vs. Scorpio Sun, Moon or Rising Sign
The Water and Water Relationship

Water: "Is my boyfriend emotionally stable and wise about our joint finances? Or will debts pile up in the first year of marriage? I need a supportive life-long lover as well as a loving one." the watery female lover thinks to herself. "Will my future spouse conserve our financial resources or spend unwisely without thought for the future? I can connect better romantically if I know that my chosen life-mate is passionate as well as mature and pragmatic." the watery male lover wonders.

Cancer Moon lovers can enjoy a highly fulfilling relationship with partners who have their Sun, Moon or Rising sign in the feelings-oriented water sign of Scorpio. Both these signs are alike but also dissimilar in their own way. Elementally, water supports water wonderfully. Pour two glasses of water into a pitcher and we will not be able to tell where one begins and the other ends; their energies will have mingled seamlessly. While this sympathetic bonding is good, water (the water sign lover), when threatened, betrayed or hurt, will freeze up and become a solid block of ice. Such emotional withdrawal can seriously damage a double water (Cancer Moon/Scorpio Sun, Moon or Rising sign) element relationship.

The only way to change this is to heat (provide attention and end further neglect of their delicate psyche) that block of ice and coax it into slowly melting. The emphasis should be on the word *slow*. Water signs are generally suspicious about instantly made promises and no follow through to back up what was said. Gradually, the frozen energy of ice changes into the fluidic, forgiving quality of water, the most emotional element of all. Cancer Moon partners are sensitive and emotional, but only with the right person will their guard come down.

There are two, specific types of the Cancer Moon personality, studying each type's requirements in love can be key to relating to them on a deeper level. The first type of Cancer Moon personality is the *careerist type* and the second is the *nurturing type*. The careerist type of Cancer Moon lover lives to work and works very diligently to earn professional success. They are intelligent, excellent at managerial tasks and can also step into major leadership positions with great ease. People will come to depend on them at work and they can remain at one place of work for years. The nurturing type of Cancer Moon lover needs to be able devote a majority of their emotional energies to stabilizing the home environment, so that both lovers as well as their children can feel secure and valued. Whatever they do in life, their main focus will usually be to draw trusted people around them, as this allows them to feel needed, protected and appreciated. The welfare of children will be of particular interest to the nurturing type of Cancer Moon lover.

Scorpio types, who are evaluators by nature, look for a lover who is intense like them or at least understands why they take certain aspects of life to heart. Scorpio types like to experience life at a deep level, which may be too deep for the average human being to adjust to, hence the search for a lover who has most of the qualities they seek. But Cancer Moon partners will know exactly how that enigmatic Scorpio heart operates and what it desires the most. Both are careful signs and their financial issues will either bring them closer or create unwanted tension between them, usually over the smallest expenditures.

This couple should never let the respect and honor between them as friends ever change, no matter how many years them remain married. The desire for a strong union that can last for decades will be evident in both partners. The Cancer Moon sign is the most sensitive of all the water signs, and is known for its patience and ability to tolerate almost anything (sometimes even an excruciatingly bad marriage). But when both partners have the same watery energy in them, neither may want to take the risk and make the first move when there are differences of opinion. Or, they might emotionalize the situation so much that reasonable communication becomes impossible.

Frequent, rational communication, even if both of them want to run to their rooms and isolate themselves, will help carry this relationship out of the dangerous waters of misunderstandings that often take too long to sort out. No matter who is wrong or right, quickly and genuinely offering the olive branch can mean the difference between a relationship between strangers who are simply attracted to each other physically, and soul companions who will never tolerate seeing something they so tenderly built, dying away due to pride. The clannish Cancer Moon mate enjoys being around their family, develops quasi-filial ties easily, enjoys being surrounded by lots of little kids and having their cherished elders near them, if family ties have been healthy in the past. This family-oriented and tradition-loving sign thrives in long-term marriages where neither partner has any doubt about the other's loyalty. And even though both partners will be sharing a double dose of water-power (both are water signs), both must still test each other out, at least in the initial phases of their courtship.

The Scorpio type mate will be either mature about using control and power in their relationships, or perhaps not be quite as wise as others think they are. It depends on what kind of partner we attract. Scorpio type lovers are not always, but can be incredibly possessive in love relationships as well as about their children or income. Most Scorpio type mates are people who personify the influence of the planet Pluto. This means that we are dealing with a lover who is both emotional as well as wise. When in love, the world completely changes for this sign and without a doubt, they will end up changing their partner's life forever as well. If their lover takes love and commitment lightly, they won't after they meet this highly interesting personality. If they do take love seriously, they will find that they have met a soul mate of sorts in their intense Scorpio mate.

The Cancer Moon lover might ask, *"How does one handle the moods of a Scorpio type lover? What do I do when my boyfriend won't talk to me for hours and won't tell me what's wrong either? I can't bear it when he won't talk to me, I'd really like to do everything I can help him sort out his problems."* The first thing to understand is that in a Scorpio type lover, we are not dealing with an average lover with transparent emotions. A careful interaction will have to be thought out, where distance and closeness will have to intermingle beautifully. Give them a lot of emotional space and never barrage them with questions. Never try to pry out their secrets but let them volunteer them. Love should feel like a protective balm to them, instead of an intrusion. Watch the signals they give out, because they will give out clear signs that mirror the condition of their hearts. Intuitive Cancer Moon lovers will easily pick up those vibes.

Both the Scorpio energy and the watery Cancer Moon lover worry about the proper management and use of money and resources, so if they're both on the same page about that, ninety percent of their problems will disappear. Cancer Moon partners love spending time in nature and their Scorpio type partner will know exactly why. Both these watery signs have a close tie to water. This will be a close and long term union because neither will carelessly destroy something that invariably takes so much out of them emotionally to build.

The only problems between them may circle around the Cancer Moon lover's tendency to see everything through sentimental eyes and the Scorpio type lover's tendency to worry and become a tad too intense about everyday matters. This combination can last forever if one of them became the stable rock of the relationship.

Cancer Moon vs. Sagittarius Sun, Moon or Rising Sign
The Water and Fire Relationship

Water: "Is my boyfriend emotionally stable and wise about our joint finances? Or will debts pile up in the first year of marriage? I need a supportive life-long lover

as well as a loving one." the watery female lover thinks to herself. "Will my future spouse conserve our financial resources or spend unwisely without thought for the future? I can connect better romantically if I know that my chosen life-mate is passionate as well as mature and pragmatic." the watery male lover wonders.

Fire: "I need romance and passion to really enjoy my relationship. Will my boyfriend be a faithful mate for life?" the fiery female partner wonders. "I want an active and freedom-loving partner. Will my girlfriend understand my need for true freedom in life or be too controlling?" the fiery male lover thinks to himself.

Cancer Moon lovers can enjoy a highly energizing relationship with partners who have their Sun, Moon or Rising sign in the philosophical fire sign of Sagittarius. But adjustments may have to be made due to how differently each sign looks at love and bonding. Each partner symbolizes an element. Understanding that element helps us delve deeper into the real personality of that partner. Fire represents a passionate interest in life, a love of adventure and a strong sense of optimism. Water represents a desire to secure, empathize, express and feel raw emotion.

There are two, specific types of the Cancer Moon personality, and each type approaches love and romance from different points of view. The first type of Cancer Moon personality is the *careerist type* and the second is the *nurturing type*. The careerist type of Cancer Moon lover seeks out professional success in life and may work incredibly hard to prove their mettle to the world. This type will want to be known as a self-made person and will enjoy independently rising up in the world. Determined, organized and ambitious, the careerist type of Cancer Moon lover will get very attached to their chosen vocation in life and can use their intuition to make the best business decisions. Settling down in life will be something they'll consider, but only when every professional battle has been won. The nurturing type of Cancer Moon lover needs to connect through caring for others and integrating intricate family structures. Love will play a big role in their lives because they derive their sense of self-esteem from what others think of them. Children and parents figure prominently in their lives.

Watery Cancer Moon mates will look for a lover who is passionate and thrives with one partner, which is something that they think quickly removes the tension and guesswork out of a new relationship usually built on shaky ground. The expansive Sagittarius energy needs a lover who is passionate but emotionally accommodating. When problems occur, Sagittarius, in other words, needs someone who doesn't make an already serious situation more frightening by becoming emotional about it, but instead, looks calmly for ways to efficiently resolve it in the smallest amount of time possible and with the least amount of fanfare.

The fiery Sagittarius partner may, at least sometimes, not want some of the same things that a security-conscious Cancer Moon lover absolutely requires to feel secure. The restless Sagittarius type mate usually focuses outside of the home sphere, while the Cancer Moon lover enjoys the security of the sanctuary of their home and focuses a major part of their life energy there (they could also be very attached to their job or business, which could mirror the importance of a home base). This relationship still has a good chance of surviving, despite these two rather disparate energies, because they could start out as good friends (Cancer Moon lovers make the most understanding confidants) and remain good friends until they are both sure that they can come up with a common ideology that will bind them to one another permanently.

Sagittarius types are sweetly romantic and will enjoy not having to wonder if their Cancer Moon lover will be faithful or not: philosophical Sagittarius can preserve the truth of a relationship if they are truly in love or have been burned many times by partners who repeatedly failed to understand them. Sagittarius types can infuse their watery Cancer Moon lover's life with excitement, a joy of travel and lots of fun experiences where both can let their guards come down and relax. The Cancer Moon lover should give their Sagittarius type lover *lots of space*, both emotional and physical, if they really want them in their life. This includes being able to spend time with their friends, be they male or female. Friendships help salve the happy and philosophical Sagittarius heart and any attempt to control their interactions with others will be thwarted.

This couple should begin to build the road to a good relationship by never letting the respect and honor between them as friends ever change, no matter how many years they remain together. The desire for a strong union that can provide an in-built sense of permanent friendship will be evident in both partners. The Cancer Moon sign is a very sensitive water sign, and is known for its patience and ability to tolerate almost anything (sometimes even an excruciatingly bad marriage, something a Sagittarius mate won't). But when neither partner can comprehend the other's agenda, neither may want to make the first move when there are differences of opinion. Frequent communication, even if both of them want to run to their rooms (or run outside, as Sagittarius mates tend to do) and mull over their problem in solitude, will help carry this relationship out of the dangerous darkness of misunderstandings that has caused many a relationship to crumble.

No matter what the disagreement may be, quickly and genuinely offering the olive branch can mean the difference between a relationship between strangers who are simply attracted to each other physically, and soul companions who will move heaven and earth to protect something they so tenderly built.

The Sagittarius energy is mutable and flexible, and will make *some* changes to accommodate their sensitive Cancer Moon partner, but they must be truly in love to go through the effort needed. This relationship can succeed if each lover is given time to acclimatize themselves to their new connection at their own emotional timetables. Sagittarius type lovers can help their Cancer Moon soul mates be more emotionally forgiving and infuse them with a Jupiter-style, live-and-let-live ideology, while the Cancer Moon essence introduces the fiery Sagittarius type lover to the comforting lunar notion of emotional stability and reliability, something they will be drawn toward in the twilight of their days, when excitement and a desire for constant change may not have the same appeal as it does today.

Cancer Moon vs. Capricorn Sun, Moon or Rising Sign
The Water and Earth Relationship

Water: "Is my boyfriend emotionally stable and wise about our joint finances? Or will debts pile up in the first year of marriage? I need a supportive life-long lover as well as a loving one." the watery female lover thinks to herself. "Will my future spouse conserve our financial resources or spend unwisely without thought for the future? I can connect better romantically if I know that my chosen life-mate is passionate as well as mature and pragmatic." the watery male lover wonders.

Earth: "Does my boyfriend manage his finances maturely or will I end up paying his bills and supporting him? I need stability and true commitment before I can enjoy the romance between us." the earthy female thinks to herself. "Will my future wife spend my hard earned cash on frivolous items at the mall or be wise enough to save up for our retirement?" the earthy male lover wonders.

C ancer Moon lovers can enjoy a highly stabilizing relationship with partners who have their Sun, Moon or Rising sign in the ambitious and hard-
working earth sign of Capricorn. The pull here will be one of marriage because
these signs are polarized. Both are alike but also dissimilar in their own way.
When the seventh sector comes into place, there will be, at some point or the
other, a desire to merge destinies on a legal level.

There are two, specific types of the Cancer Moon personality, making a clear
distinction between them can help with figuring out which one you are most
likely to find greater compatibility with. The first type of Cancer Moon personality is the *careerist type* and the second is the *nurturing type*. The careerist
type of Cancer Moon lover is determined to rise up in the world and balance
out their life through career achievements. This type really does live to work
and whatever they choose as their life's vocation, will become an integral part
of their own psyche. The nurturing type of Cancer Moon lover needs to secure
their own emotions by securing the closest relationships around them. This
type takes caring to a whole new level and there may be an interest in having
children early in life. Their early parental influences will play a big part in how
the nurturing type reacts to their own children. It is advised that they raise
their little bundles of joy according to what they think is best and not follow
another mind-set in doing so. Love relationships and their stability will be the
ultimate barometer of the nurturing type of Cancer Moon lover's level of happiness in life.

The sensitive Cancer Moon lover may sometimes unleash a great avalanche of
emotions on their lover while their earthy Capricorn mate will keep all those
feelings inside *until the dam bursts*. Frequent and honest communication could
aid them both greatly, help relieve tension and keep it from building up over
time.

Capricorn type partners are driven and ambitious and need a partner who is
emotionally sensitive but also careful about managing money and investing it.
Cancer Moon lovers are closely associated with the collection of things
(tokens, pictures, sometimes money), because they're sentimental and find
security in doing so. Capricorn type lovers usually tend toward building something that they can refer to as their personal legacy in life. This is important to
grasp. They have a deep emotional need to leave their imprint or mark on the
world so that respect and prestige are attached to their name for all time. If
they can find a lover who will not interfere with this desire, they will be elated.

Aspiring for something grand in life, Capricorn type mates work diligently
and they need a partner who can appreciate their efforts, sometimes spanning

decades of hard work. Both Cancer Moon lovers and their Capricorn type partners take life seriously, as well as the daily goings-on in their love life. Commitment is not a word their lover should be scared of because these two signs have no patience for such immaturity. The only problem to watch out for is when Cancer Moon mates become too emotional, and when their earthy lovers cannot handle it and begin to withdraw from the tension it causes.

As mentioned above, the Capricorn type mate may lean more toward keeping a lot of their feelings inside, sometimes for years at a time, which could seriously hurt their relationship. Their emotionally open Cancer Moon mate may, when stressed out, tend to unburden themselves at the wrong time, when that information cannot be properly interpreted and grasped. An emotional overload could cause the usually stable Capricorn type partner to lash out verbally or completely withdraw from discussing the problem. Timing is everything in the game of love between earth and water signs.

Capricorn types may also feel a bit depressed sometimes (something that is directly attributable to the power of their ruler Saturn, a serious and disciplined planet which can cause doubt or feelings of inferiority to arise) and this could carry itself into their watery lover's emotional world. This earth and water combination of lovers needs to feel special to their life-partner and both need to be treated with the utmost care and tenderness. Harsh words spoken in haste when tempers flare are not easily forgotten.

They could both keep in mind the following points: the Cancer Moon lover functions on purely emotional and instinctive energy and finds excessive logic and rationalization a serious roadblock to enjoying life, while the stoic Capricorn type lover may consider too much emotionality in a lover a perplexing problem which they can neither explain nor circumvent. Logic and emotion can co-exist if both lovers can learn to tone down the dosage of each according to the time and situation. The Cancer Moon lover could learn to not take the smallest problems quite so seriously, while their Capricorn type lover could learn to anticipate their lover's moods, so that both of them can reach an even playing field.

This couple's best bet is to handle each other tactfully and learn each other's fears so that any possible emotional gridlock can be eliminated before it gets out of hand. The Cancer Moon partner fears being lied to or cheated by their lover, the one person they may have trusted and loved the most in the world. The Capricorn lover fears failure when they have worked their fingers to the bone to get somewhere in life. When it comes to starting a family, this pair will make responsible parents as well as faithful companions. The Capricorn essence symbolizes the Saturn or father (protective) energy, while the Cancer Moon essence symbolizes the maternal (nurturing) Moon energy, doubled in intensity due the Moon being in Cancer. This will be a memorable and life-altering relationship in a positive way for both lovers.

Cancer Moon vs. Aquarius Sun, Moon or Rising Sign
The Water and Air Relationship

Water: "Is my boyfriend emotionally stable and wise about our joint finances? Or will debts pile up in the first year of marriage? I need a supportive life-long lover as well as a loving one." the watery female lover thinks to herself. "Will my future spouse conserve our financial resources or spend unwisely without thought for the future? I can connect better romantically if I know that my chosen life-mate is passionate as well as mature and pragmatic." the watery male lover wonders.

Air: "Is my boyfriend open-minded enough and will he appreciate my outspoken side? I need a life mate who will talk to me, communicate with me about every-thing and not clam up and brood." the airy female partner muses. "Will my girlfriend allow me to do the things I love or will she try to restrict me from openly expressing myself?" the airy male lover wonders.

Cancer Moon lovers can enjoy a highly fulfilling relationship with partners who have their Sun, Moon or Rising sign in the modern and open-minded air sign of Aquarius. This water and air combination can survive if both partners can understand what separates them and what brings them together; love means vividly different things to each. Each partner symbolizes an element. Understanding that element helps us delve deeper into the real personality of that partner. Air represents a desire for true self-expression and can display a towering intellectualism. Water represents an advanced sense of empathy, emotional purity as well as a soft and inviting sensuality.

There are two, specific types of the Cancer Moon personality, making a clear distinction between them can help with figuring out which one you are most likely to find greater compatibility with. The first type of Cancer Moon per-sonality is the *careerist type* and the second is the *nurturing type*. The careerist type of Cancer Moon lover needs to shine on the world stage and can be a wise and intelligent leader in their community. Much of their life-focus will be on making a success of themselves or being a self-made person. Capable and bright, they can do well in any field and will get very attached to their chosen occupation. The nurturing type of Cancer Moon lover thrives best when their family and children are near them and particularly when their lover is understanding of them. Finding a soul companion for life will always have more meaning for them than will winning professional acclaim. Children will be a particular source of interest for the nurturing type of Cancer Moon lover.

Aquarius type lovers need to be with a very emotionally flexible partner who forgives easily and can grasp the unusual Aquarian life philosophy. A partner who causes an emotional overload in an Aquarius type lover, will soon find that they stop communicating with them. Emotional gridlock can be avoided if both the Cancer Moon mate and their Aquarian type lover keep discussing their problems quickly and in as short an amount of time as possible. Don't go to bed angry! Each partner is sensitive about certain topics; the Cancer Moon mate is sensitive about being given enough attention and care by their lover, while the Aquarian type lover will be touchy about being controlled and being told what to do, who to meet and how to spend their cash.

Cancer Moon mates generally are tradition-minded and like to follow a set pattern in life. This is also a family-friendly Moon sign and feels, if their family relationships have been generally healthy thus far, close to their parents and siblings. Aquarian types are not the most traditional of signs and their idea of love and marriage may clash with what the Cancer Moon lover has in mind for them as a couple. Aquarian types tend to develop many quasi-filial ties over a lifetime and may spend more time and attention on friends than blood relatives. Watery Cancer Moon lovers will test out their lovers to see if they will be *trustworthy and dependable in the long run*, while Aquarian type lovers will also test their potential partners to check if they can adequately provide the *consistent level of personal freedom* they need to feel truly fulfilled in life.

Initially, there may be some confusion in the heart of the Cancer Moon partner as to how they can successfully comprehend their unflappable and intellectual lover. They may try to see the world from their point of view, at least for a while, and try to find out what their likes and dislikes are. The watery Cancer Moon partner may be trying very hard indeed to understand their airy partner but may not be able to properly interpret the sometimes, unconventional emotional language of the Aquarian type lover. The Aquarian type lover, on the other hand may think that they have a good idea of what their sensitive lover wants out of life, but that may not be true. It would take the restless Aquarian type mate a very long time indeed to fully grasp the depth of the incredibly intuitive Cancer type persona. An emotional person can gradually learn to develop an intellectual side (it is a skill that can be acquired), but an intellectual person may have trouble developing an emotional side if it doesn't feel natural to them.

For maximum compatibility, they could both keep in mind the following points: the Cancer Moon lover functions on purely emotional energy and finds excessive logic and analysis a serious roadblock to enjoying life, while the airy Aquarian type lover may consider too much emotionality in a lover a perplexing problem which they cannot find an easy solution to. Logic and emotion can co-exist if both lovers can learn to tone down the dosage of each according to the time and situation. The Cancer Moon lover could learn to not take the smallest problems quite so seriously, while their Aquarian type lover could learn to take certain issues *more* seriously, so that both of them can reach an equal playing field of daily interaction.

This couple's best bet is to handle each other tactfully and learn each other's triggers so that any possible emotional gridlock can be eliminated before it gets out of hand. The Aquarian type lover may communicate enough for both of them, therefore the Cancer Moon partner might like to be more expressive and answer their lover's questions bluntly and frankly. They should not worry about what their lover wants to hear, but should say what they really feel like saying without feeling pressured. Their fair-minded Aquarian mate will appreciate this openness.

Aquarian types have a very unique idea of what the perfect love relationship should be: they want a broad-minded lover with whom they can bond intellectually first and romantically second. Passion or mushy romance is not something they find easy to relate to, and they need to know that their partner is a best friend first and a compatible lover second. Cancer Moon partners place a high degree of emphasis on passion and emotional compatibility in a relationship, but it can only be fully expressed if their partner has already and truthfully committed to them. This combination can make their relationship work if Cancer Moon mates will allow their Aquarian type partners to express their love for them in their own way, and if the Aquarius energy learns to be more consistently attentive and sensitive to the Cancer Moon psyche.

Cancer Moon vs. Pisces Sun, Moon or Rising Sign
The Water and Water Relationship

Water: "Is my boyfriend emotionally stable and wise about our joint finances? Or will debts pile up in the first year of marriage? I need a supportive life-long lover

as well as a loving one." the watery female lover thinks to herself. "Will my future
spouse conserve our financial resources or spend unwisely without thought for the
future? I can connect better romantically if I know that my chosen life-mate is
passionate as well as mature and pragmatic." the watery male lover wonders.

C ancer Moon lovers can enjoy a highly successful relationship with partners who have their Sun, Moon or Rising sign in the sensitive water sign
of Pisces. The Pisces energy is very compatible with the watery Cancer Moon
essence because water flows and merges easily with water, and this couple will
have an easier time understanding each other's emotions. However, too much
water and emotionality can overwhelm a relationship and rob it of a firm
foundation; even water needs something stable to flow on. A stabilizing factor
will have to be introduced for maximum success.

Each partner symbolizes an element. Understanding that element helps us delve
deeper into the real personality of that partner. Water represents an ability to
effectively sympathize, as well as offer a soft and inviting sensuality. Elementally,
water supports water wonderfully. Pour two glasses of water into a pitcher and
we will not be able to tell where one begins and the other ends; their energies
will have mingled seamlessly. While this sympathetic bonding is good, water (or
the water sign person), when threatened, betrayed or hurt, will freeze up and
become a solid block of ice. Such emotional withdrawal can seriously damage
a double water (Cancer Moon/ Pisces Sun, Moon or Rising sign) relationship.

The only way to change this is to heat (provide attention and end further
neglect of their delicate psyche) that block of ice into slowly melting. The
emphasis should be on the word *slow*. Water signs are generally suspicious
about instantly made promises and no follow through to back up what was
said. Gradually, the frozen energy of ice changes into the fluidic, forgiving
quality of water, the most emotional element of all. Balancing the attributes of
this wonderful element is key.

There are two, specific types of the Cancer Moon personality, studying each
type's requirements in love can be key to relating to them on a deeper level.
The first type of Cancer Moon personality is the *careerist type* and the second
is the *nurturing type*. The careerist type of Cancer Moon lover lives to work
and works very diligently to earn professional success. They are intelligent,
excellent at managerial tasks and can also step into major leadership positions
with great ease. People will come to depend on them at work and they can
remain at one place of work for years. The nurturing type of Cancer Moon
lover needs to be able devote a majority of their emotional energies to stabi-

lizing the home environment, so that both lovers as well as their children can feel secure and valued. Their main focus will usually be to gather trusted confidants around them, as this allows them to feel needed and appreciated. The welfare of children will be of particular interest to this Moon sign type.

Nurturing Cancer Moon lovers require emotional commitment before they will let their heart wade in further into the great Piscean waters of openly expressed emotion and a frighteningly deep intuition. Pisces types are deeply emotional themselves and need a partner who can provide a firm support system on which they can blindly rely. The Pisces energy brings sensitivity and faith to a sometimes, skeptical and fearful Cancer Moon mate, while the Cancer Moon lover aids their watery soul mate in finding their voice and feeling more confident about making any life choices, particularly if it is a difficult choice to make.

Pisces type partners, more than Cancer Moon mates, need to be able to think clearly and require a lover who can bring them out of any self-doubt, which may plague them sometimes. The Pisces type partner must watch out for a tendency toward unhealthy obsessions, which could work against them if it brings them closer to a toxic personality who may be capable of deceiving them by pretending to be in love with them. Financially, Pisces types may be more impulsive when spending cash, and this may pose a problem because Cancer is a financially frugal sign and most Cancer Moon folks are very prudent about managing their resources properly, at the right time and in the right way. This is a good match provided the Pisces type lover learns not to push their watery partner's emotional buttons too often for too trivial a reason and vice versa.

Family-friendly Cancer Moon mates should help their sensitive partner express their practical side more than their trusting side. Artistic and imaginative Pisces types must also remember never to withhold any information from their Cancer Moon lover. If a Cancer Moon mate begins to doubt their partner even a little, that little doubt could spread into a full fledge suspicion and wreck the relationship.

Neptune rules the sign of Pisces, and while it can inspire and create the most beautifully haunting fantasies man can dream of, it can also cause a great deal of confusion and self-deception in the tender Pisces heart. Which is why frequent and clear communication should be a rule of this relationship. The Pisces energy lifts their Cancer Moon sweetheart out of the world of fear and confusion and puts them down into the sensual world of romance, poetry and a freely given trust. This is a good combination if a family is planned.

Chapter 17
The Leo Moon Sign Lover

Leo Moon vs. Aries Sun, Moon or Rising Sign
The Fire and Fire Relationship

Fire: "I need romance and passion to really enjoy my relationship. Will my boyfriend be a faithful mate for life?" the fiery female partner wonders. "I want an active and freedom-loving partner. Will my girlfriend understand my need for true freedom in life or be too controlling of everything I do?" the fiery male lover thinks to himself.

Leo Moon lovers can enjoy a highly successful relationship with partners who have their Sun, Moon or Rising sign in the happy and energetic fire sign of Aries. Each partner symbolizes an element. Understanding that element helps us delve deeper into the real personality of that partner. The fire element represents a desire to experience life and approach it with happy anticipation; seeking out an exquisite adventure is often an effort at seeking out great wisdom. No guts, no glory! No glory, no fun. Elementally, fire uplifts fire beautifully. A good example of this would be the magnificently glittering fireworks that light up the night sky at New Year's Eve.

This double fire relationship merges the destinies of two loving mates who yearn to live their best, be their best and love their best. Fire is one of the most important elements because without it, the world would freeze and become useless. With the gift of heat, the great oceans move, frozen icebergs melt and create more water and frozen hearts begin to feel the depth of human emotion once again.

The fire energy must also be maturely handled to bring forth its best attributes. A fire that burns too hot dies away just as quickly. Therefore, the key is to let it burn *slowly and longer*, changing it from a destructive fire to a productive fire. Too much fire can cause destruction, but if its power is controlled and tempered, it can turn into the comforting fireplace that keeps our homes so warm and cozy when the harshness of winter comes upon us. Balancing the attributes of this versatile and life-giving element is key.

There are two different types of the Leo Moon personality. It might help to know exactly which one you have given your heart to. The first type is the *lion type*; this type tends to be super-confident, dominant and ambitious while the second type is the *cub type*, which tends to be more mellow, non-aggressive and romance-seeking. If the Aries type mate is as dominant as the lion type of Leo Moon personality, they may have trouble agreeing on key issues due to power struggles. If the Aries type lover happens to be submissive, like the lamb type Aries lover, they just might get along perfectly well with the lion type of Leo Moon personality.

If you're attractive, have a great sense of humor and can quickly reciprocate someone's love and adoration, then the Leo Moon lover will want to write your phone number down pronto. Aries type lovers share the same mental and emotional circuitry as Leo Moon lovers because fire signs intrinsically understand typical fire sign life-goals. Sexual compatibility becomes an additional stabilizer and both of these lovers will get emotionally attached almost instantly. Sentimental romantics, they can be mad at each other one moment and be hugging and kissing the next. Aries types like to initiate projects and Leo Moon lovers enjoy taking charge of the decision-making process. If they can reach an agreement as to who directs and who follows, provided the partner leading has only the best interests of the relationship at heart, long-term goodwill is ensured.

The Leo Moon lover needs to make sure that their Aries type lover is never neglected (the all-or-nothing Aries energy will abruptly walk away if they have to compete for their lover's attention too often), while the occasionally reckless, Aries type lover should ensure that tact and diplomacy are used in every situation. Both are fiercely loyal to each other and yet very sensitive to rejection from each other. Leo Moon mates are fixed in habit and temperament, and the Aries essence likes to instigate change due to a fondness for excitement. The Leo Moon lover may join their Aries type mate in having fun, but may not be comfortable with *too* much change due to their fixed nature. *"You know sweetheart, there's a fine line between having fun and going a little too wild. How about if we go out and have a nice dinner, instead of hiking up the mountain a second time? I'm a little hungry."* the Leo Moon lover suggests. The rambunctious Aries energy can get a little wild and crazy now and then (there's just too much to do and see!), which will cause the Leo Moon lover to jump in and gently steer them clear of too much mischief.

The Leo Moon sign will be merry and eager to drink up life most of the time, but when they feel down in the dumps, they will have to be handled extremely carefully. Lots of TLC coupled with a special alternation of closeness and space should do the trick. Fortunately, this fiery Moon sign won't be depressed for long. The Leo Moon sign is a happy mixture of the influence of the emotive, healing Moon and the bright majesty of the Sun.

Leo Moon lovers function under the influence of the Sun, and when the Sun's magnificent and sunny energy meets up with the active, impulsive essence of Mars (the ruler of Aries), the effect will be tangibly felt in the daily life of the Leo Moon/Aries Sun, Moon or Rising sign partnership. The Sun is the central character in our solar system and all the other planets respectfully orbit it. The Leo Moon mate is a lot like the Sun, a lot of people will want to congregate around them, at work and at home. The Aries partner will have to hunker down and get used to the idea of sharing their charismatic mate with the rest of the world.

Mars, the warrior and protector planet tends to be hot-tempered and highly experimental in various areas of life. Both these forces (the Sun and Mars) are strong and, in the arena of self-expression, can be rather opinionated and blunt. If a clash of wills occurs, neither will back down without having their say. This means that one of them will have to modulate the relationship in such a way that neither has the upper hand or an unfair advantage over the other. The lover who loves the most will spend more time maintaining and fine-tuning this delicate balance so that their love can survive and flourish over many years.

The Moon sign of Leo makes for an incredibly open-minded and easy to understand partner most of the time. Their requirements are minimal but they really hope that they will be fulfilled and respected by their lover. Sometimes, there may surface a tendency in this fiery and impulsive Moon sign to begin a relationship quickly but somehow lose steam half way down the road. If their partner is very sensitive, they may not understand why the pace and direction of the relationship has suddenly changed. Therefore a casual but strong friendship is initially advised with this Moon sign, so that one of the lovers can maturely control the speed of the relationship and not let it spiral downward into disinterest from either lover too soon.

The friendship aspect of a relationship with a Leo Moon lover should not be underestimated. A gradual and regular interaction can bring both partners face to face with each other as confidants. Honor and respect are of great value to Leo Moon lovers and it must be stressed that a relationship built on mutual respect, instead of only passion will usually outlast a one-dimensional, physical relationship that could die out remarkably quickly.

Also, Leo Moon partners need to be genuinely appreciated, so the fun-loving Aries type lover shouldn't poke and prod their sensitive Leo Moon lover's ego too much. Frequent verbal appreciation will help them grow closer, as will observing those little romantic courtesies like remembering birthdays, anniversaries and Valentine's Day (no matter what their age). When both lovers share the energy of the same element, there could be an overwhelming of sorts, where there is nothing to contrast their love and balance it out. But their lighthearted natures will help carry any tension away. The couple that laughs together, stays together.

One of them will have to be the financial rock of the relationship, and make sure that financial problems don't filter into other areas of their relationship and sour them, as they often do for other couples. They're both impulse shoppers, so one of them will have to make sure that money is not spent without regard for the future and that a regular income keeps coming in. These fiery lovers share a lot in common and there may be a desire for children at some point. This is a good marriage match, particularly if both fiery lovers learn to tone down their natural impatience. If they can forgive easily, they can last a lifetime. This is a truly loving pair!

Leo Moon vs. Taurus Sun, Moon or Rising Sign
The Fire and Earth Relationship

Fire: "I need romance and passion to really enjoy my relationship. Will my boyfriend be a faithful mate for life?" the fiery female partner wonders. "I want an active and freedom-loving partner. Will my girlfriend understand my need for true freedom in life or be too controlling?" the fiery male lover thinks to himself.

Earth: "Does my boyfriend manage his finances maturely or will I end up paying his bills and supporting him? I need stability and true commitment before I can enjoy the romance between us." the earthy female thinks to herself. "Will my future wife spend my hard earned cash on frivolous items at the mall or be wise enough to save up for our retirement?" the earthy male lover wonders.

L eo Moon lovers can enjoy a healing and fulfilling relationship with partners who have their Sun, Moon or Rising sign in the dependable earth sign of Taurus. Each partner symbolizes an element. Understanding that element helps us delve deeper into the real personality of that partner. The fire element represents a nature that actively seeks out happiness and yearns to experience a once-in-a-lifetime kind of burning passion. The earth element represents a need to produce, protect and secure all aspects of a love relationship; success without longevity is meaningless to this element.

Elementally, fire and earth can support each other wonderfully. Fire needs the earth so that it has support to burn on, while the earth needs fire to give it warmth, so that the winter's last frozen touch is melted away. Fire, however, must be handled in a mature way, because it can cause destruction if not controlled, while the earth can cause a landslide to occur and rearrange the map in one stroke. When these energies mingle in appropriate amounts, the fire element warms our homes, helps cook our food and earth provides a stable base and foundation for us to create our lives on. Balancing the attributes of each element is key.

If you're cute, fiercely loyal, bright and optimistic, the Leo Moon lover will adore your company. In many ways, both these fixed signs are alike: Leo Moon lovers enjoy being in a relationship and prefer it to being 'single and looking', while Taurus type lovers work hard at keeping a good relationship afloat if their lover has most of the important qualities they seek in a life-mate. The only thing they may have to watch out for is the fiery Leo Moon's desire for appreciation and admiration. The Leo Moon partner likes to hear their partner *verbalize* that appreciation regularly and sometimes, Taurus type lovers may become complacent with the relationship and forget to do this.

Making a distinction between the two varying types of the Leo Moon persona is key to getting the right shade of compatibility. The first type of Leo Moon personality is the *lion type* while the second is the *cub type*. The lion type is very much like the proud lion it represents; they are assertive, usually dominant and very charismatic, people tend to just flock to them as though they were a rock star. The second type, the cub type of Leo Moon personality is more submissive, acquiescent and ever searching for their perfect soul mate. This type is romantic and easily hurt emotionally. The Taurus type lover may get along best with the second, cub type Leo Moon lover if they are assertive themselves. If the Taurus type lover is passive, they may find greater camaraderie with the protective, lion type of Leo Moon personality. The key is to match up the strong lovers with the supportive ones for best results.

Both Leo Moon lovers and their Taurus type mates are very loving signs and the passion they experience will be rare and unforgettable. Marriage is also a fine idea if both of them can keep a few points in mind: Leo Moon mates should never force their hard-working and faithful Taurus type partner to enter into any phase in life before they are ready. The Taurus type lover won't mind a long courtship: they like to test out their partner and feel that time is always on their side. But Leo Moon lovers may not be so patient and may take off and begin a new relationship without fully having used their precious chance to understand their earthy, tenderhearted, if slightly reticent lover.

The Taurus type mate may lean more toward internalizing a lot of their feelings, sometimes for years at a time, which could seriously hurt their relationship, not to mention their health. Their fiery Leo Moon mate, on the other hand, may tend to impulsively share too much at the wrong time, when that information cannot be properly appreciated. An emotional avalanche could cause the usually stable Taurus type partner to lash out verbally or completely withdraw from discussing the problem. Timing is everything and Leo Moon partners can be the masters of perfect timing if they wish.

Leo Moon lovers function under the influence of the Sun. When the Sun's bright and brilliant energy meets up with the passive, romantic essence of Venus (the ruler of Taurus), the effect will be strongly felt in the Leo Moon/Taurus Sun, Moon or Rising sign partnership. The Sun tends to be dominating, forceful but is also benevolent and easy to approach. It can't help being so influential, it's the mighty Sun after all, the giver of life and vitality around which all the other planets revolve. Venus, the love and relationship planet tends to be receptive, and tends to seek out approval from stronger, more aggressive personalities.

Both these planetary forces react well to true affection. If a clash of wills occurs, Venus-ruled, Taurus types may refuse to fight, but won't give in to demands from anyone either. Beautiful Venus uses silence as a weapon for showing disapproval, as will the Taurus type lover. The Sun-ruled, Leo Moon lover will keep on repeating their point of view over and over (the Sun's influence is intellectual). This means that one of them will have to fine-tune the relationship in such a way that neither has the upper hand or an unfair advantage over the other. The partner who loves more will learn to compromise sooner.

The Moon sign of Leo makes for an incredibly easy-going partner most of the time, but this Moon sign will have its moments. Their requirements are few but specific, and they really hope that they will be fulfilled by their lover; no dominating and no emotional manipulation will be tolerated. Usually, there may be a tendency in this fiery and impulsive Moon sign to begin a relationship quickly but somehow lose steam half way down the road. Their Taurus type partner is very sensitive, and may not be comfortable with the sudden change of pace and direction. Stability in all things is essential to earthy Taurus types. *"If you give someone your word, honor it. That's how you build character."* the careful Taurus type lover advises. Therefore a casual friendship is initially advised with this Moon sign before they fall into the throes of passion, so that one of the lovers can maturely control the speed of the relationship and not let it spiral downward into disinterest from either lover.

The friendship aspect of a relationship with a lover with a Leo Moon sign should not be taken lightly. A gradual but regular interaction can bring both partners face to face with each other as confidants before they become lovers too soon. Honor and respect is of great value to Leo Moon lovers and it must be stressed that a relationship built on mutual respect instead of only passion will usually outlast a one-dimensional physical relationship that could die out remarkably quickly. Taurus types will demand monogamy (Venus *never* shares her lovers) and generally, Leo Moon lovers won't have a problem with sexual exclusivity.

This couple's best bet is to handle each other tactfully and learn each other's triggers and fears so that any possible emotional gridlock can be eliminated before it gets out of hand. What does the Leo Moon lover fear? They fear falling in love with an overly dependent and fickle partner who will never value their loyalty and may try to control them by using love as a weapon. What does the Taurus type mate fear? They fear the break up of a perfectly good relationship or marriage due to an unfaithful lover who made promises they knew they'd never keep.

The Taurus type partner might want to try not to push too hard nor totally withdraw from the scene if difficulties arise in their love life. They should retreat and re-evaluate, but never stop communicating. The magnetic Leo Moon lover may feel comfortable enough to speak for both of them, therefore the Taurus type partner might like to be more expressive and speak their mind when their lover asks them a direct question, instead of saying *"Honey, why don't you decide what we should have for dessert? You know what I like."* The Leo Moon lover will be more than happy to decide, but input both from partners is better than one of them always assuming control. This will keep their relationship respectful and healthy over the long haul.

Also, Taurus type lovers need financial stability before fully committing their heart to one person and the Leo Moon energy could certainly provide that domestic tranquility and comfort. If fiery Leo Moon lovers can watch how much they spend and if pragmatic Taurus type partners can curtail how much they worry about finances, this could be a solid partnership. The Leo Moon energy brings out the romantic in their Taurus type partner, and the Taurus type lover brings out their Leo Moon lover's sensitive, practical and cautious side. This is a great long-term match.

Leo Moon vs. Gemini Sun, Moon or Rising Sign
The Fire and Air Relationship

Fire: "I need romance and passion to really enjoy my relationship. Will my boyfriend be a faithful mate for life?" the fiery female partner wonders. "I want an active and freedom-loving partner. Will my girlfriend understand my need for true freedom in life or be too controlling of everything I do?" the fiery male lover thinks to himself.

Air: "Is my boyfriend open-minded enough and will he appreciate my outspoken side? I need a life mate who will talk to me, communicate with me about every-thing and not clam up and brood." the airy female partner muses. "Will my girlfriend allow me to do the things I love or will she try to restrict me from expressing myself?" the airy male lover wonders.

Leo Moon lovers can enjoy an expressive and fulfilling relationship with partners who have their Sun, Moon or Rising sign in the gregarious air sign of Gemini. Each partner symbolizes an element. Understanding that ele-ment helps us delve deeper into the real personality of that partner. Fire rep-resents passion and desire, and a need to eagerly dive into life and experience it from every angle. Air represents freedom and a need to use self-expression in a myriad different but imaginative ways.

Elementally, fire and air can co-exist remarkably well. Fire needs the oxygen in the air to burn its brightest, while the air or the atmosphere needs the heat of fire so that the frozen energy of a merciless winter begins to thaw and melt away. Be that as it may, if the air in the form of rough winds blows too force-fully, it can extinguish a small fledgling flame that is trying desperately to become a productive fire, while fire, if it burns too hot, can rob the air of all its oxygen and change its nature completely. Balancing the attributes of each element is key.

If you're independent, self-confident and physically alluring, the Leo Moon lover will want to hover near you. Fiery Leo Moon lovers will feel energized by a Gemini type partner, as the airy Gemini energy brings forth a sense of vitality in their already adventurous, risk-loving partners. They're both flirtatious and respond very eagerly to attention from each other. The fun-loving Gemini type lover needs a partner who is a good conversationalist and understands their need to be unrestricted in everything that they do. Freedom-loving air signs don't want to be answerable to anyone, not even their soul mate, and the slightest hint of controlling behavior from a lover will make them recoil. Freedom of expression is extremely important to the talkative and mentally restless Gemini type persona. One thing that should be kept in mind with this pairing is the Leo Moon partner's occasional tendency to take control of the relationship and forget to ask their Gemini type partner how they feel about things. They may not mean to usurp power, but Gemini type partners intend to be an equal partner when *any* decision is taken and will value the courtesy of being consulted.

There are two separate types of the Leo Moon personality; one is the confident and magnetic *lion type* while the second is the soft-natured and passive, non-confrontational *cub type*. The lion type may tend to direct and lead the course of the relationship actively, while the cub type may choose to go along with the desires of a more dominant mate. The Gemini type lover is often dominant themselves, which is why they may find greater ease with the cub type, romantic and somewhat more emotionally malleable Leo Moon personality. Two highly opinionated personalities may find that it may be too hard for them to bend to the will of the other. When pride enters the picture, love and passion exit it.

Leo Moon mates may also exhibit that famous fire sign temper once in a while, but it invariably cools quickly. Their mate must note that Leo Moon lovers will accept as fact everything they are told, they take things very literally; honesty is the key link here. The Gemini type lover must make sure they never forget or omit mentioning some information that they considered inconsequential but their lover didn't.

A he-said, she-said situation can develop rapidly when the Mercury-ruled, Gemini type lover is involved (this planet rules speech). Sometimes the wrong words tumble out at precisely the wrong time and cause some serious damage. No matter who is wrong or right, quickly and genuinely apologizing can mean the difference between a relationship between strangers who can only connect physically, and soul companions who connect on emotional and spiritual levels as well. Gemini types are very loving, and will be happy to see their mate also taking an active role in reconciliation.

Leo Moon lovers function under the influence of the Sun. When the Sun's bright and powerful energy meets up with the sharp, inquisitive and brilliant essence of Mercury (the ruler of Gemini), the effect will be strongly felt in the Leo Moon/Gemini Sun, Moon or Rising sign partnership. The Sun tends to take charge but is also benevolent and protective. It can't help shining and attracting attention; it's the mighty Sun after all, the nucleus of our world. Mercury, the information and communication planet tends to be a bit high-strung, highly creative and seeks to express itself and react at every given opportunity.

If a clash of desire occurs (both are dominant and mincing words may be hard to do all the time), the Gemini type lover may argue and make a good deal of effective points but refuse to give in to demands from anyone, finally ending up doing exactly as they please; Mercury is not called the best word weaver and mental gymnast in the family of planets for nothing. The Leo Moon mate, other hand, may be the *louder* of the two, and also demand to get their way. This means that one of them will have to modulate the relationship in such a way that neither has the upper hand or an unfair advantage over the other. The lover who cares the most for the relationship's survival will spend more time maintaining a balance between two opinionated but amazingly charismatic personalities.

A little diplomacy will go a long way in soothing the nerves of both partners. They must also make sure that their financial issues don't color their relationship, because both of them will want sole control over their money and their ability to spend it. Compromise and sensitivity will save the day once again. The Leo Moon lover brings forth in their Gemini type lover a sense of high romance and courtship (Leo rules the human heart) and makes them feel good about themselves physically. The exciting and affectionate Gemini type lover stimulates their mate intellectually, and helps the Leo Moon partner feel free and unrestrained in truly expressing who they are to the world. This relationship will benefit from starting off as a solid, long-term friendship and then gradually progressing into a deeper, more significant emotional bond.

Leo Moon vs. Cancer Sun, Moon or Rising Sign
The Fire and Water Relationship

Fire: "I need romance and passion to really enjoy my relationship. Will my boyfriend be a faithful mate for life?" the fiery female partner wonders. "I want an active and freedom-loving partner. Will my girlfriend understand my need for true freedom in life or be too controlling of my chosen lifestyle?" the fiery male lover thinks to himself.

Water: "Is my boyfriend emotionally stable and wise about our joint finances? Or will debts pile up in the first year of marriage? I need a supportive life-long lover as well as a loving one." the watery female lover thinks to herself. "Will my future spouse conserve our financial resources or spend unwisely without thought for the future? I can connect better romantically if I know that my chosen life-mate is passionate as well as mature and pragmatic." the watery male lover wonders.

Leo Moon lovers can enjoy an emotionally rewarding relationship with partners who have their Sun, Moon or Rising sign in the water sign of Cancer. Each partner symbolizes an element. Understanding that element helps us delve deeper into the real personality of that partner. Fire represents a desire to meet life with an exuberance and optimism; this element refuses to let defeat claim it. Water represents a desire to exult in human emotion in its purest form, so that life feels authentic, vibrant and meaningful.

Elementally, water and fire are compatible, but adjustments have to be made for a full chance at success. Water needs fire to create an atmosphere of warmth and security, while fire needs water to cool itself off if it is beginning to burn dangerously bright. Water must be careful around fire and not completely extinguish its hopeful energy, and fire must be used carefully around water because hot water can scald. Balance between the elements is key.

The Cancer type lover should be able to distinguish with ease between the two specific types of the Leo Moon personality; this will aid them greatly in getting to know the inner workings of their lover's heart. The first type of Leo Moon personality is the rock star-like, *lion type*, while the second is the somewhat more passive and accommodating *cub type*. If the Cancer type lover is docile themselves, they will like being around the protective energy of the lion type, Leo Moon personality. The more leadership-oriented Cancer type lover may, on the other hand, gravitate toward the cub type, romantic Leo Moon personality.

Leo Moon lovers are openhearted, demand loyalty and thrive in long-term relationships where they are sure of their partner's allegiance toward them. Cancer type lovers need to know that their partner wants to build a secure future together so that they can put some roots down. *"If I go out with this man, how much security will it bring me? Is he a good and trustworthy man? Can I share my dreams with him as well as my fears? How dependable is he really?" the* curious Cancer type female wonders. *"If I ask this woman out, will she attach to me too soon and become controlling of me? Is she after my money? Is she still going out with ex-boyfriends?"* the Leo Moon male wonders.

The Leo Moon lover is dominant and eases into the position of *relationship manager* very quickly, therefore they must always do their lover the courtesy of asking for their input regularly. Giving vent to that fire sign temper at the wrong time may also contribute to needless tension. While they may not mean anything by it, it is very possible that such an outburst could seriously damage the relationship and cause the extremely sensitive Cancer type partner to begin to keep secrets and withdraw from discussing important matters openly for fear of another outburst. Cancer type partners are strong but can feel disheartened over the slightest ill-timed and harsh utterance, however innocent from the point of view of the Leo Moon partner.

The Leo Moon lover responds to the energy of the Sun, while the Cancer type mate functions under the influence of the Moon. The Sun and the Moon are an exquisite complement to each other; the Sun is male and aggressive, and the Moon is female, non-confrontational and maternal. This relationship will work even if the Cancer type partner is male and the Sun-ruled, Leo Moon lover is female. Each will invoke the nurturing qualities needed to create a successful family atmosphere, should they decide to become parents.

The sunny, Leo Moon mate seems to be loved by everyone they meet and their lover may feel a bit possessive now and then. The watery Cancer type partner may have some difficulty in trying to understand some of the long-term motivations of the Leo Moon lover. The Leo Moon lover, on the other hand may think that they know exactly what their sensitive lover needs in life, but that may not be true. *"You want someone to take care of you."* the Leo Moon lover says. *"No, I want to be understood and appreciated. I want you to love the real me."* the Cancer type mate answers. It would take the restless and fiery Leo Moon mate a very long time indeed to fully grasp the oceanic depth of the extraordinary Cancer type persona.

The Cancer type lover is emotional energy personified and finds excessive analysis and rationalization a needless distraction when trying to create a sturdy bond with their lover (*"Why do I have to tell you how I feel? Can't you see it on my face? In my eyes?"* the Cancer type lover questions), while the energetic and fiery Leo Moon lover may consider too emotional a lover a perplexing problem which they cannot circumvent (*"Why do I always have to watch what I say around you? We're lovers, you should know my temperament by now, honey, I tell it like it is."* the Leo Moon lover informs.) Logic and emotion can co-exist if both lovers can learn to tone down the dosage of each according to the time and situation. The Cancer type lover could learn to not take the smallest problems quite so seriously, while their Leo Moon lover could learn to take certain issues *more* seriously, so that both of them can reach a level playing field.

This couple's best bet is to learn each other's fears so that any possible emotional gridlock can be eliminated before it gets out of hand. What does the Leo Moon lover fear? They fear an excessively emotional lover who might try to control what they do by using their love against them. The Cancer type lover fears having to live with a mate who is consistently insensitive and cannot understand that they act out of concern, and not control.

The Cancer type lover needs a partner who can be depended on for financial assistance if ever deemed necessary in a crisis. This is because they will also support a lover who may need that same financial assistance someday; Cancer is a highly reciprocal sign. The water element thrives when there is easy and quality communication between them and their chosen partner. They should learn to use their astute intuition to read into their passionate Leo Moon lover's heart and be able to anticipate when things could get stressful. The Leo Moon essence, on the other hand, needs a physically demonstrative lover, whom he or she can show off in public and be proud of. Genuine admiration from peers is crucial to this fiery Moon sign's self-esteem. But everyone needs TLC sometimes and Cancer type lovers make understanding partners who can take tender care of their lover, and help nurture them in an environment that is safe enough for emotional nesting and trust building. The Leo Moon mate will respond by protecting their mate in every situation and being their most stalwart supporter. This is a fruitful combination.

Leo Moon vs. Leo Sun, Moon or Rising Sign
The Fire and Fire Relationship

Fire: "I need romance and passion to really enjoy my relationship. Will my boyfriend be a faithful mate for life?" the fiery female partner wonders. "I want an active and freedom-loving partner. Will my girlfriend understand my need for true freedom in life or be too controlling about the way I live my life?" the fiery male lover thinks to himself.

Leo Moon lovers can enjoy a highly revealing and rewarding relationship with partners who have their Sun, Moon or Rising sign in their own fire sign of Leo. Each partner symbolizes an element. Understanding that element helps us delve deeper into the real personality of that partner. Fire symbolizes a passion for life as well as love and intimacy. Elementally, fire supports fire beautifully. The double fire relationship helps two soul companions figure out what they need to experience true, self-worth through close relationships; Leo Moon lovers yearn to be heard and appreciated.

Fire is one of the most important elements because without it, the world would freeze and life would come to a standstill. With the gift of heat, the great oceans move, frozen icebergs melt and create more water and frozen hearts begin to feel the depth of human emotion once again. Fire energy must also be maturely handled to bring forth its best attributes. A fire that burns too hot dies away just as quickly. Therefore, the key is to let it burn slowly and longer, changing it from a destructive fire to a productive fire. Balancing the attributes of this vibrant element is key.

It would help both of these lovers if they could distinguish between the two, specific Leo Moon personality types, as it would aid with figuring out the needs of each partner, instead of jumping to conclusions about them. The first type of Leo Moon personality is the *lion type*, while the second is the *cub type*. The lion type is super-confident, ambitious and dominant by temperament, while the second, cub type, is often passive, accommodating and more interested in relationships instead of climbing the social ladder.

If both these lover's personalities resemble the lion type Leo Moon personality, then there might be some problems with both of them wanting to get their way all the time. But if one of them is the cub type and the other is the lion type Leo Moon personality, then they could achieve that delicate balance where instead of vying for power, both will be able to approach each other in their own emotional language. The cub type Leo Moon lover will enjoy the protection of the lion type Leo Moon partner, while the lion type will enjoy not having to fight to direct and control the relationship.

They will attract each other with their warmth and friendly approach to life: the attraction between these two fiery Leo type lovers will be strong, but some adjustments will have to be made for long-term compatibility. They key to a double fire relationship is for one of the two lovers to become the watchdog of the relationship from the very beginning. Two Sun-ruled, Leo lovers may express their dominant side once in a while, so one of them will have to learn to compromise. *"Why are you being so bossy with me today? All I did was ask if you mailed that payment or not!"* the Leo type lover might say. *"I'm not being bossy! I just don't want to have to keep track of everything all the time, honey."* the Leo Moon lover may answer. The more passive lover must become the rock that steers the relationship toward stable shores, or become the cooling agent when fiery tempers flare. Both of them are ardent, loving and very trusting and this camaraderie will pull them through many a problem over the years.

The only problem that could cause complications is when one of them loses their temper and impulsively blurts out things that should be either left unspoken or said at a more appropriate time. The double Sun (Leo is ruled by the Sun) vibration may create a lot of heat but too much of it might rob the relationship of contrast. Fire signs are emotionally volatile when under pressure and respond very quickly indeed to any sort of attack, even if it is from a loved one. Their reaction will be to put up a protective verbal shield immediately. Yes, forgiveness usually comes easily and they will be kissing and making up within hours, but if arguments occur too often, it could alter the original nature of the relationship in a fundamental way.

Honest communication is a good start, but it will not help unless both partners approach each other in a tender and respectful manner when complex discussions are on the agenda. Fire signs are tough as nails and do not back down from any person or situation; they have great self-confidence and make very stalwart partners. But the key will always be kindness and consistent understanding when dealing with each other, even on bad days. Passion may stabilize them, but understanding will grant them longevity.

Leo Moon vs. Virgo Sun, Moon or Rising Sign
The Fire and Earth Relationship

Fire: "I need romance and passion to really enjoy my relationship. Will my boyfriend be a faithful mate for life?" the fiery female partner wonders. "I want an active and freedom-loving partner. Will my girlfriend understand my need for true freedom in life or be too controlling?" the fiery male lover thinks to himself. Earth: "Does my boyfriend manage his finances maturely or will I end up paying his bills and supporting him? I need stability and true commitment before I can enjoy the romance between us." the earthy female thinks to herself. "Will my future wife spend my hard earned cash on frivolous items at the mall or be wise enough to save up for our retirement?" the earthy male lover wonders.

Leo Moon lovers can enjoy an intriguing and domestically rewarding relationship with partners who have their Sun, Moon or Rising sign in the analytical earth sign of Virgo. Each partner symbolizes an element. Understanding that element helps us delve deeper into the real personality of that partner. Fire represents a need for excitement, action and newness. Earth represents a need to nurture, stabilize and safeguard love so that it stands the test of time.

Elementally, fire and earth can support each other wonderfully. Fire needs the earth so that it has support to burn on, while the earth needs fire to give it warmth. Fire, however, must be handled in a mature way, because it can cause destruction if not controlled, while the earth can cause a landslide to occur and rearrange the map in one stroke. When these energies mingle in appropriate amounts, the fire element warms our homes, and earth provides a stable base and foundation for us to create our lives on. Balancing the attributes of each element is key.

Making a distinction between the two varying types of the Leo Moon persona is key to creating the right shade of compatibility. The first type of Leo Moon personality is the *lion type* while the second is the *cub type*. The lion type is very much like the proud lion it represents; they are assertive, usually dominant and very charismatic. The second type, the cub type of Leo Moon personality is more submissive, acquiescent and ever searching for their perfect life mate. This type is romantic and takes rejection very hard. The Virgo type lover may get along best with the second, cub type Leo Moon lover if they are assertive themselves. If the Virgo type lover is passive, they may find greater camaraderie with the dominant, lion type of Leo Moon personality. The key is to match up the strong lovers with the supportive ones for best results so that egos don't clash twenty-four/seven.

If the Virgo type, lover's life philosophy is properly understood by the Leo Moon lover in the initial stages of their courtship, daily compatibility could be easily achieved on many fronts. Virgo types love to bring order, purpose and daily sustenance to the relationship, while Leo Moon lovers are endearing, charismatic creatures who may sometimes lack the tact that Virgo types need from a lover. Leo Moon lovers are casual but ambitious, while the Virgo essence is goal-oriented and consistently hardworking. Love between these two vividly differing energies can survive, if Virgo type partners can teach their Leo Moon lover to slow down and limit their need to take risks, and if the Leo Moon lover can teach their Virgo life-companion to take life and its myriad problems in their stride, and remind them that worrying over the nitty-gritty could cost them their peace of mind. *"Calm down, honey, it's just a late bill, will it matter fifty years from now if it was on time or not?"* the Leo Moon lover asks. *"It will matter if someone decides to check my credit tomorrow! I need to sort this out right now, dear."* the Virgo type mate explains.

The Virgo type mate may, in typical earth sign fashion, occasionally lean more toward directing a lot of their feelings inward, sometimes for years at a time, which could seriously hurt their relationship and have a negative effect on their health. Their fiery Leo Moon mate, on the other hand, may tend to share too much at the wrong time with typical fire sign enthusiasm, when that information could have been presented more diplomatically and at a more appropriate time. A Virgo type lover seeks calm and peace in their relationships, and an emotional avalanche could cause the usually stable Virgo type partner to lash out verbally (watch out when Mercury lets those words fly!) or completely withdraw from discussing the problem. Timing is everything and Leo Moon partners might like to watch the *where* and the *when* before they tackle touchy issues.

The mentally astute Virgo energy creates a firm, dependable structure for Leo Moon mates to base their life on, while the Leo Moon lover helps lower Virgo's blood pressure by showing them that life has a lighter, happier side too. The earthy Virgo essence is dutiful and obliging, and if their tendency to correct is slightly modified, it would do them both a world of good and help bring them closer emotionally. Virgo must resist the desire to be on a constant clean up mission of their relationship; relationships can be messy and hard to control, but that's the naturalness of the process of falling in love.

The Leo Moon sign will be a bundle of joy and merriment most of the time, but if they're undergoing a blue spell, care should be taken in approaching them (absolutely no smothering! Let them come to you.). Lots of TLC coupled with a special blend of closeness and distance should do the trick. Fortunately, this fiery Moon sign won't be depressed for long. The Leo Moon sign is a fascinating mixture of the influence of the emotional Moon and the bright majesty of the Sun.

The Leo Moon mate thrives in relationships where they can enjoy regular intimacy (the fifth sign of Leo is connected to the fifth Astrological sector of romance), which is something that Virgo types will also deem important. When it comes to health and well being, the Virgo type mate would be a welcome boon to the impulsive Leo Moon lover. who has a weakness for fast food, which could injure their health and heart (Leo rules the heart) in the long run. *"How about we go grab some pizza, honey? I'm starved!"* the Leo Moon lover suggests. *"How about I make something delicious at home that might help us both lose some weight and save a few bucks too?"* the frugal Virgo lover might answer. (Note to Virgo: once in a while, pizza is okay too! Every aspect of life must not be too strictly regimented.)

Leo Moon lovers, with their natural fixity, find it hard to make big, permanent changes in their life to fit in another person, but this extra effort will pay off in a big way. Mutable Virgo types will tolerate more of their Leo Moon lover's personality and quirks than anyone else. Mercury-ruled, Virgo types will be wise to employ a regular dose of verbal appreciation to keep their fiery lover emotionally fulfilled. This relationship is based on the wine factor; it could improve and refine itself with age.

Leo Moon vs. Libra Sun, Moon or Rising Sign
The Fire and Air Relationship

Fire: "I need romance and passion to really enjoy my relationship. Will my boyfriend be a faithful mate for life?" the fiery female partner wonders. "I want an active and freedom-loving partner. Will my girlfriend understand my need for true freedom in life or be too controlling of what I do?" the fiery male lover thinks to himself.

Air: "Is my boyfriend open-minded enough and will he appreciate my outspoken side? I need a life mate who will talk to me, communicate with me about every-thing and not clam up and brood." the airy female partner muses. "Will my girlfriend allow me to do the things I love or will she try to restrict me from truly expressing myself?" the airy male lover wonders.

Leo Moon lovers can enjoy a romantic and intellectually rewarding rela-tionship with partners who have their Sun, Moon or Rising sign in the romantic air sign of Libra. Each partner symbolizes an element. Understand-ing that element helps us delve deeper into the real personality of that partner. Fire represents passion and a yearning to jump into life with both feet and grab their share of adventure, romance and happiness. Air represents an incredible intellectualism and creative genius; this element must express itself and feed its intellectual hunger to feel fulfilled and at ease with other areas of life.

Elementally, fire and air can co-exist remarkably well. Fire needs the oxygen in the air to burn its brightest, while the air or the atmosphere needs the heat of fire to eliminate the frozen energy of a bone-chilling winter. Be that as it may, if the air in the form of winds blows too forcefully, it can extinguish a small fledgling flame that is trying desperately to become a productive fire, while fire, if it burns too hot, can rob the air of all its oxygen and change its nature completely. Balancing the attributes of each element is key.

The Leo Moon personality comes in two shades; one is the *lion type* Leo Moon personality while the other is the *cub type*. The lion type is almost always ambitious, assertive and tends to actively control the direction and pace of the relationship. The cub type is the opposite; they are mellow, romantic and enjoy an easy-going reputation. If the Libra type lover is passive and supportive, they will be attracted to the lion type persona, while if the Libra type lover is as assertive as the lion type, Leo Moon lover, they will get along better with the non-aggressive, cub type Leo Moon persona. The point is to make sure that the aggressive lovers don't have to constantly match wits with equally aggressive partners and create power struggles.

If you're well dressed and attractive, can play a little hard to get at the right time and know the value of loyalty in love, the Leo Moon lover will want to draw closer to you. These two lovers will get along quite nicely if the Leo Moon lover keeps in mind the fact that the Libra type lover thrives when they are regularly appreciated, both physically and intellectually. Leo Moon lovers can be hasty and prone to losing that legendary fire sign temper, and harmony-oriented Libra personalities recoil in horror from people who shout and make a scene in an effort to get attention. Libra types should keep in mind that their Leo Moon soul mate needs to be handled tactfully and with consistent tenderness especially when they are in an occasional bad mood. Libra's natural diplomacy will help smooth out any situation, no matter how explosive.

Libra type lovers function under the influence of Venus, while Leo Moon partners are ruled by the Sun. When the Sun's explosive and magnificent energy meets up with the harmonious and anchor-seeking energy of beautiful Venus, the effect will be felt in the Leo Moon/Libra Sun, Moon or Ascendant partnership. The Sun's energy tends to be benevolent, protective but also dominating sometimes. It can't help how powerful it is, it's the mighty Sun after all, the giver of life and light. Matchmaker Venus is focused on the initiation, sustenance and improvement of interpersonal relationships, especially those that are nearing the state of marriage.

Both these planetary forces are unique and, in the arena of relationships, can be compatible. The Sun (Leo Moon) likes to protect Venus (Libra), and Venus enjoys being protected by the Sun. Each supplies a need in the other. If a clash of wills occurs, receptive Venus might back down and try another approach, while the Sun energy will keep on stressing the same point over and over. This means that one of the lovers will have to modulate the relationship in such a way that neither has the upper hand or an unfair advantage over the other. The lover who cares more will make the most of the effort at compromise.

The Moon sign of Leo makes for an incredibly open-hearted and loving partner most of the time. Once in a while, there may be a tendency in this fiery and impulsive Moon sign to begin a relationship quickly but somehow lose interest half way down the road. If their partner is very sensitive (Libra is quite sensitive to relationship ups and downs), they may not understand why the pace and direction of the relationship has suddenly changed. Therefore a casual friendship is advised with this Moon sign initially, so that one of the lovers can maturely control the speed of the relationship and not let it spiral downward into disinterest from either lover. Lady Venus, the ruler of Libra, will not tolerate prolonged disinterest from a lover, and if swift changes are not made, she will walk away from that relationship and begin a new one elsewhere. A little tact and consideration could help in avoiding this loss. Honor and respect is of great value to Leo Moon lovers and sexually compatibility alone will not fulfill them; they expect the best, they want to be fulfilled on all levels.

If the Leo Moon lover can keep the romance alive and be more affectionate with Libra types (remember birthdays, anniversaries and most importantly Venus' favorite Valentine's Day), and if the Libra type mate can give the Leo Moon lover a good degree of personal freedom and attention *when* they need it, this match will work out and last decades. This highly communicative fire and air combination can grow stronger as time passes by; they are both highly creative and hungry for life's most stimulating experiences, which they hope to share and enjoy together.

Both will effectively train one another into picking up traits that make their overall personalities well-rounded and wholesome. The Libra essence brings out their Leo Moon soul mate's romantic and tender side, while the fiery Leo Moon partner brings out their airy sweetheart's freedom-loving and assertive side. This is a romantic, passionate combination.

Leo Moon vs. Scorpio Sun, Moon or Rising Sign
The Fire and Water Relationship

Fire: "I need romance and passion to really enjoy my relationship. Will my boyfriend be a faithful mate for life?" the fiery female partner wonders. "I want an active and freedom-loving partner. Will my girlfriend understand my need

for true freedom in life or be too controlling of me and my decisions?" the fiery
male lover thinks to himself.

Water: "Is my boyfriend emotionally stable and wise about our joint finances? Or
will debts pile up in the first year of marriage? I need a supportive life-long lover
as well as a loving one." the watery female lover thinks to herself. "Will my future
spouse conserve our financial resources or spend unwisely without thought for the
future? I can connect better romantically if I know that my chosen life-mate is
passionate as well as mature and pragmatic." the watery male lover wonders.

Leo Moon lovers can enjoy a highly emotional and fulfilling relationship with partners who have their Sun, Moon or Rising sign in the deep, water sign of Scorpio. Each partner symbolizes an element. Understanding that element helps us delve deeper into the real personality of that partner. Fire represents a desire for adventure, excitement and intimacy. Fulfillment for this outgoing element is usually brought about by taking a big risk. Water represents a desire for security and passion; fulfillment for this element is brought about by creating an atmosphere of long-term stability.

Elementally, water and fire are compatible, but adjustments have to be made for a full chance at success. Water needs fire to create an atmosphere of warmth and security. While fire needs water to cool itself off if it is beginning to burn dangerously bright. Water must be careful around fire and not completely extinguish its hopeful energy, and fire must be used carefully around water because hot water can scald. Balance between the elements is key.

Differentiating between the two classic types of the Leo Moon persona is key to knowing how to approach them. The first type of Leo Moon personality is the *lion type* while the second is the *cub type*. The lion type is very much like the proud lion it is named after; lion types are assertive, usually dominant and very self-confident. The second type, the cub type of Leo Moon personality is more submissive, acquiescent and sincerely interested in finding their perfect relationship. This type is romantic and less ambitious than the first. The Scorpio type lover may get along best with the second, cub type of Leo Moon lover if they are assertive themselves. The key is to match up the strong lovers with the supportive ones for best results; power struggles needlessly disrupt love relationships.

Both these signs (Leo Moon and Scorpio) are fixed by temperament and emotional in their own ways. Leo Moon lovers *externalize* their feelings *("Hey honey, did I tell you about that awful argument I had with my Mom on the phone last night?"* the Leo Moon lover will try to share), while intense Scorpio types fiercely internalize them, (*No, I don't want to talk about that conversation I had with my Dad yesterday, honey, I just need a little time to think things over. Don't worry yourself, I'll figure something out."*). Scorpio feels everything deeply and thrives on predictability, while Leo Moon lovers need excitement and attention from their lover (and life) on a regular basis. Both are capable of great and lasting love with only the slightest modulation in approaches. The sentimental Scorpio essence brings out the tenderness in their Leo Moon lovers, while the Leo Moon energy causes the usually suspicious and careful Scorpio to lay down that ever present guard and be more joyful and worry-free.

The Scorpio essence is intense and focused, demanding total loyalty, which Leo Moon lovers can supply if their emotions are appealed to in the *right way* – with love, trust and sensitivity. They only need to watch out for letting arguments (all couples have them) get out of hand and taking each other's offhand comments too seriously. Leo Moon lovers forgive easily but the Scorpio essence may have trouble offering the olive branch, at least for a while. Their trust has to be re-won so that they can get back into the throes of the relationship with confidence.

Scorpio type partners have to be handled with the utmost care and gentility, and while it may take a lot out of the usually carefree Leo Moon partner, the extra effort will mean greater passion and intimacy. This relationship can work out beautifully if the Leo Moon lover is more verbally tactful around their Scorpio type partner, and if the Scorpio type lover can grant their fiery Leo Moon lover more room to make mistakes and more freedom by being more trusting.

The Leo Moon partner needs to share their life with a mate who is not too serious but can laugh at life's problems instead of exaggerating their gravity. As a fire sign, impetuous Leo Moon partners revel in a relationship where any problems can be talked out quickly and resolved efficiently. *"Let's get this problem behind us and get on with life! I hate going over the same issue over and over, honey."* the Leo Moon partner suggests. Scorpio types are sensitive and may not like being accused of any failure; this sign really does give a hundred and ten percent of their time and efforts in securing their primary love relationship. But they may resent having to always be the patch-up guy in their relationship, while their mate does not help and work on improving it for the long haul.

Initially, there may be some confusion in the heart of the Scorpio type partner as to how they can successfully comprehend their carefree and easygoing partner. The cautious Scorpio type female may wonder, *"We have nothing in common, he's so aggressive at times, he talks constantly and spends his cash like water. There's no way we'll get along in the future. But I still can't stop thinking about him!"* The watery Scorpio type partner may be trying very hard indeed to understand their fiery partner but may not be able to properly interpret the emotional language of the Leo Moon lover.

The Leo Moon lover, on the other hand may think that they have their sensitive lover all figured out, but that may not be true. *"I know what you want, honey, you want me to look after you."* the Leo Moon lover says. *"No, I don't sweetheart, I can take care of myself. I just want to be loved and valued in this relationship on a permanent basis."* the proud Scorpio type lover answers. It would take the lighthearted Leo Moon mate a very long time indeed to fully grasp the sheer depth of the extraordinary Scorpio type persona. Every relationship with a Scorpio type mate will prove life-changing and this relationship will be no different.

They will be able to enjoy a successful relationship, if they could both keep in mind the following points: the Scorpio type lover functions on purely emotional energy and finds carelessness and too much time spent on having fun a serious roadblock to building a stable life together, while the fiery Leo Moon lover may consider too much emotionality in a lover a perplexing problem that creates too many distances between them. Caution and fun can co-exist if both lovers can learn to tone down the dosage of each according to the time and situation. The Scorpio type lover could learn to not take the smallest problems quite so seriously, while their Leo Moon lover could learn to take certain issues *more* seriously, so that both of them can relate on any level, any time.

This couple's best bet is to learn about each other's worst fears so that any possible emotional gridlock can be eliminated before it gets out of hand. What does the Leo Moon lover fear? They fear ending up with a partner who wants to be with them because they have money or influence, and not because they love them. What does the Scorpio type lover fear? They fear being tragically betrayed by the one person they love more than anyone else in the world. The Scorpio type partner might want to try not to push too hard nor totally withdraw from the scene if there are disagreements. The irrepressible and endearing Leo Moon lover may enthusiastically communicate enough for both of them, therefore the Scorpio type partner might like to openly share the musings of their heart more often.

One final tip for Leo Moon lovers who desperately love their watery partner is to never knowingly keep any information from Scorpio types and never omit information, no matter how inconsequential it may seem to them at the time, and vice versa. Scorpio is a financial sign and takes money matters and sharing money seriously, so Leo Moon lovers may have to watch their spending habits. This relationship can last if Scorpio type mates can be less controlling and more trusting of their fiery sweetheart's behavior. They have a good chance at making this their best relationship ever.

Leo Moon vs. Sagittarius Sun, Moon or Rising Sign
The Fire and Fire Relationship

Fire: "I need romance and passion to really enjoy my relationship. Will my boyfriend be a faithful mate for life?" the fiery female partner wonders. "I want an active and freedom-loving partner. Will my girlfriend understand my need for true freedom in life or be too controlling of everything I do?" the fiery male lover thinks to himself.

Leo Moon lovers can enjoy a fun-filled and stimulating relationship with partners who have their Sun, Moon or Rising sign in the wisdom-seeking fire sign of Sagittarius. Each partner symbolizes an element. Understanding that element helps us delve deeper into the real personality of that partner. Fire brings forth a passionate zest for life and need to optimistically seek out adventure; a great adventure always brings great wisdom! Elementally, fire supports fire beautifully.

Fire is one of the most important elements because without it, the world would freeze and become useless. With the gift of heat, the great oceans move, frozen icebergs melt and create more water and frozen hearts begin to feel the depth of human emotion once again. Fire energy must also be maturely handled to bring forth its best attributes. A fire that burns too hot dies away just as quickly.

Therefore, the key is to let it burn slowly and longer, changing it from a destructive fire to a productive fire. Balancing the attributes of this useful and versatile element is key. The Sagittarius essence is very similar to the Leo Moon persona, both need a lot of freedom to grow *individually* within their relationship and require a happily given trust to fully taste the relationship from every emotional angle.

Knowing how to tell the difference between the two, separate types of the Leo Moon personality is crucial to getting to know them well enough to fall in love with them. The first type of Leo Moon personality is the dominant, super-confident, *lion type*, while the second is the romantic and passive, *cub type*. Most Sagittarius types are slightly dominant and like to set the pace of their relationship. Therefore the cub type, Leo Moon lover would be best for them, mainly because they may not compete with them or vie for control or power within the relationship. If both of them are dominant, the lion type, Leo Moon lover could easily clash with the Sagittarius type lover and both could struggle for dominance.

When it comes to setting goals, the only problem these two lovebirds might encounter is when their emotional timetables clash and create a scenario where they see no resolution but to drift apart. For example, one lover may want to start a family, while the other may not want that responsibility at that particular time in their life. Or one lover may want to get married while the other may want to focus on their career. Fire signs also have fiery tempers but traditionally they cool rapidly if even the slightest effort at reconciliation is made. Leo Moon lovers require a great deal of attention and cannot tolerate romantic neglect from a lover. Their Sagittarius mate, on the other hand, may not be able to provide that level of attention regularly; they gravitate toward the Leo Moon mate's star-like persona, but when they are called upon to play the adoring fan too often, things might get a little complicated.

When it comes to solving problems, the Sagittarius type lover needs a calm, intelligent and rational lover; they recoil from mates who use drama or ultimatums to push their needs forward or use excessive emotion to make their point. This sentiment is shared and understood by their charismatic Leo Moon mate. But since both of these lovers are fire signs, once in a while those fiery emotions will float up to the surface and demand to be dealt with. This couple's best bet is to handle each other tactfully and learn each other's weak points so that any possible emotional gridlock can be eliminated before it gets out of hand.

The Sagittarius type partner might want to try not to leave reconciliation to chance if the relationship hits a sudden roadblock. Jupiter, the ruler of Sagittarius, may sometimes make them want to take big leaps without first thinking through the consequences and make them jump to conclusions without adequate reason. The Leo Moon mate, influenced by the power of the mighty Sun, may also jump to some similar conclusions and thus, both partners could end up disrupting a relationship that could have been handled better had they both remained cool, calm and in perfect control of their emotions. They must deal with facts, not feelings.

This couple should learn about each other's hidden fears for greater compatibility. What does the Leo Moon lover fear? They fear ending up with a lover who is only in their life for selfish or monetary reasons instead of true love. What does the Sagittarius type mate fear? They fear being tied down in a bad relationship permanently and *then* meeting the love of their life who truly understands them and lets them function with the least amount of restrictions.

Both signs thrive in relationships where they get plenty of attention and romance; they both love being before an audience. Appreciation is their rocket fuel! They have big hearts and often the most miniscule of reasons get blown out of proportion with them, which is often the easiest thing to remedy. Their key is to always remain honest with each other, keep every promise they make to each other and make sure that their finances are carefully and honestly handled, because when two impulse shoppers join forces in a relationship, discussions surrounding the management of money will inevitably come up. They should never let their financial issues sour other parts of their relationship (money issues sadly lie at the heart of many lovers separating).

Intellectually well-matched and protective of one another, their friendship will never weaken, and if both are mature souls and can easily and frequently forgive, their relationship can survive the greatest storms and allow them to gracefully age together. Fiery friends who become confidants first and lovers second, will have a longer, more emotionally comfortable relationship than friends who proceed directly from the friend stage to the sexual stage. This is a winning pair!

Leo Moon vs. Capricorn Sun, Moon or Rising Sign
The Fire and Earth Relationship

Fire: "I need romance and passion to really enjoy my relationship. Will my boyfriend be a faithful mate for life?" the fiery female partner wonders. "I want an active and freedom-loving partner. Will my girlfriend understand my need for true freedom in life or be too controlling of me?" the fiery male lover thinks to himself.

Earth: "Does my boyfriend manage his finances maturely or will I end up paying his bills and supporting him? I need stability and true commitment before I can enjoy the romance between us." the earthy female thinks to herself. "Will my

future wife spend my hard earned cash on frivolous items at the mall or be wise
enough to save up for our retirement?" the earthy male lover wonders.

Leo Moon lovers can enjoy a very devoted and successful relationship with partners who have their Sun, Moon or Rising sign in the dependable and success-oriented earth sign of Capricorn. Each partner symbolizes an element. Understanding that element helps us delve deeper into the real personality of that partner. Fire represents a burning passion and a desire to take risks and challenge defeats instead of falling victim to them. Earth represents a desire to reach out and secure each vital area of life; the need to protect, enhance and strengthen will be evident.

Elementally, fire and earth can support each other wonderfully. Fire needs the earth so that it has support to burn on, while the earth needs fire to give it warmth, so that the winter's last frozen touch is melted away. Fire, however, must be handled in a mature way, because it can cause destruction if not controlled, while the earth can cause a landslide to occur and rearrange the map in one stroke. When these energies mingle in appropriate amounts, the fire element warms our homes, and earth provides a stable base and foundation for us to create our lives on. Balancing the attributes of each element is key.

The Capricorn type lover might like to ascertain whether their Leo Moon lover has a *lion type* or a *cub type* of Leo Moon personality. The lion type is assertive, dominant and charismatic, while the cub type is submissive, slightly more accommodating and more romance-oriented than ambitious. The dominant and mature Capricorn type lover will get along best with the cub type, Leo Moon lover, because they are less likely to challenge their authority and decisions.

Leo Moon lovers have great lessons to learn from the wise Capricorn type partner as well as teach them some important ones. The planet Saturn rules the sign of Capricorn. Capricorn types can make many of their Leo Moon lover's ambitions come true by sharing with them their dedication and uncommon sense of perseverance. Success and social prestige lie close to both their hearts, and finding a lover who understands and supports this life goal would be an added bonus. Primarily supportive and protective, Capricorn types can teach their Leo Moon lovers how to create a proud legacy and leave something tangible and powerful behind, while bringing to their attention the fact that preparing ahead of time for that rainy day is a good thing for a fun-loving and merry Leo Moon lover to do. But both lovers should be careful to not place personal ambition above the well-being of close relationships; being successful would mean nothing if there is no one there to share in the fruits of their labor (missing the birthdays of friends and family due to work is a serious no-no).

Leo Moon lovers become more frugal, driven and success-oriented around the Capricorn type lover. The more introverted Capricorn types should be more vocal around the fiery and dominant energy of the Leo Moon lover, while Leo Moon lovers should learn to listen carefully when the knowledgeable and karmic Saturn energy speaks through the Capricorn lover. *"Let's plan everything out for the next five years. We'll get engaged next summer, then in the fall of the year after that we'll get married and go on our honeymoon. We'll start a family three years after that, what do you think, sweetheart?"* the planning Capricorn type mate eagerly suggests.

Capricorn types receive from their Leo Moon lovers a new perspective on life, where they can be more optimistic, light-hearted and feel more sure of the steps they have to take in life (Leo Moon mates can help alleviate their Capricorn type sweetheart's occasional depression that is brought on by Saturn's influence). *"Now that we've done all the work and all the chores are complete, let's have fun, darling!"* the Leo Moon lover coaxes their dutiful and industrious mate. It will be a welcome relief.

Capricorn type lovers function under the wise influence of karmic Saturn, while Leo Moon partners are ruled by the Sun. When the Sun's explosive and bright energy meets up with the wise and serious temperament of Saturn, the effect will be tangibly felt in the Leo Moon/Capricorn Sun, Moon or Ascendant partnership. Saturn, (the planet that governs the karmic costs of all actions, good and bad, from every lifetime) the old timekeeper of the planetary family tends to be careful, strict and highly aware of the hidden karma factor that crops up between two lovers under the guise of relationship problems. Both these forces are strong and, in the arena of relationships, will refuse to give up their point of view. If a clash of wills occurs, neither will back down. This means that one of the lovers will have to modulate the relationship in such a way that neither has the upper hand or an unfair advantage over the other. The lover who loves the most will spend more time doing this, usually behind the scenes.

As for managing finances, it should be kept in mind that the Capricorn type lover is more conservative than careless, especially when it comes to a precious resource like income. *"Money doesn't grow on trees."* is a favorite phrase of theirs. Clipping coupons doesn't come easily to generous Leo Moon lovers, who should take to spending within reason and always consult their earthy partners before big purchases are made. This courtesy alone will help smooth out a majority of their problems. Together, both these dynamic energies can create a formidable empire that will stand the test of time, with Capricorn supplying the stability and direction, and the Leo Moon lover supplying the joy of romance and merriment with lots of happy times to look back on.

Leo Moon vs. Aquarius Sun, Moon or Rising Sign
The Fire and Air Relationship

Fire: "I need romance and passion to really enjoy my relationship. Will my boyfriend be a faithful mate for life?" the fiery female partner wonders. "I want an active and freedom-loving partner. Will my girlfriend understand my need for true freedom in life or be too controlling of my life and decisions?" the fiery male lover thinks to himself.

Air: "Is my boyfriend open-minded enough and will he appreciate my outspoken side? I need a life mate who will talk to me, communicate with me about every-thing and not clam up and brood." the airy female partner muses. "Will my girl-friend allow me to do the things I love or will she try to restrict me from expressing myself and living my life the way I want to?" the airy male lover wonders.

Leo Moon lovers can enjoy a very emotionally uplifting relationship with partners who have their Sun, Moon or Rising sign in the intriguing air sign of Aquarius. These signs oppose each other in the zodiac family, so there will be a marital pull between them, a desire to mingle their fate on a permanent and legal level in the form of marriage. Each partner symbolizes an element. Understanding that element helps us delve deeper into the real personality of that partner. Fire represents a need to live life and experience it without fear and pessimism; this element emphasizes the passion of the heart. Air represents a need to express oneself through a variety of mediums and help facilitate the transfer of information; this element emphasizes the passion of the mind.

Elementally, fire and air can co-exist remarkably well. Fire needs the oxygen in air to burn its brightest, while the air or the atmosphere needs the heat of fire to help thaw out the last vestiges of winter and invite spring to return. Be that as it may, if the air in the form of winds blows too forcefully, it can extinguish a small fledgling flame that is trying desperately to become a productive fire, while fire, if it burns too hot, can rob the air of all its oxygen and change its nature completely. Balancing the attributes of each element is key.

There are two, basic types of the Leo Moon personality; one is the *lion type* and the second is the *cub type*. The lion type, Leo Moon lover is polished, self-assured, assertive and rather dominant in relationships. The cub type, Leo Moon lover is passive, more accommodating and rather more focused on romance than on being ambitious and running up to take their place on the world stage. The Aquarius type lover, if assertive themselves, will gravitate toward the cub type, Leo Moon lover who will be less likely to challenge their authority. This is rather important to grasp because it will color their interactions vividly.

The first desire between these two lovers will be to create a life-long relationship. Aquarius types are unique, one-in-a-million personalities and fiery, Leo Moon mates like their lovers to be different and rare, as well as physically demonstrative. Aquarius types help their Leo Moon lovers look at life through the ideal of true individuality and lend them their signature broad-mindedness (Aquarius is the sign of universal brotherhood). If Leo is the sign of royalty, Aquarius is the sign of the people. Aquarius has the vision to succeed and a Leo Moon lover will support their lover in any quest that lies close to their heart. They will also expect the same loyalty and support back, so immediate reciprocation is crucial.

The air sign of Aquarius gifts passionate Leo Moon mates the desire to fight for the right to live their life on their own terms. The downside of this combination is that sometimes the airy Aquarian can get distracted, emotionally disconnect themselves for a short time and cause their Leo Moon partner to think that their lover has lost interest in them. Losing interest mid-stream or sending mixed signals could leave the Leo Moon soul mate confused and bewildered. Ruled by the fire element, unless that fiery Leo Moon heart is tended to carefully, it will cease to provide passion. Aquarius types must always remember that their happy and openhearted Leo Moon lover thrives on lots of attention and love, given freely, *without having to glance at your watch*. Leo Moon lovers might feel perplexed by their airy Aquarius type lover who sometimes cannot spare enough time for their relationship to blossom, but expects it to evolve on its own magically, thus bringing their love perilously close to collapsing forever. Equal input and effort will be needed to keep this love strong and vital.

Aquarian type lovers function under the influence of Uranus, while Leo Moon partners are ruled by the Sun. When the Sun's forceful and engaging energy meets up with the erratic, unconventional but original energy of Uranus, the effect will be felt in the daily give and take of the Leo Moon/Aquarius Sun, Moon or Ascendant partnership. The Sun tends to be benevolent, protective but also dominating. Uranus, the most unpredictable planet in the solar system family tends to be reform-minded, revolutionary and highly experimental in various areas of life. They are usually not very comfortable with rules and traditions that society says they *have* to follow or be left out of the mainstream. To that, the proud Aquarian type person will say, *"So be it, you can do it your way and I'll do it my way."* Both these forces are strong and loving but, in the arena of relationships, can be equally opinionated. If a clash of wills occurs, neither will back down. This means that one them will have to modulate the flow of the relationship in such a way that neither has the upper hand or an unfair advantage over the other. The partner who loves the most or derives more satisfaction from the relationship will learn this technique of subtle compromise sooner.

Leo Moon partners should not expect more attention from their Aquarian type partners than they can realistically give. Aquarius types will want to give equal attention to their friends, pet projects and other personal goals and their lover must not deny them their happiness. A partner who makes too many unrealistic demands or causes an emotional overload in an Aquarius type lover, will soon find that they close their heart to them. They will refuse to relate in an atmosphere of constant pressure.

This results in the Leo Moon lover also withdrawing for fear of being further rejected. An emotional traffic jam can be avoided if both of them keep discussing their problems instead of letting them fester under the surface. The plus side of this combination is that once an Aquarian type person has willingly committed themselves to functioning within a marital or family structure *at the right time* as a spouse or parent, or has brought children into the world, they will give a hundred and ten percent of themselves. Fixed by nature, once they have decided on a course of action, they will stick to it admirably and with more heart than other signs. The key is for them to reach that decision on their own, without any outside influence or pressure. Most Aquarian parents are every child's dream; they will treat them as equals and friends instead of looking down on them or controlling them too strictly.

Leo Moon soul mates should be more patient around the romantically unconventional (but truly loving) Aquarian energy, and Aquarian type lovers should follow through on any promises made: personal honor is a language they both cherish and understand. The Leo Moon lover brings out their Aquarian mate's tenderly protective side, which they will never share with anyone else. Together, both these energies support each other, fill each other with excitement and stand up for each other when faced by a crisis. This is a wonderful combination.

Leo Moon vs. Pisces Sun, Moon or Rising Sign
The Fire and Water Relationship

Fire: "I need romance and passion to really enjoy my relationship. Will my boyfriend be a faithful mate for life?" the fiery female partner wonders. "I want an active and freedom-loving partner. Will my girlfriend understand my need for true freedom in life or be too controlling of everything I want to do?" the fiery male lover thinks to himself.

Water: "Is my boyfriend emotionally stable and wise about our joint finances? Or will debts pile up in the first year of marriage? I need a supportive life-long lover as well as a loving one." the watery female lover thinks to herself. "Will my future spouse conserve our financial resources or spend unwisely without thought for the future? I can connect better romantically if I know that my chosen life-mate is passionate as well as mature and pragmatic." the watery male lover wonders.

Leo Moon lovers can enjoy a very emotionally uplifting relationship with partners who have their Sun, Moon or Rising sign in the spiritually inclined water sign of Pisces. Each partner symbolizes an element. Understanding that element helps us delve deeper into the real personality of that partner. Fire represents a passion for life and a refusal to let defeat have the last word; this element gets up and puts up a fight if dealt an unfair blow by life. Water represents an emotional purity as well as a soft and inviting sensuality; this emotional element yearns to create a secure and safe structure within which to relate to life.

Elementally, water and fire are compatible, but adjustments have to be made for a full chance at success. Water needs fire to create an atmosphere of warmth and security, as well as afford us those relaxing hot showers. While fire needs water to cool itself off if it is beginning to burn dangerously bright. Water must be careful around fire and not completely extinguish its hopeful energy, and fire must be used carefully around water because hot water can scald. Balance between the elements is key.

The fiery Leo Moon personality comes in two different flavors; one is the *lion type* and the other is the *cub type* Leo Moon personality. The Pisces type lover should be able to distinguish between them for maximum compatibility. The lion type, Leo Moon lover is dominant and highly ambitious, while the cub type is mellow and more docile than the lion type. The passive, Pisces type lover may feel more comfortable with the lion type, Leo Moon lover, while the more self-confident Pisces type lover will enjoy the company of the non-confrontational, cub type Leo Moon partner. Leo Moon lovers look for a mate who is attractive, refined and very loyal. Intuitive Pisces type mates can usually sense what their lover is thinking without having to ask them. The emphasis in this relationship will be on how the Leo Moon mate reacts to the Pisces type lover's *moods,* and how the Pisces type mate reacts to their fiery lover's *actions.*

Pisces type lovers function under the influence of Neptune, while Leo type partners are ruled by the Sun. When the Sun's aggressive and sunny energy meets up with the compassionate, dreamy, fantasy prone energy of Neptune, the effect will be felt in the every day give and take of the Leo Moon/Pisces Sun, Moon or Ascendant partnership. The Sun tends to be forceful in demeanor. It can't help it, it's the mighty Sun after all, life itself revolves around its power. Neptune, the most ethereal and illusory planet in the solar system family tends to be inspiring, harmony and acceptance-seeking and highly impressionable in various areas of life.

Both these forces are strong in their own way and, in the arena of relationships, can blend well if certain things are kept in mind. If a clash of wills occurs, the Sun-ruled, Leo Moon mate will insist on having their way and may dominate conversations, while the Neptune-ruled, Pisces lover will back down and remain non-confrontational, but will never forgive their more aggressive lover for forcing them into an impossible situation. This means that one of them will have to modulate the relationship in such a way that neither lover dominates the other. The partner who cares more will invest more time and energy in trying to achieve the right level of compromise.

The Pisces type lover may lean toward going along with their mate's choice in everything due to a need to please or give up desires in order to make their lover feel more contented or satisfied with them. This urge to always bend or over-facilitate must be curtailed so that a proper balance of power is achieved in their relationship; challenge-seeking Leo Moon lovers may prefer their lover to be strong and capable, not overly emotional or too eager to accommodate. Some people with Pisces placed prominently in their natal charts will sometimes suffer from low self-esteem due to the influence of Neptune.

Neptune causes doubt to surface in the delicate and emulative Pisces psyche. Therefore, the naturally self-confident Leo Moon partner will have to help bolster their water sign lover's self-image. The Pisces type partner must watch out for a tendency toward obsession, which could be unhealthy for them if it makes them vulnerable enough to invite a harmful personality into their life, who may promise love, attention (Pisces types are most susceptible to this) and protection but never deliver it. They may also deliver it but under impossible or disrespectful conditions.

Sun-ruled, Leo Moon lovers can also help protect their sensitive Pisces type mates from manipulators and troublemakers who might use their compassionate side to influence them. This could be a good romantic pairing if the Leo Moon lover, who may display a tendency to take control and make decisions, will actively invite their Pisces type mate to join them in the decision-making process. If the Pisces type lover can grant their Leo Moon partner freedom in all things, as well as a lot of attention, verbal and physical, this will be a truly comfortable and fulfilling relationship.

The soft-hearted and reflective Pisces type lover will see their Leo Moon partner as the solid anchor they were looking for their whole life, the kind who will stabilize any part of their life that may have spiraled out of control, and help them readjust to any life situation with confidence. The Leo Moon partner will view their beloved water sign, soul mate as someone they can confide in and unburden themselves to; Pisces types will be able to soften up their fiery mate's sometimes risk-loving or aggressive approach to life. This is a truly romantic combination.

Chapter 18
The Virgo Moon Sign Lover

Virgo Moon vs. Aries Sun, Moon or Rising Sign
The Earth and Fire Relationship

Earth: "Does my boyfriend manage his finances maturely or will I end up paying his bills and supporting him? I need stability and true commitment before I can enjoy the romance between us." the earthy female thinks to herself. "Will my future wife spend my hard earned cash on frivolous items at the mall or be wise enough to save up for our retirement?" the earthy male lover wonders.

Fire: "I need romance and passion to really enjoy my relationship. Will my boyfriend be a faithful mate for life?" the fiery female partner wonders. "I want an active and freedom-loving partner. Will my girlfriend understand my need for true freedom in life or be too controlling of my life and actions?" the fiery male lover thinks to himself.

Virgo Moon lovers can enjoy a very productive and close relationship with partners who have their Sun, Moon or Rising sign in the cheerful and protective fire sign of Aries. Each partner symbolizes an element. Understanding that element helps us delve deeper into the real personality of that partner. Fire represents a passionate, active approach to life. Earth represents an unmatched stability and reliability: earth is a faith in love and an undying dedication to a relationship as well as a desire to work through any problem successfully.

The Virgo Moon lover may display one of two, distinct Virgo Moon personality types; they may either be the *organizer type* or the *easy-going type*. The organizer type may be a neat freak while the easy-going type may have difficulty in maintaining some degree of order in their lives and work. The organizer type may always be on time for appointments while the easy-going type may never seem to get the hang of it. Both function well in relationships, but the organizer type may be unable to live with a messy, scruffy lover or spouse.

They will methodize everything and may find it irksome if their lover cannot follow their little "systems" of keeping their home clean and habitable.

If the core, life values of the sensitive Virgo Moon lover are properly understood by the Aries type lover in the *initial* stages of their courtship, then they can build something pure and beautiful together. Virgo Moon lovers are introspective souls who thrive on being truly appreciated by their closest loved ones, and love to bring a sense of order to the relationship, while Aries type lovers are impulsive, romantic and action-packed creatures who may sometimes lack the ability to adhere to routine that their Virgo Moon soul mates look for in a lover. Reflective Virgo Moon lovers focus *inward* in order to understand their world, while the Aries type lover may focus outside of themselves for answers to why things happen the way they happen.

Aries type lovers are ruled by the planet Mars, and their Virgo Moon partner functions under the energy of the great observer planet, Mercury. Mercury and Mars are similar in some ways and yet in some ways, stand in stark contrast to each other. Quick-witted Mercury seeks intellectual stimulation, interesting conversation and thrives with an equally communicative partner. Mercury rules communication, teaching and travel, and will therefore cause a great deal of mostly positive changes to occur in the life of the Aries type lover through their Virgo Moon mate. Muscle bound Mars, on the other hand, rules the desire for action and needs to keep moving. Restless Mars crumbles without a cause to fight for.

Both these planetary forces are powerful and therefore must be handled extremely carefully because their essence will change on the field of love and intimacy. Mercury is verbally fearless and Mars is physically reckless. Mars is a dominant force and Mercury is clever and indubitably the solar system's best word weaver. If a clash of wills occurs, Mars won't give in. Mercury, on the other hand, may back down for a while, or talk for hours but will not change how they see the situation. Two dominant people cannot exist peacefully in a love relationship unless one of them learns the subtle and often secret art of compromise and balance. The partner who is most deeply in love will learn this art sooner.

Aries types are casual in outlook and rarely get rattled (in fact, they may rattle other people a tad too often) while the Virgo Moon essence is achievement-oriented, and will get inwardly upset quite easily over the smallest things. This excessive worrying could really hurt their sensitive digestive systems in the long run (Virgo rules the digestive tract). Love between these two vividly varying energies can survive if Virgo Moon partners can teach their impetuous Aries type sweethearts how to switch gears, look before they leap and be more practical, and if the Aries type lover can teach their beloved Virgo Moon soul mate to tone down their anxiety-level about miniscule things instead of letting their many daily chores at work and home take up all their precious energy.

The Virgo Moon partner is devoted, but when their friendship progresses to the level of intimacy, they will gradually want a more committed relationship. The sign of Virgo rules the sixth sector in natal Astrology. This sixth sector rules health and hygiene and when a close relationship evolves into a passionate one, the Virgo Moon partner will need to know if their chosen mate is sexually active with anyone else. This reason for this is not mere possessiveness, but an actual concern for their own health and well-being.

Most Virgo Moon lovers will refuse to take big risks with their sexual health and will take on the responsibility of making sure their partner has a clean sexual history. The Virgo Moon partner, after marriage, will also make sure that their home is well stocked with wheat instead of white bread, fresh baby carrots instead of candy and chocolate, and freshly squeezed orange juice instead of sodas and alcohol. They will take a special interest in what their lover eats and will try to instill in them good dietary habits, something that will allow both of them to age together and be young and agile even when they are in their golden years. The Aries type mate is usually active and athletic, so this couple could use their time at the health gym or hiking trail to bond together and sweat out their daily worries. A treadmill and some free weights will definitely be found at this health-conscious couple's home.

The Aries type partner will have to bear in mind that when their Virgo Moon lover corrects them, it is usually not for any personal gain but out of a sense of caring. Aries types are very sensitive to harsh criticism (and will actively reject any efforts at being controlled or manipulated), so if the Virgo Moon partner can suggest changes gently and tactfully, their Aries type lover will not bristle and actually listen and change what they do. The magic lies in *how* Aries types are appealed to. Virgo Moon lovers are ruled by the sharp and erudite planet Mercury, so it shouldn't be too difficult for them to figure out how to make their point firmly and effectively. As long as Virgo Moon mates don't overdo their desire to constantly fix their relationship or become obsessive about changing it, things will go well. Sometimes the sheer naturalness of a relationship should be encouraged; not everything needs constant human interference or adjustment. Easy-going and dedicated Virgo Moon partners will tolerate more of their Aries type lover's fun-loving antics than anyone else. If the Aries type lover can watch their temper and tendency to jump to conclusions, this relationship will not just work, it will thrive.

Virgo Moon vs. Taurus Sun, Moon or Rising Sign
The Earth and Earth Relationship

Earth: "Does my boyfriend manage his finances maturely or will I end up paying his bills and supporting him? I need stability and true commitment before I can enjoy the romance between us." the earthy female thinks to herself. "Will my future wife spend my hard earned cash on frivolous items at the mall or be wise enough to save up for our retirement?" the earthy male lover wonders.

Virgo Moon lovers can enjoy a very emotionally rewarding and romantic relationship with partners who have their Sun, Moon or Rising sign in the earth sign of Taurus. Similar earthy energies blend well and support each other over the long haul. But they can also cause a complete standstill to occur if arguments arise. These signs are earthy, and the earth is as ancient as time.

Earth represents a desire to nurture and safeguard all that is important in life, such as primary relationships and financial stability. This element symbolizes an unmatched reliability: earth is a faith in love and an undying dedication to a relationship, and a desire to work hard and overcome any challenges that may find their way into the relationship.

The Virgo Moon lover may display one of two, distinct Virgo Moon personality types; they may either be the *organizer type* or the *easy-going type*. The organizer type will be well-dressed, well-groomed and quite familiar with the deft use of a needle and thread as well as ironing starch, while the easy-going type may be quite comfortable in jeans and a t-shirt. The easy-going type may not be able to systemize their lives like the organizer type of Virgo Moon personality, but will still get by somehow.

Elementally, the double earth vibration is very supportive. The first function of the earth element is to help other structures stand tall while carrying their load on itself. Earth is one of the strongest elements and is also the most modest when seen through the essence of earthy Moon signs (Taurus, Virgo, Capricorn). When nourished, the earth yields great bounties of food and nutrition, but when it is neglected, it becomes useless, dry and parched. When earth is in abundance, everything is stable and life continues as it should. But if that ever-dependable earth decides to move, we will see earthquakes, both physically, and in our emotional lives.

When an earth sign partner withdraws due to neglect or betrayal from a partner, it will be very difficult indeed to get them to open their hearts again.

Which is why it is best to manage everything perfectly from the start. When threatened, the earth element sits still and refuses to initiate any action. This is when they must be given time to heal and then be approached again in a sincere manner. This is the one element on which stands our whole world, which is why earth signs must be offered respect before they are offered love. Balancing the attributes of this highly supportive element is key.

Virgo Moon partners bring their detail-oriented and practical natures to every relationship and their Taurus type lover will appreciate how hard-working and genuinely attentive they are. Taurus type partners add romance and sensitivity to the union, which helps worry wart, Virgo Moon lovers express their sensual side more often, instead of keeping it under wraps all the time (keeping their romantic side too tightly bound up may cause estrangement with more outspoken, demonstrative signs). Taurus type lovers are sensitive and Virgo Moon partners must watch how they approach the strong and steady Taurus energy, because Taurus hates change, doesn't take criticism very well and might take it more seriously than was intended.

Their Virgo Moon soul mates may only be trying to help (they usually correct due to a sense of caring, not control), but they must be careful about *how* they say it. Taurus types are susceptible to kindness, and respond better to soft-spoken, non-aggressive partners who won't demand things but will approach them in a calm, controlled, rational manner. At some point, on a stressful day, Mercury may make the Virgo Moon lover very talkative or critical indeed. The Taurus type mate may lean more toward internalizing feelings, sometimes for years at a time, which could seriously hurt their relationship, not to mention their health. An ill-timed, emotional avalanche could cause the usually stable Taurus type partner to lash out verbally or completely withdraw from discussing the problem. Observant Virgo Moon partners can manage things better by working on the careful timing of broaching certain, perhaps highly touchy, subjects.

An active interest in the health of their lover and themselves will be a trademark of the Virgo Moon lover. When friendship morphs into passion, Virgo Moon lovers will worry about their chosen mate being sexually active with anyone else (Virgo rules health and hygiene). Taking risks with their sexual health is never on the Virgo Moon lover's agenda and a lover with a relatively clean sexual history will be particularly loved by them. The Virgo Moon partner will also make sure that their home is well stocked with healthy foods instead or harmful fast food. They will take a special interest in what their lover eats and will try to instill in them good dietary habits. Dessert-loving,

Taurus types may indulge in that famous sweet tooth now and then, but their careful Virgo Moon mate will ensure that they remain balanced and stay healthy.

Neither frugal lover will have to worry about the other over charging credit cards before the first of the month or forgetting to pay the gas bill. This is a stable and harmonious combination if having children is on the cards at some point, as both make devoted parents. If they can keep the lines of communication always open between them, they will surmount any temporary problems and make quite an enviable success of their love relationship.

Virgo Moon vs. Gemini Sun, Moon or Rising Sign
The Earth and Air Relationship

Earth: "Does my boyfriend manage his finances maturely or will I end up paying his bills and supporting him? I need stability and true commitment before I can enjoy the romance between us." the earthy female thinks to herself. "Will my future wife spend my hard earned cash on frivolous items at the mall or be wise enough to save up for our retirement?" the earthy male lover wonders.

Air: "Is my boyfriend open-minded enough and will he appreciate my outspoken side? I need a life mate who will talk to me, communicate with me about everything and not clam up and brood." the airy female partner muses. "Will my girlfriend allow me to do the things I love or will she try to restrict me from truly expressing myself?" the airy male lover wonders.

Virgo Moon lovers can enjoy a very expressive and intellectually stimulating relationship with partners who have their Sun, Moon or Rising sign in the active and talkative air sign of Gemini. This relationship will function under a double dose of Mercury power running through its core. Super-fast, Mercury rules both these lovers and its influence will be doubly felt in this sign combination. Gemini type lovers are optimistic, energetic, highly opinionated partners who thrive in relationships that focus more on what can be, instead of what could have been; lovers who brood or complain incessantly will not blend well with them.

The Virgo Moon lover may display one of two, distinct Virgo Moon personality types; they may either be the *organizer type* or the *easy-going type*. The organizer type may be well-dressed, ambitious, cautious and perhaps a neat freak while the easy-going type may be casual, not too concerned with outward appearances and may need help finding their niche in life. Both function well in relationships, but the organizer type may be unable to live with a messy lover or spouse who is careless about their personal appearance.

Virgo Moon mates are outwardly in control but inwardly very sensitive. Their Gemini type mate can understand this well; they have two sides to them too. Occasionally, the Gemini twins will experience two separate emotions at a time and send out mixed signals; one twin will want to go to the movies while the other may want to stay home and spend time alone. A wise, patient partner will allow Gemini types to sort through their emotions instead of yelling at them and saying *"What exactly do you want? Are we going out tonight or not? Would you make up your mind already?"*

The Gemini type person relieves stress by talking problems through, while the Virgo Moon lover relieves tension by working and fixing things, sometimes in total silence. The Virgo Moon essence lends a solid foundation to the sometimes disorganized and scattered but brilliant Gemini energy. One thing to watch out for is the Virgo Moon partner's habit of criticizing; the Gemini mate's psyche is highly sensitive to criticisms. The usually gregarious Gemini type mate may lean more toward sharing every little, private detail with most people, which could seriously hurt their relationship. Therefore discretion should be employed. The Virgo Moon mate errs on the side of caution and will generally refrain from sharing the most intimate details about money, bank accounts and their future plans with others.

The Virgo Moon partner will be able to relax more and be more comfortable if their lover watches what they eat and takes care of their health. Sexual exclusivity will be expected, but not only for romantic reasons. The Virgo Moon lover will be very curious about whether their partner has a clean sexual history (Virgo rules the sixth Astrological sector of health and hygiene). After marriage, their home will probably be well stocked with wheat instead of white bread, fresh baby carrots instead of chocolate and too many sugary sweets, and freshly squeezed orange juice instead of sodas and alcohol. Instilling good dietary habits in a lover will be important to the Virgo Moon lover. Gemini types may indulge in that famous exotic diet of theirs now and then, but their careful Virgo Moon mate will ensure that they steer them clear of harmful foods (fast food might be on the Virgo Moon lover's hit list). Mercury is highly energetic, so if both these Mercurial lovers could hit the fitness center a few times a week, it will help them bond as well as stay healthy. All that mile-a-minute, Mercurial energy has to go somewhere!

The Virgo Moon partner will lend their earthiness to ground and stabilize the jumpy Gemini energy from time to time. Ever an eager student of life, there's a lot the Gemini type partner can learn from their Virgo Moon lover, as well as teach them some crucial lessons about life in a loving, protective manner. This combination is ideal for a couple that makes their living through publishing, the literary arts and are part of the world of books, the internet, teaching, traveling and selling products or services. Mercury is the most persuasive salesman of the zodiac, and with twice the energy of Mercury in this relationship, this couple could be very successful in any business.

Virgo Moon vs. Cancer Sun, Moon or Rising Sign
The Earth and Water Relationship

Earth: "Does my boyfriend manage his finances maturely or will I end up paying his bills and supporting him? I need stability and true commitment before I can enjoy the romance between us." the earthy female thinks to herself. "Will my future wife spend my hard earned cash on frivolous items at the mall or be wise enough to save up for our retirement?" the earthy male lover wonders.

Water: "Is my boyfriend emotionally stable and wise about our joint finances? Or will debts pile up in the first year of marriage? I need a supportive life-long lover as well as a loving one." the watery female lover thinks to herself. "Will my future spouse conserve our financial resources or spend unwisely without thought for the future? I can connect better romantically if I know that my chosen life-mate is passionate as well as mature and pragmatic." the watery male lover wonders.

Virgo Moon lovers can enjoy a very close relationship with partners who have their Sun, Moon or Rising sign in the emotive water sign of Cancer. Each partner symbolizes an element. Understanding that element helps us delve deeper into the real personality of that partner. The element of earth builds and then *stabilizes* what it has created, while the element of water *emotionalizes* and then learns to purify itself with those feelings.

There are two, distinct Virgo Moon personality types; knowing more about each may help in matching lifestyles, daily habits and personal preferences when two lovers share a home together. The first type is the *organizer type* and the second type is the *easy-going type*. Neat freak would be a good word to describe the organizer type of Virgo Moon personality, while the easy-going type may have difficulty in multi-tasking as well as managing little things like mowing the yard regularly and making a permanent filing system for bills, incoming mail, etc. Both will adapt well in relationships, but the organizer type may be subject to frequent heartburn if their lover or spouse cannot follow their little "systems" of keeping their home neat, clean and presentable.

The earthy Virgo Moon energy blends nicely with the watery, emotional and anchor-seeking Cancer type lover. Both thrive in truly committed relationships and marriage is something that both could get used to once trust has been firmly established between them *over time*. Virgo Moon lovers are hardworking and need to be in a relationship where they know that they are being appreciated and needed; life, people and relationships should serve a definite purpose according to them. Virgo represents the sixth sector of service and health. Any trouble or misunderstandings with a lover could easily cause the Virgo Moon lover to have digestive problems (Virgo rules the digestive tract).

This relationship will blend the energies of brilliant Mercury (ruler of Virgo) and the mystical Moon (ruler of Cancer). Mercury's (or the Virgo Moon lover's) quick tongue becomes softer, kinder and more restrained around the caring Cancer partner, while the introverted and usually shy Cancer partner may begin to feel more self-confident around the protective Virgo Moon lover.

The Cancer type personality needs frequent and tangible assurances from their life-companion that they will be there for them when the going gets tough. If this couple is devoted to each other, there is no better combination than this for long-term compatibility, where each lover desires to take the relationship into the more comfortable and sometimes pleasantly predictable zone of marriage. Cancer type partners must also understand that too much emotionality causes a strange restlessness and confusion in the normally unflappable Virgo Moon mate's heart; they relax only around lovers who can calmly and patiently sort out problems instead of trying to inflate the significance of those issues.

Virgo Moon lovers should also keep in mind that their Cancer type lover may take their usually well-meaning criticism too hard and see it as being picked on, which may not be what the Virgo Moon partner had in mind at all. Virgo Moon companions should carefully phrase what they want to say and Cancer type lovers should learn to develop a tougher skin. Being over-sensitive may work against them in the long run and they should try to find the real cause

of their reactions, which in most cases may be a legitimate fear of abandonment due to betrayals in the past.

Cancer type lovers bring out their Virgo Moon mate's romantic and tender
side, which is there but rarely pops out. A Virgo Moon soul mate is often the
best match for a Cancer type person, and the trust between them will flow
freely if they have built their love slowly and let it blossom on its own invisi-
ble timetable. Both signs feel special if they get to nurture a mate without
being accused of trying to control them, and with this sign combination, a
true reciprocity will emerge without much prompting. This is a promising
combination.

Virgo Moon vs. Leo Sun, Moon or Rising Sign
The Earth and Fire Relationship

*Earth: "Does my boyfriend manage his finances maturely or will I end up paying
his bills and supporting him? I need stability and true commitment before I can
enjoy the romance between us." the earthy female thinks to herself. "Will my
future wife spend my hard earned cash on frivolous items at the mall or be wise
enough to save up for our retirement?" the earthy male lover wonders.*

*Fire: "I need romance and passion to really enjoy my relationship. Will my
boyfriend be a faithful mate for life?" the fiery female partner wonders. "I want
an active and freedom-loving partner. Will my girlfriend understand my need
for true freedom in life or be too controlling of my actions and decisions?" the
fiery male lover thinks to himself.*

Virgo Moon lovers can enjoy a very romantic relationship with partners
who have their Sun, Moon or Rising sign in the generous and loving fire
sign of Leo. If the Virgo Moon lover's likes and dislikes are properly understood and appreciated by the Leo type lover in the budding stages of their love
story, compatibility could be easily achieved on many fronts. Each partner
symbolizes an element. Understanding that element helps us delve deeper into
the real personality of that partner.

The Virgo Moon lover may display one of two, interesting Virgo Moon personality types; they may either be the *organizer type* or the *easy-going type*. The
organizer type may take spring cleaning very seriously while the easy-going

type may not pay as much attention to how their homes look on the outside. Both function well in relationships, but the organizer type may be unable to live with a lover or spouse who cannot see the value of cleanliness and order. The *"Everything in my house should be just so"*, organizer type of Virgo Moon will be slightly dominating by temperament.

Virgo Moon companions bring substance and simplification to a relationship, while Leo type lovers are endearing and charismatic creatures who may sometimes, or at least initially, lack the focus that their structure-oriented, Virgo Moon lover looks for in a lover. Leo types are easygoing and ambitious by turns, while the Virgo Moon essence is goal-oriented and consistently focused on results. *"How about taking today off, sweetheart? Let's go do something romantic, just you and me."* suggests the fun-loving Leo type lover. *"Sounds great, honey, but I have a huge pile of files waiting for me on my desk at work, and two new trainees to work with today, not to mention coming home and getting all the payments ready to mail tomorrow morning."* says the nearly always stressed out Virgo Moon lover. If their emotional timetables match, they could achieve something great together as a couple and this sign combination could work out well. Love between these two differing energies can survive if Virgo Moon partners open themselves up to the Leo life philosophy of enjoying fun and work in *equal* parts, and if the Leo type mate adjusts their need to take occasional risks or go overboard emotionally.

At some point, on a stress-filled day, Mercury may make the Virgo Moon lover very verbally critical indeed. The frank Leo type mate may also occasionally lean toward blurting it all out at the wrong time, which could seriously hurt their relationship. Excessive displays of emotion can rattle those delicate Virgo Moon nerves; they are best approached respectfully and calmly. The Leo type mate, on the other hand, cannot function if their lover broods and refuses to take an active part in resolving issues; this silence may be construed as a lack of love and may cause further disruptions between them.

Virgo rules the sixth sector in Astrology, which rules health and hygiene and when a friendship changes into a passion-filled relationship, the Virgo Moon partner will need to know if their chosen mate is sexually active with anyone else. A lover who takes too many unnecessary sexual risks with their health may find that their Virgo Moon lover drifts away from them. The female Virgo Moon girlfriend might say, *"If he's not concerned about his own health and welfare, how much concern will he show for my health? If he lacks that sense of responsibility, what am I doing dating him?"* Once married, the Virgo Moon partner will also make sure that their home is well stocked with healthy, nonprocessed foods and will show an interest in working out with their lover. Leo types may indulge in that famous *"I'll have a bit of everything on the buffet table, please"* appetite now and then (the Sun-ruled, lover likes to splurge), but their careful Virgo Moon mate will ensure that they maintain a balanced diet and watch their weight.

The mentally astute Virgo Moon energy creates a firm, dependable structure for Leo types to base their life's greatest ambitions on, while the merry Leo type lover brings workaholic Virgo Moon's blood pressure down by disarming them with their delectable sense of humor, something Virgo Moon mates respond to particularly well. Leo type companions, with their natural fixity, find it hard to make sweeping changes in their life to fit in another person, but this extra effort will enable them to receive a most precious love from their partner.

Mutable (emotionally adaptable) Virgo Moon mates will tolerate more of their Leo type lover's personality quirks and fulfill more of their relationship requirements than anyone else. Mercury-ruled, Virgo Moon soul mates will be wise to apply a regular dose of verbal appreciation to keep their fiery lover emotionally fulfilled. The Leo energy brings forth their Mercury-ruled sweetheart's romantic and privately sensual side. Better grab that Virgo Moon lover while you can, Leo! This may be your best chance at marital success.

Virgo Moon vs. Virgo Sun, Moon or Rising Sign
The Earth and Earth Relationship

Earth: "Does my boyfriend manage his finances maturely or will I end up paying his bills and supporting him? I need stability and true commitment before I can enjoy the romance between us." the earthy female thinks to herself. "Will my future wife spend my hard earned cash on frivolous items at the mall or be wise enough to save up for our retirement?" the earthy male lover wonders.

Virgo Moon lovers can enjoy a very close and yet revealing relationship with partners who have their Sun, Moon or Rising sign in their own earth sign of Virgo. Each partner symbolizes an element. Understanding that element helps us delve deeper into the real personality of that partner. Earth represents an unmatched stability and reliability: earth is a faith in love and an undying dedication to a relationship. Earth signs tend to not give up on close bonds until every avenue of compromise has been exhausted.

The Virgo Moon lover may exhibit one of two, unique Virgo Moon personality types; they may either be the *organizer type* or the *easy-going type*. The organizer type has a place for everything and if their lover uses something at home, like a stapler from the organizer type's desk and then forgets where they put it, it could cause some tension to build up over time. The easy-going type may have difficulty in maintaining some degree of order in their lives and work and will not take kindly to being judged as well as helped. They might say *"If you're going to come in and organize my whole apartment in one day, how on earth am I ever going to find anything when I need it? I know it looks bad but I promise, my system works!"* The organizer type of Virgo Moon lover probably won't buy it and may keep insisting on "fixing" everything. Both types function well in relationships, but the organizer type may never be able to get used to a careless or unkempt lover.

The attraction between these two earthy lovers with similar goals will be strong but some adjustments will have to be made for long-term compatibility. The earth element induces reliability, with the result that two things can occur: there may be great stability between the two Virgo type lovers (for example, a beneficial situation that doesn't require change, like a good marriage) or there might be a refusal to take any action (a negative situation like a bad, abusive relationship that continues for years on end, souring many lives). Once an earthy Moon sign person digs their heels in, there is very little that can be done to make them take any action. Mountains don't move, you see. They key to a successful double earth relationship is for one of the two lovers to become the watchdog of the relationship or the rock that steers the relationship toward moderation. The lover who loves more will learn to balance the relationship and not let little annoyances get out of hand.

The sign of Virgo rules the sixth sector in natal Astrology. This sixth sector rules health and hygiene and when the Virgo Moon partner is really close to falling in love, they will begin wondering about the effects of their lover's sexual health on their own health. Possessiveness may not be the most accurate reason for this; this Moon sign judges a lover's maturity level by how responsible they are about sexual cleanliness.

Any lover who takes too many risks with their sexual health will become a red flag to the Virgo Moon lover, who will spend a great deal of time on eating right, cooking healthy foods and paying attention to working out and watching their weight. The Virgo Moon home or apartment will be well stocked with wheat instead of white bread, fresh baby carrots instead of chocolate and too many sugary sweets, and freshly squeezed orange juice instead of sodas and alcohol. While their mate may indulge in some forbidden foods now and then, their careful Virgo Moon mate will ensure that they remain balanced and stay healthy by getting them a treadmill and some free weights for their birthday. Together, they can sort out any differences more easily if they are less stressed out, and working out regularly will certainly help facilitate that.

Both are loyal when in love and will sympathize with and understand the emblematic Virgo need for security, purpose and stability within love relationships. This Moon sign has very specific likes and dislikes and may be set in their daily habits. When another similar personality enters the picture, there is a good chance one may find the other's little idiosyncrasies irritating or annoying. This means that both of them have to be flexible enough to not alter their lover's lifestyle too much while learning to respect their choices.

The other problem that could cause complications is when one of them says some things in the heat of anger that should have been left unspoken. Problem solvers extraordinaire, Virgo Moon lovers as well as their Virgo type mates like to quickly correct critical situations that are in front of them. And while the Virgo type partner may understand why they're making their point, they may not like to be corrected *too* often. Speech maestro Mercury will create many chances for misunderstandings to arise between these two earthy lovers, but can also create an equal number of chances for clarity to quickly return. Yes, forgiveness usually comes easily and both of them will be kissing and making up within hours, but if this happens a lot, it could alter the nature of the relationship in a fundamental way. If one Mercurial lover wants to discuss something, while the other would rather not engage in a lengthy conversation at that precise time, one of them will have to bend.

Honest communication is a good start, but it will not help unless both partners approach each other in a tender manner when complex discussions are on the agenda. Earth signs will make every diligent effort to make sure the relationship is safe and healthy, and therefore make very stalwart partners. When the same energy tries to blend itself between two lovers, one will have to provide a contrast. If one of them is brooding, the other should bring out their lighter side. If one of them begins to get too distracted, the other can help bring them back on track. This double Virgo combination can be quite successful in the long run.

Virgo Moon vs. Libra Sun, Moon or Rising Sign
The Earth and Air Relationship

Earth: "Does my boyfriend manage his finances maturely or will I end up paying his bills and supporting him? I need stability and true commitment before I can enjoy the romance between us." the earthy female thinks to herself. "Will my future wife spend my hard earned cash on frivolous items at the mall or be wise enough to save up for our retirement?" the earthy male lover wonders.

Air: "Is my boyfriend open-minded enough and will he appreciate my outspoken side? I need a life mate who will talk to me, communicate with me about every-thing and not clam up and brood." the airy female partner muses. "Will my girlfriend allow me to do the things I love or will she try to restrict me from openly expressing myself and living my life the way I want to?" the airy male lover wonders.

Virgo Moon lovers can enjoy a romantic and sympathetic relationship with partners who have their Sun, Moon or Rising sign in the marriage-minded air sign of Libra. When air sign and earth sign energies combine in the game of romance, there will be a lot of banter as well as a lot of chances for sending out the wrong message. Each partner symbolizes an element. Under-standing that element helps us delve deeper into the real personality of that partner. Earth represents an unmatched stability and reliability: earth is a faith in love and an undying dedication to a relationship. The air element, when perceived through the sign of Libra, represents an incredible desire to enhance and grant longevity to love relationships, which are often their primary source of critically important self-understanding.

The Virgo Moon lover may display one of two, interesting Virgo Moon per-sonality types; they may either be the *organizer type* or the *easy-going type*. The organizer type may be a real neat freak; they may put together little methods of finding things and locating certain objects, or they may designate certain days of the week for certain household chores like laundry, vacuuming and cooking. The easy-going type may have trouble finding time to clean and vac-uum and may expect their partner to take care of that aspect. Both these types of the Virgo Moon personality function well in relationships, but the organizer type will find it rather annoying to keep picking up after a careless lover. They will methodize everything and make up little "systems" of keeping their home clean and easy to run, and anyone sharing their home with them would do well to follow those guidelines.

Of the two, the Libra type lover is more impulsive and very sensitive, especially when dealing with a love partner. The self-sufficient Virgo Moon lover may be able to go for long periods of time without being in any relationships, but it will be too difficult for marriage-oriented Libra types to do this. Both Virgo Moon partners and Libra types are strong intellectuals and frequent, earnest communication is very important to both. While they can mingle interests easily, it should be noted that the only situation in which marriage oriented Libra types begin to lose patience with their Virgo Moon lover is when they refuse to commit to a future together but won't terminate the relationship either. *"What kind of mixed message is that?"* the Libra type female wonders. *"Gosh, I'm just not ready to tie the knot just yet. I need a little more time to decide if this is the best decision for me. Will my beloved be patient with me, or walk away in anger? Their reaction to this alone will decide this question for me. If she's patient, she's the one."* the rational Virgo Moon male muses.

Usually, Libra types are known for being the best fence sitters of the zodiac, but when their hearts are involved, another's indecision may cause a lot of emotions to well up. There is a good chance that the Venus-ruled, Libra type lover is an impulse spender (glamorous Venus invented the shopping mall), so one of them will have to be the financial stabilizer and make sure that the financial aspect of their relationship doesn't cause trouble in other areas. Libra is a marriage sign, while the typical Virgo Moon lover thrives in a productive relationship first. Virgo Moon lovers need lots of time to test out their potential soul mates for long-term emotional compatibility. *"If he can't be a respectful, patient friend now, then how on earth will he make a responsible husband someday? I think he needs to mature a lot more before we can go out again."* the Virgo Moon female may reason about a lover.

This relationship is a union of Mercury (ruler of Virgo) and Venus (ruler of Libra). Mercury is clever and quick to spot a potential lover in a crowd, while as the official matchmaker of the planetary family, beautiful Venus can also zero in on a possible love match rather quickly. Intellectual Mercury loves getting to the nitty-gritty of situations and won't mind a long, steady courtship, while Venus will want to begin a successful, life long marriage within a reasonable amount of time.

"We're not getting any younger, you know. We might like to consider settling down now, honey." the Libra mate says. *"No, but we are getting smarter. Time is on our side, why rush things when we both enjoy just being together?"* the cautious Virgo

Moon lover explains. Practical Virgo Moon mates know that a *"yes"* at the alter also means a *"yes"* to sharing personal checking accounts as well as sharing their personal space. The Mercury-ruled, Virgo Moon lover will simply withdraw from an uncomfortable situation instead of standing there and be barraged by question after question. Venus-ruled Libra, on the other hand, needs to know where they stand and may walk away broken hearted if they do not get an honest answer. To Lady Venus, an undecided lover is an uninterested lover.

Libra types want to see their partner in their future and may need some tangible proof that marriage is on the cards (an engagement party with a few select friends, or a ring that they can happily display). It might help them if the romantic Libra type lover, as well as the very devoted but slightly non-committal Virgo Moon lover, began their courtship slowly and keep it from burning too hot, too fast. Gradually getting to know one another would help immensely, as would having a good idea about each other's expectations ahead of time.

The best way for this relationship to survive is for the Libra type partner to allow their Virgo Moon lover the chance to decide on their own timetable, as to what shape they want their love to take, while the Virgo Moon lover could try to understand the deeply partnership-oriented and attractive Libra partner's need for timely commitment and trust. Libra types may display a fear of loneliness, while the Virgo Moon mate may fear a failed marriage and its financial repercussions. Neither should hold back how they feel and they should be able to get to the heart of any differences quickly. The Libra energy brings out the tender romantic in their Virgo Moon lover, while the Virgo Moon lover brings out the dutiful and responsible side of their Venus-ruled partner. This is a great marriage combination.

Virgo Moon vs. Scorpio Sun, Moon or Rising Sign
The Earth and Water Relationship

Earth: "Does my boyfriend manage his finances maturely or will I end up paying his bills and supporting him? I need stability and true commitment before I can enjoy the romance between us." the earthy female thinks to herself. "Will my future wife spend my hard earned cash on frivolous items at the mall or be wise enough to save up for our retirement?" the earthy male lover wonders.

Water: "Is my boyfriend emotionally stable and wise about our joint finances? Or will debts pile up in the first year of marriage? I need a supportive life-long lover

as well as a loving one." the watery female lover thinks to herself. "Will my future
spouse conserve our financial resources or spend unwisely without thought for the
future? I can connect better romantically if I know that my chosen life-mate is
passionate as well as mature and pragmatic." the watery male lover wonders.

Virgo Moon lovers can enjoy a stable and long term relationship with partners who have their Sun, Moon or Rising sign in the deep, emotional
water sign of Scorpio. Each partner symbolizes an element. Understanding
that element helps us delve deeper into the real personality of that partner.
Earth represents an unmatched stability and reliability: earth is a faith in love
and an undying dedication to a relationship, even if there may be temperamental differences. Water represents a need to feel the very depths of human
emotion, and then strengthen oneself by its effects. Emotions help a water sign
person experience life in the most honest and authentic way.

The Virgo Moon personality may be defined by two specific, personality
types; they are the *organizer type* and the *easy-going type.* The organizer type
may take great pride in their appearance and will take care to present a clean,
wholesome look to the world. The easy-going type may be the complete opposite of the organizer type, in that they may not be too worried about what the
neighbors think of their messy front yard or unwashed car. Both these types of
the Virgo Moon personality will enjoy relationships, but if the organizer type
pairs up with a messy lover, or if the easy-going type matches up with the neat
freak, there might be trouble in paradise.

Virgo Moon lovers are privately sensitive, and only with the right person will
their guard come tumbling down. They look for specific traits in a lover; they
should be productive (they shouldn't fear hard work like it was a medieval dis-
ease), be gentle by temperament and know exactly where they're going in life.
Scorpio types like to experience life at a deep level, which may be too deep for
the average human being, hence the search for a lover who has most of the
qualities they seek. But supportive Virgo Moon partners will know exactly
how that enigmatic Scorpio heart operates and what they need to feel truly fulfilled in life.

The Scorpio type mate and the earthy Virgo Moon lover worry about the
proper management and use of money and resources, so if they're both on the
same page about that, ninety percent of their problems will disappear. Problem solvers extraordinaire, Virgo Moon lovers enjoy spending time improving
and fixing things, and their observant Scorpio type partner will appreciate
being with someone who cares equally about the relationship. Both these signs

have a close tie to each other and can often become the most important people in each other's lives.

This relationship is a union of Mercury (ruler of Virgo) and Pluto (ruler of Scorpio). Mercury is clever and quick to spot a potential lover in a crowd, while somber and wise Pluto will also be able to tell apart lovers with true, long term potential from the *"time wasters"* who won't appreciate their intensity. Intellectual Mercury loves getting to the nitty-gritty of situations and will refrain from jumping carelessly into new, untried relationships, while Pluto will want to begin a successful, life-long marriage within a reasonable amount of time. Pluto-ruled, Scorpio types seek a rock-solid stability, and marriage, they feel, will afford them that stability permanently.

When it comes to getting married, practical Virgo Moon mates know that a *"yes"* at the alter also means a *"yes"* to sharing personal checking accounts as well as sharing their personal space. If pushed for a commitment, the Virgo Moon lover will simply withdraw from an uncomfortable situation. But Scorpio types need to know where they stand with their lover and if their chosen mate is as dependable as they seem on the outside; it's all or nothing with passionate Scorpio types.

The pragmatic Virgo Moon lover creates a dependable environment for anchor-seeking Scorpio types so that their life together can unfold, while the Scorpio type lover brings workaholic Virgo Moon's blood pressure down by making them believe that they there for them, come what may. The earthy Virgo Moon mate is dutiful and obliging, and if their *tendency to correct* can be modified, it would do them both a world of good. Scorpio type companions, with their natural fixity, find it hard to make changes in their life to fit in another person, and if they do, they will expect an equal effort back and quickly. Scorpio type mates should bear in mind that they should never keep secrets from their earthy lover because once the mirror of trust cracks, it may take a lifetime to build that trust back with this Moon sign.

The only problems between them may circle around the Virgo Moon lover's tendency to see everything through logical, practical, business-like eyes and the Scorpio type lover's tendency to sometimes float away on the tides of their own emotions. Pluto may try to immerse them in resentment and repressed anger, but they must try to swim away and return from the lure of a petrified past. A non-hysterical partner who can keep their own emotions under check will be best for the Scorpio type mate; when this watery sign cannot find calm within themselves, they will reach out for stability outside of themselves.

Virgo Moon partners are goal-oriented while ambitious Scorpio types are fueled by pure emotion, with the result that their decisions are made using their heart or their moods on that particular day. Too much emotionality or intensity can shake the Virgo Moon partner's focus on getting things done and make them lose their balance. Which means that Scorpio types must be more in control of their emotions, while Virgo Moon partners must help their sensitive partners deal with life the way it is, not the way they dream it could be. This could be a loving combination.

Virgo Moon vs. Sagittarius Sun, Moon or Rising Sign
The Earth and Fire Relationship

Earth: "Does my boyfriend manage his finances maturely or will I end up paying his bills and supporting him? I need stability and true commitment before I can enjoy the romance between us." the earthy female thinks to herself. "Will my future wife spend my hard earned cash on frivolous items at the mall or be wise enough to save up for our retirement?" the earthy male lover wonders.

Fire: "I need romance and passion to really enjoy my relationship. Will my boyfriend be a faithful mate for life?" the fiery female partner wonders. "I want an active and freedom-loving partner. Will my girlfriend understand my need for true freedom in life or be too controlling of my actions and choices in life?" the fiery male lover thinks to himself.

Virgo Moon lovers can enjoy an intellectually vibrant and emotionally uplifting relationship with partners who have their Sun, Moon or Rising sign in the cheerful and openhearted fire sign of Sagittarius. But adjustments may have to be made due to how differently each sign looks at love and bonding. Each partner symbolizes an element. Understanding that element helps us delve deeper into the real personality of that partner. Fire represents a desire to take risks and learn from the challenges those risks pose; the goal is to strengthen oneself through one's ability to face and learn from danger. Earth represents a desire to create and build something that serves a specific and much needed purpose, and then permanently stabilize and protect what was created.

The Virgo Moon lover may display one of two, interesting Virgo Moon personality types; they may either be the *organizer type* or the *easy-going type*. The organizer type may be a quintessential neat freak; they may put together little systems of finding things and locating certain objects, or they may designate certain days of the week for certain household chores like laundry, vacuuming and cooking. The easy-going type may have trouble finding time to clean and vacuum and may expect their partner to take care of that aspect. Both these types of the Virgo Moon personality function well in relationships, but the organizer type will find it rather annoying to keep picking up after a sloppy lover. They will methodize everything and keep their home clean and easy to run, and anyone sharing their home with them would do well to follow those guidelines.

Virgo Moon lovers will look for a life mate who is committed and thrives with one partner, which quickly removes the tension and guesswork out of a new relationship usually built on shaky ground. The expansive Sagittarius energy needs a lover who is passionate but accommodating in every aspect of life. As a fire sign, their search is one of finding a lover who can understand their need to preserve their share of freedom within a relationship. A partner who is loving as well as independent and non-clingy will appeal to them. The mutable or emotionally flexible Virgo Moon mate may comprehend this desire for intimacy and space at specific intervals better than most.

This relationship has a good chance of surviving, despite these two rather disparate energies, because each of them is changeable and therefore can adapt rather well to the shifting peripheries of their lover's personality. Sagittarius types are idealistic and value their time alone, while the Virgo Moon mate will usually be comfortable with being self-sufficient and busy with their own life and projects. Sagittarius types have a horror of having to blend destinies with a lover who is incapable of being on their own and needs constant input or advice from their mate. Independence is a quality Sagittarius types will greatly value and their loving Virgo Moon mates will usually have no problem in allowing them that personal space.

The sign of Virgo rules the sixth sector in natal Astrology. This sixth sector rules health and hygiene and when a close relationship evolves into a passionate one, the Virgo Moon partner will lean toward sexual exclusivity. This relationship is a union of Mercury (ruler of Virgo) and Jupiter (ruler of Sagittarius). Mercury is clever and can attract lovers with their conversational skills, while Jupiter will tune in and attract lovers with his joviality and philosophical bent of mind. Intellectual Virgo Moon mates will prefer a long, steady courtship, which is something that Sagittarius types would prefer. *"The more time we have to study each other and make our friendship stronger, the better our love life will be."* observes the Sagittarius type mate rightly.

The Virgo Moon lover is very mindful of their responsibility and duty at home and work, perhaps too much sometimes. They may be unable to psychologically check out of work when they come home at the end of the day and may bring home all their work-related worries. Unnecessary responsibilities may seem tiresome to the typical Sagittarius type lover and an overly emotional mate may cause a lot of confusion in the free-flowing Sagittarius energy. At the same time, a lazy life mate who becomes a financial burden will irk the Virgo Moon mate who may expect more out of life than to have to baby sit a grown adult. If one of these two lovers can agree to stabilize the relationship (compare personal expectations ahead of time), things will proceed well in the long run. Sagittarius types need a lot of freedom to fully experience love, romance and intimacy; they tend to *live* their way into the answers they seek in life. Bind them with love and they will flee. Free them up with love and they will embrace your presence. The Virgo Moon lover may know just how to strike that magical balance.

Earthy Virgo Moon partners will help the sometimes, impatient sign of Sagittarius learn to be more responsible, complete the projects they start and conserve their financial resources. A relationship with a Virgo Moon lover will be quite a training exercise for the Sagittarius type mate, in the most positive way. The Virgo Moon lover should give their Sagittarius type lover lots of space, emotional and physical, if they really want them in their life. Sagittarius is flexible, and will make *some* changes to accommodate their equally flexible and loving Virgo Moon partner, but they must be truly in love to go through the effort needed. This relationship has a good chance of being a long-term connection, if the relationship begins as a longstanding friendship, giving each time to acclimatize themselves to each other's quirks and habits at their own emotional timetables.

Virgo Moon vs. Capricorn Sun, Moon or Rising Sign
The Earth and Earth Relationship

Earth: "Does my boyfriend manage his finances maturely or will I end up paying his bills and supporting him? I need stability and true commitment before I can enjoy the romance between us." the earthy female thinks to herself. "Will my future wife spend my hard earned cash on frivolous items at the mall or be wise enough to save up for our retirement?" the earthy male lover wonders.

Virgo Moon lovers can enjoy a wonderful and spiritually rewarding relationship with partners who have their Sun, Moon or Rising sign in the commitment-minded earth sign of Capricorn. With both partners operating under the stability of the earth energy, this could be a successful relationship in the making if they both apply themselves. Each partner symbolizes an element. Understanding that element helps us delve deeper into the real personality of that partner. Earth represents an unmatched stability and reliability: earth is a faith in love and an undying dedication to a relationship, even if there are temperamental problems to sort out. This element believes that if there is trust, love will follow with ease.

Elementally, the double earth vibration is very supportive. The first function of the earth element is to help other structures stand tall while carrying their load on itself. Earth is one of the strongest elements and is also the most modest when seen through the essence of earthy Moon signs (Taurus, Virgo, Capricorn). When nourished, the earth yields great bounties of food and nutrition, but when it is neglected, it becomes useless, dry and parched. When earth is in abundance, everything is stable and life continues without a glitch. But if that ever-dependable earth decides to move, we will see earthquakes, both physically, and in our emotional lives. When an earth sign partner withdraws due to neglect or betrayal from a partner, it will be very difficult indeed to get them to open their hearts again. Which is why it is best to manage everything perfectly from the start.

Capricorn types are driven and ambitious and need a partner who is emotionally sensitive but also careful about money management. Virgo Moon lovers are very concerned with making things run smoothly and delight in creating a goal-oriented atmosphere in which a lot of progress can be made in the shortest amount of time. Getting somewhere in life may be what brings them together, but could also tear them apart. They must remember that personal ambition should never be more important than the nurturing of personal relationships. They must place their love for each other above making a name for themselves.

Unafraid of hard work, eyes-on-the-prize Capricorn type lovers usually tend toward building something that they can refer to as their personal legacy or their greatest personal achievement, and if their life mate understands this need, it would help with creating a significant emotional bond between them. A common life goal must bind them together. This is important to grasp, especially because Virgo Moon lovers are extremely supportive of partners who work as hard as they do, to achieve something they can refer to as their joint labor of love. Success has its rewards and this success will have an enormous and tangible effect on the Capricorn type mate's self-esteem. Both Virgo Moon lovers and their Capricorn partners never take life lightly, or love casually. *"If you're in it with me, you're in it for the long haul."* these two earthy lovers promise.

This union will signify the merging of two, special planetary energies: Saturn (the ruler of Capricorn) and Mercury (the ruler of Virgo). Karmic Saturn is serious, promotes longevity, is self-controlled and prompts the Capricorn type lover to search for a stable life mate who is not frivolous, loud or combative. Mercury, when seen through the eyes of Virgo alone (and not Gemini, a sign that is also ruled by Mercury) is detail-oriented, intellectually sensitive and cautious in making important life decisions. Both of these earthy signs will wait for as long as it takes for the right moment to present itself, be it work or love; timing is everything to them and they are capable of controlling their heart's deepest desires until they get the green signal from their mates to proceed. Capricorn types and Virgo Moon lovers will prepare for every contingency; failure is not an option.

Commitment is not a word their lover should be scared of because these earth signs have no patience for such immaturity. *"If you can't commit now, how dependable will you be ten years into the marriage when we have three kids and a mortgage?"* they rightly question. Both need to feel special to their life-partner and need to be treated with the utmost care and tenderness. Harsh words spoken in haste are not easily forgotten, so the Virgo Moon partner will have to watch that Mercurial need to correct. Capricorn types will have to watch a tendency to over-reach their goals, control their relationship too strictly and should try to be more communicative, so that their proclivity for depression is kept at bay. This pair can be a very healthy addition to each other's lives and will make responsible parents as well as faithful companions. They should also remember that the couple that laughs together, stays together, therefore a night out at the comedy club or movies should be part of the plan once in a while. This is a stable and loving combination.

Virgo Moon vs. Aquarius Sun, Moon or Rising Sign
The Earth and Air Relationship

Earth: "Does my boyfriend manage his finances maturely or will I end up paying his bills and supporting him? I need stability and true commitment before I can enjoy the romance between us." the earthy female thinks to herself. "Will my

future wife spend my hard earned cash on frivolous items at the mall or be wise enough to save up for our retirement?" the earthy male lover wonders.

Air: "Is my boyfriend open-minded enough and will he appreciate my outspoken side? I need a life mate who will talk to me, communicate with me about everything and not clam up and brood." the airy female partner muses. "Will my girlfriend allow me to do the things I love or will she try to restrict me from openly expressing myself and live the way I want to?" the airy male lover wonders.

Virgo Moon lovers can enjoy an intellectual and uniquely rewarding relationship with partners who have their Sun, Moon or Rising sign in the forward-thinking air sign of Aquarius. This earth and air combination can survive if both partners can understand what separates them and what brings them together. Each partner symbolizes an element. Understanding that element helps us delve deeper into the real personality of that partner. Earth represents a desire to produce, protect and then safeguard primary relationships with an aim toward success and permanence. Air represents an incredible intellectualism and creative genius, as well as a strong desire to communicate every thought and feeling to their mate (or the world); lovers who tend to brood or sulk may not blend well with the fast-moving air element.

The Virgo Moon lover may display one of two, interesting Virgo Moon personality types; they may either be the *organizer type* or the *easy-going type*. The organizer type may pay special attention to how they look, be very methodical about household chores and always try to be on time for dates or appointments. The easy-going type may be the complete opposite of the organizer type. Both these types of the Virgo Moon personality do well in marriages or relationships, but the organizer type will find it rather annoying to keep picking up after a careless lover. One can say that if the organizer type were to date the easy-going type, they both would instantly start to criticize each other; one would call the other too controlled and the other would respond by saying that they don't have a clue about how to go through life. It could get ugly.

If you're well-groomed, responsible, always on time and have a regular job that you actually love, the Virgo Moon lover may want to get to know you a little better. Aquarius types need to be with a broad-minded, slightly unconventional and very emotionally flexible partner who is forgiving by nature and can grasp the unusual but rich Aquarian life philosophy. Virgo Moon lovers are super-pragmatists and like to follow a specific plan in life, so that the least numbers of mistakes are made. *"I don't fear mistakes, in fact I see them as learn-ing experiences."* the Aquarius type lover explains. *"I don't fear mistakes either, but I do resent that making them wastes my valuable time. I could do with a lit-tle less stress in my life. A little planning never hurt anyone."* the Virgo Moon lover counters.

Virgo Moon partners are a family-friendly sign and feel, if family relationships have been generally healthy in their past, close to their parents and siblings. Some Aquarian types may develop many quasi-filial ties during their lives and may treat their pals as close family and their family as acquaintances. Aquar-ian types are loving but not the most traditional of signs and their idea of love and marriage may clash with what the Virgo Moon lover has imagined for them as a couple, *until* they are emotional ready for that commitment them-selves. A prolonged friendship between them would help clarify expectations ahead of time.

Virgo Moon lovers will test out their partners to see if they will be trustwor-thy and *dependable* in the long run, while Aquarian type lovers will also test their potential partners to check if they can adequately provide the *consistent level of personal freedom* they need to feel truly fulfilled in life. Aquarian types have a very unique idea of what the perfect love relationship should be: they want a lover with whom they can bond intellectually *first* and romantically second. The work-is-worship, Virgo Moon mate wants a lover who yearns to better themselves and serve a specific purpose in life, as a support or inspira-tion to someone else. Life, work and personal efforts have to mean something, otherwise life would cease to make any sense to them.

Neither of these two lovers feel comfortable with too emotional, clingy or dependant a lover. Virgo Moon soul mates place a high degree of emphasis on active effort in a relationship, and their passion and devotion can only fully be expressed if their partner has no hesitation in truthfully committing their heart to them. This earthy Moon sign may have a fear of being with a lover who expects them to do all the work in keeping a relationship functioning smoothly while not contributing to its success in any way themselves. While the Aquarian type mate fears falling in love with someone who cannot under-stand that personal freedom is a crucial component within marriages that keeps them from stagnation. They will refuse to clock in and clock out with a lover; without trust, love withers.

This combination can be a good success if Virgo Moon partners will allow their Aquarian type lovers to express their love for them in their *own* way (and refrain from altering their approach), and if the Aquarius lover is more attentive and sensitive to the delicate Virgo Moon psyche (neglecting the Virgo Moon mate emotionally may not be wise). The Aquarian type lover is fixed in habit and the benefit of that fixity is that once they *do* decide to get married, start a family and settle down with a spouse, they are more like to stay the course and not abandon their lover. But they must decide that for themselves and not be influenced by any outside factors that might unduly pressurize them. Most Aquarian types make understanding parents and emotional manipulation is not a child-rearing technique they will choose when they can use the connection of friendship and tenderness instead.

These two share a strong, intellectual bond, which may get them over many a rough spot in their lives. Mercury-ruled, Virgo Moon soul mates can help airy Aquarian types learn about the incredible rewards of frugality, focus and hard work, while the Uranus-ruled, Aquarian type partner can introduce their Virgo Moon lover to being more free in mind, body and spirit, and encourage them to be more fearless and expressive without worrying about being accepted or rejected by the world. This will be a beautiful and unique kind of love story, one worth every effort.

Virgo Moon vs. Pisces Sun, Moon or Rising Sign The Earth and Water Relationship

Earth: "Does my boyfriend manage his finances maturely or will I end up paying his bills and supporting him? I need stability and true commitment before I can enjoy the romance between us." the earthy female thinks to herself. "Will my future wife spend my hard earned cash on frivolous items at the mall or be wise enough to save up for our retirement?" the earthy male lover wonders.

Water: "Is my boyfriend emotionally stable and wise about our joint finances? Or will debts pile up in the first year of marriage? I need a supportive life-long lover as well as a loving one." the watery female lover thinks to herself. "Will my future spouse conserve our financial resources or spend unwisely without thought for the future? I can connect better romantically if I know that my chosen life-mate is passionate as well as mature and pragmatic." the watery male lover wonders.

Virgo Moon lovers can enjoy a highly romantic and passionate relationship with partners who have their Sun, Moon or Rising sign in the opposite water sign of Pisces. The pull here will be one of marriage because these signs are polarized. Both are alike but also dissimilar in their own way. Each partner symbolizes an element. Understanding that element helps us delve deeper into the real personality of that partner.

Earth represents an unmatched stability and reliability: earth is a faith in love and an undying dedication to a relationship coupled with a hope that any interpersonal problems can be worked through. Water represents a need to experience raw emotion and then be purified by its intensity. Elementally, water and earth are quite compatible. Water needs the earth to give it direction and arrange the boundaries and flow of its bodies of water, while the earth needs water so that fruitful farms that feed millions, and gardens and trees grow tall and green. The earth receives true nourishment in the form of rain from the water-bearing clouds in the sky. Each element supports the other beautifully.

But care must be taken so that one element doesn't overwhelm the other. If there is too much earth in the water, it would be impossible to drink it. If there is not enough water in the earth, nothing grows anywhere. Balancing the attributes of each element is key. When the astrological seventh sector comes into play, there will be, at some point or the other, a desire to merge destinies on a legal level through marriage. The Pisces energy is very compatible with the earthy Virgo Moon essence because water and earth have an easier time understanding each other than other elements.

Virgo Moon mates are sometimes *as slow* to offer commitment, as their Pisces type lovers are quick to accept it. Pisces types are comfortable with raw emotion and extraordinary intuition, while super-logical Virgo Moon lovers view it with skepticism. Pisces types seek an anchor in life who will provide a rock-solid foundation on which they can rely, no matter how many good or bad experiences life throws at them. The Pisces energy brings sensitivity and compassion to a sometimes skeptical and pre-occupied Virgo Moon lover, while the Virgo Moon lover aids their watery soul mate in finding their true voice, being more practical and feeling more confident about any life choice that they may have to make in the years ahead.

Pisces type partners, more than Virgo Moon lovers, need to be able to think clearly and require a lover who can bring them out of any self-doubt, which may perhaps plague them at certain times in their lives. Water signs need direction; still waters run deep but tend to stagnate, while flowing water refreshes.

Financially, Pisces types may be more impulsive when spending cash, and this may pose a problem because Virgo is a financially prudent sign and most

Virgo Moon folks are very careful about managing their resources properly, at the right time and in the right way. This is a good match provided the Pisces type lover learns not to push their earthy and stable Virgo Moon lover into making any decision based on only emotion and not logic and reason. Virgo Moon mates *analyze* life, people and events while their Pisces type lovers *emotionalize* the same, therefore a balance is required so that neither partner overwhelms the other with their vividly different approaches to relationships.

Virgo Moon soul mates can help their sensitive partner express their pragmatic side more than their trusting side, in order to balance them out and give them a sense of grounding (water signs may need that earthy grounding to stabilize them), while the Virgo Moon lover can learn from their Pisces type mate to trust their gut feelings and learn to tone down that ever present sense of suspicion (earth signs may need to be more comfortable with their emotions and refrain from keeping them bound up too tightly). Pisces types must also remember never to withhold any information from their Virgo Moon lover. If the Virgo Moon soul mate begins to doubt their partner even a little, that little doubt could alter the natural course of the relationship in a negative way. The Virgo Moon lover must also remember to never neglect their Pisces type lover (for example, denying them attention or input when they really need it), no matter how busy they are and no matter how heavy that workload may be at the office, their lover should always come first.

Neptune rules the sign of Pisces, and while it can inspire and creatively fantasize, it can also cause a great deal of confusion and self-deception in the tender Pisces heart. Which is why frequent and clear communication should be a rule of this relationship. The refined Pisces energy lifts their Virgo Moon sweetheart out of the boring world of checkbooks, to-do-lists and financial planning and puts them down into the sensual world of romance and heartfelt promises, while the Virgo Moon lover becomes the Pisces type lover's strongest and ever-present support in life. This could be a fruitful combination.

Chapter 19
The Libra Moon Sign Lover

Libra Moon vs. Aries Sun, Moon or Rising Sign
The Air and Fire Relationship

Air: "Is my boyfriend open-minded enough and will he appreciate my outspoken side? I need a life mate who will talk to me, communicate with me about everything and not clam up and brood." the airy female partner muses. "Will my girlfriend allow me to do the things I love or will she try to restrict me from expressing myself and living my life according to my rules?" the airy male lover wonders.

Fire: "I need romance and passion to really enjoy my relationship. Will my boyfriend be a faithful mate for life?" the fiery female partner wonders. "I want an active and freedom-loving partner. Will my girlfriend understand my need for true freedom in life or be too controlling of my actions and behavior?" the fiery male lover thinks to himself.

Libra Moon lovers can enjoy a highly romantic and passionate relationship with partners who have their Sun, Moon or Rising sign in the polar opposite fire sign of Aries. Each partner symbolizes an element. Understanding that element helps us delve deeper into the real personality of that partner. When seen through the sign of Aries, fire represents a sense of passion, purposeful action and optimism. When seen through the eyes of the Moon sign of Libra, the air element represents a desire to express oneself through inter-personal relationships and then experience incredible personal growth as a result of it.

Compatibility might be best achieved if the Aries type lover can differentiate between the two distinct types of the Libra Moon personality. The most common type is the *marriage type*, who may focus solely on marriage and love for emotional sustenance, while the second is the *thinker type*, who is more intellectual than focused on love or raising a family. The dominant Aries type mate will find the first type a better match for them, as they will be more passive and marriage-oriented than the latter Libra Moon type. Any sense of competition in this relationship must be quickly and permanently eliminated for best results (Aries tends to compete subconsciously).

Libra Moon lovers are drawn toward marriage and relationships in a way that other signs are not. To them, relationships symbolize a critical path to clarity and self-knowledge. Libra Moon mates seek harmony *within* themselves by first creating it outside of themselves. Ever the integrator, the Libra Moon person enjoys bringing people (or ideas) together so that a base of support is created for the betterment of all. The Libra Moon lover is diplomatic, emotionally flexible and indubitably one of the romantic Moon signs of all. Aries type mates can teach their Libra Moon lovers to voice their opinions with a total lack of fear and can help them get over their apprehension over not being nice enough. *"It doesn't matter what people think, honey! All that matters is what you think."* advises the Aries type mate wisely.

These two lovers will feel the full effects of their ruling planets in their relationship. Mars (ruler of Aries) and Venus (ruler of Libra) will be inseparable lovebirds most of the time, but may experience a clash of wills on occasion. Mars (through the Aries type mate) may impetuously say too much (too loudly) and Venus (through the Libra Moon mate) may sulk or withdraw for a while if she doesn't get her way. If Venus does decide to give in, she will never let Mars forget it. If disagreements crop up, neither lover should wait too long to say they're sorry. Doubt has no place in the Libra Moon/Aries Sun, Moon or Rising sign relationship and both partners should make every effort to talk out differences the *same* day they occur. Waiting too long might cause fear to set in, which can lead to suspicions that are hard to eliminate.

These two will get along quite nicely if they can familiarize themselves with each other's fears. What does the Aries type lover fear? They fear boredom as well as being caught in a bad relationship that cuts off their sense of personal freedom; a controlling lover will keep them out of the house most of the time. What does the Libra Moon lover fear the most? They fear being witness to their primary love relationship or marriage crumbling and their not being able to do anything to salvage or protect it: romantic Libra Moon mates marry for the long haul. Marriage and relationships become their major source of trust in life and any disturbances will cause them to feel apprehensive about what might come next. *"Will my husband leave me? Is he having a mid-life crisis? Am I not as beautiful as I used to be? Why is he drifting away like this?"* worries the sentimental idealistic in them.

If the Aries type lover can keep the romance alive in their relationship and be more affectionate with their Libra Moon sweetheart (remember those special days, birthdays, anniversaries and of course, Venus' favorite day, Valentine's Day), and if the Libra Moon lover can give their Aries type lover a good degree of personal freedom (constantly questioning Aries types on their whereabouts or smothering them is a no-no), this match will work out well and last decades. The independent Aries type mate may prefer not to mingle too much with their lover's set of friends, or may prefer to spend a great deal of time on projects that do not require their lover's input, or they may decide to maintain habits from before they met and not want to give them up. The Libra Moon lover must adapt to these situations for a maximum chance at compatibility with their quirky lover and not cajole their mate into altering their way of life too greatly.

Don't-fence-me-in Aries views independence as a virtue and a Libra Moon lover likes to share activities with their mate. A balance would be ideal (it is critical that Libra Moon lovers pursue regular interests *apart* from their activities with their mate), so that both of them can maintain their autonomy as well as enjoy their love and watch it grow. The Aries type mate must not create too much of a schism between them and their mate (there's a thin line between wanting your space and being neglectful), otherwise devoted Libra Moon mates may decide to walk away in search of a lover who *does* value their charming company. This pair will be successful with only the slightest modulation in personalities; the love between them will be eternal.

Libra Moon vs. Taurus Sun, Moon or Rising Sign
The Air and Earth Relationship

Air: "Is my boyfriend open-minded enough and will he appreciate my outspoken side? I need a life mate who will talk to me, communicate with me about everything and not clam up and brood." the airy female partner muses. "Will my girlfriend allow me to do the things I love or will she try to restrict me from truly expressing myself?" the airy male lover wonders.

Earth: "Does my boyfriend manage his finances maturely or will I end up paying his bills and supporting him? I need stability and true commitment before I can enjoy the romance between us." the earthy female thinks to herself. "Will my future wife spend my hard earned cash on frivolous items at the mall or be wise enough to save up for our retirement?" the earthy male lover wonders.

Libra Moon lovers can enjoy a fulfilling and loving relationship with partners who have their Sun, Moon or Rising sign in the reliable earth sign of Taurus. Each partner symbolizes an element. Understanding that element helps us delve deeper into the real personality of that partner. Earth represents a need to stabilize key relationships in life in the favor of longevity, value and security. The air element, through the Moon sign of Libra, symbolizes a need to balance their inner worlds by balancing their primary love relationships and then letting that harmony spread, grow and flourish.

Taurus types must distinguish between the two, clear versions of the Libra Moon personality. The most common type is the *marriage type*, while the second is the intellectual, *thinker type*. The former romantic and non-combative type will blend well with the Taurus type lover. With a double dose of Venus power surging through this relationship, romance will fill the hearts and souls of this pair. Both Taurus types and Libra Moon lovers will respond quickly to the soft and alluring Venus energy. The desire for a strong union that can provide an in-built sense of permanent friendship will be evident in both partners.

Family-friendly, Taurus types possess qualities that the Libra Moon mate needs to create and preserve a firm, interactive structure on which to build a strong, loving relationship, while the Libra Moon mate has qualities that are useful for the fixed, Taurus type mate to use as they learn the artful skills of subtle diplomacy and emotional flexibility from their Libra Moon mate. The Libra Moon lover patiently shows them that it is best to unload the pressure that unexpressed emotions tend to create on the tolerant Taurus heart, while being able to enjoy the simple pleasures of life.

If the Libra Moon lover can control their legendary tendency toward indecision, it will help the Taurus heart relax because this earth sign cannot function merely on vagaries and verbal promises of commitment: they want you to put your money where your mouth is and stand by those passionate promises that were made. When it comes to commitment, Libra Moon companions will commit but perhaps take too long to make up their minds.

The Taurus type lover, on the other hand could also take too long to decide if their Libra Moon partner is best for their lifestyle, because earthy Taurus likes to be very sure of what sort of permanent situation they are getting into. Libra Moon soul mates are generally very marriage-minded which suits Taurus types just fine, *if* they are ready for matrimony themselves. If not, there could be a situation on their hands. They both need to give each other the gift of space to decide without undue pressure. This alone will bring them closer because other lovers will get impatient, get angry and stomp out of the house, vowing

254 The 12 Moon Signs in Love

never to return. Caution might tip the balance in the most patient lover's favor.

Patience is crucial to handling the earthy Taurus energy and understanding is key to relating to the romantic, relationship-oriented Libra Moon mate. If they can find a way to match their emotional timetables, this could be a successful pair, where the Taurus type partner provides the stability and their Libra Moon lover provides the fun, romance and excitement. This is a stable, loving, Venusian pair!

Libra Moon vs. Gemini Sun, Moon or Rising Sign
The Air and Air Relationship

Air: "Is my boyfriend open-minded enough and will he appreciate my outspoken side? I need a life mate who will talk to me, communicate with me about everything and not clam up and brood." the airy female partner muses. "Will my girlfriend allow me to do the things I love or will she try to restrict me from expressing myself?" the airy male lover wonders.

Libra Moon lovers can enjoy an intellectually fulfilling and productive relationship with partners who have their Sun, Moon or Rising sign in the gregarious air sign of Gemini. When two air sign energies combine in the game of romance, there will be a lot of banter as well as a lot of chances for sending out the wrong message. Each partner symbolizes an element. Understanding that element helps us delve deeper into the real personality of that partner.

The element of air, through the sign of Gemini, desires to use self-expression as a tool to bring the world its brightest ideas and bring people together through the power of inspirational oratory: when Gemini talks, the world listens. When seen through the Moon sign of Libra, the air element seeks to unify, integrate, solidify and grant longevity to marriage and relationships so that successful ambition is well matched by successful personal or romantic goals. Elementally, air supports air and blends with it seamlessly. But it should be noted that a whole lot of air going around without aim only becomes a destructive typhoon. While, when it is controlled and properly tempered, it becomes the clean, fresh air that we expect when we open the windows of our homes in the springtime.

When seen through the wisdom of Astrology, two air sign mates can make great contributions to the world. Therefore, this precious air energy must be respected and put to good use. When the air element is given a chance to be its best, the world receives brilliant orators and speakers who can move great masses of people into doing good things in a karmic sense. Balancing the attributes of this versatile element is key.

It might greatly help if a distinction was made between the two types of the Libra Moon personality. The first is the *marriage type*, who may gravitate toward relationships as their sole source of fulfillment, while the second is the independent, *thinker type*, who may not feel the need to be in love to connect to their deeper selves; they'll find other ways to gain self-wisdom. Gemini types may blend better with the latter type, who is more autonomous and does not need as much input or attention from lovers as the former.

Of the two, the attractive and charismatic Gemini type lover is more impulsive in saying the wrong thing at the wrong time, but meaning well. This may occur innocently but the repercussions will be real. Mercury, the ruler of Gemini, governs speech and swift communication (be sure to duck when those Mercurial comments fly!). Gemini talks first, and thinks later. Libra Moon lovers are very sensitive, especially when dealing with a love partner. Both are strong intellectuals and frequent, earnest communication is very important to both. While they can mingle interests easily, it should be noted that the only situation in which marriage-minded Libra Moon partners begin to lose patience with their Gemini type lovers is when they refuse to commit to a future together but won't terminate the relationship either.

Usually, Libra Moon mates are known for being the best fence sitters of the zodiac (those Libra scales dip and rise), but when their hearts are involved, another's indecision may cause a lot of emotions to come up to be dealt with. There is a good chance that both partners are impulse spenders (Mercury, the ruler of Gemini, makes split second decisions and Venus, the ruler of Libra, is a shopping guru), so one of them will have to be the financial watchdog and make sure that the financial aspect of their relationship doesn't cause trouble in other areas (money issues sadly lie at the heart of many lovers separating). Blending their individual spending styles would help.

Libra is a strong marriage sign, while the typical Gemini type lover thrives within an unfettered friendship setting first, which is wise. If they're genuinely in love, Libra Moon partners may need some tangible proof that marriage is definitely on the cards. One way to combat this clash of timetables would be for both of them, the romantic Libra Moon lover, as well as the restless but charming Gemini type lover, to begin their courtship slowly and keep it from burning too hot, too fast. Gradually getting to know one another would help immensely. Friends who become confidants first and lovers second, will have a longer, more emotionally comfortable relationship than friends who proceed directly from the friend stage to the sexual stage. This gives them a chance to make sure that their expectations match ahead of time.

A good way for this relationship to survive is for the Libra Moon partner to allow their Gemini type lover the chance to decide on their own timetable, as to what shape they want their love to take, while the Gemini type lover could try to understand the deeply partnership-oriented Libra Moon partner's heart and their need for stability with one loving partner. Refined by nature, Libra Moon folks recoil in horror from a lover who is combative, lacks delicacy of speech and a gentleness of manner. Neither should hold back how they feel (Libra Moon people must remember to stop worrying about being too nice all the time, not everyone appreciates their diplomacy) and they should be able to get to the heart of any differences quickly. This will be a highly communicative and purposeful relationship.

Libra Moon vs. Cancer Sun, Moon or Rising Sign
The Air and Water Relationship

Air: "Is my boyfriend open-minded enough and will he appreciate my outspoken side? I need a life mate who will talk to me, communicate with me about everything and not clam up and brood." the airy female partner muses. "Will my girlfriend allow me to do the things I love or will she try to restrict me from truly expressing myself and doing what I want to do in life?" the airy male lover wonders.

Water: "Is my boyfriend emotionally stable and wise about our joint finances? Or will debts pile up in the first year of marriage? I need a supportive life-long lover as well as a loving one." the watery female lover thinks to herself. "Will my future spouse conserve our financial resources or spend unwisely without thought for the future? I can connect better romantically if I know that my chosen life-mate is passionate as well as mature and pragmatic." the watery male lover wonders.

Libra Moon lovers can enjoy an uplifting and happy relationship with partners who have their Sun, Moon or Rising sign in the sensitive water sign of Cancer. Each partner symbolizes an element. Understanding that element helps us delve deeper into the real personality of that partner. The air element, through the Libra Moon vibration, symbolizes a desire to promote strong, inter-personal relationships between lovers while fostering original self-expression between them as well. The water element, through the Cancer type lover, represents a need to take human emotion to a brand new, more unique level, where two lovers can use emotions not to control each other, but to strengthen their love bond over time.

Cancer types might want to differentiate between the two separate types of the Libra Moon personality in order to find out how to approach their lover. The first is the *marriage type*, who may find self-direction only through the intimate medium of relationships, while the second is the *thinker type*, who may choose to walk on an independent path where marriage and children are not their focal point. Family-oriented Cancer types may get along best with the first category of the Libra Moon personality, which can slip into and function successfully within the home environment more easily.

With the power of Venus and the hypnotic Moon surging through this relationship, this will be a highly romantic and close union. Both Cancer type lovers and anyone with Libra prominently placed in their natal charts will respond eagerly to the soft lunar as well as romantic Venus energy. Most Cancer type lovers make faithful and capable partners and will usually want to create a dependable structure within which a family can be raised (Cancer is the sign of the mother, the primary nurturer of the whole family). Libra Moon partners are *very* visually sensitive to beauty in a woman and attractiveness in a man and will be drawn to their Cancer type partner's signature patience and tenderness.

With the double cardinal quality at play in this union, Libra Moon lovers can energize the watery Cancer type lover by infusing in them an excitement for life and new, intellectually stimulating experiences. Cancer type mates may try to gently lead their relationship towards calmer waters. Movies and music, art and book collections will be a favorite of this creative Venus/Moon couple. The only problem they might like to watch out for is the Libra Moon partner's occasional inability to make a decision, or make one and then be unable to stick to it. They may, once in a while, suffer from the grass-is-always-greener-on-the-other-side syndrome, much to their mate's chagrin.

"Is she the one for me or am I making a big mistake?" the Libra Moon male wonders. *"Is he going to be my life-long soul mate or will his eyes wander and cause our marriage to collapse?"* the female Libra Moon partner thinks to herself. This indecision could cause a lot of instability within their watery Cancer lover's

heart. *"Does he love me like he says he does or is he using me?"* the tenderhearted, Cancer type girlfriend wonders. *"Is she for real or is she going to break my heart?"* the Cancer type boyfriend ponders. Lots of questions will arise in their hearts.

Commitment-friendly, Cancer types need a definite answer, preferably written in stone so that there is a surety they can depend on. The Libra Moon lover will commit but perhaps take a little longer to check the facts before reaching the alter. The Cancer type lover, on the other hand could also take too long to decide if their Libra Moon partner is best for their lifestyle, because emotionally cautious Cancer types like to be very sure of what type of permanent situation they are getting into. Cancer type lovers are very attached to their homes, possessions and their privacy, so if they want someone to be a regular part of their lives and especially their family circle, it is an incredibly admirable leap of faith of their part to ask their lover to accept life with them.

The Libra Moon lover is generally marriage-minded which suits sensitive Cancer types just fine, if they are ready for matrimony themselves. Patience is key to handling the fluctuating lunar moods of sensitive Cancer types and understanding is key to relating to the romantic Libra Moon lover. Both these signs are very loving and get attached easily, which is why they must both indulge in a little solitude now and then. Constant closeness with a lover can distort their expectations and confuse their sense of identity, which must be preserved, no matter how much they feel like changing to suit their lover or accommodating them. Love relationships are good, but *overvaluing* any relationship may be detrimental.

A little private time can clarify a lot of things for them and allow them to return to the relationship scene refreshed and confident. The Cancer energy brings out Libra Moon's sentimental, home-loving and cautious side, while the social Libra Moon/Venus energy helps Cancer types to get back in touch with their expressive and artistic side. This is a good combination as long as one of them becomes the center of stability for the relationship and keeps it from getting mixed up in too much emotionalism.

Libra Moon vs. Leo Sun, Moon or Rising Sign
The Air and Fire Relationship

Air: "Is my boyfriend open-minded enough and will he appreciate my outspoken side? I need a life mate who will talk to me, communicate with me about everything and not clam up and brood." the airy female partner muses. "Will my girlfriend allow me to do the things I love or will she try to restrict me from truly expressing myself and doing what I want with my life?" the airy male lover wonders.

Fire: "I need romance and passion to really enjoy my relationship. Will my boyfriend be a faithful mate for life?" the fiery female partner wonders. "I want an active and freedom-loving partner. Will my girlfriend understand my need for true freedom in life or be too controlling of my behavior and actions?" the fiery male lover thinks to himself.

Libra Moon lovers can enjoy a vibrant and loving relationship with partners who have their Sun, Moon or Rising sign in the joyous and charismatic fire sign of Leo. Each partner symbolizes an element. Understanding that element helps us delve deeper into the real personality of that partner. The fire element, through the Leo vibration, represents a need to be heard, appreciated and acknowledged by a lover as well as the world. The air element, through the Libra Moon energy, seeks to integrate, bolster and blend two personalities into one so that compatibility can be achieved between lovers on a multitude of levels.

Leo types should make a clear distinction between the two varying types of the Libra Moon personality. The first is the *marriage type*, who may look to their lover for a steady stream of attention and support, while the second is the *thinker type*, whose life direction may not include the marriage or family route but may instead focus on honing their intellectual skills. The usually dominant Leo type lover will get along better with the former, more accommodating, marriage type Libra Moon lover, who may be willing to get married at some point. Leo types won't want to stay single for too long.

These two will get along quite nicely if the Leo type lover keeps in mind that the ultra romantic Libra Moon partner thrives on genuine and frequent inter-action with their chosen beloved. Brooding, sulking, secretive and introverted lovers cause the open and easy-going Libra Moon mate to feel confused and restless. Libra Moon mates are very touchy about any threat to or disturbance in their closest relationships. They will usually spend a great deal of time on maintaining their marriage or relationship; most of their energies will be devoted to trying to make their connection to their spouse or lover stronger and more comfortable for *both*. Libra rules the scales of justice; any hint of unfair behavior from a lover will register instantly on the Libra Moon heart.

Leo type partners are loving but can be temperamental sometimes (on a bad day) and prone to losing that famous fire sign temper, while Libra Moon personalities are very sensitive to any raising of the voice (they recoil from people who use shouting, yelling and screaming, especially in public, to gain attention). Libra Moon partners should keep in mind that the sunny, out-going Leo personality needs to be handled tactfully and with tenderness consistently. Each has fears the other should be aware of. What does the Libra Moon lover fear? They fear losing a chance to marry and build a happy life with the person that they love the most in the world, or getting that chance and then watching their relationship crumble due to neglect from their lover. What does the Leo type mate fear? They have a fear of being taken advantage of by a person who doesn't love them but only wants to use them financially or emotionally.

Libra Moon lovers function under the influence of Venus, while Leo type partners are ruled by the Sun. When the Sun's blindingly brilliant energy meets up with the harmony- seeking and romantic essence of the Goddess of love, the effect will be tangibly felt in the Libra Moon/Leo Sun, Moon or Ascendant partnership. The Sun tends to be powerful, benevolent but sometimes too forceful. It can't help it, it's the mighty Sun after all, the giver of life and the nucleus of our solar system. Venus, the most romantic planet in the planetary family, helps release tension and tends to make Libra Moon mates soft-spoken, physically attractive and creates a desire in them to seek out the approval of a stronger and more confident lover.

Both these forces are opposites and, in the arena of relationships, can clash if misunderstandings arise. If wires get crossed, the Venus-ruled, Libra Moon lover will back down (temporarily at least), while the Sun-ruled, Leo type lover will keep pressing their point over and over. Venus symbolizes the heart while the Sun represents the intellect. This means that one of the lovers will have to modulate the relationship in such a way that neither has the upper hand or an unfair advantage over the other. The more sensitive lover of the two will spend more time learning the art of compromise and work behind the scenes to keep everything flowing smoothly.

If the Leo type lover can keep the romance alive and be more affectionate with their Libra Moon companion (don't forget those emotionally charged days, like birthdays, anniversaries and Valentine's Day), and if the Libra Moon lover can give their fiery Leo type lover a good degree of personal freedom to do what they want, (spend time with friends and devote some time to pet projects, enjoy some alone time), this match will work out and last decades. Leo type lovers stimulate Libra Moon partners into being more vibrant and independent, while Libra Moon mates soften up any fiery aggressiveness in their endearing Leo type lover. This highly communicative fire and air combination can be successful, if they are open to understanding what makes the *other* truly happy in life.

Libra Moon vs. Virgo Sun, Moon or Rising Sign
The Air and Earth Relationship

Air: "Is my boyfriend open-minded enough and will he appreciate my outspoken side? I need a life mate who will talk to me, communicate with me about everything and not clam up and brood." the airy female partner muses. "Will my girlfriend allow me to do the things I love or will she try to restrict me from expressing myself and spending time on the things I care about?" the airy male lover wonders.

Earth: "Does my boyfriend manage his finances maturely or will I end up paying his bills and supporting him? I need stability and true commitment before I can enjoy the romance between us." the earthy female thinks to herself. "Will my future wife spend my hard earned cash on frivolous items at the mall or be wise enough to save up for our retirement?" the earthy male lover wonders.

Libra Moon lovers can enjoy a vibrant and productive relationship with partners who have their Sun, Moon or Rising sign in the earth sign of Virgo. Each partner symbolizes an element. Understanding that element helps us delve deeper into the real personality of that partner. Earth, through the Virgo type mate, desires to strengthen and fortify personal relationships in the interests of longevity (or create something as ancient as the earth itself) and stability (the foundation of the earth rarely moves). Air represents, through the Libra Moon vibration, a powerful desire to support, preserve and maintain romantic relationships and to learn about themselves from the most intimate of interactions.

Creative and bright, the Libra Moon lover is pleasant and able to get along with the most complex of personalities. They could get the shyest person to open up, as well as get the most aggressive, opinionated personality to fall silent. Known for a gentle touch, the romantic Libra Moon lover seeks harmony *outside* of themselves in order to find harmony within themselves, therefore a soft-natured, calm and sympathetic spouse would be best for their nerves. While they can mingle interests with anyone easily (Libra is a master integrator), it should be noted that the only situation in which Libra Moon lovers begin to lose patience with their Virgo type sweethearts is when they refuse to commit to a future together but won't terminate the relationship either.

Usually, Libra Moon lovers are known for being the most indecisive sign of the zodiac (those scales dip and rise), but when their hearts are involved, another's indecision may cause a lot of emotions to come up to be dealt with. Virgo types are careful about committing their hearts because it often means that they also have to commit to sharing their living space and financial resources everyday.

This careful and pragmatic earth sign will never make the mistake of letting emotion get in the way of making the best decision for their lifestyle. There is a good chance that the Venus-ruled, Libra Moon lover is generous but also an impulse spender (flirtatious Venus invented the art of shopping), while the Virgo type mate might lean toward more frugality than is necessary, so one of them will have to be the financial watchdog and make sure that the financial aspect of their relationship doesn't spill over and cause unwanted disturbances in other areas of their relationship. Libra is a marriage and companionship sign, while the typical Virgo type lover thrives on an unfettered friendship and productive relationship first. Libra Moon mates want to see that ring on their finger, while skeptical Virgo type lovers want to make absolutely sure that this union will last a few decades at least. The more intellectual variety of the Libra Moon lover may not be too marriage-oriented, but may express themselves in other creative ways. This type will have an easier camaraderie with the slightly non-committal Virgo persona.

The Virgo type mate can be a bit emotionally cool sometimes and may not be able to match the sheer abundance of romanticism that fills the Libra Moon heart. Libra rules the scales of justice and if their lover treats them unfairly, this unfairness will register very quickly with the Libra Moon lover. *Gradually* getting to know one another would help immensely. Knowing each other's fears also helps. What does the Libra Moon lover fear? They fear that they may never see their love story culminate in a happy and long marriage that could grow stronger and deeper every year. Virgo type mates fear that they may end up marrying a person who is selfish, hides their true motives from them and only wants their money. Both most fear betrayal by a lover *after* marriage.

The Virgo type lover could try to understand their deeply partnership-oriented lover's life-goals and their need for a secure marriage at the right time (to

Libra Moon lovers, an uninvolved or undecided lover is an uninterested lover, and Venus may not allow them to stick around for too long once their heart withdraws from their relationship), while the Libra Moon lover could learn to better adhere to their partner's little habits and quirks. The emotionally flexible Libra Moon mate may be one of the few Moon signs that will easily adapt to the Virgo type person's need to see things done in a particular way. The Libra Moon energy brings out the tender romantic in their Virgo type lover, while the Virgo energy brings out the dutiful and responsible side of their Venus-ruled partner. This combination makes for good marriage material.

Libra Moon vs. Libra Sun, Moon or Rising Sign
The Air and Air Relationship

Air: "Is my boyfriend open-minded enough and will he appreciate my outspoken side? I need a life mate who will talk to me, communicate with me about every-thing and not clam up and brood." the airy female partner muses. "Will my girlfriend allow me to do the things I love or will she try to restrict me from expressing myself the way I feel comfortable?" the airy male lover wonders.

Libra Moon lovers can enjoy a revealing and yet fulfilling relationship with partners who have their Sun, Moon or Rising sign in their own air sign of Libra. Each partner symbolizes an element. Understanding that element helps us delve deeper into the real personality of that partner. The air element, when filtered through the Libra Moon vibration, desires to experience original self-expression through relationships, particularly in a marriage setting. Elementally, the double air vibration can mix personalities beautifully. Air supports air and blends with it seamlessly. This precious air energy must be respected and put to good use. When the air element is given a chance to be its best, the world receives brilliant orators and storytellers who can move great masses of people into doing good things in a karmic sense. Balancing the attributes of this fast-moving and versatile element is key.

Libra Moon partners need a great deal of romance and intimate interaction in their lives (Libra is a marriage sign, after all). Lovers who are inordinately secretive, tend to brood and are non-communicative will not blend well with them. They need someone who is willing to work on the trouble spots in the relationship and solve problems quickly without letting them take root. Refinement, delicacy and gentility; these are things that only another Libra type person can embody, offer and appreciate.

Be that as it may, too much similarity is as hurtful to a love connection as are too many differences. When two authentic, Venus-ruled lovers (Libra is ruled by Venus) get together in the game of love, they will feel an incredible empathy for each other, as well as a deep understanding of one another's basic life goals. But invariably, there will be times when one says something to the other without thinking or processing it first, creating in them a confusion that is unbearable (the air element *must* express itself, but should do so with caution).

One partner has to provide the contrast of personalities without which the relationship might begin to quickly shift shape or atrophy. For example, one of these two Libra lovers will have to be prudent about expenditures or be more invested in creating a regular income. If one of them agrees to take on the responsibility of being the stabilizer in the relationship, it will take a considerable amount of pressure off the relationship. Both are romantic, sentimental and ever searching for that elusive, ideal partnership. *"I know they're out there somewhere, and one day, I'll find my perfect love."* the idealistic Libra Moon person hopes.

Venus, the harmonious matchmaker of the planetary family, likes to see people falling in love and settling down, but is not itself a practical planet. How compatible will they be six years after the vows have been said? This couple would do well to bring their relationship out of the Venus fantasy world and back onto the playing field of their daily life. Their best bet is to be infallibly honest with each other when dealing with finances and expenses (Venus is also a financial planet), encourage each other in pursuing their most cherished goals (particularly the ones that are independent of each other), and make sure that their need to please doesn't eclipse their right to be authentic versions of themselves. They must watch out for a tendency to be *too nice* or over-extend themselves, when it may not be necessary to try quite so hard to secure someone's approval. The Libra Moon vibration seeks to experience peace and harmony within their hearts by first creating it *outside* of themselves, in their closest relationships. Children will bring this pair closer, but both must be ready for that big step.

Two airy personalities may need some serious grounding if this relationship is to stand the test of time. Both lovers will have to show real maturity, be fair to each other (Libra rules the scales of justice), show tolerance and try not to judge their partner, but affirm to each other repeatedly that their love will be strong enough to weather any storm together. With Venus blessing this couple, their love is sure to endure.

Libra Moon vs. Scorpio Sun, Moon or Rising Sign
The Air and Water Relationship

Air: "Is my boyfriend open-minded enough and will he appreciate my outspoken side? I need a life mate who will talk to me, communicate with me about everything and not clam up and brood." the airy female partner muses. "Will my girlfriend allow me to do the things I love or will she try to restrict me from expressing myself?" the airy male lover wonders.

Water: "Is my boyfriend emotionally stable and wise about our joint finances? Or will debts pile up in the first year of marriage? I need a supportive life-long lover as well as a loving one." the watery female lover thinks to herself. "Will my future spouse conserve our financial resources or spend unwisely without thought for the future? I can connect better romantically if I know that my chosen life-mate is passionate as well as mature and pragmatic." the watery male lover wonders.

Libra Moon lovers can enjoy a highly fulfilling and passionate relationship with partners who have their Sun, Moon or Rising sign in the sensitive water sign of Scorpio. Each partner symbolizes an element. Understanding that element helps us delve deeper into the real personality of that partner. The air element, through the Libra Moon vibration desires to express itself as well as gain critical self-knowledge about itself through love relationships, particularly ones that have the potential to last decades. Water represents an emotional purity as well as a soft and inviting sensuality. This element represents a desire to let authentic human emotions guide the path in love relationships, so that there is no room for secrets or fear.

Scorpio type lovers place an inordinate amount of importance on the quality and durability of their love relationship, and so do Libra Moon lovers. The only difference between them is that Libra Moon lovers are a touch more emotionally flexible, while the Scorpio type mate is a bit more fixed in temperament and habit. Airy Libra Moon lovers also need an enormous degree of commitment in their relationships (Libra is a marriage sign). The emotional Scorpio type lover will hold their romantic and eager Libra Moon mate to every promise they make and carefully test them to see if they are really as involved in their love relationship as they say they are.

Libra rules the scales of true justice and will sense any hint of unfairness from a lover even it is to an imperceptible degree; Libra Moon people are sensitive that way. Scorpio types want a partner who won't get scared and run away as soon as life's more difficult situations begin emerging, but will stand beside them no matter how many complications life throws at them, and is sure of what they want in life, including them. *"If you're not sure about me now, after all this time together, then what's the point of being together? I need to know for sure, I need to know one way or the other."* the all-or-nothing Scorpio type mate warns. The Libra Moon lover will refuse to make up their mind if placed under pressure. Airy Moon signs are like the element they represent, they will rush out of a room like a breeze if too much pressure has accumulated in the room. Scorpio type lovers run on purely emotional energy, it is their daily fuel and they are unable to view life in a casual, detached manner. They may take this inability to decide rather personally.

Most Libra Moon soul mates are social creatures and want to enjoy every high point that life has to offer, and may find people who take life too seriously, too restrictive to endure on a daily basis. This difference will usually rear its ugly head when the management of finances is being discussed (money issues sadly lie at the heart of many lovers separating). While sexual compatibility will never be a problem area, each partner's style of spending money will be a topic of discussion. The Libra Moon lover is not too focused, in most cases, on learning about the benefits of extreme frugality. While watery Scorpio types will have to wrestle with a lot of recurrent heartburn if their immature mate doesn't know the difference between a need and a want.

Scorpio is a financial sign and this sign judges partners not only on how they look and how they manage their most volatile emotions, but also on *how careful they are with their cash.* Scorpio types are also easily hurt when words are used rashly. This relationship can last if Scorpio type mates can be less controlling and more trusting of their sweetheart's behavior, and if Libra Moon mates can be open to being introduced to the deeper aspects of love and intimacy; the tiniest trace of superficiality in butterfly-like, appearance-focused, Libra Moon lovers will disappear once they see love through Scorpio's eyes. Libra Moon lovers must make an effort understand their intense, watery lover's motivations and always approach them with respect and kindness, especially when tempers are about to flare.

Scorpio type mates must monitor a subconscious tendency to control people or situations, as well as a desire to influence the outcome of events. Harmony-seeking, matchmaker Venus, the ruler of Libra, likes to see people falling in love, getting to the alter to say their *"I dos"* and starting families, but Venus itself is not a practical planet. Pluto, the ruler of Scorpio, is a serious and self-controlled planet that may cause many sweeping changes to occur in the lives of their Libra Moon lovers. The emotionally malleable Libra Moon lover will, in most cases, be able to handle those changes with remarkable adaptability.

The energy of Pluto may seem like a total mismatch when placed next to the light and airy, happy and bubbly Venus energy. But both lovers (the Libra Moon mate and their Scorpio lover) can learn a great deal about life, its seriousness as well as its joy, from each other. They would do well to bring their relationship out of the Venus fantasy world, and the somber, slightly suspicious world of Pluto, and put it back onto the platform of their neutral daily life. This could be a good marriage match.

Libra Moon vs. Sagittarius Sun, Moon or Rising Sign
The Air and Fire Relationship

Air: "Is my boyfriend open-minded enough and will he appreciate my outspoken side? I need a life mate who will talk to me, communicate with me about everything and not clam up and brood." the airy female partner muses. "Will my girlfriend allow me to do the things I love or will she try to restrict me from expressing myself?" the airy male lover wonders.

Fire: "I need romance and passion to really enjoy my relationship. Will my boyfriend be a faithful mate for life?" the fiery female partner wonders. "I want an active and freedom-loving partner. Will my girlfriend understand my need for true freedom in life or be too controlling of what I want to do with my life?" the fiery male lover thinks to himself.

Libra Moon lovers can enjoy a loving and close relationship with partners who have their Sun, Moon or Rising sign in the social and active fire sign of Sagittarius. Each partner symbolizes an element. Understanding that element helps us delve deeper into the real personality of that partner. The fire element, through the sign of Sagittarius, represents a need to live life authentically and experience it without fear and pessimism; this element emphasizes the passion of the heart. Air, through the Moon sign of Libra, represents a need to express oneself truly, through a variety of mediums and help facilitate the transfer of information; this element emphasizes the passion of the mind.

A good way for the Sagittarius type lover to achieve maximum compatibility with their Libra Moon partner, is to make a distinction between the two different types of the Libra Moon personality. The most common type to be found is the *marriage type*, for whom marriage and intimacy take precedence over developing their intellectual gifts, while the second is the *thinker type*, who may find more solace in honing their intellectual gifts like writing and learning, instead of following the marriage, mini-van and maternity route. The marriage type should avoid depending on their lover for more attention than can be comfortably supplied, while the latter, bookish or writer type must learn to curtail a slightly detached attitude toward lovers.

If you're attractive, optimistic and can match your physical beauty with solid intellectual muscle, the Libra Moon lover just might fall deeply in love with you. The Libra Moon sign is emblematic of emotional moderation in all things (those Libra scales of justice sure help with figuring that out), coupled with a Venusian delicacy of manner. Partners who tend to brood, are overly emotional, inclined to be hysterical or secretive may find that the Libra Moon lover drifts away from them gradually. *"Why shout and yell when we can discuss this issue in a soft, calm tone of voice? I'm sure we can reach a fair and just resolution to everything. Let's make sure everyone leaves happy."* the fair-minded Libra Moon person might suggest. This Moon sign is cool in a crisis or emergency.

Libra Moon mates tend to get emotional about the *idea* of a relationship, rather than the relationship itself; for airy Moon signs the mind is a more frequently used romantic tool than the heart. Cool tempered, Libra Moon lovers seek harmony outside of themselves in order to build it *inside* of themselves. Sagittarius types will appreciate their Libra Moon lover's ability to accommodate and forgive easily; the malleable Libra Moon lover can adjust to almost any personality type but must make sure they don't give up control too often. More dominant by temperament than passive (Jupiter is a giant compared to Venus), Sagittarius types will lean toward actively modifying the relationship if they are truly in love, or have been burned many times by partners who repeatedly failed to understand them, manipulated them or cost them their original sense of trust.

The fiery Sagittarius type partner may *wisely* want to take the commitment side of the relationship slowly and want to test out their Libra Moon partner to see if they can really supply that rare blend of intimacy and autonomy that they need. Sagittarius types can teach their butterfly-like, sometimes immature lovers an invaluable lesson in life; that relationships are not the only avenue for self-knowledge. Patience, risk, faith and unplanned adventure are also great teachers and character builders. There are things in the world that are far greater than pleasure and pain. The slightest superficiality in the Libra Moon lover will dissipate once they envision life through their partner's eyes. Both lovers may find that the draw toward relationships will increase in intensity as they age and become more realistic and mature about balancing love with personal goals, learning to give equal time to both and be able to enjoy the many fruits of that balance.

Lady Venus (the ruler of Libra Moon) governs marriage, romance and love, while the Sagittarius type partner functions under the mega energy of Jupiter, the largest planet in our solar system family. Jupiter governs travel, foreign lands, ancient teachings, philosophy and the pursuit of a multi-faceted sense of freedom. Venus attracts Jupiter with her femininity as well as her intelligence, and Jupiter impresses Venus with his intellect and openhearted approach to life. The desire for a strong union that can provide an in-built sense of permanent friendship will be evident in both partners, but a common ideology must first bind them to each other. The average, non-confrontational Libra Moon lover thrives best in a supportive role, but must learn to voice their views fearlessly like their fiery mate. The diplomatic Libra Moon sign will *actively refuse to compete* with their lover, which takes an enormous amount of pressure off the relationship.

Libra Moon lovers must ensure that they're not too changeable (the air element cannot sit still and may become easily distracted); if a decision is made, they must stick to it. The more docile Libra Moon lover may feel tempted to give up control and let their confident mate take the lead. But this would be a mistake because in many ways, they would only be placing an additional burden on their lover's shoulders. It is crucial that the Sagittarius type lover join forces with a partner who will not become too dependent on them for everything and is strong enough to enhance their own independence within their relationship. Another, highly important thing to bear in mind is that humor and laughter are extremely necessary in keeping these lovers in the best emotional form of their lives. If a friendship takes off, their love will last.

Libra Moon vs. Capricorn Sun, Moon or Rising Sign
The Air and Earth Relationship

Air: "Is my boyfriend open-minded enough and will he appreciate my outspoken side? I need a life mate who will talk to me, communicate with me about every-thing and not clam up and brood." the airy female partner muses. "Will my girlfriend allow me to do the things I love or will she try to restrict me from truly expressing myself?" the airy male lover wonders.

Earth: "Does my boyfriend manage his finances maturely or will I end up paying his bills and supporting him? I need stability and true commitment before I can enjoy the romance between us." the earthy female thinks to herself. "Will my future wife spend my hard earned cash on frivolous items at the mall or be wise enough to save up for our retirement?" the earthy male lover wonders.

Libra Moon lovers can enjoy a highly driven and successful relationship with partners who have their Sun, Moon or Rising sign in the ambitious and success-seeking earth sign of Capricorn. This union is a mingling of the energies of air and earth. Each partner symbolizes an element. Understanding that element helps us delve deeper into the real personality of that partner. Earth represents a need to stabilize key relationships in life in the favor of longevity, value and security. The air element, through the sign of Libra, symbolizes a need to balance their inner worlds by balancing their primary love relationships and then letting that harmony spread, grow and flourish.

There are two types of the Libra Moon personality and knowing which one you're in love with could help with understanding how to approach them. The first type is the *marriage type,* for whom marriage and raising a family will be paramount, while the second is the *thinker type,* for whom finding their intellectual voice will be important. The former type will get along well with the dominant Capricorn type lover who will prefer a partner who will not thwart their efforts at building a name for themselves in society. But care should be taken that industrious Capricorn types do not place their desire for success above their closest relationships. Ambition can wait but once people's hearts shut them out, chances once lost may never be granted again. Forgetting the birthdays of family or friends because *"there's a ton of work at the office that needs to be done"* would be a serious blunder.

Libra Moon lovers have great lessons to learn from the hard-working and serious Capricorn energy, as well as teach them a few of their own. Capricorn types can build into being the most cherished ambitions that a socially conscious Libra Moon lover can envision. Primarily supportive and protective, Capricorn types can teach Libra Moon lovers how to create a legacy and leave something tangible and powerful behind, while bringing to their attention the fact that planning ahead for that rainy day is a good thing for a sunny, Libra

Moon lover to do. Capricorn places achievement before pleasure, while for Libra Moon mates, pleasure is exactly why we're here on earth.

Libra Moon lovers gradually become cautious, driven and success-oriented around the Capricorn essence. Capricorn types should be more vocal around the effervescent energy of the Libra Moon lover, while Libra Moon partners should learn to pay more heed when the wise Saturn energy speaks through the Capricorn type lover. Capricorn types receive from the Libra Moon energy a new perspective on life, where they can be more optimistic, light-hearted and feel more confident about themselves (outgoing and social Libra Moon lovers can help alleviate Capricorn's occasional depression brought on by Saturn's influence).

The Libra Moon lover can be changeable sometimes, and it is that romantically changeable part that their earth sign lover may have a problem with. Capricorn wants a partner who is a hundred percent sure of what they want in life, including them. *"If you can't make up your mind about me, then why are we together? How long does it take to decide if you love someone or not? I'm not talking about a few months, I'm talking about a lifetime together, just you and me."* the Capricorn type mate warns. And while Libra Moon partners understand that well, they may not make up their mind quickly if there is more than one prospect on the scene. Also, they will refuse to make up their mind if placed under pressure. Stability-minded Capricorn types may take this delay rather seriously.

Libra Moon lovers are ruled by Venus and their Capricorn type mates function under the influence of Saturn. Saturn is the karmic timekeeper of the planetary family and is responsible for keeping track of every person's actions across many lifetimes, whether they be positive or negative, while instilling in people a respect for discipline, honesty and hard work. Venus' relationship-minded and flirtatious energy may seem rather frivolous when compared to the strong, silent and productive Saturn temperament. But both Sir Saturn and Lady Venus need one another more than they can imagine. Venus (the Libra Moon lover) needs Saturn's grace, stability and strength while Saturn (the Capricorn type lover) needs Venus' lightness of spirit to tide it over when those deep, dark, blue spells threaten to disrupt the emotional equilibrium of their heart.

As for managing finances, it should be kept in mind that the Capricorn energy is never careless, especially when it comes to a precious resource like income. Venus loves to go shopping, so Libra Moon lovers should try to spend within reason and always consult their earthy partners before big purchases are made. This courtesy alone will help smooth out a majority of their problems.

Together, both these dynamic energies can create a formidable empire that will stand the test of time, with Capricorn supplying the stability and direction, and the Libra Moon lover supplying the joy of romance and marriage with lots of fun and laughter thrown in!

Libra Moon vs. Aquarius Sun, Moon or Rising Sign
The Air and Air Relationship

Air: "*Is my boyfriend open-minded enough and will he appreciate my outspoken side? I need a life mate who will talk to me, communicate with me about everything and not clam up and brood.*" *the airy female partner muses. "Will my girlfriend allow me to do the things I love or will she try to restrict me from expressing myself in any way that I want?" the airy male lover wonders.*

Libra Moon lovers can enjoy a highly communicative and idealistic relationship with partners who have their Sun, Moon or Rising sign in the broad-minded and intelligent air sign of Aquarius. Each partner symbolizes an element. Understanding that element helps us delve deeper into the real personality of that partner. Air represents a desire to experience life through original self-expression; when air signs speak, the world pays heed. When observed through the Libra Moon vibration, this element seeks to relate on a romantic and intimate, one-on-one level. When filtered through the Aquarius energy, this element desires to relate on a universal, all-inclusive level that breaks the barriers of gender, race, age and disability. Of the two, the latter is more karmically significant.

It might aid the Aquarius type lover if they knew exactly which of the two, distinct types of the Libra Moon personality they have fallen in love with. The first is the *marriage type*, for whom marriage and intimate companionship are a special and positive addition to life (what their lover thinks of them sometimes takes precedence over what they think of themselves). The second type is the *thinker type*; for their self-sufficient nature, romance may hold less of an attraction (this type lives in the world of ideation). They may revel in the chance to spread their intellectual wings and make significant and useful contributions to the immortal world of ideas; they may choose to fall in love with wisdom and learning. The Aquarian type lover may find an easier, pressure-free camaraderie with the thinker type of Libra Moon personality; their emotional circuitry is rather similar.

If you're attractive, out-going, an avid book lover and have a well developed sense of humor, the Libra Moon lover just might give you their number.

Aquarius type lovers want their partners to be unique, more *intellectually sensitive* than emotionally sensitive and as open-minded as they are. Whether married or not, at some point in their lives, both Libra Moon and Aquarius types will want to expand their intellectual and personal horizons. Freedom (as is dictated by the fast-moving and impossible to trap air element) is crucial to their enjoying life. A restrictive lover who is possessive, suspicious and incapable of survival without constant input from a lover will soon find themselves without the support of their airy Aquarian type mate (clingy, needy spouses will find their Aquarian type lovers finding reasons to spend more time outside the house in order to escape that atmosphere). Their search revolves around finding a lover who handles independence as gracefully as they handle deep passion, happily enjoying both and being overly swayed by neither. When we are alone, our level of trust in ourselves rises. A real relationship must leave room for the Aquarius type lover's personal interpretation of it.

Flirtatious Libra Moon lovers may, at some point, want to enjoy the world of partnership and long-term matrimony, but before they are ready for that stage, they will want to be absolutely positive that they have picked the right partner. Aquarian types, while very loving, as a general rule are not too interested in raising a family and being homebound; their focus in life usually lies *outside* of the home sector, where they feel, more progress can be achieved and more universal contributions can be made.

Be that as it may, it should be noted that when an Aquarian type lover willingly chooses to pursue the avenue of marriage or raising a family, they will do it with more sincerity and devotion than other signs. Their fixity (Aquarius is a fixed sign) will cause them to ensure that promises are honored. But is it crucial for them to reach those conclusions on their own, without being poked or prodded by an impatient lover. Most Aquarian types make sympathetic parents; they will lean toward treating their children as equals and not as though they were weaker than them; they will make little best friends out of their children and reach out to them by showering them with the gift of freedom instead of rigidly controlling their every act. Egalitarian and easy to approach, an Aquarian type mom will be able to get down to the level of her children and show a real interest in their point of view, which helps bolster their self-esteem.

As a relationship-oriented sign, most Libra Moon lovers are usually more invested in nurturing romantic involvements than the concept of childrearing (Lady Venus often makes a better wife than a nanny). A clear purpose must guide this relationship, something profound and larger than themselves must connect them. Intellectually well matched, both partners will be supportive and slightly more tolerant of each other than other signs. Finances will have to be watched as neither of them is particularly drawn to the art of coupon clipping. For the Libra Moon lover, money equals fun and pleasure (Lady Venus thinks life is one grand, never-ending party). Aquarian type lovers enjoy passion, but wisely acquiesce that there are a lot of other experiences out there, that are equally as good, even if they are non-sexual.

The thrill of living their life *their way* with minimal interference from a lover, attracts the Aquarian type lover, and the flexible Libra Moon mate will strive to create an environment that is comfortable for their spouse. Aquarians are emotionally cool but get passionate about *an idea* in a millisecond, while diplomatic Libra Moon lovers have the tact and perseverance to keep a good marriage going for decades and succeed where more temperamental lovers may have given up.

It is crucial that the Libra Moon lover watch a legendary tendency to fence-sit or over-accommodate; they must make sure they do not devote more time than is necessary to support their love relationship, but try to let it run on auto-pilot most of the time, they should maintain their independence and develop their own interests (particularly those that are outside their marriage). Aquarian types bring out a desire in the Libra Moon mate to live their life authentically, while a Libra Moon mate can cause their airy Aquarian type lover to desire intimacy and enjoy sensuality on a regular basis. A mating of their minds must occur for both of them before their bodies touch; they are both *air* signs. If this relationship is begun on the footing of friendship and is allowed to blossom slowly, the love between them will burn eternally bright.

Libra Moon vs. Pisces Sun, Moon or Rising Sign
The Air and Water Relationship

Air: "Is my boyfriend open-minded enough and will he appreciate my outspoken side? I need a life mate who will talk to me, communicate with me about everything and not clam up and brood." the airy female partner muses. "Will my girlfriend allow me to do the things I love or will she try to restrict me from truly expressing myself?" the airy male lover wonders.

Water: "Is my boyfriend emotionally stable and wise about our joint finances? Or will debts pile up in the first year of marriage? I need a supportive life-long lover as well as a loving one." the watery female lover thinks to herself. "Will my future

spouse conserve our financial resources or spend unwisely without thought for the
future? I can connect better romantically if I know that my chosen life-mate is
passionate as well as mature and pragmatic." the watery male lover wonders.

Libra Moon lovers can enjoy an emotionally rewarding and sentimental
relationship with partners who have their Sun, Moon or Rising sign in the
sensitive water sign of Pisces. Each partner symbolizes an element. Understanding that element helps us delve deeper into the real personality of that
partner. The air element, when seen through the Libra Moon sign, symbolizes
a desire to gain great personal insight through intimate relationships and more
specifically, marriage. The water element, when observed through the sign of
Pisces, needs to create a comfortable and rock-solid environment within which
human emotions can be expressed without judgment or fear, and compassion
can be expressed with the surety of quick reciprocity.

If the Pisces type lover could decipher as to which of the two, distinct Libra
Moon personalities they are feeling drawn toward, it might help them speak
each other's emotional language more easily. The most common type of Libra
Moon energy is the *marriage type*, for whom relationships may take on an
inordinately influential role in life, while the second is the *thinker type*, for
whom friendships and select intellectual involvements are a more comfortable
choice than marriage. The Pisces type mate may find maximum compatibility
with the romance-seeking, first type of Libra Moon persona as they will both
be on the same page in life with regard to most topics.

Libra Moon lovers look for a mate who is attractive, very communicative and
does not resort to secrecy, brooding or moodiness. Pisces type lovers are gregarious when in a certain mood and can attract the Libra Moon lover with
their physical beauty as well as their easily adaptable personality; even if they
have nothing in common, they both will still find ways to be together. The
emphasis in this relationship will be on frequently changing moods and
dreams (think of the oceans, they are never still), which lies in the domain of
Neptune. The Libra Moon lover is also affected by moods; but not to the deep
extent that watery Pisces is. The Pisces type lover experiences life and all its
complexities on a very psychologically deep level.

Some people with Pisces placed prominently in their natal charts will occasionally suffer from low self-esteem due to the influence of Neptune. Neptune
causes doubt to surface in the delicate and impressionable Pisces psyche, causing them to reach out to more domineering lovers who may be more confident
than them. Therefore, the Libra Moon partner will have to help bolster their

water sign lover's self-confidence. Venus-ruled, Libra Moon mates can have a significant effect on how their lover views themselves, so any effect should be molded into a positive one.

This is a couple that thrives on textbook romance, the ancient ideal of true love and a genuine sentimentality. If the Pisces type lover can grant their Libra Moon partner a lot of attention (verbal and physical) as well as freedom (Libra is an air sign), and if they can grant their Pisces type mate a lot of attention and sympathy, this will be a truly symbiotic relationship. The Piscean essence is poetic and alluring but due to a need for acceptance and regular emotional reinforcement from stronger personalities, they will have to clarify their needs in order to keep from giving up too much of their self-will when in love. Libra is cardinal and Pisces is mutable in quality; the Libra Moon lover may try to guide and the Pisces type lover may trustingly follow if their heart is involved, therefore, a careful, well-tested choice of partner is in order.

Being around a Libra Moon lover pushes Pisces types into becoming more focused on projects and begin to tap into their own sense of confidence. Pisces types help their Libra Moon lover with getting back in touch with their emotional, sensitive and dreamy side. Both partners would do well to remind each other that they must build a solid foundation first: one of friendship and most importantly, of raw honesty. Communications problems should be dealt with by being doubly clear in communicating what they both want, instead of hoping their mate will read their mind.

The Pisces type partner must watch out for a tendency toward obsession, which could be unhealthy for them if they meet up with a deceptive lover who may use them or their financial resources and never supply the attention and love they really need. Neptune rules the sign of Pisces, and while it symbolizes oceanic compassion and a natural intuition, it can also be curiously blind to the many red flags that pop up around them when a manipulative lover manages to win their confidence. Emotional moderation and a healthy sense of skepticism will prove therapeutic, as will learning the art of living alone without support, at least for short periods of time. Pisces types may become too dependent on lovers for attention and input, which could deny them that vital self-confidence that will pull them through when those mysterious, Neptunian mood-cycles descend upon their hearts. Each of these lovers supports the other selflessly and if good communication skills are learnt and effectuated early on, this could be a great relationship.

Chapter 20

The Scorpio Moon Sign Lover

Scorpio Moon vs. Aries Sun, Moon or Rising Sign
The Water and Fire Relationship

Water: "Is my boyfriend emotionally stable and wise about our joint finances? Or will debts pile up in the first year of marriage? I need a supportive life-long lover as well as a loving one." the watery female lover thinks to herself. "Will my future spouse conserve our financial resources or spend unwisely without thought for the future? I can connect better romantically if I know that my chosen life-mate is passionate as well as mature and pragmatic." the watery male lover wonders.

Fire: "I need romance and passion to really enjoy my relationship. Will my boyfriend be a faithful mate for life?" the fiery female partner wonders. "I want an active and freedom-loving partner. Will my girlfriend understand my need for true freedom in life or be too controlling of my actions and behavior?" the fiery male lover thinks to himself.

Scorpio Moon lovers can enjoy an emotionally rewarding and deeply senti- mental relationship with partners who have their Sun, Moon or Rising sign in the openhearted fire sign of Aries. Each partner symbolizes an element. Understanding that element helps us delve deeper into the real personality of that partner. The fire element represents a passionate approach to life where a desire for an exquisite adventure often results in an exquisite learning; that learning is then used to fully embrace the raw, naturalness of life. Water rep- resents a desire to use the purity of emotion to experience human relationships at a deep and subtle level, and then actively fortify those connections so that they can last a lifetime. Elementally, water and fire are compatible, but adjust- ments have to be made for a full chance at success.

The Scorpio Moon personality is divided into two, specific personality types. The first type is the self-controlled, *ambitious type* and the second type is the emotionally open, *passionate type*. The first type places professional prestige over all else while the second type places love relationships, close friendships, a happy, stable marriage above all else. Both types are private, secretive and dominant; they fall into the role of relationship manager very easily and usually, voluntarily.

The enigmatic Scorpio Moon sign is deep, emotional and thrives on stability while Aries type lovers need regular doses of heart-pumping excitement and stimulation. Both are capable of great and lasting love. The Scorpio Moon essence brings out a protective tenderness in the Aries type lover, while the Aries energy causes the usually suspicious and careful Scorpio Moon mate to lay down that ever present guard and be more trusting and openhearted.

The sign of Aries is ruled by Mars, and Pluto rules Scorpio. When the forces of Pluto and Mars match up in the field of love, we can safely assume that it will be an emotionally moving (sometimes explosive) and memorable relationship for both partners. Pluto is connected to the breakdown of belief systems that serve no purpose so that a new, better system can take its place for the benefit of all; super-detective Pluto helps zero in and test the true intentions of people. Protector Mars is associated with initiating change and causing people to pay attention to any injustice that harms more than it helps. Both these planetary energies are temperamentally vast and their volatility must be handled very carefully.

In relationships, Mars-ruled, Aries type partners will want to be free of restrictions and will actively reject every form of control, even from a loved one. Pluto-ruled, Scorpio Moon partners want their lovers to trust them when they make high-impact decisions for them, and may sometimes even make those decisions without consulting their free-spirited Aries type partners. One sign externalizes every thought, feeling and impulse, while the other (the Scorpio Moon) fiercely *internalizes* everything. Needless to say, tempers could flare and accusations could fly if wires get crossed. If this occurs too often, one or both of these passionate but opinionated lovers may decide to part ways, saying that the other is too emotional for them to handle. This will be an intense relationship and its true nature will reveal itself after many years of living together and adapting to each other.

Most Scorpio Moon mates are people who personify the influence of the planet Pluto as well as the energy of the transient Moon. They have a firm control over their emotions as well as an incredible sense of persistence. This means that we are dealing with a lover who is both emotionally powerful as well as wise enough to be aware of it. When in love, the world completely changes for this Moon sign and without a doubt, they will end up changing their partner's life forever as well. If their lover takes love and commitment lightly, they won't after they experience the educating influence of this personality. If they do take love seriously, they will find that they have met a soul mate of sorts in their intense and loving Scorpio Moon mate.

The Scorpio Moon lover is devoted and demands total loyalty, which Aries type partners can supply if appealed to in the right way – with love and sensitivity. The Aries type lover must learn to approach the sensitive Scorpio Moon heart carefully, while the Scorpio Moon lover must try to supply their fiery lover with enough freedom for them to feel comfortable. Secretly, Aries types may yearn for the approval of their mates. The only weak spot is that occasionally, due to a faulty sense of timing, both are capable of saying the wrong thing to each other, without meaning a single word of it. Aries types forgive easily but the Scorpio Moon partner may have trouble offering the olive branch, at least until the storms in their heart have subsided. Trust is everything to them.

Problems tend to roll right over the typical, jolly Aries type lover, who has a more rough-and-tumble philosophy about life. For the Scorpio Moon lover, on the other hand, problems take hold and resentments get seeded deep in their psyche (if an injustice has been inflicted, it will, sooner or later, be evaluated and addressed, it may not be avenged, but it *will* be addressed) which is why it is important to treat them with respect and kindness from the very beginning, while the slate is clean and you have their friendship.

How does one handle the moods of a Scorpio Moon lover? The first thing to understand is that we are not dealing with an average lover with transparent emotions. A careful effort will have to be made to bond with them, where distance and closeness will have to intermingle beautifully. Give them a lot of emotional space and never barrage them with questions. Never try to pry out their secrets but let them tell you what they are. Your love should feel like a protection to them, instead of an intrusion. Watch the signals they give out, because they will give out clear signs that mirror the condition of their hearts.

Pure, emotional energy is the Scorpio Moon lover's rocket fuel, and they are unable to view life in a casual manner. Aries types find people who take life too seriously very stifling and usually this difference will rear its ugly head when the management of finances is being discussed. While sexual compatibility will stabilize them, how each partner spends money will be a topic of discussion. The Aries energy is not money-minded or too focused, in most cases, on saving up or preparing that nest egg. While watery Scorpio Moon partners cannot rest knowing that they have just given their credit card to a spendthrift lover who has just pulled out of the drive way with a three page shopping list and a big, fire sign smile on their face.

The Scorpio Moon sign is a financial sign and judges partners not only on how they look and how they manage emotions, but also on how careful they are with *their* cash. This relationship can last if Aries types can be open to being introduced to the deeper, more permanent aspects of love and intimacy, something that they may have always wondered about but never actually experienced, while Scorpio Moon mates can learn to tone down their slightly possessive nature and subconscious urge to control, and allow their Aries type lover enough freedom to find their comfort zone within the relationship. The Aries type mate is like a boomerang, if you set them free, they come flying back every time. They bring out the kid in the usually serious Scorpio Moon lover, while the Scorpio Moon lover protects and helps Aries mature quickly in the ways of the world. Aries energizes while the Scorpio Moon lover stabilizes this love story. This is a loyal combination.

Scorpio Moon vs. Taurus Sun, Moon or Rising Sign
The Water and Earth Relationship

Water: "Is my boyfriend emotionally stable and wise about our joint finances? Or will debts pile up in the first year of marriage? I need a supportive life-long lover as well as a loving one." the watery female lover thinks to herself. "Will my future spouse conserve our financial resources or spend unwisely without thought for the future? I can connect better romantically if I know that my chosen life-mate is passionate as well as mature and pragmatic." the watery male lover wonders.

Earth: "Does my boyfriend manage his finances maturely or will I end up paying his bills and supporting him? I need stability and true commitment before I can enjoy the romance between us." the earthy female thinks to herself. "Will my future wife spend my hard earned cash on frivolous items at the mall or be wise enough to save up for our retirement?" the earthy male lover wonders.

Scorpio Moon lovers can enjoy a wonderful and deeply fulfilling relationship with partners who have their Sun, Moon or Rising sign in the creative earth sign of Taurus. The pull here will be one of marriage as these signs are polarized. Both are alike but also dissimilar in their own way. Each partner symbolizes an element. Understanding that element helps us delve deeper into the real personality of that partner. Earth represents an unmatched stability and reliability: earth is a faith in love and an undying dedication to a relationship. Water represents an emotional purity as well as a soft and inviting sensuality. Elementally, water and earth are quite compatible.

The Scorpio Moon personality is divided into two, specific personality types; knowing which one we're dealing with can affect our approach greatly. The first type is the *ambitious type* and the second type is the *passionate type*. The first type lives for professional successes and is assertive, while the second type is family-oriented and very tuned in to securing their closest love relationships by almost constantly tending to it. Both types will want to direct the path of their relationships in a protective capacity.

The sign of Taurus is ruled by Venus, and Pluto rules the Scorpio Moon lover. When the power of the planets Pluto and Venus match up in the field of love, we can safely assume that it will be a memorable, perhaps emotionally intense relationship for both partners. Somber Pluto helps effervescent Venus mature, while Venus helps romance the ever-serious Pluto (even Pluto deserves to let his hair down and have some fun, and Lady Venus is just the party animal to help him do it!). Pluto creates opportunities in a relationship for the raw truth to be told and accepted, no matter what the cost. Pluto rebuilds from the ground up, and needs to begin that process by first destroying the shaky, crumbling foundations of a relationship or thought system.

Pluto's formidable power within human love relationships is seen when the Scorpio Moon lover makes such a great impact on a mate, that their lover has to adopt and put into motion certain far reaching changes in their life in order to keep the love of the Scorpio Moon lover. Bubbly Venus is associated with initiating relationships between people and bringing their artistic and aesthetic sides to life. Pluto moves slower than Venus in the heavens, which means that Pluto has precedence over flirtatious Venus. Clearly, we can see who will have the upper, more dominant hand in this relationship.

In relationships, Venus-ruled, Taurus partners will want to be free to decide things on their own timetable, and will react negatively to any enforced form of control, even if a loved one is involved with exerting that control. Pluto-ruled, Scorpio Moon partners expect their lovers to trust them and will usually take on the role of financial analyst and banker in the relationship (Scorpio is a financial sign), something they are wonderfully suited to. Taurus is also a financial sign and will be deeply interested in the monetary aspects of merging their lifestyle with another, and may also want an equal say in how money is handled. Both signs are sensitive to every thought, feeling and nuance, and tend to fiercely internalize every emotion, magnifying the effect of each a hundred times over. This heightens passion but may also magnify pain. Needless to say, maturity and constant balance are needed to make this relationship a successful and *equal* one. This intense relationship will reveal its true nature after many years of experiencing and adapting to one another.

Most Scorpio Moon mates look far into the future when marriage is on the table. Will their spouse be monogamous and true? Do they have a wandering eye? Are they calm in a crisis or do they go to pieces and mismanage household funds? Obsession on part of the Scorpio Moon lover must be monitored; in their need to help a weak lover, they might give more attention or love than is needed, only to have that person walk out of their life after they've found the stability they wanted. The tender-hearted Scorpio Moon person must wisely look for telling signs before they go too far in playing protector to anyone. The Taurus type lover, on the other hand, must learn to avoid over-depending on their mate for support, while the Scorpio Moon lover must foster independence in their mate instead of assuming too much control, even if it is of a beneficial variety.

When the seventh astrological sector comes into play, there will be a desire to merge destinies on a legal level. Taurus types are stable and emotional, and may desire marriage but only when the most compatible person comes along. Scorpio Moon lovers look for a companion who understands their approach to life and won't cause too many needless changes in their life. Taurus types help neutralize the explosiveness of the Scorpio Moon lover's emotions and aid them in adhering to moderation in all things.

The proper management and use of money is crucial to the growth of trust between these two lovers, so if they're both on the same page about that, a majority of their problems will disappear. Taurus type partners are nature lovers and love spending time in nature, and their Scorpio Moon partner will know exactly why they need this rejuvenation. This will be a close and long-term union because neither will carelessly destroy something that takes so much out them emotionally to build. The only problems between them may circle around the Taurus type lover's slowness in giving the go ahead for certain projects and the Scorpio Moon lover's tendency to worry and become a tad too intense about everyday matters that are better handled in a light-hearted vein. The secret to their success is to agree to place each other above all else in the world. This combination can last forever as these two signs share the rare soul mate energy.

Scorpio Moon vs. Gemini Sun, Moon or Rising Sign
The Water and Air Relationship

Water: "Is my boyfriend emotionally stable and wise about our joint finances? Or will debts pile up in the first year of marriage? I need a supportive life-long lover as well as a loving one." the watery female lover thinks to herself. "Will my future spouse conserve our financial resources or spend unwisely without thought for the future? I can connect better romantically if I know that my chosen life-mate is passionate as well as mature and pragmatic." the watery male lover wonders.

Air: "Is my boyfriend open-minded enough and will he appreciate my outspoken side? I need a life mate who will talk to me, communicate with me about every-thing and not clam up and brood." the airy female partner muses. "Will my girlfriend allow me to do the things I love or will she try to restrict me from truly expressing myself?" the airy male lover wonders.

Scorpio Moon lovers can enjoy a stimulating and rewarding relationship with partners who have their Sun, Moon or Rising sign in the expressive air sign of Gemini. Each partner symbolizes an element. Understanding that element helps us delve deeper into the real personality of that partner. The element of air represents a desire to elevate self-expression, especially within close relationships, so that fear and secrecy are eliminated. Water represents a need to purify relationships by giving full reign to human emotions; extreme emotions are not to be feared but used to cleanse our hearts of negativity. Ele-mentally, air and water are quite compatible and can have a symbiotic rela-tionship if they make even the smallest personality adjustments.

The Scorpio Moon personality is divided into two, specific personality types. The first type is the *ambitious type* and the second type is the *passionate type*. The first type needs to achieve every success at work and is very ambitious, while the second type will draw their true strength from their marriages, fam-ilies and close friendships. Both are dominant by temperament and will have a strong desire to have their relationship go exactly where they want it to go. Both these types will usually attract passive lovers who will seek out their pro-tection and guidance.

Scorpio Moon mates function under the influence of Pluto, while Gemini type partners are governed by the energy of Mercury. Pluto symbolizes the act of transforming close relationships so that each partner's motivations and desires are clearly observed. Mercury represents the need to sort through, understand and translate many varied forms of information so that people can be educated about the world's problems. Pluto re-creates and revitalizes, while Mercury explains and analyzes. When these two planets join forces, the effects of this unique astrological merger will be evident in the Scorpio Moon/Gemini Sun, Moon or Rising sign relationship.

The average Gemini type female might say, *"My Scorpio Moon boyfriend is so intense, sometimes when he gets into one of those moods, he won't even acknowledge that I'm in the room. He just sits there all serious and seems lost in his world. How do I bring him out of it? I feel like I'm going crazy if he doesn't talk to me."* Gemini type lovers thrive with communicative, sprightly and engaging partners who are eager to talk about and discuss any problem together. Their ultimate choice will be someone who is emotionally flexible and does not take things too seriously. They love partners who are wise but also funny and can be their best friend *first* and lover second.

The stoic Scorpio Moon lover finds silence incredibly therapeutic and needs time and space to clarify their feelings independently. They will reject any help if it is offered at the wrong time, and it would be wise to not approach them when they're feeling moody. The Gemini type lover's first reaction will be to *talk* their mate out of their sadness but that may not work unless the Scorpio Moon lover is ready to share the questions that haunt their heart.

Scorpio Moon lovers are intense and take relationships and love very seriously: they're looking for a life mate who is mature and emotionally balanced; while fun-loving Gemini type lovers inevitably need an enormous degree of unrestricted freedom in their relationships, so that they can do to their relationships what they constantly do with themselves: which is re-invent, improve and restructure it. This involves change, which the Scorpio Moon lover, who is fixed in habit, may not be comfortable with. *"Change is great and welcome if it serves an important purpose. When change is used to improve, it's useful, but changes due to boredom and restlessness are pure folly, not to mention a total waste of time."* the Scorpio Moon lover says. The emotional Scorpio Moon lover will hold carefree and clever Gemini types to every promise they make and carefully test them to see if they are really as involved in their love relationship as they say they are. Gemini types are changeable but highly motivating and charismatic personalities. And it is that changeable part that their water sign lover may have a problem adapting to.

Scorpio Moon lovers look for a stalwart and reliable lover who can weather life's sudden storms with them and never even dream of deserting them. The rougher the seas of life get, the more closely they will stick by their chosen soul mate. And while fun-loving Gemini types understand that well, they may display a less intense but equally genuine way of expressing their love. Scorpio Moon lovers are super-emotional and sensitive to every change and nuance in an evolving relationship. Gemini type partners find people who take problems too seriously very tiresome, *"Life is tricky as it is, why make things worse by making a big deal out of every failure or insult?"* the Gemini type lover may reason. They make a valid point, and it should be noted that there is no one better qualified to help the Scorpio Moon lover emerge out of a blue spell than the bubbly, effervescent Gemini type life-mate. Their exquisite sense of humor may prove to be a balm that Scorpio Moon lovers will begin to count on, the closer and older they get.

While sexual compatibility will be a great stabilizer for them, how each partner spends money will be the deal-breaker. When it comes to building a nest egg or financial safety cushion, the happy-go-lucky Gemini type mate would do well to heed the advice of their watery lover. As a financial sign, Scorpio Moon lovers will relax more readily if they know that their mate shares their views on money management and investment. When it comes to self-expression, it should be noted that Scorpio Moon mates are easily bruised when words are used rashly, while Gemini type lovers have a need to always express everything very clearly and frequently. A little diplomacy on part of the verbally impulsive Gemini type mate will go a long way to soothe the easily ruffled nerves of their Scorpio Moon lover.

A-joke-a-minute, vibrant Gemini type lovers can add a much needed touch of lighthearted fun to their lover's lives. If the Scorpio Moon lover can learn to overcome their occasional possessiveness and allow their Gemini type lover enough personal freedom so that they can create, nurture and enjoy their own interests in life, this relationship last and flourish. The Gemini type mate must be granted the freedom to spend time with their own, exclusive set of friends, work on personal projects and decipher their unique path in life; they will be happier and more balanced to be around if their mate grants them this release from daily routine. Each must supply what the other needs unconditionally. If this occurs, this couple will be celebrating their golden anniversary while others are still playing the dating game!

Scorpio Moon vs. Cancer Sun, Moon or Rising Sign
The Water and Water Relationship

Water: "Is my boyfriend emotionally stable and wise about our joint finances? Or

will debts pile up in the first year of marriage? I need a supportive life-long lover
as well as a loving one." the watery female lover thinks to herself. "Will my future
spouse conserve our financial resources or spend unwisely without thought for the
future? I can connect better romantically if I know that my chosen life-mate is
passionate as well as mature and pragmatic." the watery male lover wonders.

Scorpio Moon lovers can enjoy a wonderful and meaningful relationship with partners who have their Sun, Moon or Rising sign in the intuitive water sign of Cancer. A double dose of watery energy permeates this combination, which means that one of these two lovers will have to be the stabilizing force in this relationship so that it thrives and lasts for a lifetime. Both are alike but also dissimilar in their own way.

Each partner symbolizes an element. Understanding that element helps us delve deeper into the real personality of that partner. Water represents a desire to use the purifying tendencies of human emotions to heal and fortify important love relationships. Water, through the Scorpio Moon sign, empowers and cleanses, while through the sign of Cancer, it protects and creates the most ideal conditions for emotional nesting. Pour two glasses of water into a pitcher and we will not be able to tell where one begins and the other ends, their energies will have mingled seamlessly. While this sympathetic bonding is good, water, when threatened, betrayed or hurt, will freeze up and become a solid block of ice. Such emotional withdrawal can seriously damage a double water relationship.

The only way to change this is to heat (provide attention and end further neglect of their delicate psyche) that block of ice into slowly melting. The emphasis should be on the word *slow*. Watery Moon signs are generally suspicious about instantly made promises and no follow through to back up what was said. Gradually, the frozen energy of ice changes into the fluidic, forgiving quality of water, the most emotional element of all. Balancing the attributes of this mysterious element is key.

The Scorpio Moon personality is divided into two, specific personality types. The first type is the *ambitious type* and the second type is the *passionate type*. The first type will find great fulfillment through career successes and peer adulation; power seems to follow them around sometimes, while the second type needs to create a firm foundation in life so that their primary relationships can stand the test of time. Both types are private, secretive and dominant; they fall into the role of caretaker very easily and usually, voluntarily.

Cancer types are sensitive and emotional, and seek out self-confident, often dominant lovers who can anchor them in life; their lovers must provide security, stability and financial protection. Scorpio Moon mates will enjoy an easy camaraderie with them because both of them will sense that they share many common, water-sign type, life goals. What are those goals? They may revolve around building a firm foundation of trust before love enters the picture. There may be a desire to marry and start a family, as well as actively find ways to financially support the family. Family ties will mean a lot to this devoted couple. Pluto, through the Scorpio Moon lover, will demand monogamy (powerful Pluto *never* shares his lovers) and generally, Cancer type lovers won't have a problem with sexual exclusivity, as long as all their promises are kept.

Both the Scorpio Moon energy and the watery Cancer type lover worry about the proper management and use of money and resources, so if they're both on the same page about that, ninety percent of their problems will disappear. Cancer types, whether male or female, will have a calming influence on the volatile emotions of the Scorpio Moon lover. Since their Moon sign is Scorpio, the traces of both Pluto and the Moon will be found in their emotional make-up. That indicates that not only is the Scorpio Moon lover emotional from the Scorpio side, it is also sensitive due to the effects of the ultra-emotional Moon. Moderation in reactions and feelings is extremely important in order to keep the Scorpio Moon person from helplessly flowing in and out on the fluctuating tides of these two, highly sensitive planetary bodies.

The Cancer type love thrives best in relationships where their mate openly admires them, exults in their success and freely shares their innermost thoughts with them. They may need to know on a fairly regular level if their partner loves them and will expect some verbal assurances at the very least. The Scorpio Moon lover, if caught undergoing a moody spell, may not be able to give them this. The Scorpio Moon lover, if typical of this Moon sign, will also be keenly aware of how much influence they have over their sympathetic and acceptance-seeking Cancer type mate. This is when the real acid test of their relationship begins. The Scorpio Moon lover must not, under any circumstances, cut off verbal contact with their Cancer type lover. If they do, it will create an unbearable confusion in their sensitive lover's hearts. The sign of Scorpio sometimes tends to use control in order to influence people or the outcome of certain events. They must refrain from doing so when it comes to interacting with their trusting, Cancer type mate; this is crucial to emotional bridge building.

Neither one of them has transparent emotions and the natural inclination of these two water signs will be to alternate between reaching out for immediate support when depressed or shunning it until they feel like accepting it. Cancer types are extraordinarily intuitive and will have no trouble reading the signals their Scorpio Moon lover gives off. As time goes by, the longer they remain in love, their minds and bodies will get more adjusted to the emotional rhythms of their hearts.

For best results, the Scorpio Moon lover must learn to take a more logical view of life, which will also help their loving Cancer type mate, who may try to emulate them in an effort to feel closer to them. Both of these signs tend to let pressures build and fester, especially if there are any unexpressed feelings from the past. A secure home environment or a permanent home base to function out of will be crucial for both lovers, especially for the Cancer type lover for whom the home symbolizes every security and happiness. This will be a close and long-term union and if they can make sure that their suspicions, fears and tempers remain under control, their bond will grow deeper. They're both emotionally vibrant but too much of that could create temperaments that are too sensitive to appreciate the ballet of opposites that is human relationships. Both must promise to place each other above monetary benefit, above other members of the family and friends. This sense of loyalty is crucial for them to build trust. If they could bring out each other's light-hearted side more often, it could help solidify the connection. This is a highly devoted pair.

Scorpio Moon vs. Leo Sun, Moon or Rising Sign
The Water and Fire Relationship

Water: "Is my boyfriend emotionally stable and wise about our joint finances? Or will debts pile up in the first year of marriage? I need a supportive life-long lover as well as a loving one." the watery female lover thinks to herself. "Will my future spouse conserve our financial resources or spend unwisely without thought for the future? I can connect better romantically if I know that my chosen life-mate is passionate as well as mature and pragmatic." the watery male lover wonders.

Fire: "I need romance and passion to really enjoy my relationship. Will my boyfriend be a faithful mate for life?" the fiery female partner wonders. "I want an active and freedom-loving partner. Will my girlfriend understand my need for true freedom in life or be too controlling of what I want to do in life?" the fiery male lover thinks to himself.

Scorpio Moon lovers can enjoy an intense and highly successful relationship with partners who have their Sun, Moon or Rising sign in the sweetly romantic fire sign of Leo. Both these signs are fixed by temperament and intensely emotional in their own ways. Each partner symbolizes an element. Understanding that element helps us delve deeper into the real personality of that partner. Fire represents a burning passion and a need to feel the pulse of life through adventure, excitement and pushing one's physical and emotional limits. Water represents an emotional purity as well as a soft and inviting sensuality; this element desires to feel the power of emotion within close relationships and then be strengthened by that power.

The Scorpio Moon personality is divided into two, specific personality types. The first type is the *ambitious type* and the second type is the *passionate type*. The first, ambitious type devotes their energies toward finding a way to shine in front of the world while the second type derives a large part of their fulfillment in life by stabilizing their family structure and romantic relationships. Both types are dominant in their own way and will fare best with lovers who will not second-guess their motives and can agree to let them take the lead.

Leo type lovers externalize their feelings (they enjoy sharing their fears as well as their plans) while sensitive Scorpio Moon lovers fiercely *internalize* them (the private Scorpio Moon lover might sometimes wish that their mate would be more discreet about giving out too much information to friends). The Scorpio Moon energy is deep, wise and thrives on stability while Leo type lovers need excitement and attention from their lover on a regular basis to feel fulfilled. Both are capable of great devotion. The Scorpio Moon lover needs to trust their mate beyond a shadow of a doubt, while their happy-go-lucky mate might trust too easily, before that trust has been adequately earned. Each could learn priceless life lessons from one another.

The Scorpio Moon essence is deep and focused, demanding nothing less than total loyalty, while Leo type lovers also need that same level of loyalty so that they can fully relax around their lover. Both of them are protective of each other and will be one another's strongest champions. But they must never jump to conclusions about each other's true motives. Leo type lovers forgive easily but the Scorpio Moon essence may have trouble offering the olive branch, at least for a while. The weeds of suspicion must be kept from growing within the Scorpio Moon heart lest they entwine themselves around their closest relationships.

Scorpio Moon partners have to be handled with the utmost care and gentility, while it may take a lot out of the usually carefree Leo type partner, the extra effort will bring them the relationship of a lifetime. This relationship can work out beautifully if the Leo type lover is more verbally tactful around their Scorpio Moon partner, and if the Scorpio Moon lover can grant their fiery and loving Leo type lover more room to make mistakes and more freedom by being more trusting of them. The Scorpio Moon partner must watch out for a tendency toward obsession, which could be unhealthy for them if it brings them closer to a toxic personality who may be capable of deceiving them. Obsession could blind them to red flags that might save them a lot of heartache when dealing with lovers that have not yet been tried and tested. They must also make sure that they don't become overly dependent on their lover for support; Leo types might have trouble carrying the full weight of their relationship on their shoulders alone.

The Leo type mate thrives best with a physically demonstrative lover, they're pretty touchy feely. The Scorpio Moon lover is equally passionate, but may display that passion in private only. To the Leo type mate, passion is fun, but to the Scorpio Moon lover, passion is serious business. The Leo type partner may frequently look for signs of affection from their lover; to them, these are what keep the newness of the relationship going. Remembering emotionally charged days like birthdays, anniversaries and most especially, Valentine's Day will do much to cement the relationship in the eyes of the Leo type mate.

What should the Leo type mate do when they're trying their best to coax their attractive Scorpio Moon lover to accompany them to the movies, and keep reading the do-not-disturb sign on their face? Firstly, they must back off immediately. Scorpio Moon lovers are super-sensitive, but when caught in the middle of one of their deep, Plutonic moods, they are even more sensitive. Impulsive Leo types must grant their lovers the gift of space and privacy; any lover who can do this will win greater favor with the Scorpio Moon lover. Under no circumstances should there be any tantrums or angry speeches by the Leo type mate. The more consideration they show their emotional lovers at this time, the more their lover will be eager to repay the favor when their Leo type mate is feeling blue. True compatibility is a carefully played game of reciprocity.

Control will always be an issue with a Scorpio Moon partner, and the less of it they exert the better for the long-term success of their love. The Leo type lover may unwittingly take on the prominent role of relationship manager early on in the relationship, which may cause problems with power struggles. Each lover should do the other the honor of always asking their opinion; they must not only love one another, but sincerely respect one another as well. One final tip for Leo type lovers who desperately love their watery partner is to never knowingly keep any information from their Scorpio Moon lover. Scorpio is a financial sign and takes money matters and investing seriously, so Leo type lovers may have to watch their spending habits. With a little bit of diplomacy, they have a good chance of making this their best relationship ever.

Scorpio Moon vs. Virgo Sun, Moon or Rising Sign
The Water and Earth Relationship

Water: "Is my boyfriend emotionally stable and wise about our joint finances? Or will debts pile up in the first year of marriage? I need a supportive life-long lover as well as a loving one." the watery female lover thinks to herself. "Will my future spouse conserve our financial resources or spend unwisely without thought for the future? I can connect better romantically if I know that my chosen life-mate is passionate as well as mature and pragmatic." the watery male lover wonders.

Earth: "Does my boyfriend manage his finances maturely or will I end up paying his bills and supporting him? I need stability and true commitment before I can enjoy the romance between us." the earthy female thinks to herself. "Will my future wife spend my hard earned cash on frivolous items at the mall or be wise enough to save up for our retirement?" the earthy male lover wonders.

Scorpio Moon lovers can enjoy an incredibly fulfilling and wholesome relationship with partners who have their Sun, Moon or Rising sign in the devoted earth sign of Virgo. Both are alike but also dissimilar in their own way. Each partner symbolizes an element. Understanding that element helps us delve deeper into the real personality of that partner. Earth represents a desire to give strength and longevity to close relationships, while the water element seeks to use the power of emotions to secure and safeguard those same relationships for the long haul.

The Scorpio Moon personality is divided into two, specific personality types. The first type is the *ambitious type* and the second type is the *passionate type*. The first type is very ambitious and careful in planning out their professional career while the second revels in stable love relationships and is quite maternal. Private, secretive and dominant, both will tend to guide their marriages and relationships subtly in the direction of their choosing. Passive lovers will be most successful with them, as equally assertive ones will challenge their authority often, gradually weakening in the fabric of their love.

Virgo type lovers are privacy-loving, sensitive and highly selective about who gets to enter their life and heart. Scorpio Moon partners look for a lover who is intense like them or at least understands why they get worked up about certain injustices or feel hurt by certain losses in life. Unresolved, painful memories from a long, dead, petrified part of their past may still burden them. Scorpio Moon mates envision life in a dramatically different way than do most people. But observant Virgo types will know exactly how that deep Scorpio Moon heart operates and what they need to feel comfortable and safe. Both are careful signs and their financial issues or spending personalities will be the acid test that will show true, long-term compatibility between them.

Virgo types love spending time improving and fixing things and their Scorpio Moon partner will appreciate this effort. But care must be taken that Virgo types don't become too involved in a permanent "clean up" mission of their relationship; letting it evolve along its natural pattern would also be therapeutic once in a while. This will be a close and long-term union because neither lover will walk away from this relationship without having tried to make it work with every ounce of their being.

The only problems between them may circle around the Virgo type lover's unfailing pragmatism, and the Scorpio Moon lover's tendency to emotionalize unimportant issues when their emotions are about to peak. Virgo type partners are goal-oriented while Scorpio Moon lovers driven by pure emotion, with the result that their decisions are made using their heart or their moods on that particular day. Each should learn to adopt more of the other partner's signature qualities to aid compatibility.

The Scorpio Moon lover's famous possessiveness may be perplexing to the more emotionally detached Virgo type mate. Yes, they too are sensitive, but Pluto's perceptions run far deeper than Mercury's light-hearted approach to life. The Virgo type mate may secretly wonder if their Scorpio Moon lover loves them and what their feelings are regarding permanently settling down together. But the patient Virgo type lover will wait until their partner is ready to share that information with them; Virgo types are not famous for aggressively chasing after love partners demanding to know how they feel about them. This makes the Scorpio Moon lover respect them as equals as well as keeps the Scorpio Moon lover on their toes about what the Virgo type partner is secretly thinking about the state of their union.

That the Scorpio Moon lover is a bit moody is a given. But what can the analytical Virgo type lover do about it? Quite frankly, not much, which is the best course of action. The Scorpio Moon sign needs to be able to process their feelings and then shed that burden in private without prying eyes disturbing their peace. They may look to their Virgo type mate for protection and sustenance, and if the Virgo type lover is in a balanced mood themselves, their interactions will go smoothly. Once in a while, the Virgo type mate may let loose some of those sharp, Mercurial comments, perhaps on a particularly stressful day at work, for example. This outburst may temporarily send the Scorpio Moon lover into a state of emotional withdrawal. Therefore, if the Virgo type mate can curtail giving reign to Mercury when their temper is about to flare, both of them will win.

Too much emotionality or intensity can shake the practical Virgo type partner's focus on getting things done and make them lose their usually rock-solid emotional balance. Which means that Scorpio Moon mates must be more in control of their emotions as well as their suspicions and fears which could spill out into their relationship, while Virgo type partners must help their sensitive lovers understand that sometimes it is best to let the pain of the past stay there and have faith that the future will be fruitful. They can see signs of that already; they found each other, didn't they?

Scorpio Moon vs. Libra Sun, Moon or Rising Sign
The Water and Air Relationship

Water: "*Is my boyfriend emotionally stable and wise about our joint finances? Or will debts pile up in the first year of marriage? I need a supportive life-long lover as well as a loving one.*" *the watery female lover thinks to herself.* "*Will my future spouse conserve our financial resources or spend unwisely without thought for the future? I can connect better romantically if I know that my chosen life-mate is passionate as well as mature and pragmatic.*" *the watery male lover wonders.*

Air: "*Is my boyfriend open-minded enough and will he appreciate my outspoken side? I need a life mate who will talk to me, communicate with me about everything and not clam up and brood.*" *the airy female partner muses.* "*Will my girlfriend allow me to do the things I love or will she try to restrict me from expressing myself the way I want to?*" *the airy male lover wonders.*

S corpio Moon lovers can enjoy an expressive and romantic relationship with partners who have their Sun, Moon or Rising sign in the marriage-minded air sign of Libra. Each partner symbolizes an element. Understanding that element helps us delve deeper into the real personality of that partner. The air element, when perceived through the sign of Libra, represents a desire to cultivate love relationships and use that interactive experience to understand themselves better. Water, when seen through the Moon sign of Scorpio, represents a need to purify love relationships using emotion and intuition, so that there is compatibility on more than one level.

The Scorpio Moon personality is divided into two, specific personality types. The first type is the *ambitious type* and the second type is the *passionate type*. The first type feels most alive when chasing their professional dreams and will need to be with a lover who won't mind them occasionally placing work above togetherness with their partner. The second type will be just the opposite; for them, love relationships will never play second fiddle to ambition. Both types must watch their tendency to assume total control in relationships and cause an imbalance in their marriages.

Scorpio Moon lovers are intense and are generally slow and cautious about jumping into complex relationships until they're sure of the outcome, while Libra type lovers need an enormous degree of reciprocity and commitment in their relationships. The emotional Scorpio Moon lover carefully tests their lover's loyalty as well as hopes that they will be discreet with their secrets; this Moon sign thrives best with lovers who are emotionally more calm than them, can be depended on in any crisis and can be trusted to not leave their side should difficult life problems appear out of nowhere.

The Libra type mate may occasionally suffer from the-grass-is-always-greener mentality. Too much of Libra's legendary fence sitting may pose some problems with building trust. Scorpio Moon lovers will have difficulty placing their heart and emotions in the hands of a mate who may be unable to return the sheer intensity with which the Scorpio Moon mate loves. Superficial lovers need not apply. Social Libra types want to enjoy life, take in as much fun as is allowed, and find people who take life too seriously very draining. It is a classic clash between the stability-minded watery Moon sign and the freedom-loving air sign.

The different ways in which each sign manages finances may cause some turbulence; Libra may not be as financially frugal as the Scorpio Moon lover. The pleasure-seeking and fun-loving Libra type essence is not focused, in most cases, on saving up for that nest egg, at least when younger. To them, money is a tool to use toward instant happiness, while cautious Scorpio Moon partners need to know that they can trust their lover with their hard earned paycheck. To them, money is a tool to use toward creating a solid, financial security blanket. Scorpio is a financial sign and this sign judges partners not only on how they look and how they manage their most volatile emotions, but also on how careful they are with *their* cash and assets. Both of them should consult each other before making big purchases; the more often they show each other this courtesy, the more the money demon will stay away from disrupting this love story (money issues sadly lie at the heart of many lovers separating).

Obsession may play a big, if sometimes negative role in the Scorpio Moon lover's life. There will be some lovers who will be worth the attention and sacrifices of the Scorpio Moon mate, while others will promptly leave after shattering their sense of trust, which will have a big effect on how future lovers are treated. Scorpio Moon lovers are also easily hurt when words are used carelessly; little things cut them to the core. This relationship can last if Libra types can be open to being more serious about life and tone down the romantic risks they take. Libra types must try to understand their intense lover's fears and always approach them with respect and kindness. While Scorpio Moon mates must try to lessen the amount of control they exert, even unwittingly, on their lover, whom they may have a marked tendency to protect and guide. Libra types mature under the influence of the responsible Scorpio Moon vibration, while they in turn will feel lighter in spirit when their air sign lover is around. This is a great match.

Scorpio Moon vs. Scorpio Sun, Moon or Rising Sign
The Water and Water Relationship

Water: "Is my boyfriend emotionally stable and wise about our joint finances? Or will debts pile up in the first year of marriage? I need a supportive life-long lover as well as a loving one." the watery female lover thinks to herself. "Will my future spouse conserve our financial resources or spend unwisely without thought for the future? I can connect better romantically if I know that my chosen life-mate is passionate as well as mature and pragmatic." the watery male lover wonders.

Scorpio Moon lovers can enjoy a revealing and emotionally vibrant relationship with partners who have their Sun, Moon or Rising sign in their own water sign of Scorpio. The attraction between these two watery lovers with similar goals will be strong but some adjustments will have to be made for long-term compatibility. The water element induces emotionality within an already emotional essence, with the result that two things can occur: there may be great empathy between the two Scorpio lovers or they might completely drown their relationship in their own emotionalism.

Once a water sign person shuts down their communication system for any reason, be it due a loss or a betrayal by a lover, there is very little that can be done to make them get over their sense of sadness. From a certain point of view, the falling rain, the great roaring rivers and the mighty oceans are a form of tears. And the oceans never stop weeping. The key to a successful double water (Scorpio Moon/Scorpio Sun, Moon or Rising sign) relationship is for one of the two lovers to become the watchdog of the relationship.

With so much watery energy, one of them must become the rock of moderation that supports and steers the relationship toward a healing balance. Both of these lovers are ardent, loving and very sensitive. Only with the right person will their almost constantly reinforced emotional guard come down. Scorpio Moon lovers look for a partner who is intense like them or at least understands why they react the way they do to certain things in life, and are unable to forget the betrayals and losses of their past. One can't just tell a Scorpio Moon person to snap out of it or get over something that is weighing heavily on their hearts; that would be intensely dishonoring of them. What they should be allowed to do is to take their time, relax and approach their feelings in the way they are most comfortable with (using pure solitude).

The Scorpio Moon personality is divided into two, specific personality types. The first type is the *ambitious type* and the second type is the *passionate type*. The first type devotes their energies toward rising up in the world of professional prestige while the second type derives a large part of their fulfillment in life through love relationships, close friendships, a happy, stable marriage and nurturing their families. The ambitious type must try to pair themselves up with passive partners who will not challenge them and cause disruptions in their marriage, while the passionate type will also enjoy being with a lover who trusts them and will not try to assert their dominance too often.

Scorpio Moon mates naturally respond to life at an intrinsic and meaningful level, which may be too deep for the average human being to comprehend (let alone adapt to), hence the cautious search for a lover who can match their emotional rhythms effectively. But fellow Scorpio types will find it easier than most to blend emotions with that enigmatic Scorpio Moon heart. They will know how it works its magic and what hurts it as well as exhilarates it. Both lovers will have an enormous effect on each other and there will inevitably be monumental changes that they will, knowingly or not, bring into each other's lives; Pluto transforms everything it touches.

The wise Scorpio Moon mate will and should refrain from using power in their closest relationships; it is something that just happens whenever heavy-duty Pluto is involved. But care must be taken so that neither lover takes over more control in the relationship than is necessary. Scorpio Moon lovers, are legendary for that possessiveness of theirs and when a second Scorpio influence is thrown into the mix, both will effectively get to feel what its like when someone tries to steer you one way or the other. Both lovers will be serious about where their love is headed, what shape it will take and what they will have to do to keep their connection from weakening. Pluto will urge both lovers to give a hundred and ten percent of their energies in trying to improve and protect their marriage or relationship. With two people who are actively working on keeping the relationship fresh and potent, any disputes or misunderstandings will dissolve quickly. Once powerful Pluto blesses the double Scorpio relationship, nothing will ever touch it or harm its longevity.

It would be worthwhile, however, to discuss the moods of the Scorpio Moon lover. What is the best way to handle a moody Scorpio Moon mate? The best thing to do would be to watch for signals from them, which will tell us when to approach them and when to give them their space and privacy. The feelings of this Moon sign run incredibly deep (Pluto controls all that is hidden or buried) and until the Scorpio Moon lover is ready to share the content of their hearts, it is best to go on with your life. Any attempts to force the Scorpio Moon mate to reveal how they feel before they are ready will be vigorously resisted.

Scorpio Moon partners love spending time in the wildness of nature (so that the pure wilderness in them is soothed) and their Scorpio type partner will know exactly why they need this emotional refreshment. Both of them will have a close tie to water. This will be a secure and long-term union because neither Scorpio energy lover will carelessly destroy something that takes so much out them emotionally to build. The only problems between them may circle around both their tendencies to see everything through emotional eyes. They're both emotionally sensitive and too much of that could overwhelm them. If they could bring out each other's light-hearted side more often, it could help balance and solidify the connection. This is a loving pair!

Scorpio Moon vs. Sagittarius Sun, Moon or Rising Sign
The Water and Fire Relationship

Water: "Is my boyfriend emotionally stable and wise about our joint finances? Or will debts pile up in the first year of marriage? I need a supportive life-long lover

as well as a loving one." the watery female lover thinks to herself. "Will my future spouse conserve our financial resources or spend unwisely without thought for the future? I can connect better romantically if I know that my chosen life-mate is passionate as well as mature and pragmatic." the watery male lover wonders.

Fire: "I need romance and passion to really enjoy my relationship. Will my boyfriend be a faithful mate for life?" the fiery female partner wonders. "I want an active and freedom-loving partner. Will my girlfriend understand my need for true freedom in life or be too controlling?" the fiery male lover thinks to himself.

Scorpio Moon lovers can enjoy an emotional and purposeful relationship with partners who have their Sun, Moon or Rising sign in the philosophical fire sign of Sagittarius. But subtle personality shifts may have to occur due to how differently each element looks at love and bonding. Each partner symbolizes an element. Understanding that element helps us delve deeper into the real personality of that partner. The fire element represents a need to passionately live life, take risks and then use those risks to gain an elevated perspective of themselves and their experiences. The water element desires to use the depth of emotion and its purity in order to build bridges that can connect the human heart to a superior sense of understanding within relationships.

The Scorpio Moon personality is divided into two, specific personality types. The first type is the *ambitious type* and the second type is the *passionate type*. The first type needs to make their mark on the professional scene and may sometimes choose to place love on the backburner of life, while the second type will always place love relationships, close friendships and their families above all else. Both types are private, secretive and dominant; they fall into the role of caretaker very easily and usually, voluntarily. Dominant lovers may clash with them and they might have to deal with the ugly specter of power struggles, while passive lovers will discover a high degree of compatibility with the Scorpio Moon personality.

Watery Scorpio Moon partners are the personification of intensity and when it comes to love, finding a lover is a serious task; only the very best will do. Cautious and skeptical initially, it will be years before they devote their full trust to another. The expansive Sagittarius mate needs a lover who is passionate, but also displays a certain lightness of spirit, a sense of elasticity in their ability to embrace life's almost always unpredictable course. These two may initially, perhaps, not always want the same things in life: the stable Scorpio

Moon lover may be ready to settle down while the mutable Sagittarius type lover may still need time to make sure they're with the *right* lover. Or the Sagittarius type partner may be interested in tying the knot and the Scorpio Moon lover may need more time to make certain that their choice will stand the test of time, instead of leading them to divorce court (or more terrifying to them, a division of *their* funds, Scorpio is a financial sign).

This relationship can and will survive and even thrive, if both of them can learn to handle each other's fears ahead of time. This will not only bring them closer, but also be instrumental in facilitating a more permanent, fulfilling bond between them. What does the Sagittarius type mate fear? Romance-wise, they fear ending up with a lover who exhibits one persona before marriage and another one after the closeness between them has grown; they privately recoil at having to share their life with a lover who is inflexible, overly emotional, too caught up in the nitty-gritty and fails to see the big picture. The Scorpio Moon lover fears entering into a partnership with someone they have grown to love and more importantly, trust, and then watch that intimacy crumble due to betrayal, deception or emotional dislocation due to an abrupt change of heart. The Sagittarius type lover cannot endure excessive, individuality-dissolving closeness, while the Scorpio Moon partner cannot survive without that very degree of closeness.

Finding out if your Scorpio Moon partner loves you as intensely as you adore them can be a little mysterious and tricky. Issues of control play a big role in any relationship with a Scorpio Moon mate and usually they will fall quite easily into the role of relationship supervisor. If past relationships have bruised the tender Scorpio Moon heart too often, then their present lover will have to fight off that lingering residue of mistrust. This Moon sign may display a characteristic possessiveness when it comes to their money, their children and their lover. Sagittarius types bristle at being controlled, they like to come and go as they see fit; smothering them under the pretense of caring will send them fleeing. On the other hand, this fiery sign must control their sometimes ungovernable temper (Jupiter does everything in a big way) which can temporarily distance and alienate all their supporters; moderation is crucial to keep their closest confidants safely within their circle of trust.

Most Scorpio Moon mates are emotional but can often control the depths to which they can sink. Are they moody? Yes. Can they get out of those deep, dark spells? Absolutely. Can their moods affect their relationship adversely? Only if their chosen lover is immature about their reactions to the complex and magnetic Scorpio Moon persona. At times like that, Scorpio Moon lovers need privacy and space in which to process their feelings. Scorpio Moon folks are self-sufficient and rarely ask for help. They will hope that their lover can be independent as well as close to them according to the requirements of the situation.

This love story can be successful if it begins as a long-term friendship, giving each time to acclimatize themselves to their love at their own emotional timetables. Sagittarius type lovers help their Scorpio Moon soul mates become more emotionally forgiving and infuse them with a classic, Jupiter-style, live-and-let-live ideology, while the Scorpio Moon essence introduces the fiery Sagittarius type lover to the Pluto style notion of seeking out true value in people and situations, as well as learning to relish emotional stability and reliability, something they will search for as they begin to age. Scorpio Moon partners will help the sometimes impatient sign of Sagittarius learn to be more responsible, see projects to their end and conserve more financial resources. This will be a productive union.

Scorpio Moon vs. Capricorn Sun, Moon or Rising Sign
The Water and Earth Relationship

Water: "Is my boyfriend emotionally stable and wise about our joint finances? Or will debts pile up in the first year of marriage? I need a supportive life-long lover as well as a loving one." the watery female lover thinks to herself. "Will my future spouse conserve our financial resources or spend unwisely without thought for the future? I can connect better romantically if I know that my chosen life-mate is passionate as well as mature and pragmatic." the watery male lover wonders.

Earth: "Does my boyfriend manage his finances maturely or will I end up paying his bills and supporting him? I need stability and true commitment before I can enjoy the romance between us." the earthy female thinks to herself. "Will my future wife spend my hard earned cash on frivolous items at the mall or be wise enough to save up for our retirement?" the earthy male lover wonders.

Scorpio Moon lovers can enjoy a highly successful and ambitious relationship with partners who have their Sun, Moon or Rising sign in the success-driven earth sign of Capricorn. Elementally, water and earth have a wonderfully symbiotic relationship. Water needs earth to flow on and receives direction from the geography of the land, while the earth needs water to be fertile and productive. Each feeds a need in the other.

The Scorpio Moon personality is divided into two, specific personality types. The first type is the *ambitious type* and the second type is the *passionate type*. The first type yearns to shine on the professional stage while the second type yearns to find fulfillment through intimacy. Both types must watch a tendency to secretiveness and a desire for control; they will find much happiness with lovers who will not compete with them, but support their every decision.

Sensitive and emotional are the two perfect words to describe the magnetic Scorpio Moon lover, and its hard for them to lower their emotional guard long enough to allow a new mate into their life. They react to the world through purely emotional stimuli, which makes them a sort of super-detective; they usually can hunt out and decipher the secret motives of people with relative ease, while the rest of us still trustingly make mistakes. But Capricorn types will also know a little something about being outwardly cool and poised while experiencing an emotional storm on the inside. Both are careful signs and their handling of their financial issues as a couple will either bring them closer or create unwanted tension between them, usually over the smallest expenditures.

What is the ideal way to handle the moods of a Scorpio Moon lover? This can be summed up in one word: respectfully. There is nothing transparent about their emotions and one must not jump to conclusions about what's bothering them. Distance and closeness will have to intermingle beautifully. Some privacy will prove most healing and they should not be bombarded with the whys and hows of the condition of their hearts – yet. This Moon sign will give out specific signals that will guide their mate as to how to approach them.

This water/earth relationship will signify the merging of the powerful energies of Pluto and Saturn. Pluto (the ruler of Scorpio) and Saturn (the ruler of Capricorn) are intense and focused planets. Their qualities will appear and take root in the Scorpio Moon/Capricorn Sun, Moon or Rising sign relationship. Saturn is serious and somber, and Pluto is deep and profound. Saturn types keep a tight lid on their emotions and can keep them concealed for extended periods of time, which is something Pluto types can also do. When Saturn explodes after years of repression, great changes will manifest themselves, which is something that applies to Pluto as well.

The only difference between these two planets is that Pluto causes things (abusive relationships, for example) to be destroyed so that positive changes can occur, while Saturn leans toward keeping things (such as a stable marriage, for example) from changing. They both understand the value of correct, honorable behavior, especially Saturn, who has been assigned the task of keeping a close eye on the karmic give and take of millions of lives. Pluto shatters and revitalizes while Saturn preserves and fortifies. With two serious energies at work in this relationship, one of these two lovers will have to maintain a sense of fun and ease so that not every situation becomes a life and death issue.

Some Capricorn types suffer from depression or melancholia (Saturn's perceptions of humanity are often painfully deep), and they would find great comfort in their patient and understanding Scorpio Moon mate. Capricorn types must take care to never place their closest relationships in peril by making work their only priority in life. The problems between them may circle around the Capricorn type lover's tendency to place personal ambition over important relationships (ambition can wait but estrangements are incredibly hard to eliminate) or see everything through practical and logical eyes, or the Scorpio Moon lover's tendency to emotionalize when they should have analyzed. If Scorpio Moon mates can employ moderation in their reactions (they feel everything, good or bad, so *very* acutely) and try to let certain painful memories of the past stay in the past instead of letting that pain filter into and sour the present, it will help them tremendously in their relationship.

They're both fiercely ambitious if they want to be, and will generally appreciate a lover who strives to better themselves, and rise up proudly in this competitive world. This combination can last forever if one of them becomes the stable rock of the relationship. They both make stalwart long-term marriage partners. If they could bring out the humor in each other more often, it could help solidify their connection and take some of the pressure off their relationship, helping it recreate itself when the time is right and infusing their lives with joy and the success they both so often seek. The couple that laughs together, stays together.

Scorpio Moon vs. Aquarius Sun, Moon or Rising Sign
The Water and Air Relationship

Water: "Is my boyfriend emotionally stable and wise about our joint finances? Or will debts pile up in the first year of marriage? I need a supportive life-long lover as well as a loving one." the watery female lover thinks to herself. "Will my future spouse conserve our financial resources or spend unwisely without thought for the future? I can connect better romantically if I know that my chosen life-mate is passionate as well as mature and pragmatic." the watery male lover wonders.

Air: "Is my boyfriend open-minded enough and will he appreciate my outspoken side? I need a life mate who will talk to me, communicate with me about everything and not clam up and brood." the airy female partner muses. "Will my girlfriend allow me to do the things I love or will she try to restrict me from expressing myself?" the airy male lover wonders.

Scorpio Moon lovers can enjoy a highly emotional and life-altering relationship with partners who have their Sun, Moon or Rising sign in the free-thinking air sign of Aquarius. This water and air combination can survive if both partners can understand what separates them and what brings them together. Each partner symbolizes an element. Understanding that element helps us delve deeper into the real personality of that partner. The air element, when perceived through the sign of Aquarius, represents a desire to connect people, wisdom and ideas in order to use that ideation to understand themselves better. Freedom of thought and belief are paramount to the air sign mate. Water, when seen through the Moon sign of Scorpio, represents a need to purify love relationships using emotion and intuition, so that there is a profound compatibility on more than one level.

The Scorpio Moon personality is divided into two, specific personality types. The first type is the *ambitious type* and the second type is the *passionate type*. The first type devotes a majority of their energies toward gaining professional power and prestige while the second type will look to the stability and harmony of love relationships for fulfillment in life. Private, secretive and dominant; they fall into the role of caretaker very easily and usually, voluntarily. Therefore they must watch their need to take over control when reacting to the Aquarius type lover, who may not always see the wisdom in that; a true balance of power is paramount to the airy Aquarius type lover.

If you're honest, cultured and passionate, the Scorpio Moon lover will be instantly drawn to you. Charismatic Scorpio Moon lovers are tradition-minded and thrive in a predictable setting; the focus will be on dependability more than experiencing a constant dose of heart-pounding excitement. They are secretive, fixed by nature, self-sufficient and priceless in a crisis. Aquarius types thrive with a very emotionally flexible partner who can grasp (but never try to alter) the exquisite and unique Aquarian life philosophy. Clarifications of personal expectations should occur at the beginning of the relationship due to the vividly different life goals of each sign.

Watery Scorpio Moon lovers are powerful and magnetic individuals but may benefit by learning a few of those legendary Aquarian traits. Ruled by the logical and freedom-loving planet Uranus, the Aquarian type lover places more interest in how their partner is *different* from them, rather than what they have in common. Are you an ordinary, nine-to-fiver or is there something other than your job that defines you? What makes you stand out as rare? The Aquarian type lover wants to be tempted more by the ageless ideas in their partner's mind than their physical allure, which they know can fade with time. Faces wrinkle but profound ideas remain immortal.

This relationship will signify the mingling of the energies of two powerful planetary forces: Pluto and Uranus. When the Scorpio Moon lover demands total commitment and the Aquarius type lover, if unprepared *at that precise time* in their life journey, shuts down their communication system and decides to withdraw, this might be a problem in the making. Pluto (the ruler of Scorpio) expects unquestioned loyalty, while Uranus (the ruler of Aquarius) cannot promise any form of stability, unless it is in an emotional format that they can live with.

This is not to say that Uranus-ruled, Aquarian types cannot commit and be stable and loving life mates, but that their natural inclination will be to shrink from any permanent arrangements where their personal freedom is not specifically guaranteed. Aquarian types do best in relationships where they are allowed the grace to *decide on their own* as to when and how they will tie the knot. They are fixed by nature and habit, which means that if they ever do decide to enter the world of marriage and child-rearing, they will make twice the effort of other signs. Aquarian types make easy to approach and loving parents who will use their parental influence benevolently and infuse their children with a respect for personal freedom and free will.

Scorpio Moon lovers place a high degree of emphasis on passion in a relationship, but it can only fully be expressed if they see no signs of hesitation in their lovers. The Scorpio Moon partner must watch out for a tendency toward obsession, which could debilitate them and blind them to reason. The Aquarian type lover is as logical as their sensuous Scorpio Moon mate is rooted in emotionality. If both of them can use moderation in their reactions (Aquarian types could take certain issues a tad more seriously instead of saying *"Why don't you handle it, honey?"* while the Scorpio Moon lover could take certain issues a little less seriously) it would be a boon to their relationship.

There are definite mood cycles to the Scorpio Moon persona and anyone in love with them will have to figure out a way to react to those moods. The first instinct of the Scorpio Moon lover will be to conceal their feelings from their lover, especially if the relationship is fairly new. As time wears on, their lover will have to handle their moods using a careful mix of being close as well as giving them all the time and space they need to come out of it.

An Aquarian type lover is a one-in-a-million soul mate who will need and expect a certain degree of personal freedom in a relationship or marriage; they will expect to be able to spend time with their *own* set of friends, work on pet projects that may not require their lover and be able to preserve their autonomy to a certain degree within their relationship. Their mate must not take this personally because this freedom will make their Aquarian type lover the happiest. Any lover who tries to force excessive closeness on them will slowly make the Aquarian type lover drift away.

A Scorpio Moon lover thirsts for a partner who is open to unpretentious exchanges of pure, honest emotion, the kind that can eliminate all the barriers that separate two lovers and can change and improve a person forever. Their love rises out of the depths of the powerful passion of transformative Pluto. Therefore any partner who deliberately shuts the Scorpio Moon partner's love out, will soon find that they have abruptly ended the relationship and voluntarily walked away. Emotional gridlock can be avoided if both of them keep talking out grievances instead of hoping they will disappear on their own. If things come to a temporary standstill, one of them will have to break the silence and talk about a truce based on the love that brought them together in the first place, which will always be profoundly strong. These two will change each other for the better.

Scorpio Moon vs. Pisces Sun, Moon or Rising Sign
The Water and Water Relationship

Water: "Is my boyfriend emotionally stable and wise about our joint finances? Or will debts pile up in the first year of marriage? I need a supportive life-long lover as well as a loving one." the watery female lover thinks to herself. "Will my future spouse conserve our financial resources or spend unwisely without thought for the future? I can connect better romantically if I know that my chosen life-mate is passionate as well as mature and pragmatic." the watery male lover wonders.

Scorpio Moon lovers can enjoy a highly fulfilling and spiritually vibrant relationship with partners who have their Sun, Moon or Rising sign in the emotive water sign of Pisces. The Pisces energy is very compatible with the watery Scorpio Moon essence because water flows and merges easily with water, and water signs have an easier time understanding each other's basic life-goals. However, too much water and emotionality can overwhelm a relation-ship and rob it of a firm foundation. Which means that one of them will have to be the rock of the relationship and keep it from becoming overwhelmed by too much emotionalism.

Each partner symbolizes an element. Understanding that element helps us delve deeper into the real personality of that partner. Water represents an emo-tional purity as well as a soft and inviting sensuality. Elementally, water sup-ports water wonderfully. Pour two glasses of water into a pitcher and we will not be able to tell where one begins and the other ends, their energies will have mingled seamlessly. While this sympathetic bonding is good, water, when threatened, betrayed or hurt, will freeze up and become a solid block of ice.

Such emotional withdrawal can seriously damage a double water relationship. The only way to change this is to heat (provide attention and end further neglect of their delicate psyche) that block of ice into slowly melting. The emphasis should be on the word slow. Water signs are generally suspicious about instantly made promises and no follow through to back up what was said. Gradually, the frozen energy of ice changes into the fluidic, forgiving quality of water, the most emotional element of all. Balancing the attributes of this element is key.

The Scorpio Moon personality is divided into two, specific personality types. The first type is the *ambitious type* and the second type is the *passionate type*. The first type needs to steer their life toward professional acclaim while the second type needs to find stability within love relationships to feel at total peace with the world. The Pisces type lover will gravitate toward both the ambitious type and the passionate type of the Scorpio Moon personality, sens-ing somehow that they will be able provide the strength and emotional sanc-tuary that they need in life.

Scorpio Moon lovers require unwavering emotional commitment before they will let their heart blindly immerse itself into the great Piscean oceans of feel-ing and intuition. Pisces types are deeply emotional themselves and need a partner who brings with them the priceless gifts of reason and moderation, someone who can provide a firm and healthy foundation of life on which they can rely. They subconsciously seek out lovers who are more dominant than they are and may try to emulate their strength, but must be careful to not sur-render too much control under the guise of offering someone their love. The Pisces energy brings sensitivity and faith to the sometimes, skeptical Scorpio Moon lover. The Pisces type partner as well as the Scorpio Moon lover must watch out for a tendency toward obsession or addiction to a manipulative lover, which could be unhealthy for them if it brings them closer to anyone who may be capable of deceiving them. Trust should be earned and never delivered on a silver platter to an untested or untried lover who may toss it by the wayside after their needs have been fulfilled. Reason and emotion can co-exist according to the demands of each changing situation.

One of the hardest things to have to do in a relationship with a Scorpio Moon lover is to find out if they love you. If the answer is in the affirmative, the next step is to ascertain how much. The romantic Pisces type lover will want to know every impulse in their lover's heart, they will want to be familiar with every passing feeling and will try to feel as humanly connected to their lover as they possible can. But unless they are truly ready, the Scorpio Moon mate will be Sphinx-like and give no inclination as to how they really feel. This draws lovers even closer to them.

Most Scorpio Moon mates are people who are clearly aware of the impact they have on their lovers and it will be remarkable; Pluto is a powerful influence when its energies play out in love relationships. The more docile of their part-ners may feel tempted to give up all control and let their Scorpio Moon mate take the lead. But this would be a mistake because in many ways, they would only be burdening them more. It is crucial that the Scorpio Moon lover join forces with a partner who will not become too dependent on them for every-thing and is strong enough to help balance out the relationship from time to time. Another, highly important thing to bear in mind is that humor and laughter are extremely necessary in keeping the Scorpio Moon lover in the best emotional form of their lives. The various problems and complications of life are often so draining for them that an active effort must be made to relieve some of the tension they so willingly take upon their shoulders.

The Pisces type lover will pick up those otherwise imperceptible emotional signals from their lover before anyone else (this sign hungers to seek out con-nections to their lover), their oceanic intuitiveness will be what makes the Scorpio Moon lover think that they may realistically be the best choice for them when they want to settle down. Pisces type mates will provide the emo-tional comfort zone that Scorpio Moon lovers need, as well as show them that it is okay to show emotion, as long as one is not placed under its control, because on some levels it cleanses them and makes them stronger, more authentic versions of themselves.

Financially, some Pisces types may be impulsive with finances, and this may pose a problem because Scorpio is a financial sign and most Scorpio Moon folks are very prudent about managing their resources properly, at the right time and in the right way. Scorpio Moon partners could help their sensitive watery partner express their practical side more than their trusting side. On the other hand, the Scorpio Moon mate must control their sometimes, ungovernable Plutonic temper which can temporarily distance all their supporters; moderation in reactions is crucial to keeping their closest confidants closer.

Pisces types must also remember never to withhold any information from their Scorpio Moon lover. If Scorpio Moon mates begin to doubt their partner even a little, that little doubt could spread into a full fledge suspicion and wreck the relationship. Together, this romantic pairing is artistic, loving and will try to make every effort to handle each other's moods with tenderness and respect. This is a good combination if a family is planned. But both must agree to place their love for one another far above all else in this world.

Chapter 21

The Sagittarius Moon Sign Lover

Sagittarius Moon vs. Aries Sun, Moon or Rising Sign
The Fire and Fire Relationship

Fire: "I need romance and passion to really enjoy my relationship. Will my boyfriend be a faithful mate for life?" the fiery female partner wonders. "I want an active and freedom-loving partner. Will my girlfriend understand my need for true freedom in life or be too controlling?" the fiery male lover thinks to himself.

Sagittarius Moon lovers can enjoy a comfortable and romantic relationship with partners who have their Sun, Moon or Rising sign in the passionate fire sign of Aries. Each partner symbolizes an element. Understanding that element helps us delve deeper into the real personality of that partner. Fire represents spiritual purification, a burning passion and an unshakeable optimism. Elementally, fire supports fire beautifully. Toss a few logs into the fireplace on a snowy night and watch that heat morph into a bright, blazing, heart-warming fire; that's the fire energy at its best.

The Sagittarius Moon sign can be separated into two, distinct personality types. Learning to distinguish between them can help the Aries type lover understand the deeper nature of this Moon sign. The first type of Sagittarius Moon personality is the *sage type* while the second is the *adventurer type*. There is a quiet wisdom about the sage type Sagittarius Moon lover; they're wise, tolerant and have a professor-like air to them. Indeed, they may own more tomes than clothes, which is admirable and impressive. The sage type adjusts well to the stability required in a long-term marriage and a life-long friendship between lovers, but will always place intellectual pursuits and personal freedom above all else.

The second type of Sagittarius Moon lover is the adventurer type. This type is delightful and easy to talk to, as well as extremely restless and is happiest while looking danger in the eye. Hungering for adventure and new, exciting relationships, the adventurer type will love to travel and be free of responsibilities that don't resonate with their values. Both these Moon sign types are assertive and will tend to fall easily into the role of relationship manager. Therefore, if the Aries type lover is also aggressive, there might be some clashes over who gets to make the big decisions. However, if the Aries type lover is passive, compliant and non-confrontational, they will be able to fit quite snugly into the hearts of both these Sagittarius Moon personality types.

If you're friendly, open-hearted, generous and a bit of a dare devil, the Sagittarius Moon lover will desire your company. The Sagittarius Moon personality is very similar to the fiery Aries type persona: both tend to seek lovers who can make them laugh and display courage in the face of life's problems. Abundant personal freedom is a non-negotiable factor for the Sagittarius Moon lover. The expansive Sagittarius Moon mate needs a self-sufficient lover who is comfortable with independence and will not overly depend on them for input on every little thing. For philosophical Sagittarius Moon lovers, self-preservation (personal space) in relationships is an incredibly necessary condition for authentic self-understanding. Someone who flows with the natural rhythms of life's inevitable ups and downs, doesn't complain incessantly or exaggerate issues will lift their spirits. As a fire Moon sign, their search is one of finding a lover who can understand the intricate concept of maintaining healthy personal boundaries within the narrow spheres of human passion. This means that they need to be able to freely re-invent and follow their own life path without having to alter its truth too much for a lover whose life agenda may not match theirs.

The only problem this couple might encounter is when there is a mismatch of personal timetables or if distractions occur and one of them feels the other is not focused enough for their love to survive (examples are one partner wanting to finish school while the other wants to settle down, or one wanting to start a family and the other needing more time to adjust to additional responsibilities). Fire signs also have fiery tempers but traditionally, their hearts can 'olive branch' their way through most problems. Both these active and happy-go-lucky signs understand a fundamental truth in life that others may miss; that there is splendor in adventure and depth in risk.

They're both idealists and being more observant of each other's moods and cognizant of each other's unspoken desires could help in getting over potential trouble spots in their relationships. Jumping to conclusions about each other's real desires would be a mistake; clarifying everything as often as possible is recommended. Intellectually bonded and protective of one another, their friendship will never perish, and if both are mature souls and can easily and frequently forgive, their relationship can survive the greatest storms and reach the safety of the shore of old age.

It might help the Aries type lover to understand their relationship through the eyes of the Sagittarius Moon mate. The fiery Sagittarius Moon sign hungers for fresh experiences and rare interactions in life. But when the lunar vibration is felt through Sagittarius, there could also be an imperceptible but powerful emotionality about the Sagittarius Moon partner. It would do their mate a lot of good if they applied themselves and learned to read the signals their partner gives out. Sagittarius Moon lovers may find maximum camaraderie with the ram/lamb Aries personality, because this combination can display strength when needed, and more importantly, never feel the need to compete with them or dominate them.

How do you handle a Sagittarius Moon lover who is in an inky blue mood and does not respond to your best jokes and funniest one-liners? The key is to not try too hard and let them absorb their emotions undisturbed. Space and distance are the Sagittarius Moon lover's best and most reliable friends. They depended on these two friends before their current lover entered their life, and even though their lover may want to speed up their healing and help them come out of their mood quickly, it really is better to let them be, and let them re-adjust their emotional compass themselves. A lover who does not intrude too much and over-extend themselves when assistance is not yet needed, during certain Sagittarian Moon moods, will be most loved by this Moon sign. Neither the Aries type mate nor the Sagittarius Moon lover like to be excessively mothered.

Studying the triggers and fears of each sign might help explain their desires. What does a Sagittarian Moon lover fear? They fear being in a relationship with a lover whose personality or nature completely changes after they have grown close and begins restricting their freedom in order to control or manipulate them for their own gain. What does the Aries type lover fear? They fear having to slow down for their mate and not being able to live their lives exactly the way they want, due to pressure or disapproval from their lover.

Sagittarius Moon lovers help impetuous Aries types to be more emotionally forgiving and infuse them with a Jupiter style, free-flowing approach to life, while the Aries type lover introduces the Sagittarius Moon mate to the idealistic Mars style, *"Let's go do stuff!"* notion of action and achievement. The happy Sagittarius Moon energy needs a lover who is passionate but also *temperamentally large* or accommodating enough to fit in the wide-angle or all-encompassing Sagittarius Moon life theme.

The fiery Sagittarius Moon partner may, at least sometimes, not want some of the same things that an Aries type lover absolutely requires to feel secure. But if timetables match, they will thrive. Both signs depend more on stable friend-ships rather than over-dramatized relationships. If one of them can stabilize their love over time, learn to compromise and practice patience, their love will remain undiminished by the tides of time.

Sagittarius Moon vs. Taurus Sun, Moon or Rising Sign
The Fire and Earth Relationship

Fire: "I need romance and passion to really enjoy my relationship. Will my boyfriend be a faithful mate for life?" the fiery female partner wonders. "I want an active and freedom-loving partner. Will my girlfriend understand my need for true freedom in life or be too controlling?" the fiery male lover thinks to himself.

Earth: "Does my boyfriend manage his finances maturely or will I end up paying his bills and supporting him? I need stability and true commitment before I can enjoy the romance between us." the earthy female thinks to herself. "Will my future wife spend my hard earned cash on frivolous items at the mall or be wise enough to save up for our retirement?" the earthy male lover wonders.

Sagittarius Moon lovers can enjoy an emotionally uplifting and stable rela-tionship with partners who have their Sun, Moon or Rising sign in the strong, silent earth sign of Taurus. But adjustments may have to be made due to how differently each sign looks at love and bonding.

The Sagittarius Moon sign is divided into two different personality types. Knowing which one mirrors their love partner can really clarify things for the Taurus type lover. The first type of Sagittarius Moon personality is the *sage type* while the second is the *adventurer type*. The sage type is mature, has a well-developed intellect and yearns to learn as much about the world, its people, its cultures and perhaps even the different religions of the world as they can. They may admire an attractive lover but may not be too eager to change their whole lives for some light flirtation. If they get married, their chosen life mate (who will have to be equally intellectual by nature) will have to give this Moon sign type their space and independence. This type adjusts rather well to the disci-pline needed to maintain a happy and equality-based marital union.

The second type of Sagittarius Moon lover is the *adventurer type*. This happy-go-lucky type is attracted to adventure like kids to a roller coaster. Risk-taking comes naturally and they will yearn to glean as much stimulation out of life as humanly possible. Travel and education (both ruled by Jupiter) serve an important purpose: they aid them in drawing closer to the meaning of life. The sage type as well as the adventurer type are dominant and strong personalities. Therefore, if the Taurus type lover is equally dominant, there might be some confusion as to who sets the pace and direction of the relationship. An easy-going and accommodating Taurus type lover might be a great match for both these variations of the Sagittarius Moon lover.

Sagittarius Moon lovers are attracted to partners who have a great respect for the outdoors, nature as well as the naturalness of life. Unpretentious Taurus types are particularly drawn toward protecting the natural world and this common love of nature will bind these two lovers together. Taurus types are practical and will look for a lover who is willing to build something permanent and strong with them, much like the earth element that represents them (Taurus is a sensitive earth sign). They *actualize* what their lover envisions.

The expansive Sagittarius Moon partner needs a lover who is passionate but emotionally flexible. The life-needs of the fiery Sagittarius Moon partner may, at least sometimes, not be same as the needs of a Taurus type lover; they both need specific things (seeking excitement for one can be inviting danger to the other) to feel absolutely secure. This relationship still has a great chance at success, despite these two rather disparate energies, because they could use their blooming friendship to analyze each other until they are both sure that they can recognize some of the qualities that are needed to keep their union a close, comfortable one.

The fiery Moon sign of Sagittarius hungers to zoom through life like a super fast spaceship and experience as much of it as possible in a very short amount of time. But when the lunar vibration is felt through Sagittarius, there could also be an unmistakable emotionality about the Sagittarius Moon partner. If their lover could pay a little more attention to the emotional rhythms of this Moon sign and learn to work with their partner's moods, it would smooth the road toward greater trust between them. What should the Taurus type lover do when their lover is in the throes of a particularly blue mood? In two words: absolutely nothing. The key is to not try too hard to help and let them absorb their emotions undisturbed. Privacy, solitude and peace are the key words.

Studying the triggers and fears of each sign in this relationship might help explain their desires. What does a Sagittarian Moon lover fear? They fear being in a relationship with a lover who begins restricting *their* freedom in order to feel more secure themselves, without thought to their undeniable and daily need for total personal freedom. The Sagittarius Moon lover needs to be in a relationship that leaves enough room for their individual interpretation of its significance in their life. What does the Taurus type lover fear? They fear the dissolution of their way of life and also fear betrayal from a lover when they have already gotten used to them emotionally and trusted them financially (Taurus is a financial sign).

Coming back to the topic of the Sagittarius Moon lover's moods, it should be noted that any partner who can understand their need for solitude when they are feeling depressed will be most loved by them. Space and distance are crucial to the Sagittarius Moon lover's comprehension of their emotions. As with all moods, this too will disappear on it's own. The Taurus type lover is equally private in wanting to sort out their feelings without much fanfare. Be that as it may, it really is therapeutic for this earthy sign to have someone with whom to unburden their heart once in a while. Internalizing their deepest, most troubling thoughts will become unbearable to them as time goes by. Their fiery lover will be more than happy to listen and be a sympathetic ear. The Sagittarius Moon lover might like to keep in mind the fact that sometimes their Taurus type partner only wants to be listened to and may not want them to dive in and rescue them. They may only be venting and not asking for advice.

What kinds of lovers does the Sagittarius Moon person look for? For starters, Sagittarius Moon partners may not enjoy dating clones of themselves, and are rather attracted to athletic and physically strong lovers with whom they can share a favorite sport or two (Jupiter is connected to sportsmanship). A tendency to compete with each other must be watched though, because in the field of sports, a proud Sagittarian Moon partner will not hold back their athletic prowess so that their lover can keep up.

The Sagittarius Moon sign is mutable and flexible, and is quite capable of making *some* changes to accommodate their Taurus type sweetheart, while the fixed sign of Taurus may need some convincing as to why those changes are needed. This relationship has a good chance, if it begins as a long-term friendship, giving each time to adjust themselves according to their own emotional timetables. Taurus types bring stability and peacefulness to this earth and fire love story, while Sagittarius Moon partners bring a love of freedom and adventure to their sensitive and earthy life companions. Both will make good, indulgent parents should they choose to start a family.

Sagittarius Moon vs. Gemini Sun, Moon or Rising Sign
The Fire and Air Relationship

Fire: "I need romance and passion to really enjoy my relationship. Will my boyfriend be a faithful mate for life?" the fiery female partner wonders. "I want an active and freedom-loving partner. Will my girlfriend understand my need for true freedom in life or be too controlling?" the fiery male lover thinks to himself.

Air: "Is my boyfriend open-minded enough and will he appreciate my outspoken side? I need a life mate who will talk to me, communicate with me about everything and not clam up and brood." the airy female partner muses. "Will my girlfriend allow me to do the things I love or will she try to restrict me from expressing myself and living my life the way I want?" the airy male lover wonders.

Sagittarius Moon lovers can enjoy a highly idealistic relationship with partners who have their Sun, Moon or Rising sign in the expressive air sign of Gemini. Each partner symbolizes an element. Understanding that element helps us delve deeper into the real personality of that partner. Fire represents a need to push the envelope, take calculated risks and then learn from them; courage builds character, it makes us stronger and more resilient. Air represents a desire to nurture original self-expression between people so that the secrets between them dissolve. Elementally, fire and air can co-exist remarkably well.

If you're in love with a partner who has Sagittarius as their Moon sign, you might to familiarize yourself with the two, distinct personality types that make up this Moon sign's persona. Which one does your lover mirror best? The first type of Sagittarius Moon personality is the *sage type* while the second is the *adventurer type*. The sage type is often incredibly smart, ambitious and places the search for meaning and wisdom in their lives above most other things. The sage type will often be found working in the capacity of trusted educator or instructor, where they can pass on what they have learnt about life, onto others who may improve their lives by it. This type does well in a marriage, provided their chosen lover is as freedom-loving as they are as well as a good, broad-minded conversationalist.

The second type of Sagittarius Moon lover is the *adventurer type*. They roam both physically and mentally, and almost never rest. This happy, friendly personality will talk fast, walk fast and think even faster. Travel, salesmanship and higher education play a big role in their lives; the giant planet Jupiter governs those areas. Any relationship with the adventurer type of Sagittarius personality will work out great as long as their lover lets them do exactly what their description suggests: freely roam, so that they can pick up the very pulse of life and feel energized by moving through life at the speed of light. Both these Moon sign types are focused on what they want out of life and would fare best with a lover who was mellow and non-combative, instead of the kind that could challenge their authority.

A lover who is a balanced blend of self-control and an erudite grasp over language might tempt an intellectual and curious Sagittarius Moon lover, for whom wisdom is a gift to be secured from any person or situation. A partner who is too introverted or too overly gregarious may not engage them for too long. Neither the Sagittarian Moon lover nor their Gemini type mate can keep secrets as they are both openhearted and love to share. The pull here will be one of marriage because these signs are polarized. Polar opposite signs may not agree on everything (oppositions have to be worked through), but the willingness to overcome problems will be genuine. Gemini types love frank, freedom loving partners who will not restrict them in life and not place them under any emotional pressure to do things. Sagittarius Moon lovers revel in relationships that allow them the grace of complete, self-expression as well release them from responsibilities that they feel do not fit in with their core values in life.

Communication and lots of it will keep this relationship strong and engaging. Sagittarius is a fire sign, so their emotions always run close to the surface. Verbally spontaneous Gemini type lovers love to blurt out whatever they feel (mincing words is not their forte) and sometimes this may cause some feelings to get trampled on. Gemini type lovers want a partner who is so accommodating that they never have to watch what they say around them. Which means that sometimes Sagittarian Moon lovers may have to hear some interesting comments from their partner. The Sagittarian Moon lover, on the other hand, must keep a tight control over their Jupiterian temper. Jupiter does everything in a big way, so when something angers the Sagittarius Moon lover, they won't sit on their ever-building frustrations. Blarney stone Gemini types also might let some Mercurial words loose and add to the fracas. Patience and calm will save the day every time.

Studying the triggers and fears of each sign might help explain their desires. What does a Sagittarian Moon lover fear? They are afraid of being bound in a love relationship that has deteriorated from being a once good exchange of affection, to a now restrictive and demanding relationship where they have to be accountable to someone else for their freedom. What does the Gemini type lover fear? They are afraid for meeting a lover who says one thing but does another, who promises something but never delivers, and most of all, who restricts their strong desire to communicate with whoever they want, whenever they feel like it.

The Moon sign of Sagittarius makes for an incredibly open-minded and adaptable partner. They are also slightly dominant by temperament and may, knowingly or not, tend to guide the relationship along a certain path. Sometimes, there may be a tendency in this fiery and impulsive Moon to begin a relationship quickly but somehow lose interest somewhere down the line. If their partner is very sensitive, they may completely misunderstand the motives of their Sagittarius Moon lover (they may only need some space but their lover might think its over between them). A casual friendship is advised with this Moon sign, so that one of the lovers can maturely control the direction of the relationship and not let it spiral downward due to sudden detachment from either lover.

The Sagittarius Moon sign is more emotional than the air sign of Gemini and if matrimony is ever discussed, both will have to make an extra effort to keep the union going. Any prolonged separation without timely and heartfelt clarifications could cause their connection some serious damage. Sagittarius Moon lovers can help keep the relationship afloat by encouraging their Gemini type sweethearts to be more philosophical, and Gemini type lovers can help by reminding their happy-go-lucky, fiery Moon sign lovers that they needn't take everything they say to heart (Gemini types must always state all the facts and never keep any information from their fire sign lover and vice versa). One of them will have to be the stabilizing factor for the love to survive. They should spend more time enjoying each other instead of questioning each other. If their emotional rhythms match, no matter how long it takes, the rest of their journey will end up exactly where they want it to; straight into each other's hearts.

Sagittarius Moon vs. Cancer Sun, Moon or Rising Sign
The Fire and Water Relationship

Fire: "I need romance and passion to really enjoy my relationship. Will my boyfriend be a faithful mate for life?" the fiery female partner wonders. "I want an active and freedom-loving partner. Will my girlfriend understand my need for true freedom in life or be too controlling?" the fiery male lover thinks to himself.

Water: "Is my boyfriend emotionally stable and wise about our joint finances? Or will debts pile up in the first year of marriage? I need a supportive life-long lover as well as a loving one." the watery female lover thinks to herself. "Will my future spouse conserve our financial resources or spend unwisely without thought for the future? I can connect better romantically if I know that my chosen life-mate is passionate as well as mature and pragmatic." the watery male lover wonders.

Sagittarius Moon lovers can enjoy a vibrant and emotive relationship with partners who have their Sun, Moon or Rising sign in the sentimental water sign of Cancer. But adjustments may have to be made due to how differently each sign looks at love and bonding. Each partner symbolizes an element. Understanding that element helps us delve deeper into the real personality of that partner. Fire represents a desire to take an active approach to life; life isn't something that happens to you, it's what you make of it. Water represents an emotional approach to life; our emotions cleanse us and show us how strong or weak we really are.

If you're honest, adventurous, passionate as well as compassionate, the charismatic Sagittarius Moon lover might want to spend time with you. Watery Cancer types will look for a lover who is not afraid of the emotional give and take within close relationships, but takes these interactions in their stride and learns from them. The larger-than-life, Sagittarius Moon partner needs a lover who is loving and generous but also *emotionally flexible* enough to weather any personality changes in the mutable Sagittarius Moon persona. *"The reality of life is that no one remains the same forever, our experiences change us and make us wiser and better human beings. Change is good and should be encouraged."* the Sagittarius Moon lover teaches. *"Change is only good if it is a positive change. When people change and grow, that's good. But when people abruptly change and cause someone's trust to shatter, that is negative change."* the equally wise Cancer type lover counters.

The Sagittarius Moon sign comes in two, interesting flavors: knowing which one your lover most resembles could help with compatibility on a variety of levels. The first type of Sagittarius Moon personality is the *sage type* while the second, more restless type is the *adventurer type*. The sage type is the quintessential teacher or educator type and for them, accumulating wisdom and experiencing life in its raw and natural state is important. Distributing that wisdom is also equally important to them, and the fields of higher education, travel, sports, religion, teaching or writing books will figure prominently in their lives. The sage type is inspiring but also dominant in relationships: therefore a passive lover with a cool but intellectually sensitive temperament would match best with them. Marriage will probably not be treated lightly and responsibilities will be taken to heart by this Sagittarius Moon type.

The second type of Sagittarius Moon lover is the *adventurer type*. This type is an eternal student; they will be happy to be able gain wisdom from everyone, including children, their lovers, their parents, their friends as well as from books. But their most influential teacher will be adventure and risk. Travel and higher learning or teaching will figure prominently in their lives. The sage type as well as the fun-loving, adventurer type tend to be assertive and will often take charge of a relationship. Therefore, a verbally careful, diplomatic as well as patient and passive lover might be able to have a longer relationship with them than an equally impulsive and dominant lover.

The fiery Sagittarius Moon partner may have entirely different needs, from an emotional point of view, from their watery Cancer type partner: they may need more personal time away from their lover periodically (intimacy may have to alternate with independence), while their Cancer type lover may need *more* time with their lover. This relationship can still prove to be a durable match, because both these lovers are wise in their own way. The fiery Sagittarius Moon lover is willing and open-minded enough to be educated by someone who makes a logical and reasonable point. The Cancer type lover is accommodating enough to appreciate another's opinion without forcing them to change how they see the world. To reach the heart of the Sagittarius Moon mate, we must approach them via wisdom, while the emotional Cancer type lover can be influenced via their feelings. Touch their heart and they'll be all ears.

The most important thing for the mutable or emotionally flexible Sagittarius Moon partner to realize is that their sensitive mate is unlike anyone they have ever met or loved. The ultra-intuitionist Cancer type mate must always be approached with care and gentility; their hearts are easily bruised and they have a hard time battling the myriad, lunar-influenced fears and suspicions that are caused by this fast-moving and often uncaring world of ours. A lover who can maturely control the fury of their temper will blend well with the Cancer type lover, which is why the Jupiter-influenced, Sagittarius Moon lover must watch that legendary temper of theirs at all times. Anger can send the sensitive Cancer type lover back into their emotional cocoon and cut off the lines of communication between them, which could send this beautiful relationship spiraling downwards toward estrangement.

The emotive Cancer type partner must not misinterpret their Sagittarius Moon lover's need for occasional solitude as a rejection of their love. In fact, their fiery lover may love them more than words can express. But when the Moon is in the fire signs (Aries, Leo and Sagittarius), there is invariably a desire to experience certain parts of life alone, so that they can comprehend and absorb the entire experience in their own way, in the purest format. If this need for space can be respected and honored, their relationship will grow closer over time, because no other lover will be prepared to understand the Sagittarian Moon lover the way their caring Cancer type partner can; this sign cares in a way that no other sign can (it is the sign of the eternal, oft forgotten mother).

When truly in love, the fiery Moon sign of Sagittarius will move heaven and earth for their lover, but if the experiences of the past have left too many painful scars on their trusting hearts, their new lovers will have to weed through the residue of the pain caused by former lovers. Always ready to make a fresh start with a new love, the undying optimism of this Moon sign is one of its greater gifts. Studying the triggers and fears of each sign might help explain their desires. What does a Sagittarian Moon lover fear? They are afraid of being caught in a relationship where they cannot express their thoughts freely and go where they want without the approval of a clingy and temperamental lover. What does the Cancer type lover fear? They are afraid of their closest and primary romantic relationship failing, or their marriage ending even though they did their best to save it from peril. Being betrayed by a lover or watching their family structure disintegrate is perhaps their biggest fear of all (Cancer is the sign of the family).

Sagittarius Moon lovers help Cancer types to be more emotionally forgiving and help them bury resentments that may have eaten away at their emotional personalities, while the Cancer essence introduces their fiery Sagittarius Moon sweetheart to the lunar notion of emotional self-expression and patience, something they will need to balance themselves as they begin to age. The energy of the Moon will help the Sagittarian Moon lover be more imaginative and artistic as well as sharpen their intuitive side. This is a loving combination.

Sagittarius Moon vs. Leo Sun, Moon or Rising Sign
The Fire and Fire Relationship

Fire: "I need romance and passion to really enjoy my relationship. Will my boyfriend be a faithful mate for life?" the fiery female partner wonders. "I want an active and freedom-loving partner. Will my girlfriend understand my need for true freedom in life or be too controlling of my actions and behavior?" the fiery male lover thinks to himself.

Sagittarius Moon lovers can enjoy a joyous and highly rewarding relationship with partners who have their Sun, Moon or Rising sign in the charismatic fire sign of Leo. Each partner symbolizes an element. Understanding that element helps us delve deeper into the real personality of that partner. Fire represents courage and daring, it creates an attraction for adventure; that hunger for adventure is often synonymous with a hunger for true wisdom, the kind that has to be experienced alone, no matter what the cost. Elementally, fire supports fire beautifully.

Sagittarius Moon lovers are most comfortable with confident, optimistic and supportive lovers. Their secret need to take risks and push the envelope will be mirrored in their Leo type love mate. Both these lovers will understand that life is not lived fully unless it is lived without any restrictions and conditions. That's the way they feel about love too; it should be unconditional, or its not love, but a compromise. Leo type lovers are ultra-romantics and thrive best with a lover who can remember those critical romantic niceties. Remembering their love mate on emotionally charged days like birthdays, anniversaries and especially, the day of love, Valentine's Day, is a smart way to go. The Leo type lover says *"If you love me, honey, show it! I don't want to have to guess."*

There are two fascinating versions of the Sagittarius Moon sign personality. Learning to tell them apart can help the Leo type lover understand the real nature of this Moon sign. The first type of Sagittarius Moon personality is the *sage type* while the second is the *adventurer type.* The sage type is brilliant, mature and ambitious and will be particularly attracted to vocations that involve writing, learning, teaching, healing, traveling, religion and even philosophy. The sage type will want to give back the wisdom that they found, to the world so that it lives on forever. Marriage and relationships will take a back seat to self-expression, but once a marriage has occurred, an honest sense of responsibility and devotion will not be lacking.

The second type of Sagittarius Moon lover is the *adventurer type.* This type is a dynamo on legs (or wheels) and they will almost constantly be in motion. Will they ever find the time to fall in love and settle down? Probably, but they must decide when and how without any interference. If their lover pushes for a marriage, they are very likely to delay it, but if they're ready for it emotionally, it will not scare them as much. The adventurer type roams and travels because they intuitively sense that in order to become the total and well-rounded human being they need to morph into, they have to get moving and start chasing the gods of wisdom, who may come in the form of people, love, passion, jobs, education and personal ambition. Neither of these two Sagittarius Moon personality types will be able to exist in a marriage where their partner is as dominant as they are, therefore a non-aggressive lover may seal the deal, unless their assertive lover can learn to completely stop competing with them. When competition enters the picture, passion will leave forever.

How do you show a Leo type lover you adore them? Be demonstrative! They're touchy feely and like lovers who are not bashful about showing their love in public. How do you show a Sagittarius Moon lover you find them absolutely irresistible? Well, there are lots of ways, actually. You could begin by finding out what they really want from life, which will help you learn about their approach to love. If you're possessive, know that the Sagittarius Moon lover will recoil from having to clock in with a lover. *"I want you to trust me honey, no matter what I do. And if I'm away from you, know that you're in my heart all the time."* the Sagittarius Moon mate explains. Set them free and they will boomerang right back into your heart. Both these forces of Sagittarius and Leo are strong and, in the arena of relationships, can be equally opinionated. If a clash of wills occurs, neither will back down from expressing their view. This means that one of the lovers will have to modulate the relationship in such a way that neither has the upper hand or an unfair advantage over the other.

The Sagittarius Moon essence is very similar to the Leo type personality; both need lovers who are cheerful, fun-loving and don't take life too seriously. The only problem they might encounter is when one feels the other is not focused enough on the welfare of the relationship. Ill-will could surface if one partner feels that the other is deliberately putting the entire responsibility of keeping their love on the right track on their shoulders, while the other only shows up for dates and goes through the motions without really interacting or being actively involved. Fire signs also have fiery tempers but traditionally they dissipate rapidly before too much damage is done.

The Leo type lover should bear in mind that when the Moon is in the sign of the Centaur, its manifestation could involve great, undiluted emotion. When the emotional Moon's energy mixes with the vibration of Jupiter, the effect will be clearly witnessed in the Sagittarius Moon lover's behavior. Jupiter causes each emotion to be felt in a big way, its effect will be magnified. So, if they're a little blue, they will need some space and distance within which to work through their feelings. If they're sad or upset, Jupiter will cause that frustration to be let out in a massive explosion; there's nothing delicate about the celestial giant, Jupiter. If he's happy, he'll be on top of the world, but if he's down in the dumps, he'll need a careful mixture of TLC and distance to get out of it. Any lover who does not intrude too much or try to smother them (a major no-no) under the guise of caring for them, during certain moods will be cherished by this Moon sign.

Studying the triggers and fears of each sign might help explain their desires. What does a Sagittarian Moon lover fear? They have a fear of not being able to get out of a bad relationship and being bound to an irrational lover by a tie of too many, burdensome responsibilities. What does the Leo type lover fear? They fear merging their life with a partner who cannot understand them and their needs despite being together for many years. They most fear falling in love with a partner who is only interested in their monetary assets. If they can become aware of each other's emotional rhythms and life-expectations ahead of time, it would help immensely. This is a loyal and amazing pair!

Sagittarius Moon vs. Virgo Sun, Moon or Rising Sign
The Fire and Earth Relationship

Fire: "I need romance and passion to really enjoy my relationship. Will my boyfriend be a faithful mate for life?" the fiery female partner wonders. "I want an active and freedom-loving partner. Will my girlfriend understand my need for true freedom in life or be too controlling of my actions and wishes?" the fiery male lover thinks to himself.

Earth: "Does my boyfriend manage his finances maturely or will I end up paying his bills and supporting him? I need stability and true commitment before I can enjoy the romance between us." the earthy female thinks to herself. "Will my future wife spend my hard earned cash on frivolous items at the mall or be wise enough to save up for our retirement?" the earthy male lover wonders.

Sagittarius Moon lovers can enjoy a productive and comfortable relationship with partners who have their Sun, Moon or Rising sign in the devoted earth sign of Virgo. But adjustments may have to be made due to how differently each sign looks at love and bonding. Each partner symbolizes an element. Understanding that element helps us delve deeper into the real personality of that partner. Fire represents a passionate, fearless approach to life; adversity is seen as a challenge and no challenge will go unanswered. Earth represents need for stability and reliability: patience and caution as seen as the most effective tools to go through life with.

The curious Virgo type lover will be eager to know which one of the following two, specific, Sagittarius Moon personality types their lover most resembles: are they like the *sage type* or are they more like the *adventurer type*? Let's discuss each and see which one is the best fit. The first type of Sagittarius Moon personality is the sage type. Why are they called that? It could perhaps be because they are a mature, responsible and ambitious version of the second, more fun-loving and light-hearted type of Sagittarius Moon personality. The sage type is more mentally and philosophically adventurous than physically adventurous. This type is drawn toward the intellectual arts, as well as teaching, traveling and perhaps even being part of the world of religion, as all these fields are under the giant teacher, Jupiter's domain.

The second type of Sagittarius Moon personality is the *adventurer type*. This type is a ball of pure energy and needs to always be on the move. Mentally as well as physically restless, the roaming adventurer makes sense of his or her world by extracting precious life-knowledge in a million different formats. Romantically, this type may feel more fulfilled by being free of societal pressures or convention. They'll fall in love and get married when they're good and ready. But their lover had better be prepared for lots of adventure! The adventurer type sees risk-taking as opportunities for personal growth and clarity, not as things to be avoided like they were the bubonic plague. The adventurer type of Sagittarius Moon personality is a happy, upbeat and exciting lover to be around. A cool-tempered, emotionally controlled and non-confrontational partner would be best for both of the above mentioned Sagittarius Moon personality types, particularly if they don't plan on trying to assert their authority or their dominance.

The Virgo type partner's pragmatism and analytical nature will attract the Sagittarius Moon lover. Virgo types will look for a lover who is as committed to the success of their relationship as they are, and will actively help sort out communication problems as well as all the other issues that can arise between couples. The wisdom-seeking Sagittarius Moon partner needs a lover who is passionate but broad-minded or accommodating in every aspect of life. The fiery Sagittarius Moon partner may, at least in some situations, not have the same life-plan as the Virgo type lover, but they will have many things in common that could solidify their love for decades. Among them will be a thirst for knowledge, an interest in health and healing (Virgo rules the health sector) as well as keeping in touch with all the latest news (this will be an intellectual bond). The Virgo type lover makes an amazing best friend, and it is their capable, friendly energy that the Sagittarius Moon partner will enjoy the most.

When two lovers with mutable (or flexible) energy decide to merge lives, one of them will have to provide a stability to their union and try to understand what type of future connection they can expect. If a common life-goal, like starting a business, raising a family or settling down together can bind them together, they will be able to find a greater, surer camaraderie. Studying and anticipating each other's mood patterns may also solidify their bond. Usually happy and cheerful, sometimes the Sagittarius Moon mate may need a careful blend of TLC and distance to get them through their blue moods. When Jupiter's vibration filters through the feeling energy of the Moon, the result will be a very touchy and sensitive Sagittarius Moon lover (at least temporarily). Any depression will be deeply felt because Jupiter is a giant of a planet and its influence is often felt in direct proportion to its size.

The secret to helping this relationship survive is to promote a balanced contrast, because too much similarity (there is a common changeability to both of them through the mutable quality) may cause the connection to stagnate or burn out. Studying the triggers and fears of each sign might help explain their desires. What does a Sagittarian Moon lover fear? They have a fear of losing their freedom to enjoy life in their own style due to a demanding and over-emotional lover who does not comprehend their desire for worry-free autonomy. What does the Virgo type lover fear? They fear seeing their marriage fail due to a partner who refuses to work on it, keeps secrets from them and betrays their life long trust. Practical Virgo type mates know that a *"yes"* at the alter also means a *"yes"* to sharing personal checking accounts as well as sharing their personal space.

The fiery Moon sign of Sagittarius is honest and will not mince words under pressure. *"You know me, sweetheart, I tell it like it is, take it or leave it."* the Sagittarius Moon lover informs. The inwardly sensitive Virgo type mate may not leave it, but they will wish that their lover was a bit more verbally diplomatic. The Virgo type lover, on the other hand, functions under the direct, celestial influence of chatty Mercury, the blarney-stone planet. So, the Sagittarius Moon lover better know when to duck when a stressed out Mercury-ruled, Virgo type partner lets those comments fly across the room. It takes a lot out of the Virgo type person to create a smooth-flowing routine in life. A-place-for-everything Virgo types methodize parts of their life in an effort to gain more control over their environment. The more they can control the routines and systems around them, the fewer mistakes are made. But their casual and rough-and-tumble Sagittarius Moon lover may feel stifled when faced with a routine that doesn't make any sense to them; freedom to live their life without excessive interference is a non-negotiable factor for them.

The Virgo type lover is duty-conscious and will not shirk their responsibility in most cases. Their optimistic Sagittarius Moon lover will have no problem with duty, but it should have a valid meaning in their life and it should connect to them directly. It will be difficult for this fiery Moon sign to accept responsibility for something that doesn't engage their heart and soul. For example, a Virgo type mate is more likely to move to a city in search of a job that they have earned a specific degree for, while the freedom-loving Sagittarius Moon lover is more likely to move to a city because their senses relax there or if they have a lot of helpful friends there. One sign is likely to place work over fun while the other sees more value in emotional comfort over the stress of setting up a daily routine. *"Rules help us make progress and save time."* the reliable Virgo type mate advises. *"Rules are made to be broken. If it doesn't make any sense to me, then those rules should be revised."* the philosophical Sagittarius Moon lover counters. Both have valid life-philosophies and will have to learn to be a little like each other for maximum success.

The Sagittarius Moon lover can be instrumental in showing their hard-working but easily wound up Virgo type partner that a balanced approach to life is essential for emotional stability; all work and no play make Virgo develop unnecessary digestive problems (Virgo rules the digestive tract). And the ever-dependable and goal-oriented Virgo type mate can show their impulsive but honest Sagittarius Moon lover that building a nest egg for their future is a splendid idea, and that while they may not slow down and become as cautious as they are, they could benefit tremendously from choosing their battles wisely and taking calculated risks instead of blindly jumping in due to boredom. If they can adjust to each other's habits and quirks, if they can make sure that their individual spending styles do not cause other problems in their relationship and above all, if they can pledge to each other to give one another the freedom to interpret their love story in their own way, this relationship will thrive and blossom.

Sagittarius Moon vs. Libra Sun, Moon or Rising Sign
The Fire and Air Relationship

Fire: "I need romance and passion to really enjoy my relationship. Will my

*boyfriend be a faithful mate for life?" the fiery female partner wonders. "I want
an active and freedom-loving partner. Will my girlfriend understand my need for
true freedom in life or be too controlling?" the fiery male lover thinks to himself.*

*Air: "Is my boyfriend open-minded enough and will he appreciate my outspoken
side? I need a life mate who will talk to me, communicate with me about everything and not clam up and brood." the airy female partner muses. "Will my
girlfriend allow me to do the things I love or will she try to restrict me from
expressing myself?" the airy male lover wonders.*

Sagittarius Moon lovers can enjoy a romantic and compatible relationship with partners who have their Sun, Moon or Rising sign in the intellectual and relationship-oriented air sign of Libra. Each partner symbolizes an element. Understanding that element helps us delve deeper into the real personality of that partner. Fire represents a burning passion and a desire to take risks and challenge defeats instead of falling victim to them. Air represents a desire to nurture true self-expression in relationships so that there is no room for secrets or fear.

The relationship-minded Libra lover should be able to distinguish between the two, varying types of the Sagittarius Moon personality, in order to make their interactions more significant. There are two variations on the Sagittarius Moon personality theme. The first type is called the *sage type* and the second is known as the *adventurer type*. The sage type of Sagittarius Moon lover is mature and embodies the qualities of an old but very learned and wise teacher or professor. This type is driven by a need to acquire wisdom, the kind that has a far reaching influence on many areas of life, like healing, teaching, traveling, philosophizing, writing books and above all, being an eternal, ever respectful student of life. The sage type proves to often be a balanced presence in married life, capable of both supporting as well as inspiring their lover and spouse for years to come.

Let's take a closer look at the more fun-loving and easy-going version of the Sagittarius Moon personality. The adventurer type of lover is highly energetic, restless and an equally eager student of life. This type thrives in a progressive and active environment and has a weakness for excitement and adventure. When it comes time to choose a marriage partner, this version of the Sagittarius Moon personality will ensure that their chosen life-mate is emotionally secure, independent and has a great sense of humor. This type must be given the time and space in which to come to a decision about marriage, and their partner will have to make many adjustments to their style of living and learning. A life-mate who is dominant and likes to get their way on critical issues will clash with both types of the Sagittarius Moon personality because both of those types happen to be equally dominant themselves. The more accommodating and slightly passive type of Libra lover might fit well into the equation, because they may not feel the constant need to challenge their self-confident lover, but might focus more on a peaceful resolution of conflict.

If you're a good conversationalist, are well read, open-minded and enjoy a good joke, the Sagittarius Moon lover will warm up quickly to you. The expansive Sagittarius Moon energy needs a lover who can be loving without being controlling and can be a friend without trying to parent them too much. This will be a relationship of equals; the Sagittarius Moon lover treats everyone with the same, unassuming friendliness while the Libra type partner may show an equally egalitarian approach to life and people. Libra types are ultra romantic and relationship-oriented and while both these lovers may not immediately think of relationships when they meet each other, the draw toward an open, loving friendship will always be there.

Sagittarius Moon mates are philosophically sensitive as well as emotionally sensitive, and they can help preserve the underlying truth of their relationship: that physical beauty is a fleeting illusion and that simplicity is true beauty (important for appearance-oriented Libra types to keep in mind). The fiery Sagittarius Moon lover will show their Libra type partner and that there are other things in life that are more important than hum drum relationships and run-of-the-mill romances. To them, a relationship built on mutual respect instead of only passion will usually outlast a one-dimensional physical relationship that could die out remarkably quickly. The romantic Libra type mate should take care to never overvalue their relationship; they tend to take any threat to their marriage or closest relationship very seriously. The air sign of Libra represents the seventh sector in Astrology, and this sector governs marriage and the legal bond between two lovers. Which is why Libra types are almost always a little more worried about the general health of the relationship than easy-come-easy-go Sagittarius Moon lovers.

Studying the triggers and fears of each sign might help explain their desires. What does a Sagittarian Moon lover fear? They are afraid of being in a relationship with someone who cannot function on their own and needs to be around their lover all the time. What does the Libra type lover fear? They have a fear of being part of a relationship where they are the only one working on it; a lack of positive interaction from a lover produces a strange sadness in the usually self-controlled Libra heart. Invariably, Libra types will jump in to save the relationship from dissolution by utilizing their skills of adaptability and compromise, which should not be over-done.

The Libra type mate's Venus energy that surges through this relationship will help this couple feel empathy for each other, as well as lead to a deep understanding. The only problem that might cause a stirring of negative emotions is when one of them is ready to commit to a marriage or long-term relationship and the other still harbors doubts. When this occurs, both partners need to handle the situation with extreme caution. If one of them is sure they've found the love of their life, the battle is half won already. The best thing to do is to give the partner who is still making up their mind, some space and freedom. They both need to give each other the gift of time to decide without undue pressure. This alone will bring them closer because other lovers will get impatient, get angry and stomp out of the house, vowing never to return. Caution might tip the balance in the most patient lover's favor.

Sagittarius Moon lovers can infuse their airy and communicative Libra type lover's life with a love of higher learning, travel to foreign nations and bring them into touch with their higher mental capabilities (understanding the various aspects of spirituality or world religions, for example). The Libra type lover can help the freedom-loving Sagittarius Moon partner ease into a healthy relationship by helping to remove the stigma of difficulty that may be associated with love in their minds, due to the careless actions of former partners who may have left more than one scar on the Sagittarius Moon heart.

Sagittarius Moon vs. Scorpio Sun, Moon or Rising Sign
The Fire and Water Relationship

Fire: "I need romance and passion to really enjoy my relationship. Will my boyfriend be a faithful mate for life?" the fiery female partner wonders. "I want an active and freedom-loving partner. Will my girlfriend understand my need for true freedom in life or be too controlling?" the fiery male lover thinks to himself.

Water: "Is my boyfriend emotionally stable and wise about our joint finances? Or will debts pile up in the first year of marriage? I need a supportive life-long lover as well as a loving one." the watery female lover thinks to herself. "Will my future spouse conserve our financial resources or spend unwisely without thought for the

future? I can connect better romantically if I know that my chosen life-mate is passionate as well as mature and pragmatic." the watery male lover wonders.

S agittarius Moon lovers can enjoy an intense and emotionally invigorating relationship with partners who have their Sun, Moon or Rising sign in the enigmatic water sign of Scorpio. But adjustments may have to be made due to how differently each element looks at love and bonding. Each partner symbolizes an element. Understanding that element helps us delve deeper into the real personality of that partner. The element of fire represents passion and an assertive spirit; being defeated by life's problems is not an option and a desire to get up from the dust and fight will be pronounced. The water element represents a gentle, non-confrontational approach to life; the urge to make peace with situations that are beyond our control will be evident. Water is calm while fire is active.

The Scorpio type lover would benefit by finding out which of two, interesting types of the Sagittarius Moon personality they may have fallen in love with, as it would help with creating more closeness. The first type of Sagittarius Moon personality is the *sage type*, while the second is the *adventurer type*. The sage type is intellectual, emotional and strives to stand out in a crowd. The adventurer type takes life a little less seriously than the sage type, and may invest more time and energy in chasing excitement and freedom.

The Scorpio type lover is usually mature and this may aid them in finding a more permanent love connection with the sage type of the Sagittarius Moon personality, mainly because this type will take love and marriage a little more seriously than the adventurer type. This will be music to the ears of commitment-minded Scorpio who longs to put down roots when the time is ripe. If the Scorpio type lover happens to have lost their heart to the charismatic and fast-moving energy of the adventurer type, they can still enjoy a good relationship with them and it might even end up in a long and stable marriage, provided the Scorpio type lover relaxes some of their expectations and let their lover roam, learn and evolve on their own timetable.

If you're attractive, self-sufficient, a little aloof but friendly if approached, the Sagittarius Moon lover might ask to write your phone number down. Watery Scorpio type lovers will look for a partner who is passionate and loyal, intelligent as well as graceful under pressure and the Sagittarian Moon lover just might fit the bill. Falling in love with a Scorpio type partner is super easy; not many can resist that Plutonic magnetism. Getting them to fall in love with you may be a little perplexing, though. Could it be that the Scorpio type lover keeps their mates guessing on purpose?

As one of the most charismatic but stoic signs in the zodiac family, trying to figure out how they feel about their lover may prove challenging for their fiery mate. Their Sagittarian Moon lover may be easier to read emotionally, but the Scorpio type partner must refrain from using control as a tool of influence in relationships, *"Tell me what you really think of me, sweetheart, I can take it on the chin."* the daring Sagittarius Moon lover might suggest. *"Give me some time, honey, I want to get to know you on as many levels as I can. That takes time, but if I can trust you totally, I can love you more intensely. If you're mature and patient, you're the one."* the emotional Scorpio type mate might answer.

The Sagittarius Moon lover will not stay long in any relationship where they feel like they are being controlled even to the slightest degree. This freedom-loving Moon sign will rather give up the love of their life than be manipulated by them. Scorpio type lovers are not always, but can be incredibly possessive in love relationships as well as about their children, their money and their beliefs. This possessiveness may be observed after their love has deepened over time, and this is the most important difference between these lovers.

Obsession may play a key role in the love life of the Scorpio type partner, and they must watch out for a tendency to let emotion reign over logic in every emotional charged situation. The all-or-nothing Scorpio type lover gives their all if they're truly in love, but must beware of lovers who might suddenly disappear after they have used their sensitive Scorpio type mate to fulfill their agenda. For an intuitive sign like Scorpio, it is curious how they might sometimes choose to ignore the red flags that might pop up signaling the unsuitability of a lover. Emotions aren't always an accurate barometer of what we should do in love; sometimes reason could truly save us from heartache. But the Scorpio type lover must be willing to see that for themselves. Fixed by temperament, they may not listen to reason if passion or obsession (or fear and suspicion) have already taken root. The Sagittarius Moon partner must also be more careful in forming love bonds, as an emotional lover might cause them to lose clarity or control over their lives.

The expansive Sagittarius Moon lover needs a partner who can easily adapt to the evolving phases of life; a partner who makes serious situations even more frightening by being too emotional about them will drive them away instead of closer to them. The Sagittarius Moon lover is cheerful and displays an amazing elasticity of spirit, which is something the Scorpio type mate could learn to emulate as time goes by. The fiery Sagittarius Moon partner may, at least sometimes, not want some of the same things that a Scorpio type lover absolutely requires to feel secure. What one sign sees as boredom the other views as much needed stability.

Studying the triggers and fears of each sign might help explain their desires. What does a Sagittarian Moon lover fear? They have a fear of being restricted by a domineering lover who may have their own insecurity issues, but prevents them from living their lives fully and freely. What does the Scorpio type lover fear? They have a fear of being betrayed by a lover whom they had taken into their world and trusted them with their emotional secrets and vulnerabilities. If one of these two lovers can agree to stabilize the relationship, things will proceed well in the long run. The Sagittarius Moon sign needs a lot of freedom to fully experience love, romance and intimacy. Bind them with love and they will flee. Free them up with love and they will embrace your presence.

The Sagittarius Moon vibration is mutable and flexible, and is capable of making some changes in life for their lover, but the fixed quality of the sign of Scorpio may have trouble with sudden change. They have to be eased into big changes slowly. This relationship has a good chance of success, if a friendship is allowed to morph into a love relationship gradually, so that each lover can get used to the other's emotional needs. This will be a close and loving pair.

Sagittarius Moon vs. Sagittarius Sun, Moon or Rising Sign
The Fire and Fire Relationship

Fire: "I need romance and passion to really enjoy my relationship. Will my boyfriend be a faithful mate for life?" the fiery female partner wonders. "I want an active and freedom-loving partner. Will my girlfriend understand my need for true freedom in life or be too controlling of my actions and behavior?" the fiery male lover thinks to himself.

Sagittarius Moon lovers can enjoy a highly stimulating and romantic relationship with partners who have their Sun, Moon or Rising sign in their own sign of Sagittarius. Each partner symbolizes an element. Understanding that element helps us delve deeper into the real personality of that partner. Fire represents a desire to live life without any trace of fear or pessimism, while embracing it, risk and all, whenever the face of life brings about unplanned changes. Elementally, fire supports fire beautifully.

The Sagittarius Moon personality is divided into two separate versions, and knowing which one is which might help the loving, Sagittarius type lover to acclimate to them better as well as be able to draw emotionally closer to them. Hey, if you're in love, this extra effort will be worth it! The first type of Sagittarius Moon personality is the *sage type* while the second type is the *adventurer type*. One can safely say that there is a little bit of both in each type. The sage type is mature, has a well-developed intellect, seeks to understand his or her world through the pursuit of education, healing, travel, religion, spirituality or law. This type adjusts rather well to the demands of marriage and maintaining a close bond with their spouse over time, particularly if their chosen partner is able to grant them total freedom to steer their life the way they want.

The adventurer type of the Sagittarius Moon personality is also wise and bright, but their focus in life is highly experimental. This type thrives on being totally free of unnecessary responsibilities that bear no meaning in their life and will want to explore the fields of sports, teaching, philosophizing and tapping into the raw, naturalness of life by never turning any experience down. Restless and ever-eager, this eternal student of life is easy-going, adaptable and non-judgmental, which makes them a good candidate for relationships. They are less likely to jump into the state of matrimony just for the sake of physical attraction and are wise enough to know that multi-level compatibility is extremely crucial to be able live with their spouse on a day to day level.

These two dominant, larger-than-life Jupiter-ruled personalities will love each other sincerely. They may also clash on occasion (mighty Jupiter, when aroused and instigated never backs down from a fight) but also forgive each other easily, which is a trademark of all fire sign combinations. Sagittarius Moon sign lovers are intellectually sensitive and their search for a life partner may bring to them into contact with many different types of personalities. Their ultimate choice will be someone who is emotionally flexible and does not take difficult situations too seriously, but can remain calm and cheerful in a crisis. Their ability to maintain a solid sense of humor will tide these lovers over many a rough spot in their relationship. They react best to love partners who are wise but can also be their *best friend* first and lover second.

When they're having fun, life will be a ball, but when two lovers with the Sagittarius energy decide to exhibit their fiery tendencies at the same time, one of them will have to be the rock of that union and try to understand what kind of undercurrents they're dealing with. Usually happy and optimistic, sometimes even they may need some TLC to get them through their moods. Learning to pre-read the patterns of their moods would be beneficial. The secret to helping this relationship survive is to promote contrast, because too much similarity may cause the connection to stagnate or atrophy. If one Jupiterian lover wants to discuss something, while the other would rather not engage in a lengthy conversation at that precise time, one of them will have to bend and approach them at a later, less emotionally explosive time.

The fiery Moon sign of Sagittarius may be ambitious, intellectually sharp and most especially, have a secret love of religion or spirituality. The mystic within them can survive side by side with the humorist or wisdom-seeker. Sagittarius Moon partners may not enjoy dating clones of themselves, and are rather attracted to athletic and physically strong lovers with whom they can share a favorite sport or two (Jupiter is connected to sportsmanship). A tendency to aggressively compete with each other must be watched, because that subtle competitiveness might easily spill into their love life and threaten to disrupt its delicate equilibrium. The partner who is willing to sacrifice more will spend more time smoothing out problems areas and making compromises. There is a time and place for competition and the world of romance is an ill-fit arena for it.

The Sagittarius Moon lover as well as the Sagittarius type mate are inspirational personalities as well as dominant by nature; the patience factor is key to long-term happiness, because the fast, furious and fiery Moon sign of Sagittarius may not want to have to slow down too often for another. Another important and helpful point for these loving partners is to make sure that their spending styles match properly. The freedom to express opinions without excessive finger-pointing by a lover is crucial. Both of these two lovebirds will make wonderful and loving parents; their children will probably connect to them happily and without fear. Both of them are teachers disguised as lovers and have a lot to learn from each other through the medium of love. Marriage is a great idea as long as one of them agrees to be non-aggressive, non-combative and a follower, while the other can lead and chart a road ahead for their relationship. If one of these two lovers can agree to be the compromiser in the relationship, things will proceed wonderfully in the long run. This is a winning pair!

Sagittarius Moon vs. Capricorn Sun, Moon or Rising Sign
The Fire and Earth Relationship

Fire: "I need romance and passion to really enjoy my relationship. Will my boyfriend be a faithful mate for life?" the fiery female partner wonders. "I want an active and freedom-loving partner. Will my girlfriend understand my need for true freedom in life or be too controlling?" the fiery male lover thinks to himself.

Earth: "Does my boyfriend manage his finances maturely or will I end up paying his bills and supporting him? I need stability and true commitment before I can

enjoy the romance between us." the earthy female thinks to herself. "Will my future wife spend my hard earned cash on frivolous items at the mall or be wise enough to save up for our retirement?" the earthy male lover wonders.

Sagittarius Moon lovers can enjoy a highly successful relationship with partners who have their Sun, Moon or Rising sign in the ambitious and dependable earth sign of Capricorn. The Capricorn type lover likes to be a hundred percent sure that when they tie the knot, they will have picked the very best life-mate they could find for their lifestyle. Which is why it is important for them to be able to distinguish between the two different types or shades of the Sagittarius Moon personality.

The first type is the classic *sage type* while the second is the easy-going, *adventurer type*. The sage type is an intellectual animal and needs to keep their energies constantly engaged in the pursuits of the mind. This type may be drawn to teaching, law, travel, writing, healing or religion and may perhaps be able to supply the maturity that the Capricorn type lover would need to see in a lover who is about to become an equal partner in their life.

The second type of the Sagittarius type personality is the happy-go-lucky, adventurer type. Their goal in life is to be a student for the ages, to glean knowledge out of every person or situation, no matter how unusual or painful and above all, to keep moving. Their undeniable restlessness may create some turbulence in their relationships, but if their lover learns to adjust to them over time, a relationship could work out well. The Capricorn type lover may find more in common with the sage type of the Sagittarius Moon personality, but must make sure they let this type enjoy total freedom in life; there should be no unnecessary restrictions placed on them and they should be free to come and go as they please for the maximum in emotional compatibility.

Sagittarius Moon lovers function under the influence of Jupiter while Capricorn type partners are ruled by the ancient and karmic time-keeper of the solar system, Saturn. When Saturn's cautious and wise energy meets up with the vast and far-reaching essence of Jupiter, the effect will be felt in the Sagittarius Moon/Capricorn Sun, Moon or Ascendant partnership. Saturn sometimes tends to be dominating. It can't help it, it's the wisest planet after all, the giver of stability and the planet that keeps a strict account of every person's good or bad karmic activity across many lifetimes. Jupiter, the largest planet in the planetary family tends to be expansive, intellectually hungry and highly experimental in various areas of life. Both these forces are strong and, in the arena of relationships, can be equally opinionated. If a clash of wills occurs, neither will back down. This means that both of them need to bear in mind that when a couple argues, its not two people at war, but two philosophies at work.

Each lover can teach the other a few important traits that are common to their own sign. For example, the industrious Capricorn type lover can show the Sagittarius Moon mate how to methodize and simplify certain aspects of life instead of just leaving them to chance. The inspirational Sagittarius Moon lover can help their conscientious mate look at life through brand new eyes; fun and hard work can co-exist successfully together. Supportive and protective, some Capricorn types tend to parent their lovers; their goal is to help improve their lives and make their connection mean something. Success in all things draws the earthy Capricorn type lover.

"Where is this relationship going? What do we mean to one another? Can I depend on you for strength and support when I need it? Am I number one in your life?" the cautious Capricorn type lover may want to know. The Sagittarius Moon lover makes for an exciting partner and spouse. Marriage is something they will definitely want to try at some point in their life, but their spouse must first reflect at least a few of their signature qualities. A partner who is easy-going, not so emotional that it blinds them to reason, and an upbeat friend will attract them instantly. Make the Sagittarius Moon lover laugh, and they will pledge their heart to you for life.

Reading each lover's mood patterns may be a key to better compatibility. It should be mentioned that sometimes Capricorn types may undergo a blue spell. It may or may not happen often, but if it does, they will like to know that their normally happy and bubbly life-partner will show the maturity needed to handle such moods. Under no circumstances should such depressions be taken lightly; Saturn sometimes places a great and often impossibly heavy burden on the emotional shoulders of the Capricorn type lover. Their mate should never ask them to *"snap out of it"* or *"get a hold of themselves"*. Saturn is a serious planet and as the designated celestial ruler of Capricorn, will cause the inwardly sensitive earth sign to need some time and space in order to wade their way out of those deep spells. Care and tenderness and understanding from a lover will soothe them until they are ready to come out and share the weight of their emotions with their soul mate. Until then, patience is the key word.

Sagittarius Moon lovers are impulsive and will have to train themselves to adequately handle the emotional needs of their loving and devoted mate. If this occurs, they will have achieved a great breakthrough. Capricorn types receive from their Sagittarius Moon lovers a new perspective on life, where they can be more optimistic, light-hearted and feel more confident about themselves (Sagittarius Moon mates can help alleviate Capricorn's occasional depression or melancholia with their joviality). Capricorn slows down the fast-paced, brilliant but occasionally scattered Sagittarius Moon energy and causes it to double check all the facts before it makes those big, Jupiter-sized deals in the sky. Capricorn will make sure that those idealistic attempts bear fruit and culminate successfully and benefit their fiery mates.

The Sagittarius Moon lover will want to successfully attempt bigger and better things with the aid of the guidance of Capricorn and use their time more constructively. With the earthy Capricorn energy to support happy-go-lucky Sagittarius Moon lovers, they can change their outlook on life and place ambition or personal goals above fun and adventure once in a while. The only problem between them could be the Capricorn type lover's tendency to put too much pressure on their Sagittarius Moon partner to achieve something (they will refuse to function under pressure). As for the freethinking Sagittarius Moon partner, their ultimate choice in a life mate will be someone who is emotionally flexible and can take difficult events in their stride. When it comes to managing finances, it should be kept in mind that the Capricorn energy is more frugal than careless, especially when it comes to a precious resource like income.

Impulsive Sagittarius Moon lovers might like to spend within reason and always consult their earthy partners before big purchases are made. This courtesy alone will help smooth out a majority of their problems. On the other hand, Capricorn type lovers should try not to clamp down too hard on their fiery mates if they went out and bought a few extra boxes of chocolate or an extra tray of sushi rolls. Sagittarian Moon mates do not take very kindly to being told how to spend their money and will expect to be respected by their partner and trusted enough to make the right financial decisions.

Studying the triggers and fears of each sign might help explain their desires. What does a Sagittarian Moon lover fear? They have a fear of ending up with a lover who places more faith in what the world says than in what they feel, while they try to control the level of the freedom they enjoy in life. What does the Capricorn type lover fear? They fear being bound in a marriage by a lover who cannot handle them with sensitivity and makes them feel guilty if they work hard at work to make something of themselves. Together, both these lovers can create an important and significant relationship, with Capricorn supplying the stability and direction, and the Sagittarius Moon lover supplying the joy of adventure and fun to keep their relationship fresh, buoyant and ultimately successful.

Sagittarius Moon vs. Aquarius Sun, Moon or Rising Sign
The Fire and Air Relationship

Fire: "I need romance and passion to really enjoy my relationship. Will my boyfriend be a faithful mate for life?" the fiery female partner wonders. "I want an active and freedom-loving partner. Will my girlfriend understand my need for true freedom in life or be too controlling of my actions and behavior?" the fiery male lover thinks to himself.

Air: "Is my boyfriend open-minded enough and will he appreciate my outspoken side? I need a life mate who will talk to me, communicate with me about every- thing and not clam up and brood." the airy female partner muses. "Will my girlfriend allow me to do the things I love or will she try to restrict me from truly expressing myself?" the airy male lover wonders.

Sagittarius Moon lovers can enjoy a highly successful relationship with part- ners who have their Sun, Moon or Rising sign in the unique and forward- thinking air sign of Aquarius. Each partner symbolizes an element. Understanding that element helps us delve deeper into the real personality of that partner. Fire represents a need to assertively and energetically shape life and achieve cherished goals; passion pushes fire sign mates into making quick changes in their lives without waiting for circumstances to change. Air repre- sents a desire to connect people and use original communication to build bridges between those entities that have become estranged; air seeks to express itself and desires to be heard at all costs.

If the Aquarius type lover ever feels like they're ready to jump into the world of romance and passion with their Sagittarius Moon sweetheart, they would greatly profit from knowing exactly which of the two, distinct Sagittarius Moon personalities their lover most mirrors. The first type is the *sage type* and the second type is the *adventurer type*. The sage type is mature, reflective, ambitious, and drawn toward higher learning as well as healing, teaching, travel and may even have an interest in the law or justice system. The sage type will feel comfortable in the marriage setting as long as they can experience the full measure of freedom that they think they need in life.

The second type, the adventurer type of Sagittarius Moon personality, is a fun- loving, restless, super-energized version of the first. This type has an easy-going attitude about life and handles problems in a light-hearted but capable manner. There may be a pronounced desire to take risks and fly through the more difficult situations in life, perhaps because this type views risk as an untapped avenue for greater personal growth. A great elasticity of emotions is required when one is at the brink of jumping into the unknown, but if anyone can do it with grace, it's the adventurer type of the Sagittarius Moon sign. This type in particular, needs to be able live their life freely and may not be able to exist in a relationship where they have to be answerable to a controlling spouse. They will want their spouse to come across as an equal partner, and not try to parent them in any way. They can gift their partner an open heart as well as a solid sense of trust and freedom, but will expect that favor to be returned wholeheartedly.

If the Aquarius type lover is self-confident and assertive, they may have to learn to compromise and choose the middle ground when power struggles arise, if they're in love with either type of assertive Sagittarius Moon personality. A passive, non-confrontational but intelligent lover will be able to fit in beautifully with both types of the Sagittarius Moon personality.

If you're adventurous, bright, laugh easily and have a generous spirit, the Sagittarius Moon lover will fall quickly for you. The first desire between these two amazing signs (Sagittarius Moon and Aquarius) will be one of creating a life-long, love relationship that is based on an even stronger, ever-present friendship. The Aquarius type mate is open-minded, charismatic and highly idealistic. This sign strives to find their own voice in life and be able to live freely without pressure from lovers. Fixed by temperament (Aquarius is a fixed sign), once they make up their mind about something, they may not easily change their position. If they do decide to change their view however, it will be done in typical Uranus-fashion: lightning fast.

The Sagittarius Moon lover's mutability (emotional malleability) will be a welcome relief to the Aquarius type mate. This fiery Moon sign can accommodate any person and get along with even the most complicated personality. Their sense of humor is their greatest asset and makes a great icebreaker. Fiery Sagittarius Moon lovers like their partners to be physically demonstrative, so their Aquarian type mates might to make sure that they can regularly supply this need in them. To the Sagittarius Moon lover, a detached lover is an uninterested lover, so the Aquarius type partner must make sure that they don't neglect the intimate side of their relationship too often. The Sagittarius Moon lover who is verbally and regularly appreciated by a partner will choose to be near them, because they will bolster their self-esteem and make them feel good about their life together. Fiery Moon signs love to be noticed, attention is their rocket fuel!

The benefit of this particular sign combination is that Aquarius types bring out in their Sagittarius Moon lovers a need to look at life through the ideal of friendliness, equality and fairness for all people; this helps tone down their slightly judgmental side (Sagittarius rules justice and law). If they can find a common goal, the Aquarius type mate has the vision and the Sagittarius Moon lover supplies the energy. Both these lovers are capable of creating a solid support system for each other, which they will increasingly depend on as they age and mature.

The Sagittarius Moon lover may sometimes prove to be a bit more emotional than the emotionally cool and logical Aquarius type mate. The influence of the Moon, when seen through the magic of the celestial super-giant Jupiter, might create a personality that experiences each mood in a big, all-consuming wave. If they're ecstatic about something, Sagittarius Moon lovers will generously want the whole world to join in their happiness. If they're a bit despondent or depressed, they might become a little annoyed at a partner who cannot seem to grasp the fact that they need privacy and not excessive emotional closeness at a time like that. But their bubbly personalities will not stay under a spell of moodiness for too long. Before long, they'll be back with their fighting spirit intact and ready to go. *"Bring it on!"* they'll say, this daring Moon sign will be ready for round two in no time.

The downside of this sign combination is that sometimes the airy Aquarian can get distracted (by projects or people, or maybe even some passing moodiness) and cause their Sagittarius Moon partner to feel some bewilderment due to the Aquarian type mate's temporary desire for a change of pace in life. Losing interest mid-stream could leave this fiery Moon sign confused and without direction. A lack of attention from their mate may not have a good effect on the normally, emotionally flexible Sagittarius Moon lover. Aquarius types must always remember that their joyous and cheerful Sagittarius Moon lover thrives on lots of attention and love, *given happily,* without hesitation. Quick and genuine reciprocity is key to keeping the fires burning within this loving relationship.

Studying the triggers and fears of each sign might help explain their desires. What does a Sagittarian Moon lover fear? They have a fear of being with a lover who cannot appreciate the genuineness of their emotions and have to deal with their detachment, instead of a happily shared intimacy. What does the Aquarius type lover fear? They fear being with a lover who cannot understand their need for total freedom to interact with whoever they want, whenever they wish. Neither of them will tolerate being mothered by a lover, and neither will be agreeable to clocking in with a partner either. *"You either trust me or you don't, honey. It's up to you, not me."* they might say.

On the other hand, Sagittarius Moon partners should not expect more attention from their Aquarian type partners than they can realistically give. A partner who causes an emotional avalanche in an Aquarius type lover, and causes them to have to wrestle too much with emotional gridlock, may find that they start spending more and more time away from them. This needn't happen. Talking out grievances instead of hoping they will disappear on their own will secure this love story for a long time. This pair of lovers can build something strong and viable together; their love can easily last a lifetime.

Sagittarius Moon vs. Pisces Sun, Moon or Rising Sign
The Fire and Water Relationship

Fire: "I need romance and passion to really enjoy my relationship. Will my boyfriend be a faithful mate for life?" the fiery female partner wonders. "I want an active and freedom-loving partner. Will my girlfriend understand my need for true freedom in life or be too controlling?" the fiery male lover thinks to himself.

Water: "Is my boyfriend emotionally stable and wise about our joint finances? Or will debts pile up in the first year of marriage? I need a supportive life-long lover as well as a loving one." the watery female lover thinks to herself. "Will my future spouse conserve our financial resources or spend unwisely without thought for the future? I can connect better romantically if I know that my chosen life-mate is passionate as well as mature and pragmatic." the watery male lover wonders.

Sagittarius Moon lovers can enjoy a highly emotive and spiritually energizing relationship with partners who have their Sun, Moon or Rising sign in the poetic and soft-natured water sign of Pisces. Each partner symbolizes an element. Understanding that element helps us delve deeper into the real personality of that partner. Fire represents passion, action and a searching curiosity; this is the element of true heroism. Water represents sympathy, emotional purity and trust; this is the element of an all-pervading compassion.

The Pisces type lover might be interested to know that there are two versions of the fascinating Sagittarius Moon personality, and knowing how each one approaches love and intimacy might help them to bond with them more closely. The first type is the *sage type* and the second is the *adventurer type*. The sage type of Sagittarius Moon personality is intellectually driven, ambitious, mature and can slip comfortably into the role of spouse. The adventurer type of the Sagittarius Moon personality is a fast and furious version of the first; they seek connectivity to life through the medium of adventure and taking chances is an integral part of their emotional language. Fearless and optimistic, the adventurer type is open-hearted, a good conversationalist and thrives with independent, emotionally secure and freedom-loving partners who can promise to never fence them in with restrictions and responsibilities that don't resonate with their free and vast approach to life. Pisces type lovers, particularly those who seek stronger and dominant life-mates, will enjoy an easy courtship and marriage with both types of the Sagittarius Moon personality, provided they agree to grant their fiery lovers as much personal freedom as they wish.

If you're intelligent, adventurous and optimistic about life, then the Sagittarius Moon mate might like to get to know you better. The Piscean essence is poetic, alluring and extends an easy sympathy toward lovers. Being around a Sagittarius Moon lover pushes Pisces types to become more confident and trust their instincts with greater surety. The Pisces type lover helps their Sagittarius Moon mate into getting back in touch with their emotional, sensitive and dreamy side. This is a highly creative sign combination. Both partners would do well to remind each other that they must build a solid foundation first: one of friendship and most importantly, of raw honesty. Friends who become confidants first and lovers second, will have a longer, more emotionally significant relationship than friends who proceed directly from the friend stage to the sexual stage.

Sagittarius Moon lovers function under the influence of Jupiter while, Pisces type partners are ruled by Neptune. When Neptune's inspirational and artistic energy meets up with the far-reaching essence of Jupiter, the effect will be clearly felt in the Sagittarius Moon/Pisces Sun, Moon or Ascendant partnership. Neptune tends to be passive and sometimes, gives in too much too often, creating an unequal or unbalanced relationship. It can't help it, its work is to promote harmony through compassion and self-sacrifice after all. But this tendency could cause more complications than are desirable in love relationships, mainly because Sagittarius Moon lovers want their partners to be reasonable but not over-compliant and weak.

Jupiter, the largest planet in the planetary family tends to think big, is wisdom seeking and highly experimental in various areas of life. Both these forces experience a strong attraction but their relationship may be rather lopsided due to the passivity of Neptune and the dominance of Jupiter. If this can be corrected, then their road ahead is free and open for as far as they both dare to see. If a clash of wills ever occurs between them, the Neptune-ruled, Pisces type lover will probably back down most of the time, which will mean that the Jupiter-ruled, Sagittarius Moon lover could get disconnected from what the other lover really feels but won't share, due to unexplainable fears. One of the lovers will have to modulate the relationship in such a way that neither has the upper hand and the channels of frank communication are always open.

The Pisces type lover is attractive, highly emotive and will lean toward seeking out or being around more assertive personalities with whom to stabilize their life. That need for a dependable anchor or reliable lover will always be there, perhaps because they know deep inside that their fluidity (Pisces is a water sign) must be matched with the solidity of the character of their ideal soul mate.

Unfortunately, this desire to seek out strength sometimes results in harmful relationships with people who look the part, talk the part and promise those exact things that a true, life-partner would, but may never deliver those things to the trusting Pisces type lover. Therefore, the urge to merge instantly must be tempered, and new lovers must be tested out thoroughly before commitment is offered. The Pisces type partner may also have a fear of loneliness or abandonment, and perhaps this fear may sometimes be so heightened that compromises are made and the wrong lover is accommodated in an effort to avoid being without a lover. The Sagittarius Moon partner admires lovers who are as comfortable with independence as they are with boundary-dissolving closeness between two, passionate lovers.

Studying the triggers and fears of each sign might help explain their desires. What does a Sagittarian Moon lover fear? They have a fear of losing their freedom to an emotionally dependent lover who cannot function without their partner at all, and keeps following them around instead of living their own life. What does the Pisces type lover fear? They fear never being able to enjoy a stable and joyous life with their chosen soul mate due to interferences and unexpected changes of heart.

The Pisces energy brings out the Sagittarius Moon lover's compassionate side, while the Sagittarius Moon energy causes the watery Pisces person to be more in-tune with how life is, instead of how they fantasize it could be (Neptune rules fantasy and the dream world). No one mood will be constant with the watery, Pisces type lover and no one emotion will last forever, which is good because it gives them a chance to get over problems easily without brooding about them. The Pisces type lover is emotional, so once again, one of the most gregarious signs in the entire zodiac will have to use more tact and sensitivity when talking to their soft-hearted Pisces type lover. This is a romantic and expressive combination and they can achieve great success by administering the slightest changes in their personalities for maximum compatibility.

Chapter 22

The Capricorn Moon Sign Lover

Capricorn Moon vs. Aries Sun, Moon or Rising Sign
The Earth and Fire Relationship

Earth: "Does my boyfriend manage his finances maturely or will I end up paying his bills and supporting him? I need stability and true commitment before I can enjoy the romance between us." the earthy female thinks to herself. "Will my future wife spend my hard earned cash on frivolous items at the mall or be wise enough to save up for our retirement?" the earthy male lover wonders.

Fire: "I need romance and passion to really enjoy my relationship. Will my boyfriend be a faithful mate for life?" the fiery female partner wonders. "I want an active and freedom-loving partner. Will my girlfriend understand my need for true freedom in life or be too controlling?" the fiery male lover thinks to himself.

Capricorn Moon lovers can enjoy a highly successful and ambitious relationship with partners who have their Sun, Moon or Rising sign in the passionate and assertive fire sign of Aries. Each partner symbolizes an element. Understanding that element helps us delve deeper into the real personality of that partner. Fire represents a desire to seek out excitement and adventure; these in turn provide opportunities for greater emotional growth through risk-taking. Earth represents a need to build, protect and secure that which is most important, which would be stable, long-term relationships: earth is a faith in love and an undying dedication to a relationship.

There are two separate types of the Capricorn Moon personality; one is the *teacher type* and the other is the *follower type.* Let's look at each one closely. The teacher type of Capricorn Moon personality is super-ambitious, diligent, intelligent and dominant by temperament. The follower type is more likely to seek fulfillment through relationships rather than climbing the never ending, social ladder. Both adapt well to relationships and marriage, as long as the teacher type lover is paired up with a non-combative and peace-loving partner who will not challenge their authority, and as long as the follower type Capricorn

Moon lover is matched up with a protective, assertive lover whose approval they will tend to rely on.

If you're soft-spoken, cultured by temperament, refined and graceful, the Capricorn Moon lover just might fall in love with you. Aries types have great lessons to learn from the stable Capricorn Moon energy. Capricorn Moon lovers can inspire their fiery mates into believing in themselves and bolster their self-confidence on many levels. Primarily supportive and protective, Capricorn Moon lovers can guide Aries type lovers into learning to incorporate the most important and best qualities of Saturn into their natures: caution, wisdom and fair judgment. Aries types become more frugal and success-oriented around the Capricorn Moon life-mate.

The Capricorn Moon lover functions under the influence of Saturn while the Aries type lover is governed by the energy of Mars. Mars and Saturn are true opposites in the planetary family; Saturn symbolizes caution, stability and knowledge, while Mars is representative of action, bold energy and a fearless sense of adventure. When these two differing energies join forces in the game of love, it will be an interesting union, where both lovers will end up picking up some of the signature traits belonging to the other over time.

If interpersonal problems arise, as they are bound to in any relationship, neither of them should wait too long to say they're sorry. Doubt has no place in the Capricorn Moon/Aries Sun, Moon and Rising sign relationship and both partners should make every effort to talk out differences the *same* day they occur. Love cannot be burdened by suspicion, for then, love would be nothing more than a fleeting conversation that is easily forgotten. Waiting too long might cause fear and resentment to set in, and there may be no cure for that. The Capricorn Moon lover stabilizes the relationship while their impetuous Aries type mate energizes it and brings it to life.

The Capricorn Moon lover slows down the fast-paced, and sometimes, scattered Aries type energy and causes it to look before it takes those giant leaps into nowhere in particular. Capricorn Moon lovers will make sure that the 'nowhere in particular' becomes somewhere very important. The Aries type lover will want to successfully attempt bigger and better things with the aid of the guidance of their beloved Capricorn Moon lover and use their time more constructively. *"Life is short, sweetheart, figure out what you want to do with your time."* advises the Capricorn Moon lover.

Saturn can sometimes make the Capricorn Moon partner want to control the speed at which the relationship is progressing, so that it can be allowed to blossom *carefully*. The Aries type partner may not initially comprehend the slowing down of the relationship and may mistakenly see it as a rejection. The Capricorn Moon male lover may perhaps suddenly go from dating someone four to five times a week to about two or three times a week. The Capricorn Moon female may try the same thing by limiting the number of phone calls to her boyfriend, which means that he ends up calling her more often and thinking about her a lot more intensely than before. The Saturn energy is wise and there is always a reason behind their actions, even if it takes the other person some time to come to grips with it.

Mars is the planet of instant gratification and could reactive negatively, at least in the beginning, to this change of pace. Which is why the Capricorn Moon partner will have to assure them of the genuineness of their feelings, but still remain firm with their schedule. Fiery Aries type lovers will respect a partner more if they are not running back and forth to please them, but have their own life and their own reasons for doing what they wish. Letting a love relationship fall second to a job or other pursuits is typical of the earthy Capricorn Moon lover's style, who is gently testing the patience level of their lover. *"If he can't take the pressure now, how will he deal with the ups and downs of a real married life? Being married will mean that both of us will have to work at our relationship a lot more often than we do now in the dating stage. How does my boyfriend bear up under difficulties? Does he up and run, or does he hunker down and try to fix the problem?"* the Capricorn Moon female is likely to ask.

The Aries type lover could completely misconstrue their lover's thoughts and erroneously begin to think that they are no longer in love with them or are trying to avoid them. The fiery lover wants to spend *all* their time with their partner, but the Capricorn Moon partner knows that this would be the easiest way to prematurely kill their love relationship. Aries types fall in love at the speed of light. But their lovers pay the price when the Aries type lover falls out of love equally quickly and never looks back, usually leaving a half-lived but potentially good relationship in their wake. Patience is a virtue and it is also a great training tool the Capricorn Moon lover uses deftly in trying to keep their relationship safe from early burnout.

The Capricorn Moon lover thinks far into the future, while the impulsive Aries type lover will spend more time in the here-and-now, rather than be bothered with thinking about a day that hasn't even dawned yet. Their earthy lover may disagree. When the Moon is in an earth sign (Taurus, Virgo and Capricorn), it creates in them a desire for maintaining higher standards, even at the risk of losing a lover.

With the earthy Capricorn Moon energy to support happy-go-lucky Aries type lovers, they can change their outlook on life and become drawn to their

348 The 12 Moon Signs in Love
348   The 12 Moon Signs in Love

ambitious side more than their purely experimental side. The only problem could be the Capricorn Moon lover's putting too much pressure on their Aries type partner to achieve something they don't want to. As for managing finances, it should be kept in mind that the Capricorn Moon energy is more frugal than careless, especially when it comes to a precious resource like income. Impulsive Aries type lovers should take to spending within reason and always consult their earthy partners before big purchases are made. This courtesy alone will help smooth out a majority of their problems.

Another important tip revolves around the spells of sadness that sometimes come over the typical Capricorn Moon lover; at times like that the impetuous Aries type lover should step back and give their partner lots of space and a steady supply of TLC. Together, both these cardinal energies can create a formidable empire that will stand the test of time, with the Capricorn Moon lover supplying the stability and direction, and the Aries type lover supplying the joy of romance and togetherness.

Capricorn Moon vs. Taurus Sun, Moon or Rising Sign
The Earth and Earth Relationship

Earth: "Does my boyfriend manage his finances maturely or will I end up paying his bills and supporting him? I need stability and true commitment before I can enjoy the romance between us." the earthy female thinks to herself. "Will my future wife spend my hard earned cash on frivolous items at the mall or be wise enough to save up for our retirement?" the earthy male lover wonders.

Capricorn Moon lovers can enjoy a highly stable and fulfilling relationship with partners who have their Sun, Moon or Rising sign in the affectionate and romantic earth sign of Taurus. With both partners operating under the stability of the earth energy, this could be a successful relationship in the making if they both apply themselves. On the other hand, if the powerful influence of the earth element is not contrasted with something to balance it out, the relationship might stagnate and be unable to improve itself over time.

When the Capricorn Moon lover and their Taurus type mate match up in a love story, it will be a memorable one indeed. The double earth vibration creates a sense of familiarity and compatibility. Saturn, the ruler of Capricorn and Venus, the ruler of Taurus couldn't be more different. Usually, the Saturn or Capricorn Moon lover will hold more sway in the relationship, because Saturn is considered to be the more senior planet in the planetary family. Venus gives off an easy-going and relaxed, *"after-hours"* vibe, while Saturn, the wise and serious karma-related planet, gives off a more controlled vibe that tells us to work hard, be cautious, and trust someone only when that trust is truly deserved.

A clash of emotions is inevitable, but not insurmountable by any means. The Capricorn Moon partner may begin to train, in some sense, their fun-loving Taurus type partner into being a more refined version of themselves. While the Venus-ruled, Taurus type lover will help their stressed-out Capricorn Moon lover to loosen up over time and encourage them to talk problems through first before they begin to obsess over them and suffer through migraine after migraine.

The Capricorn Moon lover and their Taurus type mate may lean more toward keeping a lot of their feelings inside, sometimes for years at a time, which could seriously hurt their relationship. An emotional overload could cause these usually stable earth sign partners to lash out verbally or completely withdraw from discussing the problem. Timing is everything and both of them will benefit by paying extra attention to how they address the more volatile issues between them (like their respective money spending styles).

Capricorn Moon lovers are driven and ambitious and need a partner who is emotionally sensitive but also careful about managing money and investing it. Taurus types are closely associated with the money factor, because Taurus is a financial sign. Capricorn Moon lovers yearn to leave their personal imprint on the world, toward building something that they can refer to as their personal legacy, which is important to grasp. They have a deep, emotional need to work so diligently that respect and prestige can be linked to their name forever. A partner with a similar bent of mind will be a gift to this easily stressed out Moon sign, who may need verbal encouragement from a trusted confidant now and then.

Capricorn Moon lovers need to be reminded that all work and no play makes them overly emotional and unable to cope with problems in a calm, rational manner. The need to bury themselves at work and become so totally focused on achieving results may become so great that they may begin to neglect certain, more important parts of their life, like staying in touch with family and friends. Missing birthdays or special days like anniversaries will be detrimental to building trust with lovers; once a loved closes the door to their hearts, the Capricorn Moon person may experience an unutterably painful rejection. Ambition should be balanced with all the other facets of life that are equally important.

There are two kinds of Capricorn Moon personalities that a lover might like to be aware of; one is the *teacher type* and the other is the *follower type*. Capricorn Moon partners will either be very dominant and assertive (like the teacher type) or they might be struggling to express their aggressive side (like the follower type).

If the Taurus type lover is in love with the dominant, *teacher type* of Capricorn Moon lover, then one of them will have to make sure that their assertiveness doesn't become a barrier in their love relationship. If the easy-going and passive, *follower type* of Capricorn Moon partner is involved, then the Taurus type mate might be the more aggressive one. Therefore, it would be best if the more passive and emotionally flexible partner from each sign is matched up with the stronger, protective personality from each sign. Two assertive lovers may end up challenging each other's authority on certain issues, which could seriously disrupt the delicate equilibrium of their relationship. The more passive lover could teach the more take-charge lover the benefits of compromise, while the stronger mate could teach their lover the benefits of feeling their strength and power and becoming more self-confident. Always ready to invest in their joint future, this pair will make responsible parents as well as faithful companions. This pair is rock-solid!

Capricorn Moon vs. Gemini Sun, Moon or Rising Sign
The Earth and Air Relationship

Earth: "Does my boyfriend manage his finances maturely or will I end up paying his bills and supporting him? I need stability and true commitment before I can enjoy the romance between us." the earthy female thinks to herself. "Will my future wife spend my hard earned cash on frivolous items at the mall or be wise enough to save up for our retirement?" the earthy male lover wonders.

Air: "Is my boyfriend open-minded enough and will he appreciate my outspoken side? I need a life mate who will talk to me, communicate with me about everything and not clam up and brood." the airy female partner muses. "Will my girlfriend allow me to do the things I love or will she try to restrict me from expressing myself?" the airy male lover wonders.

Capricorn Moon lovers can enjoy a highly fulfilling and expressive relationship with partners who have their Sun, Moon or Rising sign in the active and open-minded air sign of Gemini. If you have a pleasant, emotionally flexible personality, know where you're going in life and are careful with cash, the Capricorn Moon lover may want to get to know you a little better. Earthy Capricorn Moon lovers are very concerned with where they are going in life and need a partner who is comfortable with walking through life together with them, as one unit. The Gemini type lover may have a problem with the word unit because it might symbolize to them a loss of personal freedom after a relationship begins. This may or may not be true, but differences between both signs must be noted and understood. Gemini type lovers want their life partner to be active, quick and have a burning desire to get out and enjoy life instead of being homebound. Generally, this air sign's entire focus in life lies outside of the home sector.

It should be mentioned for the sake of clarity, that there are two, specific kinds of Capricorn Moon personalities that a lover might be dealing with. Capricorn Moon partners will either be like the *teacher type*, be very dominant and instantly take charge of the relationship by leading it subtly into the direction of their choosing, or they might be like the soft-natured, amiable *follower type* of Capricorn Moon personality, who may still be trying to figure out their role in the world. If the Gemini type lover is in love with the dominant, teacher type of Capricorn Moon person, then one of them will have to make sure that their assertiveness doesn't become an unwanted roadblock in their love relationship. The follower type of Capricorn Moon partner is of a more docile and passive variety, and the Gemini type mate might be the more aggressive one.

Therefore, it would be helpful if the more passive and emotionally flexible partner from each sign is matched up with the dominant personality from each sign. Two leadership-oriented lovers may each want to lead the relationship toward their chosen direction, which means that power struggles would be the order of the day. While two extremely submissive lovers would not be able to decide where the relationship should go, each would depend on the other to make all the important decisions and be reluctant to take the first step.

Capricorn Moon lovers can only relax in a relationship if promises are made and kept; they want their lover to be comfortable with spending the rest of their lives as their mate. The slightest doubt in a lover will be quickly sensed by the Capricorn Moon partner, and this will make them want to back out of the relationship in a hurry, bringing to a rather hasty close quite a promising love connection. Earthy Capricorn Moon partners can privately introduce Gemini types to passion and tenderness, as well as a very reassuring stability, while the Gemini type lover can aid their earthy lover in spreading their intellectual wings and learning to express how they really feel instead of keeping it all bottled up inside.

Capricorn Moon lovers are ruled by Saturn, the ancient planet of karma, while their Gemini type lovers are influenced by Mercury, the fastest and most mentally agile planet in the planetary family. The energies of slow and deliberate Saturn may clash easily with the fast and furious energy of Mercury. Saturn advises, *"Let's think about everything carefully before we commit."* While the Mercurial energy responds by saying *"Life's too short to double check everything! Who's got that much time? Let's just jump in with both feet and let the chips fall where they may."*

Saturn-ruled, Capricorn Moon lovers will try to instill their own life philosophy in their Gemini type lover by saying: *"Let's plan for the future, let's open some IRAs and let's save up for our retirement and maybe we could spend our golden years lying on a beach in Hawaii someday. What do you think, honey?"* The Gemini type lover would respond by saying *"Retirement? We haven't even gotten engaged yet! I love you and want to live with you, travel with you, explore every horizon with you. Why think about our old age when we can enjoy our youth now? You think too far into the future. How about living in the here and now?"* Both will effectively train one another into picking up traits that make their overall personalities well-rounded and wholesome.

This is a good, romantic pairing as long as the Gemini type lover refrains from keeping secrets from their Capricorn Moon lover, and the Capricorn Moon mate can handle their air sign lover's need for personal freedom without taking it too personally. Capricorn Moon lovers are also financially frugal and Gemini type partners will not appreciate being told what to spend money on and what to hold back on. Gemini types need to be more diplomatic around their inwardly sensitive Capricorn Moon sweethearts, while Capricorn Moon lovers can benefit from the fun-loving and merry Gemini type persona, which helps with their tendency toward occasional melancholia or depression due to Saturn's influence on them. This couple could be quite successful if they try even a little to understand each other.

Capricorn Moon vs. Cancer Sun, Moon or Rising Sign
The Earth and Water Relationship

Earth: "Does my boyfriend manage his finances maturely or will I end up paying his bills and supporting him? I need stability and true commitment before I can

enjoy the romance between us." the earthy female thinks to herself. "Will my future wife spend my hard earned cash on frivolous items at the mall or be wise enough to save up for our retirement?" the earthy male lover wonders.

Water: "Is my boyfriend emotionally stable and wise about our joint finances? Or will debts pile up in the first year of marriage? I need a supportive life-long lover as well as a loving one." the watery female lover thinks to herself. "Will my future spouse conserve our financial resources or spend unwisely without thought for the future? I can connect better romantically if I know that my chosen life-mate is passionate as well as mature and pragmatic." the watery male lover wonders.

Capricorn Moon lovers can enjoy an emotionally strong relationship with partners who have their Sun, Moon or Rising sign in the emotive and intuitive water sign of Cancer. It might help the Cancer type mate if they could narrow down which of the two Capricorn Moon personality types they have fallen deeply in love with. The first type of Capricorn Moon lover, the *teacher type*, will display marked leadership tendencies; they will be undeniably ambitious, focused and have their whole life planned out by age twenty-five. The second type of Capricorn Moon personality, the *follower type*, is acquiescent and searches out stronger lovers with whom they can emotionally anchor themselves. If the Cancer type mate is passive themselves, they will be attracted to the dominant, teacher type of Capricorn Moon lover. If the Cancer type partner is of an assertive nature, then they will find easy camaraderie with the more docile, follower type of Capricorn Moon personality. It will be a classic case of the attraction between opposites; each supplies what the other needs rather well.

The signs of Cancer and Capricorn are opposites on the astrological wheel, therefore there will be a desire to take the relationship into the sphere of marriage at some point. Cancer types may unleash a great deal of emotions on their lovers, while their earthy mates will keep it all inside until that emotional overload causes the wall of tolerance to come tumbling down. Frequent communication and regular emotional unburdening could aid them greatly.

Capricorn Moon lovers are driven and ambitious and need a partner who is emotionally sensitive but also careful about managing money and personal assets. Cancer types are closely associated with the collection of things (tokens, pictures, sometimes money), and Cancer types are sentimental and family-friendly. Ambitious Capricorn Moon lovers will usually desire to make a success of themselves in their chosen field; achieving that level of success may become, in some cases, like an obsession to them. Capricorn Moon lovers work really hard and they need a partner who can appreciate their single-minded dedication to success for themselves and their family; after all, every one will want to get in on the fun when the Capricorn Moon lover makes their first million. Both Cancer type lovers and their Capricorn Moon partners take life as well as their love life seriously.

When a Capricorn Moon lover falls in love with a Cancer type lover, the true energies of Saturn (the ruler of Capricorn) and the Moon (the ruler of Cancer) create an interesting interplay of emotions. Saturn is associated with *practical* wisdom and karmic interactions, while the Moon is connected to *emotional* wisdom, where the mind, the intellect and reason are viewed as nothing but blockages to true intuition and spiritual connectivity between loving soul mates.

Saturn will cause the Capricorn Moon lover to sometimes try to control the pace of the relationship with an iron hand, perhaps because the emotive nature of their Cancer type lover may make them feel like things are spinning out of control. But it is important that the Cancer type partner, no matter how emotional on a bad day, is not restricted too harshly. The Capricorn Moon lover feels comfortable around people who keep their feelings neatly tucked inside; they may have a fear of looking weak in front of their foes, so the earthy Capricorn Moon partner seldom shows their real emotions to anyone. Over time, this unreleased energy could blow up and cause more problems. Therefore, it is best for them to not keep such a tight lid on their natural emotions and also let the Cancer type lover express their own feelings.

The sensitive Cancer type lover must, on the other hand, bear in mind that showing too much emotion is as detrimental to a relationship as not interacting enough on an honest level with each other. They might like to keep in mind that too many episodes of over-sensitivity to comments and the smaller transgressions between couples, could cause their earthy lover to shut down all communication systems and begin to gradually withdraw from their relationship. Any partner who has an earthy Moon sign (Taurus, Virgo and Capricorn) will take a long time to open up their hearts again, once they decide to shut them down. Therefore, feelings should be expressed honestly around them, but not so emphatically that it makes them feel uncomfortable and embarrassed.

Commitment is something both of these lovers will be happy with, because it will take out most of the ambiguity and tension from their relationship. A

Capricorn Moon lover will be able to provide their lover with everything material but needs to learn to stop worrying and risk letting that tendency spread to their mate. This sign combination will make responsible parents as well as faithful companions.

Capricorn Moon vs. Leo Sun, Moon or Rising Sign
The Earth and Fire Relationship

Earth: "Does my boyfriend manage his finances maturely or will I end up paying his bills and supporting him? I need stability and true commitment before I can enjoy the romance between us." the earthy female thinks to herself. "Will my future wife spend my hard earned cash on frivolous items at the mall or be wise enough to save up for our retirement?" the earthy male lover wonders.

Fire: "I need romance and passion to really enjoy my relationship. Will my boyfriend be a faithful mate for life?" the fiery female partner wonders. "I want an active and freedom-loving partner. Will my girlfriend understand my need for true freedom in life or be too controlling?" the fiery male lover thinks to himself.

Capricorn Moon lovers can enjoy a wonderful and passionate relationship with partners who have their Sun, Moon or Rising sign in the charismatic and generous fire sign of Leo. Capricorn Moon lovers will be instantly attracted to potential partners who seem well read, carry themselves with soft-spoken grace and can be self-confident as well as kind. Leo type lovers would benefit from knowing exactly which of the two different types of Capricorn Moon personalities they have become attracted to. The first type is the *teacher type*; the dominant and confident Capricorn Moon lover who is aggressive and will tend to lead openly or indirectly; they will want their lover to fit a certain pattern. The second type of Capricorn Moon persona is the *follower type*, the passive, compliant partner who will be emulative of stronger lovers; this type will be automatically drawn toward the protection of dominant, take-charge personalities.

Therefore it would be best for the relationship if the more passive, anchor-seeking partner were matched up with the stronger personality. This will go a long way in preserving the peace and balance of the relationship. Two aggressive lovers may not be able to carry the whole weight of the relationship on themselves because compromise may not be their forte.

Capricorn Moon lovers function under the influence of Saturn, the serious, careful and karmic planet, while Leo type partners are ruled by the energy of the bright and powerful Sun. When a Capricorn Moon person meets and falls in love with a Leo type lover, they bring into focus the power of both Saturn and the Sun in their relationship. The Sun's energy is strong and ancient, while Saturn keeps a close eye on what people do and what kind of karma they are accumulating through actions taken in various relationships. Since both the Sun and Saturn are dominant forces, once in a while, there might be a clash of wills. Some Leo types are dominant and know exactly what they want, while Capricorn Moon partners think far into the future and lean toward planning meticulously for their life ahead.

Sometimes, the Leo type lover will be temperamental and bossy, or perhaps annoyed and tend to brood. The Capricorn Moon lover may try to, out of a fear of the relationship failing, hold on tighter than they should. The Leo type lover cannot function under suspicion or confusion and needs an openhearted partner by their side. And while the earthy Capricorn Moon partner may have only the best intentions at heart, they may at some level cause more damage to their union than they may be aware of, by internalizing their emotions or being too strict with themselves or their mate.

The key to success and happiness is for this couple to keep the lines of honest communication open no matter how stressful the issue. Perhaps the impulsive Leo type lover should speak less and listen more, and the Capricorn Moon partner could express their real feelings more often instead of agreeing with their lover to keep the peace while disagreeing with them in their hearts. Both these lovers are stronger than they give each other credit for and with the slightest effort, they can achieve their dreams of having each other in their lives for a long time.

Leo types become more frugal, driven and success-oriented around the Capricorn Moon essence. Leo types should perhaps learn to practice being more patient and refrain from jumping to conclusions, which is a fire sign trait. Capricorn Moon lovers receive from sunny Leo types a new perspective on life, where they can be more optimistic, light-hearted and feel more confident about themselves (merry Leo types can help alleviate their Capricorn Moon lover's occasional depression brought on by Saturn's heavy influence with their wonderful sense of humor). As for managing finances, it should be kept in mind that the Capricorn Moon energy is conservative, especially when it comes to a precious resource like income. Leo type lovers should take to spending within reason and always consult their earthy partners before big purchases are made. This courtesy alone will help smooth out a majority of their problems. This will be a faithful, compatible pair.

Capricorn Moon vs. Virgo Sun, Moon or Rising Sign
The Earth and Earth Relationship

Earth: "Does my boyfriend manage his finances maturely or will I end up paying his bills and supporting him? I need stability and true commitment before I can enjoy the romance between us." the earthy female thinks to herself. "Will my future wife spend my hard earned cash on frivolous items at the mall or be wise enough to save up for our retirement?" the earthy male lover wonders.

Capricorn Moon lovers can enjoy a passionate and productive relationship with partners who have their Sun, Moon or Rising sign in the devoted and trusting earth sign of Virgo. When Saturn (the ruler of Capricorn) and Mercury (the ruler of Virgo) meet at the crossroads of life for the purpose of forming an unbreakable romantic union, the core energies of these two planets will come into focus. Saturn is the most cautious, hard working and commitment-loving planet, while Mercury, when filtered through the sign of Virgo, is energetic, result-oriented and analytical. Yes, both of them may want the same things in life and may also achieve them with greater ease than most if they can support each other. But these two lovers must not put too much pressure on each other to achieve anything (or be anything), unless they can make sure that their love is still strong and the tenderness between them remains.

This is a love story of two over-achievers who might initially relegate love and romance to the second level of life, along with fun, excitement and happiness. Waiting too long until the time is right to enjoy these things may be a mistake that neither lover should let the other commit. They must keep their romantic side alive and keep their passion true, or their relationship may feel more like a business meeting than a romance. They should work hard, be successful, do their best and shine in front of the world, but never forget to nurture the softer side of their love, or it will surely perish from neglect and a lack of attention.

A Capricorn Moon lover will be able to provide their lover with everything material but needs to learn to stop worrying or risk letting that tendency spread to their mate. It might help the Virgo type lover if they could clearly distinguish between the two varying types of the magnetic and duty-conscious

Capricorn Moon personality. The first is the assertive, super-ambitious and dominant Capricorn Moon lover, also known as the *teacher type*. The second is the submissive, less ambitious and more creative Capricorn Moon partner who will actively seek out lovers who can help them define their own personalities in some way; this one is known as the *follower type*.

If the Virgo type lover is passive themselves, they will feel attracted to the teacher type, take-charge, dominant type of Capricorn Moon lover. If the Virgo type lover is slightly assertive themselves, they will draw the more passive, compliant, follower type of Capricorn Moon lover toward themselves. This combination of signs could work out quite well, but when the same earthy energy duplicates itself in the Capricorn Moon/Virgo Sun, Moon or Rising sign relationship, a balance will have to be maintained so that things don't get stuck in a rut and the relationship can be kept fresh and resilient.

Capricorn Moon lovers yearn to be able to make a significant contribution to the world and that might involve placing duty over desire many times. They'd hate to come home and hear their spouse say, *"Honey, do you know what day it is today?"* At the same, the Capricorn Moon person should bear in mind that success will mean nothing if the closest people around them have turned away from due to regular neglect and abandonment. This is important to comprehend, especially because Virgo type lovers are extremely supportive of partners who work as hard as they do to achieve something worthwhile, but definitely need their lover in their life every day so that they can interact and enjoy each other's company without having to rush about trying to be on time for appointments and meetings with total strangers.

The Virgo type partner, who may be ideal, if not perfect for the Capricorn Moon lover, will have to watch that tendency to correct which may seem like criticism to their mate if over done. Capricorn Moon mates will have to watch a tendency to over-reach their goals and try to be more communicative, so that their proclivity for depression is kept at bay. This pair can be a very healthy addition to each other's lives and will make responsible parents as well as faithful companions.

Capricorn Moon vs. Libra Sun, Moon or Rising Sign
The Earth and Air Relationship

Earth: "Does my boyfriend manage his finances maturely or will I end up paying his bills and supporting him? I need stability and true commitment before I can enjoy the romance between us." the earthy female thinks to herself. "Will my

future wife spend my hard earned cash on frivolous items at the mall or be wise enough to save up for our retirement?" the earthy male lover wonders.

Air: "Is my boyfriend open-minded enough and will he appreciate my outspoken side? I need a life mate who will talk to me, communicate with me about every-thing and not clam up and brood." the airy female partner muses. "Will my girlfriend allow me to do the things I love or will she try to restrict me from expressing myself?" the airy male lover wonders.

Capricorn Moon lovers can enjoy a pleasing and uplifting relationship with partners who have their Sun, Moon or Rising sign in the relationship-ori-ented and artistic air sign of Libra. There are two separate types of the Capri-corn Moon personality; one is the *teacher type* and the other is the *follower type*. The teacher type of Capricorn Moon personality is super-ambitious, hard-working, bright and dominant by temperament. The *follower type* is more likely to seek fulfillment through relationships rather than worry about soci-etal prestige, bank balances and fancy cars. Both variations on the Capricorn Moon personality adapt well to relationships and marriage, as long as the teacher type lover is paired up with a non-confrontational and harmony-seek-ing partner who will not challenge their authority, and as long as the follower type of Capricorn Moon lover is matched up with a protective, assertive lover whose approval they will invariably seek out.

The Capricorn Moon lover is drawn toward lovers who have a touch of unavailability about them, can be a good conversationalist as well as a faithful friend. Glamorous, Venus-ruled, Libra type lovers will be attracted to the accomplished-looking Capricorn Moon lover, because success and honor can be very attractive to this socially conscious air sign. Capricorn Moon lovers can bring to life any dreams that a Libra type lover can envision. Primarily sup-portive and protective, Capricorn Moon lovers can teach Libra types how to create their own personal legacy and help them bring all their talents in front of the world.

When stern Saturn (the ruler of Capricorn) and flirtatious Venus (the ruler of Libra) meet at the crossroads of life for the purpose of forming an unbreakable romantic union, the core energies of these two planets will come into focus. Saturn is the most cautious, hard working and commitment-seeking planet, while Venus, when filtered through the sign of Libra, is even-tempered, rela-tionship-oriented and peace loving. Lady Venus' has her own agenda and Sir

Saturn's agenda never changes, so one of these two lovers will have to bring in a contrast so that they can create a mutually satisfying direction for their relationship to take.

Venus-ruled, Libra lovers are not all mushy romance and no ambition; when they find the right cause or the right field, they are veritable dynamos and can prove hard to beat. The Capricorn Moon lover will see life in two shades: work and family. You might have noticed that work comes before family. Love would come in at number three, because they believe that they can do without it *most* of the time. The Libra type partner will love their work and vocation and feel thrilled when they are successful, but always put love on the top of their priority list in life. But if their love life begins to show the faintest signs of deterioration, the relationship-oriented Libra type lover will not be able to concentrate on work, no matter how hard they try.

Venus causes Libra type partners to try to sort out any relationship problems quickly so that things don't escalate into more serious issues. They could become more serious issues however, if the Capricorn Moon lover forgets to nurture their love relationship and expects their partner to take care of it and put in all the effort, while they go off into the world to make a success of themselves or their business. The sensitive Libra type lover will see this as an unfair situation and will want their partner to be an equal player in keeping their relationship healthy and enjoyable for both. *"Why do I have to do all the work? Why doesn't he care enough to show up on time for our anniversary dinner? Doesn't our love mean anything to him? Will work always come before our love?"* the Libra type female will wonder.

Her Capricorn Moon lover *does* care about their love relationship, but thinks that he can trust her to be accommodating enough to understand that he may be doing something else that can't wait. *"It's just a party, honey. How many of those have we given and attended? Didn't I go with you all those times? Wasn't I by your side? We're married now, I'm not going anywhere, but sometimes work issues have to be sorted out before things get worse."* the Capricorn Moon male reasons with his beautiful Libra type lover.

Libra type partners become frugal and supportive around the Capricorn Moon partner. Capricorn Moon lovers should be more vocal around the outspoken energy of the Libra type lover, while Libra types should learn to listen more when the wise Saturn energy wants to confide in them (Saturn rules Capricorn). Capricorn Moon mates receive from their Libra type life mate a new perspective on living and viewing life, where they can feel free to be more optimistic, light-hearted and more confident about themselves (gentle Libra types can also help alleviate Capricorn's occasional depression brought on by Saturn's influence).

As for managing finances, it should be kept in mind that the Capricorn Moon energy is never careless, especially when it comes to money. Venus loves to go shopping, so Libra type lovers should try to spend within reason and always consult their earthy partners before big purchases are made. This courtesy alone will help smooth out a majority of their problems. Together, both these dynamic energies can create a relationship or marriage that will stand the test of time, with the Capricorn Moon energy supplying the stability and direction, and the Libra type lover supplying the joy of the perfect romance.

Capricorn Moon vs. Scorpio Sun, Moon or Rising Sign
The Earth and Water Relationship

Earth: "Does my boyfriend manage his finances maturely or will I end up paying his bills and supporting him? I need stability and true commitment before I can enjoy the romance between us." the earthy female thinks to herself. "Will my future wife spend my hard earned cash on frivolous items at the mall or be wise enough to save up for our retirement?" the earthy male lover wonders.

Water: "Is my boyfriend emotionally stable and wise about our joint finances? Or will debts pile up in the first year of marriage? I need a supportive life-long lover as well as a loving one." the watery female lover thinks to herself. "Will my future spouse conserve our financial resources or spend unwisely without thought for the future? I can connect better romantically if I know that my chosen life-mate is passionate as well as mature and pragmatic." the watery male lover wonders.

Capricorn Moon lovers can enjoy an emotionally empowering relationship with partners who have their Sun, Moon or Rising sign in the intense and emotive water sign of Scorpio. There are two separate types of the Capricorn Moon personality; one is the *teacher type* and the other is the *follower type*. The teacher type of Capricorn Moon personality is ambitious and feels exhilarated by hard won success. This type is methodical, thinks far into the future and is dominant by temperament. The follower type of Capricorn Moon personality is less intellectually intense by more emotionally intense. This type seeks and finds true fulfillment through intimate relationships rather than pushing for public acclaim. Both types adapt well to relationships and marriage, as long as the teacher type lover is paired up with a non-combative and peace-loving partner who will not challenge their authority, and as long as the follower type of Capricorn Moon lover is matched up with a protective, assertive lover whose approval they will seek out in order to feel more secure about themselves.

If you're passionate and graceful, ambitious as well as respected by your peers, if you're patient and serious, the Capricorn Moon partner may find a way to be near you. Scorpio type lovers are all this and more. Sensitive and emotional, the Scorpio type lover has a lot in common with the Capricorn Moon lover. Firstly, they're both quite intense. Determined and impossible to sway, the Capricorn Moon/Scorpio Sun, Moon or Rising sign combination could be a power couple with a future (maybe even political success). Like their Capricorn Moon partners, Scorpio types know that the person they finally end up with will not be the average, run-of-the-mill romance seeker, but a person who is worthy of their time, attention and total respect.

When Saturn (the ruler of Capricorn) and Pluto (the ruler of Scorpio) meet at the crossroads of life for the purpose of forming an unbreakable and satisfying relationship, the core energies of these two planets will come into focus. Saturn is the most cautious, industrious and disciplined planet, while Pluto, when filtered through the sign of Scorpio, is eager to transform, from the ground up, any system or relationship they think needs to be improved and changed for the better. Yes, both of them may want the same things in life and may also achieve them with greater ease than most, if they can support each other. But these two lovers must not put too much pressure on each other to do anything, unless their love is strong enough and the tenderness between them remains. With two serious planets affecting this relationship, fun and happiness must be regularly experienced by both lovers in order to take some of the edge off.

Pluto-ruled, Scorpio may tend to bring out the most extreme emotions in their earthy Capricorn Moon lover. As a result, this will be a very intense relationship, where both lovers will have to force themselves, in some cases, to make adjustments that are quite difficult for them to make. But the pay off will be worth it, because when it comes to commitment, both loyal Scorpio type lovers and their devoted Capricorn Moon partners will want it more than anything else. Both these lovers may be of a dominant temperament, therefore one of them will have to understand this difference and regulate their give and take of closeness in such a way that neither partner ends up controlling the relationship too restrictively.

Both the Scorpio type lover and the earthy Capricorn Moon lover worry about the proper management and use of money and resources, so if they're both on the same page about that, ninety percent of their problems will disappear. Their all time favorite motto might be *"A penny saved is a penny earned."* Some Capricorn Moon lovers suffer from depression or melancholia, and they would find great comfort in their patient and understanding Scorpio mate. This will be a close and long-term union because neither will carelessly destroy something that takes so much out them emotionally to build.

The only problems between them may circle around the Capricorn Moon lover's tendency to be practical about everything when they could have let a little emotion seep into the picture, and the Scorpio type lover's tendency to worry about everyday matters that are better handled with ease and a calm, capable temperament. They're both fiercely ambitious if they want to be, and will generally appreciate a lover who strives to better themselves, and rise up proudly in this competitive world. This combination can last forever if one of them becomes the stabilizing factor in the relationship. They both make stalwart long-term marriage partners. If they could bring out each other's lighthearted sides more often, it could help solidify the connection and bring them closer.

Capricorn Moon vs. Sagittarius Sun, Moon or Rising Sign
The Earth and Fire Relationship

Earth: "Does my boyfriend manage his finances maturely or will I end up paying his bills and supporting him? I need stability and true commitment before I can enjoy the romance between us." the earthy female thinks to herself. "Will my future wife spend my hard earned cash on frivolous items at the mall or be wise enough to save up for our retirement?" the earthy male lover wonders.

Fire: "I need romance and passion to really enjoy my relationship. Will my boyfriend be a faithful mate for life?" the fiery female partner wonders. "I want an active and freedom-loving partner. Will my girlfriend understand my need for true freedom in life or be too controlling?" the fiery male lover thinks to himself.

Capricorn Moon lovers can enjoy a fruitful and intellectually stimulating relationship with partners who have their Sun, Moon or Rising sign in the cheerful and expansive fire sign of Sagittarius. Each partner symbolizes an element. Understanding that element helps us delve deeper into the real personality of that partner. Fire represents desire, daring and inspiration while the element of earth symbolizes stability, protection and productivity.

The industrious Capricorn Moon partner will be easily drawn toward the star-like quality of the fiery Sagittarius type person. Sagittarius type lovers will admire the hard-working and stable Capricorn Moon partner, perhaps because they can sense that their earthy mate can do things that they have trouble accomplishing sometimes; like sticking to a routine, keeping their emotions under lock and key and looking toward the future by meticulously planning out every detail ahead of time. Capricorn Moon lovers can assist their Sagittarius type lover in realizing any dream they can envision. Strongly devoted and supportive once their love has been pledged with confidence, Capricorn Moon mates can teach Sagittarius types how to create a personal legacy and shine in front of the whole world, while bringing to their attention the fact that completing any projects that they start is a useful thing for a fun-loving, Sagittarius type mate to do.

Capricorn Moon lovers function under the influence of Saturn, the serious, careful and karmic planet, while Sagittarius type partners are ruled by the energy of the large, powerful and philosophical planet Jupiter. When a Capricorn Moon person meets and falls in love with a Sagittarius type lover, they bring into focus the power of both Saturn and Jupiter in their relationship. Jupiter's energy is strong, idealistic and dominant, while Saturn keeps a close eye on what people do and what kind of karma they are accumulating through actions taken in various relationships.

Once in a while, there might be a clash of desire between the elements of earth and fire. Sagittarius types are dominant and know exactly what they want, while Capricorn Moon partners are intensely focused on furthering their personal goals; for them, fun can take a back seat to purpose for a while. Sometimes, the Sagittarius type lover will be willful and a tad too independent, or perhaps not focused enough on the relationship they share. The Capricorn Moon lover may try to, out of a fear of the relationship failing, hold on to their lover tighter than they should. The openhearted Sagittarius type lover cannot function under suspicion or doubt and needs a more trusting and friendly partner by their side. And while the earthy Capricorn Moon partner may have only the best intentions at heart, they may at some level, cause more damage to their union than they know.

It might help the Sagittarius type lover to figure out exactly which of the two types of Capricorn Moon partner they have lost their heart to. The first is the assertive and ambitious type of Capricorn Moon person, or the *teacher type*, while the second type is the more submissive, acquiescent kind of Capricorn Moon partner, or the *follower type*. The second may be more family-oriented and less ambitious than the first. If the Sagittarius type lover is assertive themselves, they may clash with the aggressive, teacher type of Capricorn Moon lover, while if the Sagittarius type person is of a more passive variety, they may bond more quickly with the stronger, take-charge Capricorn Moon lover.

The key to success and happiness is for this couple to keep the underlying friendship between them alive at all times for any interaction to be fruitful. And the Capricorn Moon lover must not needlessly test the fidelity of their Sagittarius type partner if their loyalty has already been proven, because Capricorn Moon lovers may become too suspicious of their partners if their relationship has been neglected for a prolonged period of time.

Sagittarius types become more frugal, goal-driven and success-oriented around the Capricorn Moon lover. Capricorn Moon mates receive from Sagittarius types a new perspective on life, where they can let their hair down more often and shed the burden of worry that Saturn may have permanently placed on their reliable shoulders (Sagittarius types can help alleviate Capricorn's tendency toward occasional depression or melancholia with their excellent sense of humor, Jupiter is the most jovial planet in the solar system family and will help the Sagittarius type lover heal their mate with laughter and much needed fun).

The only problem they could face could be the Capricorn Moon lover's tendency to place too high an emphasis on achievement in a relationship, urging their lover to get that higher paying job, pushing them to further their career or sometimes simply reach for a higher status than they may have now. This would be a terrible mistake because putting too much pressure on their Sagittarius type partner is the easiest way to lose their trust. As for managing finances, it should be kept in mind that the Capricorn Moon energy is more conservative and will not tolerate a spendthrift lover without letting them know their feelings on the matter; but this should be done tactfully, the proud and independent Sagittarius type lover will refuse to be educated on how to spend their income.

Impulsive Sagittarius type lovers should take to spending within reason and always consult their earthy partners before big purchases are made. This will create more respect between them, as well as a greater measure of trust. Honest dialog alone will help smooth out a majority of their problems. This stellar couple must never forget the power of humor to soothe the trouble spots in their relationship and should make the time to hit the comedy club or see a comedy movie once in a while. Together, both these lovers can create and enjoy a wonderfully supportive relationship that can stand the test of time.

Capricorn Moon vs. Capricorn Sun, Moon or Rising Sign
The Earth and Earth Relationship

Earth: "Does my boyfriend manage his finances maturely or will I end up paying his bills and supporting him? I need stability and true commitment before I can enjoy the romance between us." the earthy female thinks to herself. "Will my future wife spend my hard earned cash on frivolous items at the mall or be wise enough to save up for our retirement?" the earthy male lover wonders.

Capricorn Moon lovers can enjoy a revealing and yet successful relationship with partners who have their Sun, Moon or Rising sign in their own earth sign of Capricorn. The attraction between these two earthy lovers with similar goals will be strong but some adjustments will have to be made for long-term compatibility. The earth element induces stability within earth, with the result that two things can occur: there may be great stability between the two Capricorn lovers or there might be a refusal to get anything done. Once an earth sign person digs their heels in, there is very little that can be done to make them take any action. Mountains don't move, and they can't be pushed around, either.

The key to a successful double earth element relationship is for one of the two Capricorn energy lovers to become the watchdog of the relationship. They must become the rock that steers the relationship toward balance if communication problems occur between them. Both of them are ardent, loving and hard-working. The only problem that could cause complications is when one of them pushes the other too hard or creates an atmosphere of pressure and tension. The Capricorn Moon energy likes to see results and desires that their partner also pitch in and feel their urgency in seeing things progress quickly and successfully.

Capricorn Moon lovers function under the influence of Saturn, the serious, careful and karmic planet, while their partners are ruled by the same industrious energy. When a Capricorn Moon person meets and falls in love with a Capricorn type lover, they bring into focus twice the power of Saturn in their relationship. Ancient Saturn keeps a close eye on what people do and what kind of karma they are accumulating through actions taken in various relationships. Once in a while, there might be a clash of wills due to the cardinal quality of this sign that likes to direct and actively choose a path for the relationship to take.

There are two basic variations on the Capricorn Moon personality; the first is the dominant, *teacher type* of Capricorn Moon partner, whose focus in life will be to rise higher in the world by using the support of sheer will power and personal stamina. Like a little engine that knows no rest, this type will yearn to climb up the social ladder and make something of themselves. Their secret and powerful desire is to be respected, admired and seen as superior than the rest of their circle.

The second is the more passive and compliant, anchor-seeking, *follower type* of Capricorn Moon lover, for whom ambition may not be the be-all-and-end-all of life that is it for the teacher type of this Moon sign. The follower type will be more comfortable when they're not in the lead, but standing next to an aggressive, protective and leadership-oriented partner who functions with more surety in life than they do. The follower type may need a little help with shoring up their self-esteem now and then.

If both partners are dominant, then both will want to lead and direct the course of their relationship, which means that one of them will go to bed angry. If the assertive, teacher type of Capricorn Moon lover is paired up with a lover who actually seeks out a dominant, protective lover, then there could be an understanding between them. There should be no competition between them and neither should challenge the other's control. Capricorn is ruled by Saturn, and Saturn is the "father" planet. Once in a while, at least, father really does know best.

Capricorn Moon partners think far into the future and lean toward planning cautiously for the life ahead. Sometimes, both these earthy lovers will be temperamental and bossy, or perhaps become depressed if their lover cannot understand them at their level. The Capricorn Moon lover may try to, out of a fear of the relationship failing, cling to it and hold onto it tighter than they should. And while the earthy Capricorn Moon partner may have only the best intentions at heart, they may at some level cause more damage to their union than they know.

They should watch for a tendency to be too suspicious of each other's motives as well as the tendency to put so much pressure on each other that they cannot function freely due to burdensome obligations. The Capricorn Moon lover may need some time to adjust and may not like to be pushed into anything until they are ready. Yes, forgiveness usually comes easily and they will be kissing and making up within hours, but if this happens a lot, it could alter the nature of the relationship in a fundamental way. Honest communication is a good start, but it will not help unless both partners approach each other in a tender manner when complex discussions are on the agenda.

Earth signs will make every effort to make sure the relationship is safe and healthy, and therefore make very stalwart partners. As with other Capricorn Moon sign pairings, humor is absolutely essential in keeping this relationship afloat; Saturn's double vibration in this love story may bring out this pair of lover's somber, worry-wart side more often than their cheerful and optimistic sides. That's exactly why the comedy club was created; spending time laughing together will prove more powerfully therapeutic than being romantic. This is a loving, devoted pair indeed.

Capricorn Moon vs. Aquarius Sun, Moon or Rising Sign
The Earth and Air Relationship

Earth: "Does my boyfriend manage his finances maturely or will I end up paying his bills and supporting him? I need stability and true commitment before I can enjoy the romance between us." the earthy female thinks to herself. "Will my future wife spend my hard earned cash on frivolous items at the mall or be wise enough to save up for our retirement?" the earthy male lover wonders.

Air: "Is my boyfriend open-minded enough and will he appreciate my outspoken side? I need a life mate who will talk to me, communicate with me about everything and not clam up and brood." the airy female partner muses. "Will my girlfriend allow me to do the things I love or will she try to restrict me from expressing myself?" the airy male lover wonders.

Capricorn Moon lovers can enjoy an enlightening and supportive relationship with partners who have their Sun, Moon or Rising sign in the forward-thinking and exploratory air sign of Aquarius. If you're attractive, bright, can play hard-to-get once in a while and are reliable by temperament, the Capricorn Moon lover will be intrigued by you. Aquarius types are unique, Uranus-ruled personalities but are not very flexible emotionally, and their fixity may close some doors for them in the field of love. Capricorn Moon lovers are attracted to partners who are focused and will apply themselves with every ounce of their being to get what they want out of life.

"Do you work to live or do you live to work? Do you favor quantity over quality? Do you expect the best out of life or do you settle for mediocre?" the Capricorn Moon lover may ask. These earthy lovers give a hundred and ten percent of their attention to everything they do and falling in love will be no exception. But intellectual Aquarius types may not be as tuned in to their version of love, and may need space and distance in order to fully understand their lover's emotional patterns. The Aquarius type mate shrinks away from excessive emotionality, hysterical lovers as well as those who cannot seem to find their way around life without the constant input and approval of their love mate. Aquarius types prize independence over all else; independence always comes at a cost but it is worth it.

It would help the Aquarius type lover if they could make a distinction between the two different types of the Capricorn Moon personality. The first type is the dominant and confident type of Capricorn Moon lover (the *teacher type*), whose driving sense of ambition may place love and romance on the back burner of life. The second is the more docile or even-tempered Capricorn Moon partner (the *follower type*), who may not be too ambitious, but may instead focus on relationship building and stabilizing their marriage or nurturing an assertive spouse or watching over their family. Their family becomes their career in some sense.

The broad-minded Aquarius type of lover is usually more attached to friends and may even consider people who are not connected to them by genealogy, their primary family. They are open-hearted enough to do this successfully. If the Aquarius type partner is dominant by temperament, they will fare better with the submissive, easy-to-approach, *follower type* of Capricorn Moon lover, who might, at least to some extent, let them shape parts of their life. However, if the Aquarius type lover is passive and still looking for their own voice in life, they could blend energies well with the *teacher type* or assertive type of Capricorn Moon persona – as long as they don't try to take too much of the leadership role away from the Aquarius type partner.

The Capricorn Moon partner functions under cardinal energy, which means that they like to be able to guide the path of the relationship. The Aquarius energy is very freedom loving and may not be able to make too many adjustments in order to keep their lover in their life. Which means that the Capricorn Moon partner will have to be the compromiser and stabilizer and carry the relationship toward safer shores. Capricorn Moon partners are careful about finances and money management, and Aquarian types focus more on idealism and less on pragmatism. This couple's best bet is to carefully study what habits they can live with and what they will not be able to tolerate in the long term.

Sometimes, the Aquarian type lover will be temperamental and moody, or perhaps aloof and deliberately distant and uncommunicative. The Capricorn Moon lover may try to, out of a fear of the relationship failing, hold on for dear life. The Aquarian type lover cannot function under restriction or confusion and needs an extraordinarily understanding partner by their side. And while the earthy Capricorn Moon partner may have only the best intentions at heart, they may at some level cause more damage to their union than they can see.

If the Aquarian type lover someday, voluntarily wants to enter into the traditional and conventional world of marriage and raising children, then they will be capable and wise about it; the only condition is that *they* should powerfully desire it. If their lover is ready to get married and if the Aquarius type lover is not, they will not enter into that setting no matter how much they are prodded or pushed. This is a good match if the fixed Aquarian type lover makes an effort to understand their partner's practical and ambitious side, while the earthy Capricorn Moon partner should try to understand that their air sign sweetheart cannot survive in a very controlled relationship, which is something that could keep it from progressing to the point of marriage. Aquarian type partners bring out their Capricorn Moon lover's expressive and freethinking side, while the Capricorn Moon energy can show their airy lover the benefits of prestige, recognition and diligent hard work.

Capricorn Moon vs. Pisces Sun, Moon or Rising Sign
The Earth and Water Relationship

Earth: "Does my boyfriend manage his finances maturely or will I end up paying his bills and supporting him? I need stability and true commitment before I can enjoy the romance between us." the earthy female thinks to herself. "Will my future wife spend my hard earned cash on frivolous items at the mall or be wise enough to save up for our retirement?" the earthy male lover wonders.

Water: "Is my boyfriend emotionally stable and wise about our joint finances? Or will debts pile up in the first year of marriage? I need a supportive life-long lover as well as a loving one." the watery female lover thinks to herself. "Will my future spouse conserve our financial resources or spend unwisely without thought for the

future? I can connect better romantically if I know that my chosen life-mate is passionate as well as mature and pragmatic." the watery male lover wonders.

Capricorn Moon lovers can enjoy an emotionally fulfilling and close relationship with partners who have their Sun, Moon or Rising sign in the poetic and sensitive water sign of Pisces. Each partner symbolizes an element. Understanding that element helps us delve deeper into the real personality of that partner. Earth represents permanence and predictability while the element of water represents a fluidic nature and an ability to adapt easily to life's ever-changing panorama.

Let's begin by distinguishing between the two, distinct types of the Capricorn Moon personality. The first type is the *teacher type*, while the second is the more easy-going, relaxed and un-ambitious type of Capricorn Moon partner or the *follower type*. Capricorn Moon lovers react well to the emotional Pisces type lover, and can respond successfully to its most important need: to be protected and loved. Be that as it may, the watery Pisces lover should bear in mind that their Capricorn Moon partner is inwardly as emotional as they are, but does not show it as freely as they do. When the Pisces type lover is feeling blue or moody, the earthy support of their Capricorn Moon partner can bring them the solace they need. But when their Capricorn Moon lover feels melancholic, they will need a lot of space (emotional and physical) in order to come out of it. Prodding and pushing them into sharing what ails them will make them reach deeper into their sadness, but leaving them alone and gifting them solitude will be of enormous help to them. TLC should be offered but only when it is the right time.

Capricorn Moon lovers function under the influence of Saturn, the serious, careful and karmic planet, while Pisces type partners are ruled by the energy of the inspirational and dreamy planet Neptune. When a Capricorn Moon person meets and falls in love with a Pisces type lover, they bring into focus the power of both Saturn and Neptune in their relationship. The energy of Neptune is expressive, imaginative and artistic, while Saturn emphasizes hard work, control, discipline and stability. Neptune dreams, while Saturn protects.

Pisces types are usually passive, accommodating (perhaps too much so) and may seek out the approval of a stronger personality, while Capricorn Moon partners are assertive and like to plan out the specific steps they may have to take in the future. *"If I'm prepared, I could handle anything in life. If I'm careful, I could overcome any difficulty with ease. If I remain honest and disciplined, success will be mine when the time is ripe."* the fascinating Capricorn Moon person thinks to themselves. Sometimes, the Pisces type lover will be temperamental and evasive, or perhaps too sensitive and dependent on approval or attention. The Capricorn Moon lover, on the other hand, may try to control the relationship more than is good for it. The Pisces type lover cannot function under too much restriction (which leads to long-term emotional pressure) and needs a more easy-going and even-tempered partner by their side. And while the earthy Capricorn Moon partner may have only the best intentions at heart, they may at some level cause more damage to their relationship than they can comprehend, by having expectations that may become too high to fulfill.

The key to success and happiness is for this couple to keep talking to each other and give each other a regular status report on the current conditions of their hearts. Perhaps the Pisces type lover should take into account their Capricorn Moon partner's desire for success in all areas of life (including relationships) and could express their real feelings more often, instead of agreeing with their lover to keep the peace while disagreeing with them privately. The Capricorn Moon lover could try to let their relationship grow and blossom independently of any repeated intervention, instead of pushing it into a set pattern (Capricorn Moon partners like to methodize). Both these lovers can successfully acclimate to each other's needs, but may need time to do so.

Each of these two lovers expresses emotions differently and if they study each other's style, it will pay off in a big way, promising them long-term compatibility. The Capricorn Moon partner is typically frugal and careful with finances, while the more emotional Pisces type partner may be a bit of an impulse shopper. Being around their earthy lover will make the Pisces type lover more cautious and pragmatic. Being around the sensual and romantic Pisces energy will bring out in the Capricorn Moon lover, a most touching tenderness and sensitivity. This is a good romantic pairing if each becomes a little like the other. If they're planning a family, the maternal essence of watery Pisces and the fatherly influence of the Capricorn Moon lover will create a secure home environment.

Chapter 23

The Aquarius Moon Sign Lover

Aquarius Moon vs. Aries Sun, Moon or Rising Sign
The Air and Fire Relationship

Air: "Is my boyfriend open-minded enough and will he appreciate my outspoken side? I need a life mate who will talk to me, communicate with me about everything and not clam up and brood." the airy female partner muses. "Will my girlfriend allow me to do the things I love or will she try to restrict me from expressing myself?" the airy male lover wonders.

Fire: "I need romance and passion to really enjoy my relationship. Will my boyfriend be a faithful mate for life?" the fiery female partner wonders. "I want an active and freedom-loving partner. Will my girlfriend understand my need for true freedom in life or be too controlling of my actions?" the fiery male lover thinks to himself.

Aquarius Moon lovers can enjoy an emotionally fulfilling and close relationship with partners who have their Sun, Moon or Rising sign in the idealistic fire sign of Aries. Each partner symbolizes an element. Understanding that element helps us delve deeper into the real personality of that partner. Fire represents a need to live life without restrictions or limits; this passionate element emphasizes the need to take risks in order to fully assess how high their faith in themselves can let them fly. Air represents a need to use self-expression as a means to open not one, but a myriad different doors in order to bring remarkable people, brilliant ideas and useful discoveries together.

If you're unique, can look beyond the exterior of a person, believe in contributing to something greater than yourself and have a pronounced social conscience, the Aquarius Moon lover will want to draw closer to you. If you're deeply in love with an Aquarian Moon partner, it would greatly help you to distinguish between the two different Aquarian Moon personalities, as this will aid you in deciphering and cracking the secret code to this fascinating Moon sign.

The first type of Aquarian Moon personality is the *intellectual activist type.* This type is charismatic, assertive, original in manner and thought, and usually places their entire life focus on goals that are not conventional or run-of-the-mill. The intellectual activist type of Aquarian Moon partner is friendly without letting anyone get too close, needs a near constant stream of intellectual stimulation and will choose to direct their emotional and spiritual faculties toward a cause or belief-system that, in the grand scheme of things, has far greater value than the things that the average person busies themselves with in life. Emotionally draining environments or individuality-dissolving relationships will cause this type to choose their autonomy over coupling under too many restrictions or unreasonable demands.

The second type of Aquarian Moon persona is the friendly, open-minded *social butterfly type.* This type is likely to devote a majority of their energies toward fun-filled activities with friends and acquaintances. Their focus is to be out of the house and working on pet projects that involve all their buddies. The social butterfly type of Aquarius Moon lover will adjust better to the give and take involved in mature love relationships and may be capable of making the adjustments needed to stabilize a good marriage. The key here is that they *alone* get to decide, without pressure from an impatient partner, when and how the relationship morphs into a marriage.

If the Aries type lover happens to be dominant and assertive by temperament, they might have some difficulty in getting along with the equally dominant, intellectual activist type of Aquarian Moon personality. Two forceful people will demand to get their way when problems arise, and a repeat performance of that could weaken the fabric of the relationship over time. If the Aries type lover is patient, submissive or compliant by nature, they may have a better, harmonic way of getting along with the intellectual activist type of Aquarian Moon partner.

The social butterfly type, or the more pliant and acquiescent, second category of the Aquarian Moon partner may be able to blend energies nicely with both the aggressive Aries type as well as the dominant Aquarian Moon type of lover. The signs of Aquarius Moon and Aries can be a wonderful addition in each other's lives if each makes an effort to figure out each other's expectations instead of assuming they know them, because conclusion jumping could cause unnecessary confusion in their hearts. Most Aquarian Moon lovers are intense individuals and often focused toward loftier ideals that would allow them to make a significant intellectual offering to the world of ideas. This, they feel, would be the easiest way to immortalize their thoughts before the world community. A supportive but independent lover would simplify their life instead of complicate it by demanding more attention than they are capable of giving in a relationship.

The Aries type partner is affectionate, full of energy and this attracts the airy Aquarian Moon lover to their side. Aries types are very mindful of how their partner restricts or enhances their freedom. This is beneficial because Aquarian Moon partners also want a lover who can strike a healthy balance between closeness and distance, between intimacy and personal autonomy; these two share the same mental wiring, so to speak. The Aquarian Moon lover wants to be tempted more by the ageless ideas in their partner's mind than their physical allure; which they know can fade with the passage of time.

It will take a bright and freedom-loving partner to grant their beloved Aquarian Moon lover the space and independence they need to be happy. When it comes to success, both the Aries type lover and the Aquarian Moon partner will not display the slightest jealously toward each other and will actually encourage each other and feel proud of their various achievements. Each open-heartedly exults in the other's success. The wise Aquarian Moon soul actively refuses to be pigeon-holed and yearns to break away from the concrete jungle. They know that the human spirit is born free, and should remain unfettered by the strict rules of society. Aquarius Moon lovers are ruled by the renegade planet Uranus, and this planet embodies very much the same qualities as Mars, the "bad boy" member of the planetary family that rules Aries type lovers. Both place great importance on a life that is truly and freely lived.

The best way to show an Aquarian Moon lover that you adore them is to bind them up—with freedom. A partner who is more of a friend than a passionate one-night encounter will be more valued by the Aquarian Moon lover, because this airy essence comprehends the universal medium of friendship more easily than human passion that often narrows the peripheries of personal freedom. Easily able to develop many quasi-filial ties over a lifetime, this friendly Moon sign sees the faces of family in friends and places their friends higher up on the chain of importance than family. The Aquarian Moon lover should keep in mind that their antsy and impatient Aries type lover may have a temper but is honest and respects partners who are straightforward, non-manipulative and loyal. The Aquarius Moon partner places emphasis on universal achievement while their energetic and child-like Aries type lover places emphasis on fun and pleasure. They should create a solid and faithful friendship first and passion will follow with ease.

Aquarius Moon vs. Taurus Sun, Moon or Rising Sign
The Air and Earth Relationship

Air: "Is my boyfriend open-minded enough and will he appreciate my outspoken side? I need a life mate who will talk to me, communicate with me about every-thing and not clam up and brood." the airy female partner muses. "Will my girlfriend allow me to do the things I love or will she try to restrict me from expressing myself?" the airy male lover wonders.

Earth: "Does my boyfriend manage his finances maturely or will I end up paying his bills and supporting him? I need stability and true commitment before I can enjoy the romance between us." the earthy female thinks to herself. "Will my future wife spend my hard earned cash on frivolous items at the mall or be wise enough to save up for our retirement?" the earthy male lover wonders.

Aquarius Moon lovers can enjoy a stable and rewarding relationship with partners who have their Sun, Moon or Rising sign in the careful and dependable earth sign of Taurus. Elementally, air and earth can be compatible and helpful to each other. Air is movement and restless ingenuity while the earth is ancient and immovable.

The Taurus type lover could establish greater compatibility with their Aquarian Moon mate if they could distinguish between the two distinct types of Aquarius Moon personality. The first is the *intellectual activist type* and the second is the *social butterfly type*. The intellectual activist type is smart, hip, dominant and drawn toward devoting their energies toward humanitarian goals, while the social butterfly type is accommodating, plaint and more focused on friendships and light romances. The Taurus type lover may get along with the social butterfly type of Aquarius Moon lover more easily; both will at some point contemplate marriage and sharing a life.

When an Aquarian Moon lover falls in love with an earthy Taurus type lover, both will learn valuable lessons from each other. The airy Aquarian Moon lover will learn to enjoy a lover who is honest and reliable in times of crisis, while the Taurus type lover will enjoy a partner who is different, intellectually superior to all their other lovers and also has a faithful side. Traditionally, the Aquarian Moon partner will subconsciously search for a lover who is attractive, but not only physically. Their heart will pull them toward a mate who has a strong social conscience and is willing to fight for that they believe in (Aquarius is the eleventh sign which is connected to the eleventh sector of humanitarianism in astrological charts).

The relationship-oriented Taurus type partner will, when the time is right to settle down with a life-companion, look for a lover who is a good blend of stability and sensuality. Taurus types need to have a regular partner in life with whom they can enjoy intimacy. To the Aquarian Moon partner, intimacy will not follow unless there is a meeting of the minds first, because they need to be admirers of the way their lover thinks, lives and expresses their creativity. This airy lover will refuse to comply with society's fickle views of what is acceptable or not, and will instead try to create their own set of rules that better suit their life-philosophy. The earthy Taurus type lover wants to find a life-mate who can be depended on and unless it is the right time, the Aquarian Moon lover will not make an effort to solidify their bond.

When that occurs, the earthy Taurus type partner must not force the issue or misunderstand their airy lover's feelings. Yes, their Aquarius Moon lover does desperately love them, but needs to figure out their next move based on their own emotional timetable. Both signs are fixed and will not budge unless they think the conditions are ripe to take action. This relationship can survive, even thrive, if both of them agree to disagree on certain issues, while learning to give each other what they really need emotionally. What does an Aquarian Moon lover really need? They need a life-companion who has a buoyant temperament, forgives easily and will adjust to their unique outlook on life. Friends who become confidants first and lovers second, will have a longer, more emotionally comfortable relationship than friends who proceed directly from the friend stage to the sexual stage. What does the sensual Taurus type partner need? They need to create a love story of their own that can stand the test of time and brave any storm, no matter how mighty. They need freedom too; the freedom to admit that they need stability and commitment from their lover.

The key to success and happiness is for this couple to keep the lines of honest dialog always open. Perhaps the Aquarian Moon lover should understand that if all the adjustments are made to come from their lover, it could cause them to feel undervalued. The Aquarian Moon partner will not meddle with a relationship if they feel it is functioning relatively smoothly, and things will have to get quite complicated before they realize that the relationship is in dire danger of ruin. Waiting too long to jump in and pacify their lover would be a tricky step to take. The Taurus type partner should worry less about where the relationship is going, while the Aquarian Moon lover should not neglect doing their fair share of work on their union. Both these lovers are supportive of one another and hope to have each other in their lives for a long time. As with other romantic pairings, this relationship should begin as a strong, long term friendship before it blossoms into something deeper. This is a stellar couple!

Aquarius Moon vs. Gemini Sun, Moon or Rising Sign
The Air and Air Relationship

Air: "Is my boyfriend open-minded enough and will he appreciate my outspoken side? I need a life mate who will talk to me, communicate with me about every-thing and not clam up and brood." the airy female partner muses. "Will my girlfriend allow me to do the things I love or will she try to restrict me from expressing myself?" the airy male lover wonders.

Aquarius Moon lovers can enjoy an intellectually strong relationship with partners who have their Sun, Moon or Rising sign in the expressive and curious air sign of Gemini. Elementally, a double *air,* romantic pairing can be successful if certain adjustments are made by both lovers. Air supports air and blends with it seamlessly. But it should be noted that a whole lot of air going around without aim only becomes a destructive typhoon. While, when it is controlled and properly tempered, it becomes the clean, fresh breeze that we expect when we open the windows of our homes in the springtime.

The Aquarius Moon personality is divided into two distinct personality types; the first is the *intellectual activist type* and the second is the *social butterfly type.* The intellectual activist type of Aquarius Moon lover is bright, assertive, outspoken and devoted to humanitarian causes. The social butterfly type is more submissive, thrives on many different friendships and enjoys the thrill of romance. If the Gemini type partner is dominant, they may run into power struggles with the self-confident, intellectual activist type, but find more in common with the non-aggressive, social butterfly type of Aquarius Moon personality.

Two air sign lovers can be gregarious and active, but they will need the stability of the earth element to secure them, the heat of the fire element to expose them to passion and a touch of the water element to keep them in touch with their feeling sides. Aquarius Moon lovers are inspirational partners who are dedicated to their convictions and as fixed signs, they cannot alter the way they live and think just to fit into a relationship. The Gemini type partner understands that notion and sympathizes with it, but also may feel like settling down some day with a lover who can fit into their lifestyle without too much adjustment.

Both these air signs enjoy spending time with lovers who are interesting but not too traditional in their outlook. Aquarius Moon lovers need a lot of space apart from their lovers; the space to think and enjoy their solitude *their* way, without having to come home to a lover who will question them, call them incessantly on the phone, and try to control their activities too tightly. Gemini type lovers are the same way but may, on occasion, be a little too outspoken (Mercury is the blarney stone planet) with their Aquarian Moon sign sweetheart, who may instead prefer to speak using silence.

Another important point worth noting is that one of these two lovers will have to be the financial watchdog of the union. Arguments about financial responsibility may create unwanted tension between them and sour their affection, which can be totally avoided. Gemini types must also remember that they should never withhold any information, no matter how inconsequential it may seem, from their Aquarian Moon lover and vice versa.

An emotional traffic jam can be avoided if both of them keep talking out grievances instead of hoping they will disappear on their own. Trust will be a primary given between them and preserving its purity must never be taken lightly. These two air sign lovers will be bonded by a love of intellectual pursuits and will encourage each other to fully and fearlessly express whatever is in their hearts at any given time. This freedom must be emphasized. This is a wonderful combination and can last if the relationship is allowed to take its own shape without too much interference from either lover. This is a truly loving couple!

Aquarius Moon vs. Cancer Sun, Moon or Rising Sign
The Air and Water Relationship

Air: "Is my boyfriend open-minded enough and will he appreciate my outspoken side? I need a life mate who will talk to me, communicate with me about everything and not clam up and brood." the airy female partner muses. "Will my girlfriend allow me to do the things I love or will she try to restrict me from expressing myself?" the airy male lover wonders.

Water: "Is my boyfriend emotionally stable and wise about our joint finances? Or will debts pile up in the first year of marriage? I need a supportive life-long lover

as well as a loving one." the watery female lover thinks to herself. "Will my future spouse conserve our financial resources or spend unwisely without thought for the future? I can connect better romantically if I know that my chosen life-mate is passionate as well as mature and pragmatic." the watery male lover wonders.

Aquarius Moon lovers can enjoy an emotionally fulfilling and stimulating relationship with partners who have their Sun, Moon or Rising sign in the sensitive and intuitive water sign of Cancer. When in love, the Aquarius Moon lover could display one of two, specific personality types in a relationship. Learning to tell them apart could greatly enhance compatibility.

The first type is the *intellectual activist type* while the second is the *social butterfly type*. The first type is intelligent, dominant, charismatic and lives in the world of ideation and activism. The second, social type of Aquarius Moon lover is fun-loving, less intense, loves their friends and enjoys a good romance. If the Cancer type lover is aggressive and dominant, they may have trouble relating to the intellectual activist type of the Aquarius Moon sign. However, if they're passive and anchor-seeking, they will want to hover around the protective energy of the intellectual activist type of Aquarius Moon personality.

A successful relationship can be achieved if both partners belonging to each element try to study what the other is really like. The Cancer type of lover is emotional and moody, while the Aquarian Moon partner can be detached as well as intense by turns. Getting used to those rhythms can be difficult, but is not impossible if you're really in love. The Cancer type lover will be able to relate to their Aquarian Moon sweetheart's intense side, but feel terribly out of place with their aloof side. The airy Aquarian Moon lover is driven by beliefs and ideals that their tradition-minded Cancer type lover may not always share. Be that as it may, the watery Cancer type lover will still try to be as supportive as they can be, because the clannish Cancer energy nurtures and protects its loved ones despite difficulties (the sign of Cancer symbolizes the often forgotten, eternal Mother).

The Aquarian Moon partner will subconsciously search for a lover who can be supportive without being too controlling and can understand their need to mold their relationship into one that emphasizes personal freedom instead of unnecessary responsibilities that fulfill neither partner. This Moon sign's needs are simple; they want to be able think as well as live without restrictions.

Aquarian Moon partners will appreciate their caring lover's tendency to protect and be understanding, but to really stabilize this union, each lover will have to supply the things their partner desperately needs but is unable to openly or adequately ask for. What does the watery Cancer type lover need? They want a lover who is completely comfortable with their emotions as well as those of their partner, and can pledge their love to their lover without doubts or the subconsciously lingering fear of potential failure. What does the freedom-loving Aquarian Moon partner need? They want their lover to be easy to talk to, as well as comfortable with occasional solitude; their own as well as their partner's.

The Cancer type lover usually hopes to put together a home base from which they can respond to the world and its demands. The home has a special significance for the sensitive Cancer type lover; it represents not only a roof with four walls, but a secure place where they can begin the ancient process of emotional nesting. The Cancer type lover may privately battle a fear of losing their main support systems in life and in an effort to protect what they do have from dissolution, they cling to their lovers even tighter and more desperately.

Self-confidence could help the Cancer type partner come out of those magical but often emotionally debilitating lunar moods, during which they may reach out to a spouse, their mother, or their children with even greater ferocity. If a Cancer type lover decides to fall in love, they will want their efforts to mean something tangible and permanent. If their most important support systems in life are not permanent, how can they be of any help or value to them in a crisis? A reliable lover might fill that need, if they can be sensitive enough to understand the core, emotional makeup of the amazing Cancer type personality.

The Aquarian Moon lover, on the other hand, is terrified of ending up with a living, breathing cliché of a partner who has done nothing interesting with their life and would prefer to live out a bland existence just like every other person on earth. Studying one's partner takes more than just eyesight. So, they must find the triggers (enjoying a non-critical lover is crucial to the Aquarian Moon lover) and fears (the Cancer type lover's fear of abandonment and loneliness) and work with them. A partner who causes an emotional overload in an Aquarius type lover, will soon find that they slowly drift away from them. Gridlock can be avoided if both of them discuss their problems instead of hoping their lover will take care of them. This union has a good chance of being successful if both lovers can agree to meet each other half way. If they're both truly in love, doing this will be easy. This will be a devoted pair.

Aquarius Moon vs. Leo Sun, Moon or Rising Sign
The Air and Fire Relationship

Air: "Is my boyfriend open-minded enough and will he appreciate my outspoken side? I need a life mate who will talk to me, communicate with me about everything and not clam up and brood." the airy female partner muses. "Will my girlfriend allow me to do the things I love or will she try to restrict me from expressing myself?" the airy male lover wonders.

Fire: "I need romance and passion to really enjoy my relationship. Will my boyfriend be a faithful mate for life?" the fiery female partner wonders. "I want an active and freedom-loving partner. Will my girlfriend understand my need for true freedom in life or be too controlling?" the fiery male lover thinks to himself.

Aquarius Moon lovers can enjoy an engaging and exhilarating relationship with partners who have their Sun, Moon or Rising sign in the open-hearted and cheerful fire sign of Leo. These two signs are polarized (opposed), so the attraction here will lean toward marriage and setting up a home together at some point. There may be oppositions to each other's plans but the desire to overcome differences will also be strong.

The Leo type lover should note that there are two, distinct types of the Aquarius Moon personality. Knowing which one you've fallen in love with could aid with developing a closer bond. The first is the *intellectual activist type* while the second is the *social butterfly type*. The intellectual activist type is self-assured, assertive, drawn to humanitarian causes and has a well developed social conscience. The second, social butterfly type is less intense, is focused on friendships and is out-going, light-hearted and drawn to romance and merriment. If the Leo type lover is dominant, they will clash with the intellectual activist type of Aquarius Moon lover, but if they are passive, they will gravitate toward their charisma.

Leo type lovers are positive, happy and optimistic souls who thoroughly enjoy being part of a couple. Forever searching for that one perfect companion, Leo type lovers will be instantly attracted to the elusive Aquarian Moon personality. Aquarian Moon partners are one-in-a-million souls who possess a broad-minded view of life and people, and can understand that there are many different things that you can do with your life. Often, the traditional family and children path that some people take in life may be unsuitable for the intellectually sensitive Aquarian Moon lover who may want more out of life. Be that as it may, the romance-seeking social butterfly type of Aquarian Moon lover will slip with greater ease into the marriage mode, if their spouse will promise never to parent them or smother them.

The intellectual activist type of Aquarian Moon partner believes that there are other, more intellectual pursuits that can lift a person out of the boring shell of their daily life and truly immortalize them; deep down most Aquarian Moon people want to shine and make a difference in a humanitarian capacity. The Leo type lover will have absolutely no problem with their attractive Aquarian Moon partner wanting to be appreciated, because they know how exhilarating it can be to be noticed. Leo type lovers bond closely with partners who understand their secret need to be genuinely loved and admired. A verbally careful lover, who will take care to not wound the sensitive Leo type lover's self-esteem will do very well with them.

Most Aquarian Moon lovers are intellectual purists who are enamored of the act of falling in love and experiencing true romance, but something in them fears that if they surrender themselves to this intoxicating feeling, they might have to lose their freedom to live their life according to their own rules. Their secret hope is to find that rare soul who understands their needs; their need for emotional space as well as emotional closeness at carefully timed intervals; their need to converse with intelligent lovers and their need to drive their lives toward that one goal that will make a big difference in someone's life. A partner who causes an emotional system overload in an Aquarius type lover, will soon find that they begin to refrain from including them in their life. Communication gridlock can be avoided if both of them keep making their thoughts known frequently.

The key to success and happiness is for this couple to keep their friendship, even more than their romance, alive at all costs. If marriage is on the cards, then both of them should be prepared to compromise, adapt and adjust, particularly because they are both fixed by temperament (Aquarius and Leo are fixed in quality). A secure home environment may allow both of them to ease into a whole new facet of exploring each other. The Leo type lover does rather well in the family environment; they will adore their children and be sure to include any parents or caretakers (if they have a good history with them) into the family circle of security. The Aquarian Moon lover will observe and want to join in, and if their own family relations have been good or neutral, they will also enjoy the closeness that can develop within the emotionally well-balanced members of a family.

A Leo type lover will admire the well-intentioned and pure Aquarian Moon soul, but may sometimes wonder if life could contain a little more passion, a little more sensuality and maybe even some soul mate talk. The Aquarian Moon partner may be able to respond to these needs in their demonstrative partner some of the time, but will have difficulty doing so all the time. Keeping a Leo type lover engaged is hard work and the airy Aquarian Moon lover will definitely try. But in the end, these two fixed signs will have to decide who the stabilizer of the relationship will be. Power sharing is key. This romantic pairing can merge life-paths rather well, if each lover carefully studies what their partner *must* have and what they can realistically do without. This will be a loving match!

Aquarius Moon vs. Virgo Sun, Moon or Rising Sign
The Air and Earth Relationship

Air: "*Is my boyfriend open-minded enough and will he appreciate my outspoken side? I need a life mate who will talk to me, communicate with me about everything and not clam up and brood.*" *the airy female partner muses.* "*Will my girlfriend allow me to do the things I love or will she try to restrict me from expressing myself?*" *the airy male lover wonders.*

Earth: "*Does my boyfriend manage his finances maturely or will I end up paying his bills and supporting him? I need stability and true commitment before I can enjoy the romance between us.*" *the earthy female thinks to herself.* "*Will my future wife spend my hard earned cash on frivolous items at the mall or be wise enough to save up for our retirement?*" *the earthy male lover wonders.*

Aquarius Moon lovers can enjoy a productive and devoted relationship with partners who have their Sun, Moon or Rising sign in the hard-working and commitment-minded earth sign of Virgo. The interesting Aquarius Moon sign comes in two flavors; one is the *intellectual activist type*, while the second is the *social butterfly type*. Learning to differentiate between them will greatly aid in enhancing compatibility. The intellectual activist type is bright, unique, drawn toward humanitarian causes and is rather self-controlled in love. The second, social butterfly type is docile, less intense, friendship-oriented, outgoing and seeks romance. The Virgo type lover, if assertive and dominant themselves, will get along better with the social butterfly type, or non-aggressive type of Aquarius Moon personality. If passive and anchor-seeking, the intellectual activist type's independent manner will draw them into seeking their protection.

When an Aquarian Moon lover falls in love with an earthy Virgo type lover, both will have a favorable effect on each other's lives. Usually, the Aquarian Moon lover will first look for a mate who can be a good friend and *then* secretly evaluate their worth as a lover. To this air sign, the concept of personal freedom is not something that all people can grasp and appreciate like they can. The first thing they will think of when they're standing on the verge of a potential relationship, will be if their chosen partner will allow them what they need to feel secure, which would be unrestricted personal freedom to pursue their goals *outside* of the relationship.

This airy Moon sign desperately needs a lover who is not over-sensitive and can easily forgive innocent mistakes instead of making them into emotionally explosive situations. The one thing that an Aquarian Moon lover can safely commit to is a true and faithful friendship. Which is why it is always important to first comprehend what they are uncomfortable with, and then find out what they love. A partner who causes an Aquarius Moon lover to undergo repeated, relationship-related stress, will soon find that they curtail interacting with them. An emotional standstill can be avoided if both of them actively keep talking out grievances instead of letting them fester and double in size.

Traditionally, the Aquarian Moon partner will subconsciously search for a lover who is emotionally flexible and has a good control over their more volatile emotions. *"Will my boyfriend go to pieces simply because he's stuck in a traffic jam? Or will he remain calm and in perfect control? If we end up having children, will he run out of the house when they all start screaming at the same time? Or will he help me in calming them down without resentment?"* the Aquarian Moon female may secretly wonder to herself. The Aquarian Moon lover is terrified of ending up with a living, breathing clone of a lover who has nothing original about them. Studying one's partner needs more than just a set of eyes. So, they must find the triggers (having the freedom to do what they want, when they want, without having to clock in with a lover is crucial to the Aquarian Moon lover) and fears (the Virgo type lover's fear of their relationship or marriage failing despite all their efforts) and work with them.

Most Aquarian Moon partners are unique souls who understand that there are many different things that they can do with their life and that they don't necessarily have to follow the herd instinct. Virgo type lovers are mentally quick and never miss a thing. They will study their easy-going Aquarian Moon lover and mentally take notes. When truly in love, Virgo type lovers are tender, trusting and totally devoted to their lover, sometimes even at great personal cost. When it comes to love, the Virgo type lover may actually enjoy slowing things down a couple of notches. This is because it allows them to enter into their own comfort zone and understand their lover on their own timetable. The Aquarian Moon partner will be awed by the typical Virgo type lover's dedication to their work, their attention to detail, and their ability to keep a very clean and organized home base.

As a thinking sign, the Aquarian Moon partner cannot abide a disorganized abode and will soon prefer spending time out of the house and not inside it, because it might prove too distracting to them. This is a good combination if the Virgo type lover can remember that their Aquarian Moon lover can only function on one timetable; their own. And if the airy Aquarian Moon lover could bear in mind that once they make a promise to their Virgo type sweetheart, this caring and tenderhearted sign will hope that they will keep that promise. Intellectually bonded, a great honor is shared between these two signs and they will begin by respecting one another's abilities, before falling in love. This takes their love to an even higher level. What a great match!

Aquarius Moon vs. Libra Sun, Moon or Rising Sign
The Air and Air Relationship

Air: "Is my boyfriend open-minded enough and will he appreciate my outspoken side? I need a life mate who will talk to me, communicate with me about everything and not clam up and brood." the airy female partner muses. "Will my girlfriend allow me to do the things I love or will she try to restrict me from expressing myself?" the airy male lover wonders.

Aquarius Moon lovers can enjoy an intellectually uplifting relationship with partners who have their Sun, Moon or Rising sign in the relationship-oriented and literary air sign of Libra. There are two distinct types of the fascinating Aquarian Moon personality. Knowing which one they're dealing with might aid the Libra type lover with creating a deeper sense of compatibility. The first type is the *intellectual activist type* and the second is the *social butterfly type*. The first type is wise, dominant, has a well-developed social conscience, and is comfortable with their hard won independence. The social butterfly type is easy-going, passive, focused on fun-filled friendships and is intrigued by the thought of a new romance. The romance-seeking Libra type lover may find more fulfillment with the social butterfly type of Aquarian Moon personality, while the thinker type of Libra partner might have more in common with the intellectual activist type of Aquarian Moon lover.

These two air sign lovers (Aquarius Moon/Libra Sun, Moon or Rising sign) are smart and active, but they will need stability, passion and understanding to fully make use of their coupling. Aquarius Moon lovers are inspirational partners who are dedicated to their own way of living life and as a fixed sign, they find it difficult if not impossible to alter the way they live and think just to accommodate a relationship. The Libra type partner is a romantic creature who dreams of union with their one perfect lover. Intellectual and sensual by turns, Libra types thrive on lots of friendships and enjoy the feeling of being what could be termed *amor*iented. The Libra type lover is emotionally flexible enough to fit into any relationship, but they must take care to not give up too much for the sake of companionship. If a relationship ever ceases to be light and pleasant, they might like to weigh its true value in those Libra scales of justice, and be open to accepting a more free-flowing and compatible relationship down the road. The urge to accept any relationship offer due to boredom or insecurity must be resisted for best and balanced results.

Aquarian Moon lovers will be attracted to partners who have a well-developed intellectual side, a strong sense of convictions, as well as an appealing physique. And before any passion can be developed between them, there has to be a friendship bond that can be solidified properly. A very understanding and freedom-loving partner will have to be chosen so that they can grant their beloved Aquarian Moon lover the space and independence they need to be truly happy. Society often has unrealistic expectations of human beings, and the wise Aquarian Moon soul comprehends that the fewer restrictions man is made to live with, the more substantial his contributions to the world of selfless karmic acts become. Aquarius Moon lovers are ruled by the renegade planet Uranus while Libra type partners are ruled by Venus. Uranus needs to be *free to live*, while Venus needs to be *free to love*. Both intellectual Aquarius Moon mates and their social Libra lovers usually place their life-focus *outside* of the home sector. This can allow them to share in assisting with each other's pet projects without becoming an interference or hindrance in their work.

Both the Libra type partner and the Aquarian Moon lover need to feel that their lover can grant them the full measure of freedom that they are comfortable with – unconditionally and on a daily basis. This includes the freedom to come and go as they please, explore their world through their own eyes and follow their own life philosophies. For example, the attractive Aquarian Moon girlfriend may perhaps not want to have children, so that she can devote most of her time to more important projects that may bring her satisfaction in a way that raising a family may not. The Libra type boyfriend must respect her wishes and not force her to enter into motherhood if she finds that it doesn't resonate with her spiritual core. Aquarian Moon partners are amazing souls who refuse to be typecast, to use a Hollywood term, and this individuality should be encouraged, particularly after marriage, as that would be the true acid test of their love.

The flexible Libra type lover can comfortably blend themselves into any situation, but feels more fulfilled by the right relationships than by anything else. Libra as a marriage sign is more romance-oriented than maternal. Both the Aquarian Moon partner and their Libra type lover can thrive as a couple if they keep a few things in mind; the Aquarian Moon partner needs to know that their lover is a best friend first and a lover second, while the Libra type partner needs to be connected to their partner through a strong, equality-based marriage. This romantic pairing can do well if they keep the lines of communication always open between them. The couple that laughs together, stays together.

Aquarius Moon vs. Scorpio Sun, Moon or Rising Sign
The Air and Water Relationship

Air: "Is my boyfriend open-minded enough and will he appreciate my outspoken side? I need a life mate who will talk to me, communicate with me about everything and not clam up and brood." the airy female partner muses. "Will my girlfriend allow me to do the things I love or will she try to restrict me from expressing myself?" the airy male lover wonders.

Water: "Is my boyfriend emotionally stable and wise about our joint finances? Or will debts pile up in the first year of marriage? I need a supportive life-long lover as well as a loving one." the watery female lover thinks to herself. "Will my future spouse conserve our financial resources or spend unwisely without thought for the future? I can connect better romantically if I know that my chosen life-mate is passionate as well as mature and pragmatic." the watery male lover wonders.

Aquarius Moon lovers can enjoy an emotionally vibrant and spiritually powerful relationship with partners who have their Sun, Moon or Rising sign in the intense and emotionally strong water sign of Scorpio. There are two different facets to the Aquarian Moon personality. The first type is the *intellectual activist type* and the second type is the *social butterfly type*. The first type is independent, has a humanitarian bent of mind, is assertive and self-sufficient. The second, social butterfly type is a more mellow version of the first; they're fun-seeking, feel revitalized by many friendships, can be romantic and can acclimate to marriage if their lover does not impose it on them. The Scorpio type lover is often of a magnetic and dominant temperament, therefore they may experience too many power struggles when matched up with the intellectual activist type of Aquarius Moon personality. They could find greater compatibility with the less aggressive, non-confrontational social butterfly type of Aquarian Moon personality. A marriage might also work out well between them.

The Scorpio type lover is passionate about everything and makes a very loyal and involved partner. The Aquarius Moon lover is also intense, but may not display that intensity about some of the things the Scorpio type lover feels strongly about. Both these signs are fixed in quality, meaning that they are fixed in belief and habit and will bond only in certain ways and under certain conditions. Knowing the nature of that bonding pattern is key to making their love connection stronger. The watery Scorpio type lover thrives in an emotionally charged and often dramatically intense relationship atmosphere, where the depth and power of both partners is summoned forth and experienced on many levels, on more than one occasion.

The Scorpio view of love is very concentrated and intense, because to them, passion is not synonymous with fun, but with the true beauty of human feeling, which should be valued and not treated casually. A partner who cannot grasp, leave alone match their temperament will feel as though they are not getting the best of their Scorpio type partner's love. The airy Aquarian Moon lover can get very passionate about an ideal or cause, but may lack the watery depth of Scorpio type lovers. Their sensitivities are spread out over many projects and many people, while the Scorpio type lover zeros in like a laser on one or two people at a time. The Scorpio type lover is very comfortable in their emotional skin and accepts the fact that their emotions are the most authentic part of them. Their powerful emotions cause them to undergo many changes in their lives and their lovers will indubitably feel some of them up close and personally.

The Aquarian Moon partner will search for a lover who is attractive, but that physical beauty may not mean everything to them. Their heart will pull them toward a rare personality, an intellectually driven, *emotionally balanced* mate who has a strong social conscience and is willing to fight for that they believe in. Aquarius Moon lovers are life- partners who are dedicated to their particular way of life, their convictions, and as fixed signs, they will find it hard to adapt too easily to someone else's life-trajectory. The Aquarian Moon lover is afraid of ending up with a partner who has no outside interests apart from their relationship. Observing one's partner takes more than just looking at them; one has to dig beneath those emotional layers. Therefore, they must find and work with the fears that each has to deal with privately. The Aquarius Moon lover fears being controlled by a manipulative lover whose fears, suspicions and insecurities constantly get in the way of their love, while the Scorpio type partner fears ending up with a partner who is superficial, cannot keep their promises, lacks character and takes risks with their money (Scorpio is a strong financial sign).

The Aquarian Moon partner may feel as though too much emotionality creates an undue pressure on them and their relationship. They will try their best to understand their wise but emotional partner, but may never completely comprehend why their watery lover reacts to things in a certain way. A partner who consistently causes an emotional overload in an Aquarian Moon lover, will soon find that they will begin to withdraw from spending time with them. Total emotional gridlock can be avoided if both of them keep talking out their problems instead of hoping the other lover will take care of them; this is certainly not a one-man job when two fascinating personalities are involved.

The Aquarian Moon personality revels in autonomy and their emotions are most stable when they know that they are not being held back by their lover in any way. The Scorpio type lover enjoys intimacy and closeness, and feels that this is the most relaxing and pleasing part of their relationship, while their airy Aquarian Moon lover might need some time to be by themselves after prolonged intimacy. This need for space is not a reflection on their relationship or on their passionate Scorpio type lover, but an indication of the need for balance in their lives. The freedom-loving planet Uranus is more responsible for this than anything else.

Aquarius is an air sign, and the air can't be confined in a closed space for too long. Crack open the window and it will rush out in a frenzy. A lover who can grant their Aquarian Moon partner the unfettered freedom to come and go, while promising to always stay in touch, will be able to sustain a long and faithful relationship with them. Neither partner should knowingly push each other's emotional buttons, but always treat each other as intellectual equals and most importantly, as the best of friends. If this happens, they will be compatible enough to share a long life together. This will be a passionate pair!

Aquarius Moon vs. Sagittarius Sun, Moon or Rising Sign
The Air and Fire relationship

Air: "Is my boyfriend open-minded enough and will he appreciate my outspoken side? I need a life mate who will talk to me, communicate with me about everything and not clam up and brood." the airy female partner muses. "Will my girlfriend allow me to do the things I love or will she try to restrict me from expressing myself the way I want?" the airy male lover wonders.

Fire: "I need romance and passion to really enjoy my relationship. Will my boyfriend be a faithful mate for life?" the fiery female partner wonders. "I want an active and freedom-loving partner. Will my girlfriend understand my need for true freedom in life or be too controlling of everything I do?" the fiery male lover thinks to himself.

Aquarius Moon lovers can enjoy an active and exciting relationship with partners who have their Sun, Moon or Rising sign in the outgoing and knowledge-seeking fire sign of Sagittarius. There are two interesting variations on the Aquarian Moon personality. Compatibility would be better gauged if we could tell them apart. The first type is the *intellectual activist type* and the second is the *social butterfly type*. The first type is super-confident, can be ambitious, is usually assertive and leans toward making a difference in the world.

The second type is an easy-to-approach, relationship-friendly, more pliant but less intense version of the first. The social butterfly type of Aquarian Moon lover is immersed in spending time with friends, seeking out excitement and can adjust well to romance if not emotionally bombarded by an over-sensitive partner. If the Sagittarius type lover is dominant by temperament, they may run into power struggles with the intellectual activist type of Aquarian Moon personality. They would fare better with the romance-seeking, non-confrontational, social butterfly type of Aquarian Moon personality. A marriage between them would work out wonderfully too.

Each of these fire and air signs can be a wonderful aid in each other's lives if balance is employed. Aquarian Moon partners will find a ready friend and companion in their Sagittarian type partners. Both are diligent seekers of knowledge and love to share information. In love relationships, their temperaments will be mostly on the same plane. Aquarian Moon lovers will seek the same degree of freedom in personal relationships as their fire sign counterparts. Of the two, the airy Aquarian Moon partner, on occasion, needs to spend more time by themselves and enjoy their solitude.

Both are intellectual purists, and will have a lot of interesting things to talk about or teach each other. But a partner who causes stress or causes emotional pressure to build in an Aquarius Moon lover, will soon find that they will begin to recoil from communicating with them. Complete emotional gridlock can be avoided if both of them keep letting one another know where they stand emotionally, instead of hoping their issues will disappear on their own. The Sagittarius type partner may not be as independent as their Aquarian Moon sweetheart, and may on occasion, demand more time and attention from them than they can comfortably give.

Both signs know the deep and undeniable need for freedom in each other's hearts, and both of them greatly fear giving their heart away in haste to a lover who may be sexually compatible with them, but may not be a good, emotionally compatible match by a long shot. When it comes to creating a solid bond that can last years, both partners would do well to begin their new relationship and then step back without forcing it into any specific mold. The slower they let their blossoming love evolve, the better the chances for it to become something they both will cherish, instead of fearing how it will slow them down.

Usually, the Sagittarius type lover has a secret religious side and may want there to be a joining of lives on a legal front. The ninth sign of Sagittarius rules the law as well as religion. This is where there might be a clash of sorts, which can be easily avoided if both partners investigate the inner depths of each other's expectations well in advance. The airy Aquarian Moon mate is a unique and idealistic person, who needs to know that their chosen life partner understands all the intricate inner-workings of their mind and is amenable to being accommodating and sympathetic.

Fiery Sagittarius is a mutable and flexible sign, and therefore may be able to fix this problem. Aquarian Moon partners understand that there are many different things that you can do with your life. *"Getting married and settling down to have a few kids and moving to the suburbs works for some people, but this nine to five existence just doesn't feel like the perfect choice for me right now."* the intellectually sensitive Aquarian Moon person honestly observes. When the Aquarian Moon does become ready for the path of marriage and sharing a home, they will be the first to let their adoring Sagittarius type lover know it.

Another note that might help this couple revolves around the Sagittarius type partner's emotions. Jupiter rules the Sagittarius sign and controls, to a large extent, how this sign processes emotions. For the most part, Jupiter makes Sagittarius types rather intense in their own way and prone to experiencing every emotion in a big way. If an argument occurs, it would be very beneficial if the subject is broached calmly and peacefully, as this will have a better effect on their logical Aquarian Moon partner, who shrinks from outbursts and loud accusations. A patient and cool-tempered Sagittarian type partner will be able to enjoy a long and successful relationship and marriage with their fascinating Aquarius Moon sweetheart. This is a stellar pair!

Aquarius Moon vs. Capricorn Sun, Moon or Rising Sign
The Air and Earth Relationship

Air: "Is my boyfriend open-minded enough and will he appreciate my outspoken side? I need a life mate who will talk to me, communicate with me about everything and not clam up and brood." the airy female partner muses. "Will my girlfriend allow me to do the things I love or will she try to restrict me from expressing myself?" the airy male lover wonders.

Earth: "Does my boyfriend manage his finances maturely or will I end up paying his bills and supporting him? I need stability and true commitment before I can enjoy the romance between us." the earthy female thinks to herself. "Will my future wife spend my hard earned cash on frivolous items at the mall or be wise enough to save up for our retirement?" the earthy male lover wonders.

Aquarius Moon lovers can enjoy a successful and fulfilling relationship with partners who have their Sun, Moon or Rising sign in the hardworking and ambitious earth sign of Capricorn. The Capricorn type lover might like to note that there are two, separate types of the Aquarius Moon personality. The first is the *intellectual activist type* and the second is the *social butterfly type*. The intellectual activist type is bright, smart, assertive and very keen to contribute to the world of ideas. The social butterfly type of Aquarian Moon lover is more in tune with spending time with friends, seeking light-hearted romances and spending time on pet projects. Of the two, the latter type is more submissive and may find it easy to adapt to marriage and a family. The intellectual activist type is dominant and self-assured, which means that they may sometimes clash with the dominant Capricorn type lover when control issues arise. The Capricorn type lover may enjoy greater compatibility with the accommodating, romantic, social butterfly type of Aquarius Moon personality.

When an Aquarian Moon lover falls in love with an earthy Capricorn type lover, both will alter each other's personalities in unseen but significant ways. The Capricorn type lover responds to the influence of Saturn, the planet of wisdom, honor and true purpose in life. Saturn is sometimes able to teach important life lessons to lovers *through* the Saturn-ruled people closest to them. Aquarian Moon partners may be attracted to and admire the discipline and self-control of their earthy Capricorn type partner. The Capricorn type lover will feel moved by their airy lover's personal convictions and ability to live their lives freely, without fear of being accepted or rejected by society.

Fearless and unafraid of hard work, Capricorn type lovers are successful and focused people who often have a clear direction in life. A lot can be achieved if these two amazing people join forces in a relationship. They can realize their greatest ambitions (be they personal or humanitarian), which is something the Aquarian Moon lover will enjoy, as well as receive a lot of prestige, which the Capricorn type partner will relish. The only roadblock they might hit is the Capricorn type partner's tendency to be too serious about certain life issues, and the Aquarian Moon lover's deliberate detachment in discussing them out of a fear of being pressured or cornered. Sometimes, it may seem as though the Aquarian Moon partner is drifting away and is not interested or invested in their carefully built relationship with their earthy Capricorn type lover, causing them to want to give up and withdraw.

But it would be wise of the Capricorn type partner, who is of a very stable and usually unflappable bent of mind, to wait and let their airy Aquarian Moon partner ride out their moods. No sudden decisions should be taken by either of them and if good communication skills are effectuated, they might have an easier time helping the relationship grow and blossom. The earthy Capricorn type lover tends to worry if results are not immediately forthcoming, and if they find they can't connect to their lover, they may become terribly depressed and inconsolable. Therefore, promises must be kept so that the light of honor is never extinguished from their love. Both of these lovers are basically honest and if they make the smallest effort to compromise, they can stay together and their relationship can work out well in the long term.

The key to success and happiness is for this couple to keep confiding in each other. Both should bear in mind that if all the adjustments are made to come from only one person, it could cause them to feel like they're being taken for granted. The Aquarian Moon partner will not bother with a relationship if they feel it is functioning relatively smoothly, they believe in the old *"If it ain't broke, don't fix it."* adage. Which means that things will have to get quite complicated before they realize that the relationship is in dire danger of ruin. Waiting too long to jump in and pacify their lover would be a risky step to take. The Capricorn type partner should worry less about the direction the relationship is taking (they must try not to *overvalue* it), while the Aquarian Moon lover should not neglect doing their fair share of work on their connection.

The Aquarian Moon partner will search for a lover who is attractive to look at, but also has an equally attractive mind. Their heart will pull them toward a mate who is an original personality, lives their life on their own terms, has a strong social conscience and will not settle for same-old-same-old when they can have an exotic experience. Aquarius Moon lovers are inspirational partners who are dedicated to their vision of life, and as a fixed sign, they usually cannot alter the way they live and function just to accommodate a love relationship. The Aquarian Moon lover is apprehensive about ending up with a run-of-the-mill partner who cannot function outside of their relationship and constantly needs to cling to their mate for direction. Studying each other's long term expectations is a step in the right direction. They must find out what each one of them fears and then work with eliminating those fears; the Aquarian Moon lover fears having their natural freedom taken away by a controlling, insecure and needy partner, and the Capricorn type lover fears undergoing loss, watching their marriage fail despite their best efforts to protect it.

The Capricorn type lover is confident and very sure of what they can or cannot do, so when they pledge to do their best in the relationship, they really will apply themselves and hope that their mate will also give a hundred percent. A partner who creates issues in order to gain the attention of their Aquarian Moon lover, or causes them to experience an emotional overload, will soon find themselves out of their circle of trust. A total communication standstill can be avoided if both of them make efforts on their part and try at least half as much as their mate is trying to save their love.

The Aquarian Moon partner will act according to the moods of Uranus, which is an unconventional planetary entity, and might end up causing big changes to occur (sometimes one after the other in typical Uranus fashion) in the life of a mate who is not emotionally balanced enough to handle this influence *through* the Aquarian Moon lover. Uranus may be testing them to see exactly how much they can take and how emotionally flexible they really are. Be that as it may, the Aquarian Moon partner has a terrific sense of honor and will not let down their partner on purpose. If the friendship between them can be bolstered before the passion between them is allowed to play itself out, and if the Capricorn type lover can be more tolerant and patient with their unusual but loving partner, theirs will be a marriage to enjoy for a lifetime, while others are still playing the dating game.

Aquarius Moon vs. Aquarian Sun, Moon or Rising Sign
The Air and Air Relationship

Air: "Is my boyfriend open-minded enough and will he appreciate my outspoken side? I need a life mate who will talk to me, communicate with me about everything and not clam up and brood." the airy female partner muses. "Will my girlfriend allow me to do the things I love or will she try to restrict me from truly expressing myself?" the airy male lover wonders.

Aquarius Moon lovers can enjoy a fulfilling and highly revealing relationship with partners who have their Sun, Moon or Rising sign in their own air sign of Aquarius. The double air vibration (Aquarius Moon/Aquarius Sun, Moon, Rising sign) will come alive with an energetic exchange of idealism and true feeling. This airy pair will express the passion of the mind before the passion of the senses can be expressed. There are two different types of the Aquarian Moon personality; the first is the *intellectual activist type* and the second is the *social butterfly type.* The intellectual activist type of Aquarian Moon lover is serious about work and has to be engaged through a common ideal or cause, a pursuit so important, that the personalities of the lovers come second to it.

According to humanitarian Uranus, the ruler of Aquarius, there are things in this world that are far more valuable and meaningful than fleeting public acclaim, fancy cars and fat bank balances; one must work hard to leave behind a powerful legacy of selfless acts in order to feel true, age-transcending fulfillment. The Aquarius type lover will grasp this philosophy beautifully and be a great support to the Aquarius Moon partner, who will be unlike anyone they've ever met.

The intellectual activist type of Aquarian Moon partner will pay less attention to a humdrum romance or managing a difficult relationship, and place long-term friendships based on broad-mindedness at the top of their list. Hungry for mental stimulation, and born with an ability to be everyone's friend (the sign of Aquarius governs universal brotherhood and sisterhood), the Aquarian Moon mate will search for a partner who will never tie them down or try to use guilt and manipulation to keep them around. The social butterfly type of Aquarian Moon personality also feels hemmed in by too much control from a lover but will adjust better to making adjustments due to a passive and non-confrontational way of doing things.

If the Aquarius type lover is docile, they will be drawn toward the intellectual activist type of Aquarian Moon personality. If the Aquarius type partner is as dominant and as forceful as the intellectual activist type lover, there might be some head-butting on certain issues. When two aggressive people fall in love, one of them will have to acquiesce and give in. But if the ego gets in before love can find a way to their heart, there might be some problems. Therefore, it is best if the assertive lover pairs up with the more easy-going one in order to let the exquisite ballet of opposites that is human relationships, play itself out without interruption.

The renegade planet Uranus will instill in the Aquarius Moon lover or the Aquarius type partner, a sort of "freedom radar" that will alert them instantly if they are being used by a lover for selfish needs. The best way to approach the Aquarian Moon lover, if you have the same sign placed prominently in your natal chart, is to be their friend. The freedom to come and go (without being answerable to anyone), as well as express themselves and reinvent their personalities in any way they see fit, is key to their continued emotional stability.

The key to success and happiness is for this couple to always keep discussing issues and not let complaints fester for too long. As air signs, frequent and honest communication will be their biggest strength in this relationship; friendships place fewer restrictions on people, while relationships often demand changes that cannot occur unless they happen at the right time and under the right circumstances. The Moon sign of Aquarius will be happy to grant their partner and more importantly, their friend, as much personal space as they need; this is the one sign that adequately comprehends the concept of freedom (especially that which is granted devoid of the taint of suspicion) within marriages and relationships.

The Aquarian Moon partner needs to be with a lover who is good looking but can also match that with a formidable intellect. Their heart will pull them toward a mate who is fearless, independent, lives by their own rules and bows to no one. They admire and will try to emulate strength and independence. The Aquarian Moon lover hopes they won't have to end up with a partner who either looks like everyone else, or talks and behaves like everyone else and has nothing original about them; Uranus tends to zero in on the rare and unavailable. The Aquarius type lover as well as the Aquarian Moon lover's greatest fear in life may be the loss of a *good friend* if a relationship happens to crumble, therefore the more time they spend studying one another's expectations, the more successful they will be.

Aquarian Moon partners as well as their devoted Aquarius types life-mates understand an important secret of life; that you don't have to be exactly like the Joneses and copy everything they do or don't do. Changes often occur in lighting-fast fashion in the lives of these two lovebirds, and thankfully, Uranus, their ruler, will also grant them the emotional malleability to flow with those changes and improve their lives. When both of them are single, their secret hope will be to find that rare soul who understands their very specific but simple needs; their need for emotional space as well as emotional closeness at carefully timed intervals; their need to converse with intelligent friends and maintain all their friendships, and their need to drive their lives toward that one particular goal (personal or professional) that they receive maximum emotional strength, hope and sustenance from – with their non-judgmental, faithful and understanding lover as well as best friend by their side. This will be a beautiful love story!

Aquarius Moon vs. Pisces Sun, Moon or Rising Sign
The Air and Water Relationship

Air: "Is my boyfriend open-minded enough and will he appreciate my outspoken side? I need a life mate who will talk to me, communicate with me about everything and not clam up and brood." the airy female partner muses. "Will my girlfriend allow me to do the things I love or will she try to restrict me from expressing myself?" the airy male lover wonders.

Water: "Is my boyfriend emotionally stable and wise about our joint finances? Or will debts pile up in the first year of marriage? I need a supportive life-long lover as well as a loving one." the watery female lover thinks to herself. "Will my future spouse conserve our financial resources or spend unwisely without thought for the

future? I can connect better romantically if I know that my chosen life-mate is passionate as well as mature and pragmatic." the watery male lover wonders.

Aquarius Moon lovers can enjoy a unique and emotionally enlightening relationship with partners who have their Sun, Moon or Rising sign in the sensitive and alluring water sign of Pisces. The Aquarian Moon lover will display one of two personality types; the first is the *intellectual activist type* (who is drawn to humanitarian causes and is dominant by temperament and in the relationship setting) and the second is the *social butterfly type* (who is drawn toward fun, friends and creativity). Learning to distinguish between both these specific personality types may greatly enhance compatibility over the long-term.

The Pisces type of lover is emotional and highly sensitive, while the intellectual activist type of Aquarian Moon partner is detached as well as intensely focused on them by turns. What can a Pisces type person do to win the heart of their elusive Aquarian Moon sweetheart? It won't be easy, but it is not impossible either. First, the poetic, watery Pisces partner could study how they are similar to or different from their Aquarian Moon lover. A good deal of information would be gained by trying to observe things that cannot be seen by human eyes. This is where the intuitive Pisces type lover comes into familiar territory. The Pisces type lover may find the most fulfilling compatibility with the second type of the Aquarius Moon personality or the social butterfly type, as this type can acclimate to a marriage more readily than the first type can. More often than not, the Pisces type lover will be attracted to the notion of marriage and permanence and will hope their lover does too.

The Pisces type lover is very emotionally in-tune with what they hear from people as well as what they don't hear. They will be able to quickly sense that their airy Aquarian Moon lover has a veritable dread of being cloistered into a relationship that will take away that one thing in the world that they are truly unable to live without - their autonomy. Personal space and freedom are things that the Aquarian Moon sign cannot survive without, and this applies to the daily give and take between them as well. An insecure, suspicious partner will soon find that their Aquarius Moon lover will begin to withdraw from being around them, in order to avoid that atmosphere at home. Care must be taken in how they are approached.

The key to success and happiness is for this couple to be open about addressing each other's needs without sounding like they're doing each other a favor, but out of love and genuine respect. The Pisces type partner should not obsess about their romance quite as much as they do, while the Aquarian Moon lover should not neglect doing their fair share of work on their union. This connection can last, even flourish, if they both make an effort to adjust instead of trying to change each other.

The brainy Aquarian Moon partner will hope to find a lover who is either handsome or beautiful, but can also back up that beauty with an amazing mind. They will be drawn toward a mate who is a strong, independent personality and does not depend on the world for its opinion on anything. Therefore, one has to observe what's going on behind the scenes with regard to the Pisces type lover's heart. If past relationships have been hard on the delicate Pisces psyche, and if previous lovers have caused more pain than left them with sweet memories, the Pisces type lover will hold onto their present partner even tighter and perhaps not even realize they are doing this. The Aquarian Moon lover fears too excessive a display of emotionality, while the Pisces type partner will fear abandonment and loneliness despite having a lover in their life.

Aquarian Moon partners are rare souls who understand that they can steer their life toward many goals, their only requirement is that those goals be chosen by them alone (this Moon sign vigorously rejects any enforced parenting by a lover). Often, the traditional family and children path that some people take in life may be something that the intellectually sensitive Aquarian Moon person accepts later in life, while the Pisces type lover can function within the close, trusted family environment better than being alone.

Aquarius Moon lovers are ruled by the renegade planet Uranus, while Neptune rules the Pisces type mate. Watery Neptune governs ethereal beauty, illusions, an extraordinary intuition and leans toward a desire to be self-sacrificing. Interpersonal communication glitches can be avoided if both of them can pin point what keeps them apart as well as together. The Pisces type partner is able to understand this, but also must face their own needs. They thrive in relationships where their lover enjoys emotional and physical closeness as much as they do. There is no limit to how much tenderness a water sign partner can give or receive, and while this is good for them, a more intellectual lover will experience any excessive closeness as an emotional overload that takes their sense of balance away.

Moderation in all things is key; what would work out best for this loving duo is if one of them (the Pisces type lover) balances how much love they give and attention they need, and if the other lover (the Aquarian Moon partner) gives their partner a little more attention and caring than they expect. Truly bonded by their sense of passion, this couple can, with the slightest of efforts, bring their love connection back to life by trying to view life through their lover's eyes once in a while. The Pisces type lover brings out in their airy Aquarian Moon lover a sense of poetry and soft, hypnotic sensuality, while the Aquarian Moon lover brings out in their watery Pisces lover a desire to shed the heavy burdens of fear and embrace the freedom of fearlessness. This couple can become truly devoted over time.

Chapter 24

The Pisces Moon Sign Lover

Pisces Moon vs. Aries Sun, Moon or Rising Sign
The Water and Fire Relationship

Water: "Is my boyfriend emotionally stable and wise about our joint finances? Or will debts pile up in the first year of marriage? I need a supportive life-long lover as well as a loving one." the watery female lover thinks to herself. "Will my future spouse conserve our financial resources or spend unwisely without thought for the future? I can connect better romantically if I know that my chosen life-mate is passionate as well as mature and pragmatic." the watery male lover wonders.

Fire: "I need romance and passion to really enjoy my relationship. Will my boyfriend be a faithful mate for life?" the fiery female partner wonders. "I want an active and freedom-loving partner. Will my girlfriend understand my need for true freedom in life or be too controlling of what I do?" the fiery male lover thinks to himself.

Pisces Moon lovers can enjoy an energizing and romantic relationship with partners who have their Sun, Moon or Rising sign in the passionate and energetic fire sign of Aries. There are two separate facets to the alluring Pisces Moon personality. The first type is the *beauty seeker type* and the second is the *spirit seeker type*. The beauty seeker type of Pisces Moon lover is tender hearted, impressionable and often accepts relationships as their sole, driving focus in life. They seek beauty, which might lead them to harmony and balance. The beauty seeker type of Pisces Moon lover is expressive, poetic and alluring. This type seeks out stronger, more dominant characters whose approval will mean a lot to them, sometimes even more than what they think of themselves.

The second type, or the spirit seeker type of Pisces Moon partner is more spiritually inclined and finds an emotional anchor in giving of themselves rather than seeking out the approval of lovers who may be impossible to please sometimes. This type is particularly drawn toward the pure avenues of spirituality, ancient mysticism and religion. They will seek to connect to the ancientness within themselves and this type of the Pisces Moon persona is deep and magnetic.

Being around an Aries type lover pushes Pisces Moon lovers into becoming more focused on projects and begin to tap into their own latent fighting spirit. The Pisces Moon lover can help the Aries type lover into getting back in touch with their emotional, sensitive and dreamy side. Both partners would do well to remind each other that they must build a solid foundation first: one of friendship and most importantly, of raw honesty.

If the Aries type lover is assertive and decides to grab hold of the reins of their relationship (Aries is a cardinal sign of leadership), the independent, spirit seeker type of Pisces Moon lover will have a problem with it. But the dominant Aries type of lover will find a wonderful compatibility with the romantic, passive, beauty seeker type of Pisces Moon personality, who may gravitate toward the fiery Aries lover's willingness to protect and guide.

Communication problems can plague a Pisces Moon mate and their partner. The Pisces Moon energy is forgetful sometimes and omits mentioning details while Aries types may be too distracted and never ask to see them. Or the aggressive Aries type lover could say a lot but convey very little. Both should speak clearly to each other and encourage one another to communicate their feelings frequently to avoid misunderstandings. Pisces Moon mates want their lover to be as intuitive as they are, but most people have no idea about true intuition. Aries types are usually quite blunt in their observations and should be very patient with their Pisces Moon lover, while handling them with tenderness as their feelings could be easily hurt. The Pisces Moon energy brings out their Aries type partner's artistic side, while the Aries type energy encourages the watery Pisces Moon person to be more hardnosed about life's setbacks and feel empowered in making important decisions.

No one mood will be constant with the watery Pisces Moon lover and no one emotion will last forever, which is good because it gives them a chance to mull over problems easily without letting them fester. The Pisces Moon lover is sensitive enough to pick up the true emotion behind spoken words, even if those intentions are deliberately being cloaked. Some people with Pisces placed prominently in their natal charts, particularly the beauty seeker type of the Pisces Moon personality, will sometimes suffer from low self-esteem or have an unclear sense of who they really are due to the influence of Neptune.

Neptune's influence is inspirational in most cases, but sometimes causes doubt to surface in the delicate and impressionable Pisces Moon psyche. If a lover is ambivalent about their future together, or purposely neglectful of their Pisces Moon mate, this could translate into a terrible emotional trauma. The Pisces Moon partner must watch out for a tendency toward placing more faith in a new lover when that trust may not yet be warranted. Patience is key in falling in love, because a manipulative lover could easily find their way into the sometimes overly dependent Pisces Moon lover's heart.

The love between the signs of Pisces Moon and Aries is a classic attraction between opposites. Studying the power of the oceans can give us a lot of important information about the true personality of the appealing Pisces Moon lover. Substantive but ultimately shapeless, water can fit into any vessel, be it a glass, a bowl or even the human eye. Tears are also a form of the oceans, as is the falling rain. The Pisces Moon mate is similar to the water element; they can find a way to make themselves fit into any relationship, get along with any lover and seem like the best addition to any family.

If there are occasional miscommunications between them, neither of these lovers should wait too long to say they're sorry and should try to walk right back into their lover's circle of trust. Pride has no place in the Pisces Moon/Aries Sun, Moon or Rising sign relationship and both partners should make every effort to talk out differences the *same* day they occur. Waiting too long might cause mistrust to set in, which can be hard to get rid of. Mars-influenced, Aries type mates can have a positive effect on the path their Pisces Moon lover chooses in life. The Pisces Moon energy softens up their rough and tumble Aries type sweetheart considerably. Each can understand the other successfully over time, and if good communication skills are learnt and put into place early on, this could be a great relationship.

Pisces Moon vs. Taurus Sun, Moon or Rising Sign
The Water and Earth Relationship

Water: "Is my boyfriend emotionally stable and wise about our joint finances? Or will debts pile up in the first year of marriage? I need a supportive life-long lover as well as a loving one." the watery female lover thinks to herself. "Will my future spouse conserve our financial resources or spend unwisely without thought for the future? I can connect better romantically if I know that my chosen life-mate is passionate as well as mature and pragmatic." the watery male lover wonders.

Earth: "Does my boyfriend manage his finances maturely or will I end up paying his bills and supporting him? I need stability and true commitment before I can

enjoy the romance between us." the earthy female thinks to herself. "Will my future wife spend my hard earned cash on frivolous items at the mall or be wise enough to save up for our retirement?" the earthy male lover wonders.

Pisces Moon lovers can enjoy a stable and loving relationship with partners who have their Sun, Moon or Rising sign in the romantic and reliable earth sign of Taurus. The Taurus type lover might like to be able to distinguish between the two varying types of the beautiful Pisces Moon personality, as this extra effort might allow them to bond with them at a particularly intimate level. The first type of Pisces Moon persona is the *beauty seeker type*. This type is ultra-romantic, giving and tends to idolize lovers as well as the idea of love and relationships. They seek beauty, through which they seek purity and harmony.

The second type of the Pisces Moon persona is the *spirit seeker type*. This type is more assertive and less inclined to give up control in untested relationships. The spirit seeker type of Pisces Moon person is bright, intellectual, self-sufficient and can be successful in their chosen career field with great ease. This type will be drawn to the rare beauty of nature as well as be more comfortable with solitude than the former, beauty seeker type of Pisces Moon personality. Spirituality, religion and mysticism will intrigue them throughout their life, perhaps because they are drawn toward the purity of these ancient disciplines.

The element of water is a magnificent creation of nature, and we can learn a great deal about the watery Pisces Moon personality by observing this element closely. If we try to hold this uncontrollable element in our hands, it will find a way to slip through our fingers and find itself a stronger support. If we place the water element near the soil, the earth drinks it up. If we leave it in a bowl by an open window, the air element causes it to evaporate. Everywhere we go, the water element seeks a stable foundation on which to flow and exist. The water element craves direction and the element of earth, like an ancient riverbed, can provide that direction with ease. The Pisces Moon mate is similar to the water element; they seek out a foundation of sorts in their lover and can fit perfectly into any relationship, get along with any lover and seem like the best addition to any family.

The Pisces Moon energy is very compatible with the earthy Taurus essence because water and earth have an easier time understanding each other than other signs. Neptune, the ruler of Pisces and Venus, the ruler of Taurus are planets with similar qualities, both tending toward passive harmony. Taurus types require a good degree of emotional commitment before they will let their watery Pisces Moon lover get too close to their hearts. Pisces Moon mates are deeply emotional themselves and need a partner who can provide that rock-solid foundation on which they can rely. They need a life mate who is there to tell them that things can be better, not worse. The Pisces Moon energy brings sensitivity and faith to a sometimes, skeptical Taurus type partner, while the Taurus type lover aids their watery soul mate in building up their sense of self-confidence.

Taurus types should help their sensitive watery partner express their practical side more than their trusting side, because they do tend to think with their heart more than their head. This is good in the artistic or romantic setting, but in the harsh reality of daily living, cunning people may not often pass up the chance to take advantage of a Pisces Moon person. The Pisces Moon lover must also remember never to withhold any information from their Taurus type lover and vice versa. Be it the saving of the smallest receipt or opening each other's personal mail, both lovers must maintain the strictest boundaries of respect throughout this relationship.

If Taurus types begin to doubt their partner even a little, that little doubt could have negative consequences later on, and one never gets a second chance at making a good, first impression on a Taurus type partner. The Pisces Moon mate must also be careful about who they take into their confidence (they like to share and confide), as their secrets may not always be safe. When it comes to giving their partner some personal freedom, their sense of suspicion (common to water signs), fired up by the more impressionable vibrations of Neptune could morph into a full-fledged misunderstanding and wreck the relationship. Trust is the quality that will save the day every time. These two lovers must never let a third party, however well meaning, come between them and must always give precedence to each other above all others. This is a good combination if a family is planned.

Pisces Moon vs. Gemini Sun, Moon or Rising Sign
The Water and Air Relationship

Water: "Is my boyfriend emotionally stable and wise about our joint finances? Or will debts pile up in the first year of marriage? I need a supportive life-long lover as well as a loving one." the watery female lover thinks to herself. "Will my future spouse conserve our financial resources or spend unwisely without thought for the future? I can connect better romantically if I know that my chosen life-mate is passionate as well as mature and pragmatic." the watery male lover wonders.

Air: "Is my boyfriend open-minded enough and will he appreciate my outspoken side? I need a life mate who will talk to me, communicate with me about everything and not clam up and brood." the airy female partner muses. "Will my girlfriend allow me to do the things I love or will she try to restrict me from expressing myself?" the airy male lover wonders.

Pisces Moon lovers can enjoy an exciting and expressive relationship with partners who have their Sun, Moon or Rising sign in the out-going and communicative air sign of Gemini. But due to the wide differences in both personalities, emotional adjustments will have to be made on both sides.

The Pisces Moon personality is divided into two, separate and intriguing parts, and the Gemini type lover will benefit from learning how to tell them apart. Their lover may display either the *beauty seeker type* of Pisces Moon personality, or the *spirit seeker type* of Pisces Moon persona. The beauty seeker type seeks harmony and connectivity through beauty and goodness, yearns to find their true soul mate and is prone to trustingly slip into new, untried relationships with emotionally untested lovers rather quickly, while the spirit seeker type might be more suspicious of instant promises from a new partner. Both the beauty seeker type as well as the spirit seeker type can enjoy relationships and the stability of marriage.

The spirit seeker type of this Moon sign will be drawn to the harmony in nature and spirituality and is quite capable of being a very able and successful businessperson. They will seek spiritual connections during the various stages of life and maybe either very religious or very mystical by temperament. This open-minded type of the Pisces Moon persona may be less susceptible to the wildness of the planet Neptune, whose control over the great oceans mirrors its power over the Pisces Moon person's deepest emotions.

The Pisces Moon mate is similar to the water element; they can acclimatize to any relationship, merge easily into the lifestyle of any lover and will want to happily give more than their fair share of effort on building their relationship or marriage into something that will stand the test of time.

Gemini type lovers look for a mate who is physically attractive, very communicative and can play a little hard to get once in a while (Gemini loves excitement!). The emphasis in this relationship will be on how each lover handles their own changing moods as well as their lover's. Both the Pisces Moon partner as well as their loving Gemini type mate are born under mutable signs, or signs that can weather change with more grace than other astrological signs. The Gemini type lover is slightly changeable; they will vacillate between being very chirpy one morning and want to be left alone by the afternoon. This is mainly due to the hot and cold influence of Mercury, which rules the sign of the twins. The equally changeable Pisces Moon lover is able to understand the dualism in their mate, because they have traces of that duality within their own natures; the two Pisces fish seem to swim in opposite directions.

No one like or dislike will be constant with either lover and no one emotion will last forever, which is very good for the relationship. But the mutability factor within this love match demands a strong foundation, a stability of nature that can support them and help them trust each other as the years roll by. The Pisces Moon lover is emotional and very affected by what their partner thinks of them on any given day, therefore their mate might have to bolster their self-esteem regularly, verbally as well as through their actions by giving them steady doses of kindly attention. This is because some people with Pisces placed prominently in their natal charts (in the Sun, Moon or Rising position, for example) will sometimes wonder if they deserve the love they receive from their engaging Gemini type lover. They do deserve it as well as deserving a lot of love and caring.

The influence of Neptune has a lot to do with this feeling of not being enough because this planet has associations with illusion, dreams and the subconscious and can blur their ability to see reality from a dream (which may be why this soft-natured Moon sign may miss or choose to ignore seeing the relationship red flags that pop up now and then to help keep them safe from harm). For the Pisces Moon vibration, love is sacrifice. But self-sacrifice can drain a person and cause them to view their partner as a larger than life figure, *which they may not be in reality*. They may just be a normal person who happens to be in love with them, and may have their own idiosyncrasies. Therefore, the Pisces Moon lover will, at some level, need to view their lover with normal eyes, instead of placing their expectations too high for them too meet.

This could be a good romantic pairing if the Pisces Moon lover learns not to be so sensitive and learns to be more fearless about life, while the Gemini type partner will have to learn to handle the moods and emotions of their partner with greater diplomacy. If the Pisces Moon lover can grant their Gemini type partner personal freedom in all things, this will be a truly fulfilling relationship.

Pisces Moon vs. Cancer Sun, Moon or Rising Sign
The Water and Water Relationship

Water: "Is my boyfriend emotionally stable and wise about our joint finances? Or will debts pile up in the first year of marriage? I need a supportive life-long lover as well as a loving one." the watery female lover thinks to herself. "Will my future spouse conserve our financial resources or spend unwisely without thought for the future? I can connect better romantically if I know that my chosen life-mate is passionate as well as mature and pragmatic." the watery male lover wonders.

Pisces Moon lovers can enjoy a highly successful relationship with partners who have their Sun, Moon or Rising sign in the nurturing water sign of Cancer. The Pisces Moon energy is very compatible with the watery Cancer type essence because water flows and merges easily with water, and this double water sign couple will have an easier time understanding each other's emotions. However, too much water and emotionality can overwhelm a relationship and rob it of a firm foundation. Which means that one of them will have to be the rock of the relationship to support it. Each partner symbolizes an element. Understanding that element helps us delve deeper into the real personality of that partner.

Water represents an emotional purity as well as a soft and inviting sensuality. Elementally, water supports water wonderfully. Pour two glasses of water into a pitcher and we will not be able to distinguish between them, their energies will have mingled seamlessly. While this sympathetic bonding is good, water, when threatened, betrayed or hurt, will freeze up and become a solid block of ice. Such emotional withdrawal can seriously damage a double water relationship. The only way to change this is to heat (provide attention and end further neglect of their delicate psyche) that block of ice into slowly melting.

The emphasis should be on the word slow. Water signs are generally suspicious about instantly made promises and no follow through to back up what was said. Gradually, the frozen energy of ice changes into the fluidic, forgiving quality of water, the most emotional element of all. Balancing the attributes of this element is key. Maternal and caring Cancer types require emotional commitment before they will let anyone near their heart. Pisces Moon lovers are deeply emotional themselves and need a partner who can be a pillar of strength for them and provide the frequent nurturing that they need.

The devoted Cancer type lover should bear in mind that the enigmatic Pisces Moon personality is made up of two, distinct personality types. Distinguishing between them might aid them with learning more about their lover's needs as well as their fears. The first type of Pisces Moon personality is the *beauty seeker type*. This type is relationship-oriented, marriage-minded, accommodating and generally passive in relationships. Their purpose is to seek beauty and love through harmony within relationships. The second type of Pisces Moon personality is the *spirit seeker type*. This type is more comfortable with their solitude, adapts to relationships easily but is also quite comfortable with their autonomy. The spirit seeker type seeks to connect to their higher selves through religion, nature, spirituality and mysticism; the goal is to find value and meaning in their life.

The Pisces Moon energy brings sensitivity and faith to a sometimes, skeptical Cancer type lover who may battle many fears privately, while the Cancer type lover aids their watery lover in being able to make any life decision with confidence. Pisces Moon partners, more than Cancer types, need to be able to think with clarity and require a lover who can bring them out of a tendency to defeat themselves, if things don't go a certain way. Financially, Pisces Moon lovers may be impulse shoppers, and this may pose a problem because Cancer is a financially frugal sign and most Cancer type folks are very prudent about managing their resources in the proper format, so that a dependable bridge (a financial nest egg) is built toward the future.

This is a good match provided the Pisces Moon lover, in an emotional state of mind, tries not to push their watery partner's emotional buttons. Family-friendly Cancer types should help their sensitive partner express their practical side more than their trusting side. Imagination can be the Pisces Moon lover's biggest ally as well as their biggest foe. Neptune rules the sign of Pisces, and while it can help them dream and imagine, it can also cause a great deal of confusion and self-deception in the gentle, trusting Pisces heart. Which is why frequent and clear communication should be a rule of this relationship. The Pisces Moon partner as well as the Cancer type lover must watch out for a tendency toward *overvaluing* their lover, spouse or relationship. Expectations should not be so impossibly high that they become too difficult to meet. Also, both these water signs need to be able to observe themselves *outside* of their closest relationships, in which they may lose their identity rather easily. They will fit into the family structure quite well and may thrive in the protection that close families can sometimes provide.

This is a good sign combination if a family is planned because these lovers have the power to come quite spiritually close to each other in a way that no one else can. The Pisces Moon lover lifts their Cancer type sweetheart out of the world of fear and suspicion and gently puts them down into the sensual world of romance, poetry and true love. The Cancer type lover creates a sense of security and an emotional comfort zone for their lover, where their home will be their private sanctuary. This is a loving pair!

Pisces Moon vs. Leo Sun, Moon or Rising Sign
The Water and Fire Relationship

Water: "Is my boyfriend emotionally stable and wise about our joint finances? Or will debts pile up in the first year of marriage? I need a supportive life-long lover as well as a loving one." the watery female lover thinks to herself. "Will my future spouse conserve our financial resources or spend unwisely without thought for the future? I can connect better romantically if I know that my chosen life-mate is passionate as well as mature and pragmatic." the watery male lover wonders.

Fire: "I need romance and passion to really enjoy my relationship. Will my boyfriend be a faithful mate for life?" the fiery female partner wonders. "I want an active and freedom-loving partner. Will my girlfriend understand my need for true freedom in life or be too controlling?" the fiery male lover thinks to himself.

Pisces Moon lovers can enjoy a very emotionally fulfilling relationship with partners who have their Sun, Moon or Rising sign in the happy and generous fire sign of Leo. But due to the wide differences in both personalities, emotional adjustments will have to be made on both sides. The Pisces Moon personality can be separated into two distinct sections. Knowing which one reflects their partner most accurately can enable the Leo type mate to derive a clear idea of their lover's needs and wants in their love relationship. The first type of Pisces Moon personality is the *beauty seeker type*; this type is passionate, somewhat submissive in love relationships, takes what their lover says rather seriously and revels in their approval. This type acclimates to the marriage setting easily and makes a very accommodating spouse and lover. They seek beauty, and through beauty, they seek harmony. Their goal is to harmonize their world as much as possible, particularly through the avenue of intimate relationships.

The second type of the Pisces Moon persona is the *spirit seeker type*. This fascinating type is self-sufficient, smart and in control of their emotions. Managing a business, caring for a family, pursuing their passion in life; they can do it all. This type seeks harmony in life, and they may look for it through the mediums of spirituality, religion, mysticism or humanitarian work where the oceanic compassion of Neptune comes into its own.

Studying the power of the oceans can help the loving Leo type lover observe the true personality of the appealing Pisces Moon lover. The oceans are vast and span most of the planet earth. When observed through the filter of water signs, the water element symbolizes pure emotion. Water can take the exact shape of the vessel that holds it and then can change its shape when the vessel's shape changes. Similarly, the Moon sign of Pisces can change and morph itself into becoming any person's ideal love. The key is to maintain their own individuality during that process, so that they don't end up placing all their control and decision making skills squarely into the hands of another person.

Leo type lovers look for a mate who is attractive, fiercely loyal and very sensual. Pisces Moon lovers are expressive and talkative if you catch them in the right mood and can charm the fiery Leo type lover into forgetting what time of day it is. Whether they are male of female, the force or strength of the Sun-ruled, Leo type lover will be especially drawn to the calm, cool and hypnotic Pisces Moon persona that is never obvious in their attempt to catch their fiery lover's attention.

When it comes to understanding each other enough to build something of value between them, the changeability of the mutable Pisces Moon has to be comprehended. This watery Moon sign has an unutterable inner yearning to meet that one special person with whom they won't have to try quite so hard to find real, everyday compatibility. The Leo type lover is also affected by moods; but not to the deep extent that the Pisces Moon lover is. Pisces is ruled by the oceans or the seven seas and the element of water is ancient, as well as highly unpredictable.

The Moon has a bond with the ocean and its effects are seen here on earth, sometimes through the personalities of those whom we love. When the Moon is in the constellation of the Fish, the emotionality factor builds and doubles; there is an emotional out-pouring through the influence of the Moon as well as mighty Neptune. Without stability, the Pisces Moon person could helplessly drift in and out with the tides and fall victim to manipulative lovers who might not give up the chance to exploit their vulnerability if they are in a particularly sensitive mood.

Pisces Moon mates love to help and support their lover. But they may first need to find their own identity or voice before they start seeing themselves as a permanent part of someone else's life. The dominant Leo type partner will not want to deal with a lover who they may feel is a tad too needy or weak. And on the other hand, a passive life mate may not be able to provide the strength or support the Pisces Moon lover will someday need. Therefore, a partner who is strong but knows when to let the Pisces Moon lover step forward and shine would ideal. A wise and protective personality like that may be hard to find, but they are out there, searching for their one-in-a-million Pisces Moon soul mate.

If the Leo type lover feels like they could fill those shoes, they should go right on and try. They will probably succeed as well. Fire will heat up water and bring it to life by its sheer presence. If the Pisces Moon lover can trust their Leo type partner in all things, as well as shower them with a lot of attention, verbal and physical, this will be a truly memorable love story.

Pisces Moon vs. Virgo Sun, Moon or Rising Sign
The Water and Earth Relationship

Water: "Is my boyfriend emotionally stable and wise about our joint finances? Or will debts pile up in the first year of marriage? I need a supportive life-long lover as well as a loving one." the watery female lover thinks to herself. "Will my future spouse conserve our financial resources or spend unwisely without thought for the future? I can connect better romantically if I know that my chosen life-mate is passionate as well as mature and pragmatic." the watery male lover wonders.

Earth: "Does my boyfriend manage his finances maturely or will I end up paying his bills and supporting him? I need stability and true commitment before I can enjoy the romance between us." the earthy female thinks to herself. "Will my future wife spend my hard earned cash on frivolous items at the mall or be wise enough to save up for our retirement?" the earthy male lover wonders.

Pisces Moon lovers can enjoy a highly romantic and passionate relationship with partners who have their Sun, Moon or Rising sign in the devoted and trustworthy earth sign of Virgo. The pull here will be one of marriage because these signs are polarized. Both are alike but also dissimilar in their own way.

The earthy Virgo type lover might like to be able to distinguish between the two varying types of the beautiful Pisces Moon personality, as this extra effort might allow them to bond with them at a particularly intimate level. The first type of Pisces Moon persona is the *beauty seeker type*. This type is ultra-romantic, giving and tends to idolize lovers as well as the idea of love and relationships. They seek beauty, through which they seek purity and harmony.

The second type of the Pisces Moon persona is the *spirit seeker type*. This type is more assertive and less inclined to give up control in untested relationships. The spirit seeker type of Pisces Moon person is bright, intellectual, self-sufficient and can be successful in their chosen career field with great ease. This type will be drawn to the rare beauty of nature as well as be more comfortable with solitude than the former, beauty seeker type of Pisces Moon personality. Spirituality, religion and mysticism will intrigue them through out their life, perhaps because they are drawn toward the purity of these ancient disciplines.

When the seventh sector comes into play, there will be, at some point or the other, a desire to merge destinies on a legal level. The Pisces Moon energy is very compatible with the earthy Virgo essence because water and earth signs have an easier time understanding each other than other signs. Virgo types tend to work hard to achieve everything and their love lives will be no different. They will require emotional commitment before they will let their heart float away like a leaf on the great Piscean waters of intuition and sensitivity. Pisces Moon lovers are easily moved emotionally, and need a partner who is strong enough to provide a rock-solid foundation on which they can place their full trust.

For the Virgo type lover, honorable actions, respectfulness and faithfulness must come before they can trust anyone, while for the Pisces Moon lover, pure trust uncontrollably flows out even before the first *"I love you"* has been exchanged between them. The Pisces Moon mate feels things that the practical and logical Virgo type lover may need some time to comprehend. It is a classic clash between the intuition of the Pisces Moon lover and the pragmatism of the Virgo type partner. Indeed, the Pisces Moon lover may spot a soul mate before they even know their first name. It just happens, this strange and powerful sort of inner knowing.

After they've been married for twenty years, the Virgo type husband will shake his head and say, *"So, how did you know you'd end up marrying me before we'd even gone out on our first date? I was wondering what all this true love business really is like, seems you were a few steps ahead of me the whole time, honey."* The Pisces Moon lover feels everything acutely, while the earthy Virgo type lover needs proof before they can be sure. But they're trainable, the Pisces Moon lover thinks. And, they may be right. Once a Virgo type partner finds fulfillment and happiness with a Pisces Moon lover, once they know for sure that their trust will be returned, perhaps a hundred times more intensely than they imagined, that earthy Virgo suspicion may begin to crumble a little everyday.

The Pisces Moon energy lends a great sensitivity to a sometimes cynical, pre-occupied or almost always overworked Virgo type lover, while the Virgo type lover aids their watery partner in finding their voice, being more practical and feeling more confident about any life choices. Pisces Moon partners, more than their Virgo type lover, need to be able to think clearly and require a lover who can help them battle a fleeting sense of inferiority sometimes. They need to know that their lover thinks they are more than worthy of their love and attention, which is certainly true. Financially speaking, Pisces Moon lovers may be a little more impulsive when spending cash, and this may pose a problem because Virgo is a financially prudent sign and most Virgo type folks are very careful about keeping track of unnecessary expenditures. Being pragmatic about money will help this couple sort out *other* problems in the long run. The key is to keep money discussions from spiraling out of control.

This is a good match provided the Pisces Moon lover learns not to push their earthy and stable Virgo type lover into making any decision based on emotion and not logic. Analytical Virgo types should help their sensitive watery partner express their trusting side less often and learn to ask pointed questions of people who they may be suspicious of. The trust between *them* must be unshakeable, however. Doubt has no place in the eventually trusting Virgo type lover's heart because it will have taken them too long to be able to finally trust someone in life.

The most important tip for this couple is to always talk things out, if possible on the same day, and to maintain a strong sense of closeness where even their own relatives will not have any influence over their view of each other. Pisces Moon partners are very susceptible to misinformation (Neptune sometimes blurs the lines between truth and fiction) and they must not instantly believe everything they hear, much less act on it. This is a good combination if a family is planned because both of them will make devoted parents.

Pisces Moon vs. Libra Sun, Moon or Rising Sign
The Water and Air Relationship

Water: "Is my boyfriend emotionally stable and wise about our joint finances? Or will debts pile up in the first year of marriage? I need a supportive life-long lover as well as a loving one." the watery female lover thinks to herself. "Will my future

spouse conserve our financial resources or spend unwisely without thought for the future? I can connect better romantically if I know that my chosen life-mate is passionate as well as mature and pragmatic." the watery male lover wonders.

Air: "Is my boyfriend open-minded enough and will he appreciate my outspoken side? I need a life mate who will talk to me, communicate with me about every-thing and not clam up and brood." the airy female partner muses. "Will my girlfriend allow me to do the things I love or will she try to restrict me from expressing myself?" the airy male lover wonders.

Pisces Moon lovers can enjoy an emotionally rewarding and sentimental relationship with partners who have their Sun, Moon or Rising sign in the relationship-oriented air sign of Libra. But due to the wide differences in both personalities, emotional adjustments will have to be made on both sides.

The Pisces Moon personality is divided into two, separate and intriguing parts, and the romantic Libra type lover will benefit greatly from learning how to tell them apart. Their lover may display either the *beauty seeker type* of Pisces Moon personality, or the *spirit seeker type* of Pisces Moon persona. The beauty seeker type seeks harmony and connectivity through beauty and goodness, yearns to find their true soul mate and is prone to trustingly slip into new, untried relationships with emotionally untested lovers rather quickly, while the spirit seeker type might be more suspicious of eagerly made promises from a new partner. Both the beauty seeker type as well as the spirit seeker type of Pisces Moon lovers can enjoy relationships as well as the stability of marriage.

The spirit seeker type of this Moon sign will be drawn to the harmony in nature and spirituality and is quite capable of being a very able and successful businessperson. They will seek spiritual connections during the various stages of life and maybe either very religious or very mystical by temperament. This open-minded type of the Pisces Moon persona may be less susceptible to the wildness of the planet Neptune, whose control over the great oceans mirrors its power over the Pisces Moon person's outlook on life.

Libra type lovers look for a mate who is physically graceful, socially active and a good conversationalist. Pisces Moon lovers can charm the airy Libra type lover right off their feet with that fitly spoken compliment. Libra types are ruled by Venus, and their Pisces Moon lovers are influenced by Neptune, lord of the seven seas. In many ways both these planetary influences are alike; both symbolize beauty and harmony within relationships. The signs of Pisces and

Libra are at their very best when in compatible love relationships, because they can better understand themselves through their interactions with partners. Neptune is the higher vibration of Venus, or its higher octave.

The Venus/Libra energy focuses on personalized love (*"We will love each other forever, I will offer you my love and hopefully you will return it."*), while the Neptune/Pisces Moon energy draws our attention to love in terms of self-sacrifice (*"I will love you forever, even though you don't love me and may never love me."*). There are some important differences between them as well. Libra is the sign that rules relationships and the marriage bond, while the Pisces Moon is connected with the true expression of compassion. When Moon is in Pisces, its essence mingles with the power of Neptune, producing in the Pisces Moon partner, a pronounced emotionality and intuition.

With this Venus/Neptune effect on a Pisces Moon and Libra type relationship, one partner will be sure to lead (the cardinal quality of Libra) while the other will be willing to follow the dominant partner (the mutable quality of Pisces). As long the stronger lover has only the best intentions at heart, this will be a good and harmony-oriented connection. If there is ever an imbalance of power, the Pisces Moon lover will have to try extra hard to come out of the vicious cycle and strengthen themselves into taking back their power in the relationship. They must trust but employ caution in deciding *whom* to trust; this especially applies to the impressionable, beauty seeker type of Pisces Moon personality described in the beginning of this analysis.

Some people with Pisces placed prominently in their natal charts will sometimes suffer from low self-esteem due to the influence of Neptune. The Pisces Moon psyche may have to face the monster of doubt in all his different and subtle shades. Therefore, the Libra type partner will have to help strengthen their water sign lover's self-confidence. Being around a Libra type lover pushes Pisces types to become more focused on projects and begin to tap into their own creative spirit. Both partners would do well to remind each other that they must build a solid foundation first: one of friendship and most importantly, of raw honesty. Friends who become confidants first and lovers second, will have a longer, more emotionally significant relationship than friends who proceed directly from the friend stage to the sexual stage.

Both of these lovers should speak clearly to each other and encourage one another to communicate their feelings frequently (never beat around the bush in this romantic combination, say what you feel). Pisces Moon partners like intuitive lovers but most people are unable to respond to their partner in the special language of human intuition. Wires could get crossed easily. Libra types need to be very patient with their Pisces Moon lover and handle them with tenderness as their feelings could be easily offended. The Pisces Moon energy brings out the cardinal Libra type lover's desire to guide their mate and protect them, while the airy Libra energy encourages the watery Pisces Moon lover to be more trusting of their many talents and abilities. Each supports the other selflessly and genuine reciprocity will be the signature trait of this love connection. This could be a fulfilling and loving relationship!

Pisces Moon vs. Scorpio Sun, Moon or Rising Sign
The Water and Water Relationship

Water: "Is my boyfriend emotionally stable and wise about our joint finances? Or will debts pile up in the first year of marriage? I need a supportive life-long lover as well as a loving one." the watery female lover thinks to herself. "Will my future spouse conserve our financial resources or spend unwisely without thought for the future? I can connect better romantically if I know that my chosen life-mate is passionate as well as mature and pragmatic." the watery male lover wonders.

Pisces Moon lovers can enjoy a highly fulfilling and spiritually vibrant relationship with partners who have their Sun, Moon or Rising sign in the emotive water sign of Scorpio. The Pisces Moon energy is very compatible with the watery Scorpio type essence because water flows and merges easily with water and watery signs have an easier time understanding each other's emotions. However, too much water and emotionality can overwhelm a relationship and rob it of a firm foundation. Which means that one of them will have to be the rock of the relationship to support it.

The Pisces Moon personality can be separated into two distinct types. Knowing which one reflects their partner most accurately can help the passionate Scorpio type mate to get a clear idea of their lover's desires in their love relationship. The first type of Pisces Moon personality is the *beauty seeker type*; this type thrives most when they are in a romantic relationship, is somewhat submissive (preferring to seek out dominant lovers), takes what their lover says rather seriously and revels in their approval. This type acclimates to the marriage setting easily and makes a very accommodating spouse and lover. They seek beauty, and through beauty, they seek harmony. Their goal is to harmonize their world as much as possible, particularly through their intimate relationships.

The second type of the Pisces Moon persona is the *spirit seeker type*. This fascinating type is strong, independent, a good blend of intellectualism and emotionality, and is quite capable of supporting others. Managing a business, caring for a family, pursuing their passion in life; they are truly an all-rounder. This type seeks a connectivity to something greater than themselves, and they may rely less on relationships to do so, preferring to look for it through the ancient mediums of spirituality, religion, mysticism or humanitarian work.

Scorpio type partners tend to be dominant and self-assured; therefore they might find greater compatibility with the beauty seeker type of the Pisces Moon personality. The key is to make sure that two aggressive partners don't constantly clash when it comes to the distribution of power within relationships. Matching up the supportive lovers with the protective ones might be a winning formula.

Scorpio types require unwavering emotional commitment before they will let anyone come close to becoming their true beloved. Pisces Moon lovers are deeply emotional themselves, and can bring the gifts of concern, compassion and sensitivity to the Pisces Moon/Scorpio Sun, Moon or Rising sign relationship. Trust doesn't come easily to the skeptical Scorpio type lover. According to them, it has to be earned gradually over time, so that they can test it and monitor its growing effects on the relationship.

Neptune, the ruler of Pisces, may exert its power over the Pisces Moon partner in one of two ways: it might make them incredibly artistic and creative (like the *spirit seeker Pisces Moon type*), or perhaps lean toward repeatedly picking obviously unsuitable life-partners or untrustworthy friends (like the *beauty seeker Pisces Moon type*). Neptune represents the creative urge in man, while super-serious Pluto, the ruler of the Scorpio type partner, represents the complete breakdown of a system in order to expose the truth about its corrupt inner state. Pluto then goes about rebuilding and revitalizing it completely. If a relationship is based on manipulation where one partner consistently betrays the other and takes them for granted, Pluto creates situations where the persecuted lover can break free of the vicious cycle that may be demoralizing them day after day. When the Neptune/Pluto combination joins together in the game of love, it can be an exhilarating and eye-opening experience for both lovers.

The Scorpio type lover will open their Pisces Moon partner's eyes to things that can be changed in their lives in order to make it more authentically representative of their true inclinations. *"What's real about this situation? How much of a good friend is your best friend, really honey? If she calls herself your best friend, then how come she's never remembered your birthday in 5 years? You remember hers, don't you?"* the Scorpio type lover enlightens their Pisces Moon mate. For example, a Scorpio type partner may draw the Pisces Moon partner's attention to friends who are more destructive and selfish than friendly, leading them to terminate their connection to people who take advantage of them. Scorpio types expect their lovers to make these sometimes, difficult changes if they really trust them.

The Pisces Moon partner will also have an incredible effect on their Scorpio type lover. If there are parts of their Pluto-ruled lover's life that are selfish, or if the Scorpio type lover becomes too domineering toward their friends and family, the Pisces Moon lover will show them the diplomatic compassion that could be employed, so that the sometimes volatile Scorpio type lover doesn't end up unnecessarily making more enemies than good friends.

"I know you're mad at your brother after what he did to you last week, sweetheart, but someday we might need his help. Just take it easy at the party we're going to today, but if he comes up to you, then at least say hello. Don't worry honey, things will get better soon, I promise. If we're respectful, we will have the moral high ground." advises the Pisces Moon lover who tends to harmonize and soothe more than antagonize.

Financially, some Pisces Moon mates may be more impulsive with finances, and this may pose a problem because Scorpio is a financial sign, and most Scorpio type folks are very prudent about managing their resources properly. Together, this romantic pairing is artistic, intuitive and will try to make every effort to handle each other's moods with tenderness and respect. This is a good combination if a family is planned.

Pisces Moon vs. Sagittarius Sun, Moon or Rising Sign
The Water and Fire Relationship

Water: "Is my boyfriend emotionally stable and wise about our joint finances? Or will debts pile up in the first year of marriage? I need a supportive life-long lover as well as a loving one." the watery female lover thinks to herself. *"Will my future spouse conserve our financial resources or spend unwisely without thought for the future? I can connect better romantically if I know that my chosen life-mate is passionate as well as mature and pragmatic."* the watery male lover wonders.

Fire: "I need romance and passion to really enjoy my relationship. Will my boyfriend be a faithful mate for life?" the fiery female partner wonders. "I want an active and freedom-loving partner. Will my girlfriend understand my need for true freedom in life or be too controlling?" the fiery male lover thinks to himself.

Pisces Moon lovers can enjoy a highly emotive and spiritually energizing relationship with partners who have their Sun, Moon or Rising sign in the wisdom-seeking and open-hearted fire sign of Sagittarius. The fiery Sagittarius type lover might like to be able to distinguish between the two specific types of the hypnotic and mysterious Pisces Moon personality, as this extra effort might allow them a deeper glimpse into their emotional needs. The first type of Pisces Moon persona is the *beauty seeker type*. This type is ultra-romantic, self-sacrificing and tends to idolize lovers as well as the very idea of love and relationships. They seek beauty, through which they seek purity and harmony. This type is very visually sensitive to attractiveness in a potential lover, more than are most people.

The second type of the Pisces Moon persona is the *spirit seeker type*. This type is more assertive and less inclined to trustingly give up control in new relationships. The spirit seeker type of Pisces Moon person is bright, intellectual, self-sufficient and can be successful in their chosen career field with great ease. This type will be drawn to the rare beauty of nature as well as be more comfortable with solitude than the former, beauty seeker type of Pisces Moon personality. Spirituality, religion and mysticism will intrigue them throughout their life, perhaps because they are drawn toward the purity of these ancient disciplines. This type seeks to build a connection to their more spiritual self.

If the Sagittarius type lover is of an aggressive or dominant temperament, they may encounter power struggles with the spirit seeker type of Pisces Moon personality. If, however, the charismatic Sagittarius type lover were matched up with the more pliant and passive, non-aggressive, beauty seeker type of Pisces Moon personality, they may find it easier to blend energies with them. The point is to pair up the protectors types with the meeker, anchor-seeking types so that each supplies what the other needs and neither will have to compete with each other for power.

The Pisces Moon lover is gentle and refined. Being around a Sagittarius type lover will intrigue the emulative Pisces Moon lover to learn to be more adventurous and take more risks, even with their own heart. The Pisces Moon mate helps the Sagittarius type lover into getting back in touch with their intuitive, sensitive and compassionate side. Both partners would do well to remind each other that they must build a solid foundation first: one of friendship and most importantly, of raw honesty. Friends who become confidants first and lovers second, will have a longer, more emotionally comfortable relationship than friends who proceed directly from the friend stage to the sexual stage.

Communication problems could crop up in this relationship due to Neptune's secretiveness and Jupiter's lack of attention to details. The Pisces Moon lover sometimes forgets and unknowingly omits mentioning important little details, while the Sagittarius type lover may be too pre-occupied or trusting to question them. Clear channels of communication will help this water/fire couple keep their relationship out of the dangerous waters of misunderstandings. The Pisces Moon partner must watch out for a tendency toward giving up their point of view too often to please their lover and falling victim to obsession, which could be unhealthy for them if it brings them closer to a treacherous personality who may be capable of deceiving them in the guise of a friend or lover, and in the most tragic cases, a spouse. Neptune's negative effects can blind them to seeing the real face of people, even if there are red flags galore.

Pisces Moon lovers have an unutterable inner yearning to find a lover who can connect with them intuitively, a quality most partners will usually lack. Impulsive Sagittarius types need to be very patient with their Pisces Moon lover and handle them with tenderness as their feelings could be affected by careless or blunt remarks. The Pisces Moon energy brings out their Sagittarius type lover's mellow, softer side, while the Sagittarius type energy causes the watery Pisces Moon person to be more assertive and result-oriented. This couple combines the energies of the planet Jupiter (ruling Sagittarius) and Neptune (ruling Pisces). Wisdom-hungry and expansive by temperament, jovial Jupiter and compassionate Neptune can blend energies beautifully as long as the Sagittarius type lover keeps their sometimes extravagant reactions under control and can match them to the appropriateness of the time and place, while the Pisces Moon lover could learn to manage their fears and never let them get out of hand and begin to control them instead of them letting them control their life.

The Pisces Moon lover is emotional and very easily upset, so once again, one of the most assertive signs in the entire zodiac will have to use more tact and sensitivity when talking to their softhearted Pisces Moon lover. Some people with Pisces placed prominently in their natal charts will sometimes express a lack of clarity about who they really are due to the influence of Neptune. Neptune, which also rules illusion and self-deception, causes doubt to surface in the delicate and impressionable Pisces Moon psyche. Therefore, the Sagittarius Moon partner will have to be the support system for their mate and infuse in them that legendary Sagittarius optimism and self-confidence. The Pisces Moon energy softens up any hard edges in their Sagittarius Moon sweetheart considerably. This is an expressive and loving combination.

Pisces Moon vs. Capricorn Sun, Moon or Rising Sign
The Water and Earth Relationship

Water: "Is my boyfriend emotionally stable and wise about our joint finances? Or will debts pile up in the first year of marriage? I need a supportive life-long lover as well as a loving one." the watery female lover thinks to herself. "Will my future spouse conserve our financial resources or spend unwisely without thought for the future? I can connect better romantically if I know that my chosen life-mate is passionate as well as mature and pragmatic." the watery male lover wonders.

Earth: "Does my boyfriend manage his finances maturely or will I end up paying his bills and supporting him? I need stability and true commitment before I can enjoy the romance between us." the earthy female thinks to herself. "Will my future wife spend my hard earned cash on frivolous items at the mall or be wise enough to save up for our retirement?" the earthy male lover wonders.

Pisces Moon lovers can enjoy an emotionally fulfilling and close relationship with partners who have their Sun, Moon or Rising sign in the ambitious and prestige-seeking earth sign of Capricorn. Capricorn type lovers react well to the emotional Pisces Moon lover and can respond successfully to its most important need: to be protected and loved.

The Capricorn type lover might like to be able to make a distinction between the two individual types of the hauntingly beautiful Pisces Moon personality, as it might bring them closer to understanding what makes them tick. The first type of Pisces Moon persona is the *beauty seeker type*. This type is ultra-romantic, giving and tends to idolize lovers as well as the idea of love and relationships. They seek beauty, through which they seek purity and harmony.

The second type of the Pisces Moon persona is the *spirit seeker type*. This type is more assertive and less inclined to give up control in untested relationships. The spirit seeker type of Pisces Moon person is bright, intellectual, self-sufficient and can be successful in their chosen career field with great ease. This type will be drawn to the rare beauty of nature as well as be more comfortable with solitude than the former, beauty seeker type of Pisces Moon personality. Spirituality, religion and mysticism will intrigue them throughout their life, perhaps because they are drawn toward the purity of these ancient disciplines.

If the Capricorn type lover is aggressive and leadership-oriented by nature, they may find an easier meeting of the minds with the first category of the Pisces Moon persona – the beauty seeker type. This is because Capricorn is a cardinal sign and naturally leans toward providing direction and protection to those who look to them for support. The soft-natured and support-seeking, beauty seeker type of Pisces Moon lover may automatically gravitate toward the take-charge personality of the Capricorn type partner.

The watery Pisces Moon lover should bear in mind that their Capricorn type partner is inwardly as emotional as they are, but does not show it as freely as they do. When the Pisces Moon lover is feeling blue or moody, the earthy support of their Capricorn type partner can bring them the solace they need. But when their Capricorn type lover feels melancholic (Saturn can sometimes bring about a strange depression in Capricorn lovers), they will need a lot of space (emotional and physical) in order to come out of it. Prodding and pushing them into sharing what ails them will make them reach deeper into their sadness, but leaving them alone and gifting them solitude will be of enormously help to them.

When this Pisces Moon/Capricorn Sun, Moon or Rising sign couple falls in love, they will awaken the energies of Neptune and Saturn within their relationship. Neptune is the ruler of Pisces, while Saturn governs Capricorn. The Capricorn type lover may exhibit some of the qualities of Saturn: they may be more in control of the relationship from the beginning, they may have an obvious effect on what their Pisces Moon lover thinks of themselves, and they might frown on any excessive emotionality in their watery Pisces Moon lover.

The Neptune energy is vast, ethereal and fluidic. It can help the Pisces Moon lover reach the heights of inspiration artistically, or cause them to feel defeated and unable to summon up the strength to make big and beneficial changes in their lives. The earthy Saturn-ruled, Capricorn type lover will be called upon to steer this delicate relationship toward the calm waters of commitment and stability, while Neptune will cause the Pisces Moon mate to yearn to break free of any unreasonable expectations or restrictions their partner might place on them. When the artistic dreamer who lives in the clouds high above mortal man (Pisces Moon) mingles forces with the stoic strategist who hopes to rise up in the world and be admired by the world community for their contributions (Capricorn Sun, Moon or Ascendant), the result will be a relationship that is refreshingly novel but one that also needs constant and mature balancing.

Each of these two lovers expresses emotions differently and if they study each other's style, it will pay off in a big way, promising them long-term compatibility. The Capricorn type partner is typically frugal and careful with finances, while the more emotional Pisces Moon type partner may be a bit of an impulse shopper. Being around their earthy lover will make the Pisces Moon lover more driven and focused, as well as practical and emotionally well balanced. Being around the sensual and romantic Pisces Moon energy will bring out in the earthy Capricorn type lover a most touching tenderness and sensitivity. This is a good romantic pairing if each lover becomes a little like the other.

Pisces Moon vs. Aquarius Sun, Moon or Rising Sign
The Water and Air Relationship

Water: "Is my boyfriend emotionally stable and wise about our joint finances? Or will debts pile up in the first year of marriage? I need a supportive life-long lover as well as a loving one." the watery female lover thinks to herself. "Will my future spouse conserve our financial resources or spend unwisely without thought for the future? I can connect better romantically if I know that my chosen life-mate is passionate as well as mature and pragmatic." the watery male lover wonders.

Air: "Is my boyfriend open-minded enough and will he appreciate my outspoken side? I need a life mate who will talk to me, communicate with me about everything and not clam up and brood." the airy female partner muses. "Will my girlfriend allow me to do the things I love or will she try to restrict me from expressing myself?" the airy male lover wonders.

Pisces Moon lovers can enjoy a unique and emotionally enlightening relationship with partners who have their Sun, Moon or Rising sign in the freedom-oriented and open-hearted air sign of Aquarius. The Aquarius type lover might like to be able to distinguish between the two varying types of the romantic Pisces Moon personality, as this extra effort might allow them to bond with them at a particularly intimate level. The first type of Pisces Moon persona is the *beauty seeker type*. This type is ultra-romantic, giving and tends to idolize lovers as well as the idea of love and relationships. They seek beauty, through which they seek purity and harmony.

The second type of the Pisces Moon persona is the *spirit seeker type*. This type is more assertive and less inclined to give up control in untested relationships.

The spirit seeker type of Pisces Moon person is bright, intellectual, self-suffi-cient and can be successful in their chosen career field with great ease. This type will be drawn to the rare beauty of nature as well as be more comfortable with solitude than the former, beauty seeker type of Pisces Moon personality. Spirituality, religion and mysticism will intrigue them throughout their life, perhaps because they are drawn toward the purity of these ancient disciplines.

When the Pisces Moon lover joins forces with the Aquarian type lover in the game of romance, both of them will learn an incredible amount of informa-tion in a relatively short time. Uranus rules the Aquarian type lover, while Neptune governs the emotions of the Pisces Moon partner. Neptune expresses its dreamy and ethereal qualities through the Pisces Moon lover, while rene-gade and unpredictable Uranus will color the thinking of the Aquarian type lover.

This Neptune/Uranus bond will be unusual but memorable. The Pisces Moon lover looks for a stable partner in life but also one who can express their imag-inative and daring side, as well as their sensitive and poetic side. The Aquarius type partner will certainly be unusual and therefore attractive, but may also cause a strange restlessness in the Pisces Moon mate. The Pisces Moon female may describe her Aquarian type lover with words such as, *"He makes me feel totally alive; I feel like I could touch the stars when he's with me. But something about him makes me feel like I will never really know him. I just can't put my fin-ger on it."* The Aquarian type lover may be saying *exactly* the same thing about the hard-to-define Pisces Moon lover: *"I love being around her, she's so feminine and more beautiful than anyone I know. But there is definitely a part of her that she deliberately keeps secret from me. I want her to open that corner of her heart to me. Will she ever trust me enough?"*

The Uranus energy is one that can only relate to a lover if they let them come and go, if they let them feel free enough to express their *whole* personality, no matter how radical or different it may be, without letting it get colored by what society thinks a good life-mate should be. Fortunately, Pisces Moon lovers are emotionally flexible and may be able to withstand most of the twists and turns of the unconventional but loving Aquarian personality.

What would work out best for this duo is if the Pisces Moon lover makes sure that they don't distort their relationship's real value by *overvaluing* it, and if the Aquarian type partner gives their lover a little more attention and becomes sensitive to how their actions affect their moods. Egalitarian to the core, Aquarius type lovers will surely understand the tone of equality in this situa-tion. Truly bonded by their sense of passion (but reflecting different versions of that passion) this couple can, with the slightest of efforts, bring their love connection back to life by trying to think like their lover. The Pisces Moon lover brings out in their airy Aquarian type lover a sense of poetry and soft sensuality, while the Aquarian type lover brings out in their watery Pisces Moon lover a sense of freedom to live, think and be what they most want to be without being answerable to anyone. This is a devoted pair.

Pisces Moon vs. Pisces Sun, Moon or Rising Sign
The Water and Water Relationship

Water: "Is my boyfriend emotionally stable and wise about our joint finances? Or will debts pile up in the first year of marriage? I need a supportive life-long lover as well as a loving one." the watery female lover thinks to herself. "Will my future spouse conserve our financial resources or spend unwisely without thought for the future? I can connect better romantically if I know that my chosen life-mate is passionate as well as mature and pragmatic." the watery male lover wonders.

Pisces Moon lovers can enjoy a revealing and emotionally vibrant relationship with partners who have their Sun, Moon or Rising sign in their own sign of Pisces. The attraction between these two watery lovers with similar goals will be strong but some adjustments will have to be made for long-term compatibility. The water element induces emotionality within an already emotional essence, with the result that two things can occur: there may be great empathy between the two Pisces lovers or they might completely drown in their own watery mystery, causing each other to over-react to the smallest transgressions.

There are two, individual types of the Pisces Moon personality. Knowing which one mirrors their lover, might help the Pisces type partner get a much better idea about how to approach them. The first type of Pisces Moon personality is the *beauty seeker type*. This type is relationship-oriented, marriage-minded, accommodating and generally passive in relationships. Their purpose is to seek beauty and love through harmony within relationships. The second type of Pisces Moon personality is the *spirit seeker type*. This type is more comfortable with their solitude, adapts to relationships easily but is also quite comfortable with their autonomy. The spirit seeker type seeks to connect to their higher selves through religion, nature, spirituality and mysticism; the goal is to find real value and meaning in their life.

Neptune, the ruler of Pisces, is a vast and highly idealistic planet. If there is any Moon sign that will idealize their lover, no matter how unsuitable or wrong they may be for their life, it is the Pisces Moon sign. Sometimes Neptune causes the Pisces Moon lover to refuse to see faults in their lover when they are right before them. *"I know he has a temper, but I'm sure he doesn't mean it when he says he'd rather be with his ex. I know he loves me, even though he doesn't say it to me. What I feel in my heart is enough proof for me that we will last forever."* the hopeful Pisces Moon lover reasons. This hope is good but in some situations it might bring them perilously close to harming their own lives with their own hands. Sometimes one must acknowledge those pesky red flags, they're there for a reason — to keep the Pisces Moon lover safe from emotional manipulation, which may present itself under the guise of love.

In many ways, this Moon sign cannot stand by and watch even a toxic relationship end, it may cause too heavy an emotional overload in them. But they are stronger than they think and have the inner resolve to weather the most unmanageable storms that life can send their way. The only thing a Pisces Moon lover asks for, dreams for, is to be able to weather those storms with a life partner who is as concerned about them as they are for their welfare. They have an unutterable inner desire for a lover who can alternate between being their emotional rock, their best friend and their soul mate.

When two lovers join hearts in the game of love and romance, and if they are both functioning under the powerful influence of Neptune, then is it extremely important that one of them take over the responsibility of steering this relationship towards safer waters. Neptune can cause a pair of Pisces type lovers to become confused, forget their way and perhaps lose touch with each other's real personalities if they lack the direction and assistance of a stable foundation. Neptune is no ordinary planet. It can cause great compassion to take root in any heart, but can also blur the lines between reality and fantasy if people are not mature enough to begin with. Its essence has to be handled with care in a double Pisces relationship.

Fellow Pisces types will know exactly what that mysterious Pisces Moon heart needs to feel secure. The Pisces Moon lover worries about not being able to express their deepest emotions with a partner because their lover may try to shy away from the real expression of human feelings. So if both partners are on the same page about that, ninety percent of their problems will vanish.

Both the Pisces Moon lover, as well as their Pisces type partner are emotionally vibrant and too much of that could cause stagnation to occur. If they could bring out each other's light-hearted side more often, it could help balance and solidify the connection. These two share the rare karmic soul mate energy, and must always trust each other above all other friends and family members.

Part III
The Romantic Expectations of the 12 Moon Signs

Each Moon sign has certain expectations of their lover; find out what your lover may really want from you when they're speaking in the secret, emotional language of their Moon sign.

The Moon in Fire Signs (Aries, Leo, Sagittarius) To the optimistic, fiery Moon sign mate, life's romantic possibilities are virtually endless and the road ahead is open for as far as the eye can see. To a fiery Moon sign lover, their partner should be a happy, passionate and positive life influence on their life.

The Moon in Earth Signs (Taurus, Virgo, Capricorn) To the stable, earthy Moon sign mate, chances for romantic success must be carefully cultivated for a certain period of time if anything worthwhile is to be gained from it. To the earthy Moon sign lover, their life partner should remain a practical and dependable influence, no matter how their lives together are influenced and altered by time.

The Moon in Air Signs (Gemini, Libra, Aquarius) To the intellectual, airy Moon sign mate, life is full of opportunities for love and time must not be wasted if chances present themselves. To the airy Moon sign lover, their life mate should be a mentally stimulating and exciting, as well as open-minded and friendly influence.

The Moon in Water Signs (Cancer, Scorpio, Pisces) To the emotional, watery Moon sign mate, each possibility must best tested out first before it is blindly accepted, because a lot might be at stake. To the watery Moon sign lover, their partner should be a supportive, unquestionably loyal and protective influence.

What does love mean to each of the Moon signs?

To a fiery Aries, Leo or Sagittarius Moon sign partner, love is non-stop joy, laughter and intense passion. These lovers say, "Make me happy and I'll make you *happier.*"

To an airy Gemini, Libra or Aquarius Moon sign partner, love is an uplifting intellectual friendship first and a physical, sensual bonding second. These lovers say, "Engage my *mind* and I'll engage your heart."

To an earthy Taurus, Virgo or Capricorn Moon sign partner, love is an open-heartedly accepted responsibility, true, steadfast devotion and a sense of joint achievement as a couple. These lovers say, "Build a future with me and I'll *provide* for you."

To a watery Cancer, Scorpio or Pisces Moon sign partner, love is long-term emotional security and physical, emotional and spiritual protection. These lovers say, "*Trust* me and I'll protect you."

The Moon Sign Gift Guide

Okay, so it's your sweetheart's birthday in 3 days and you're out shopping and checking out store after store, and even went shopping online, trying to find that perfect gift. You want your gift to stand out; what do you pick? Read the Moon sign gift guide below for some excellent, time-tested ideas on how to wow your lover on their special day.

The Aries Moon Lover

The daring and outdoorsy Aries Moon male will love a black or brown faux leather bomber jacket, a sturdy pair of hiking boots, or even a pair of tickets flying him out to hike in the Grand Canyon. It has to be exciting! Adventurous Aries rules the head, so a cool pair of sunglasses will also do the trick. Hats and caps with the logos of favorite teams may also be ideal. The Aries Moon female will love a gift certificate to get her hair done at the most expensive and fashionable hair salon in town (Aries rules the head). Is your captivating Aries Moon female lover athletic and not into hair and nails? Try a beautiful red silk blouse (or red jacket with the logo of her favorite sports team), a six month pass to her local rock climbing gym so she can practice those killer bouldering moves, or season tickets to her favorite sporting event. NHL anyone? Adventure DVDs on their favorite sports will also be a hit.

The Taurus Moon Lover

The Taurus Moon male or female will love a gift of music: a portable CD player, some music CDs or even a sound system for their home or car. Taurus rules the throat and singing or listening to music will be close to their heart. Taurus is ruled by the planet Venus, and Lady Venus loves to be wined, dined and attended to. So, a recipe or dessert book would be ideal. If your Taurus Moon partner doesn't like to enter the kitchen except to get a glass of water, an elegant dinner at the most fashionable eatery in your city will seal the deal. Venus has a sweet tooth, so don't forget to order a scrumptious dessert! Taurus is an earth sign, and finds the outdoors exhilarating, so a book on hiking, gardening or growing exotic miniature tea roses will be appreciated. An Ansel Adams wall calendar will not go amiss, either. Taurus is also a money sign, so any book on proper financial investing will be read with eagerness. Nature DVDs featuring wide-open landscapes or mountains will also be a hit. A small but exquisite pair of gemstone earrings would be perfect for the Taurus Moon female.

The Gemini Moon Lover

The Gemini Moon lover is an attractive braniac, so you could never go wrong with the gift of books or art. This Moon sign is the most communicative of all and the gift of a subscription to a brand new, multi-feature cell/video phone will be very much appreciated. A laptop will be even more appreciated and enjoyed. Mentally insatiable Gemini Moon partners will love playing word games, video games, toying with puzzles and going to the movies too, so movie tickets are a perfect gift idea. The Gemini Moon male and female will enjoy a chance to take their first flying lesson (Gemini is an air sign). Also, many Gemini Moon partners are salespeople, business leaders or teachers and authors, so books on how to make more money, grow their business and biographies of famous and successful people will be eagerly read. Travel DVDs will be a hit. The Gemini Moon female might love tiny earrings (the kind that don't get in the way) or rings for their hands and toe-rings for their feet.

The Cancer Moon Lover

The Cancer Moon sign has close links with the past, the mother figure and the family. A large, elegantly framed picture of the matriarch of the family (or their parents or grandparents) will be loved. A family portrait will also do the trick (Cancer is a family-friendly sign, so get those cute, little grandkids in the image too). This Moon sign is also very attached to their home, so a gift certificate for some home improvement projects will be enjoyed a great deal. Cancer Moon mates also love to collect things: stamps, antique books, coins and vintage images, and perhaps old history volumes and old maps. History, home improvement DVDs or movies with a romantic or family theme will be a hit. A delicate pair of authentic pearl earrings will not go amiss with the Cancer Moon female. Pearls lie at the bottom of the sea, and the sea has close ties to the Moon, the ruler of Cancer.

The Leo Moon Lover

The Leo Moon mate loves being the center of attention and clown around, so the gift of a book on party jokes would be ideal. Leo rules the entertainment industry, so tickets to the movies or the theater will be thoroughly enjoyed. Leo Moon mates love to play director, and will like the gift of a video camera, so that they can create their own memories of their family events or get-togethers with old friends. The Leo Moon female will love a small but exquisite piece of gold jewelry (real jewelry, guys, this woman is truly worth it) or an elegant party dress, handbag or shoes designed by late Leo fashion designer Coco Chanel, will draw their attention to their lover's sense of thoughtfulness and their appreciation for a beautiful woman. Expensive perfume will also be a hit with the Leo Moon sign ladies.

The Virgo Moon Lover

The hard-to-please Virgo Moon mate will love a gift certificate instead of a gift. They're picky and discriminating and may prefer to pick out their own gift. Virgo is the sign of health, hygiene and work, so any book on healthy eating, fitness and cooking will score points. A new treadmill that saves them trips to the fitness gym may also be appreciated. Many Virgo Moon folks are successful business owners, so books on how to improve their business and invest their earnings will be enjoyed. Virgo Moon mates like to look well groomed, so an at-home hair grooming aid will be a hit. It's cost-efficient and convenient as well, which will get this frugal Moon sign's instant attention. Books are also always a favorite of this intellectual Moon sign. Work stress will undoubtedly affect the over-worked Virgo Moon mate, so a therapeutic massage will relax them wonderfully, even if they initially decline the offer to get one. If anyone needs one, it's these hardworking souls!

The Libra Moon Lover

The Libra Moon partner will appreciate a gift that soothes their body *and* mind, because Libra is an intellectual air sign. Romantic Libra Moon partners love books on poetry, art, decorating, architecture, world cultures, biographies as well as books on relationship improvement, such as this one. For most Libra Moon mates, their marriage or partnership will be their most important relationship in life, and giving them any aid that can help them clarify important interpersonal issues will be appreciated. For the more independent, career-oriented Libra Moon person, a gift subscription to their favorite magazine will be loved, as will a gift of CDs, a laptop and other communications aids. Tickets to the art gallery or museum will also be loved.

The Scorpio Moon Lover

The Scorpio Moon mate is secretive and guards their privacy jealously. But Scorpio is also a financial sign, so books on intelligent investing, or tickets to seminars that that can teach them how to increase their income potential will be enjoyed by them. It may be a bit baffling to find the perfect gift for this Moon sign; they have particular tastes and seldom share their preferences with people other than their closest confidants. But since they are usually concerned with the value or true worth of things (and people), a well-chosen gift of *real* jewelry for the Scorpio Moon female wouldn't go amiss. It should be real because it will symbolize your love, which is also real. For the male Scorpio Moon lover, a vacation near the ocean will do the trick. Scorpio is a water sign and has a close tie to water, as well as water sports like swimming and kayaking or sailing. Books on political intrigue and unsolved mysteries will also be enjoyed. Offer to get this Moon sign's car windows tinted to protect their privacy, and they will never forget this particularly thoughtful gesture.

The Sagittarius Moon Lover

The Sagittarius Moon lover is an endearing sea-gypsy at heart. The obvious gift for them would be tickets to a far away land that they have only read about but never visited (Europe, Africa and the Far East are always a favorite). Travel and foreign language books, road maps or a convenient holder for maps in their car will be appreciated, as will a sleek digital camera, binoculars and a lightweight, waterproof backpack. The Sagittarius Moon female will love an exotic, free flowing Egyptian kaftan, Kholapuri sandals, an African Cowry shell necklace or a hand-knitted cardigan from Ireland. The Sagittarius Moon male will enjoy showing off his comfortable Indian cotton kurta, which he will wear over jeans and top it off with his dapper Aussie Bush hat. This Moon sign can wear a newspaper get away with it; they can carry off any style of dress because they have an interesting, confident personality to match. Imported goods will be enjoyed more than local, hum-drum department store or drug store items like key chains and nail sets. Adventure DVDs and books on personal accounts in foreign lands will be read with eagerness.

The Capricorn Moon Lover

The Capricorn Moon partner may appear serious on the outside, but you will find a person who thoroughly enjoys every moment of life right under that stoic surface. This Moon sign is very aware of the proper etiquette involved in gift giving, so be prepared to be judged by the quality of your offering. This earthy Moon sign will enjoy tickets to the opera, or theater or tickets to exotic shows like Cirque du Soleil. If they're not that highbrow, then tickets to any movies that have a period or political theme will be enjoyed by them. They will dress well wherever they go, so a small but expensive and high-quality present will get their attention. The Capricorn Moon male will love a pair of silver cufflinks or a graceful tweed blazer. While their female counterpart will delight in a silk scarf, a small but expensive pair of diamond earrings (if you've been dating a little above a year) or a practical gift like a soft cashmere wrap or winter coat (if you live in the colder climes). The Capricorn Moon male will enjoy an exclusive membership to a golf club as well as books on how to invest their money successfully.

The Aquarius Moon Lover

The Aquarius Moon mate is a creature that is unlike any other, thankfully for us. Getting them that perfect gift may be a bit daunting, but it is not impossible to wow them with something they've never had before. This researcher Moon sign enjoys reading about the occult, astronomy and science or anything off the beaten path. A gift subscription to the Scientific American, the National Geographic, Parabola or any cable channels that shed light on these subjects will be enjoyed. The latest technological advances and the newest gadgetry (Aquarian Moon gals will love these too) will be interesting to them, as will issues pertaining to the care of the environment. A laptop will be thoroughly enjoyed too. The Aquarian Moon lover will become a proponent of a favorite cause early in their lives, and that can help with deciding on that ideal present for them. It needn't be expensive, but it should be exotic and not easily obtainable.

The Pisces Moon Lover

The Pisces Moon mate will be drawn to music, nature and water. Neptune, the ruler of Pisces, governs the medium of film, so movie passes will always be appreciated. A gift of original art (something you've painted yourself) as well as a trip to museums and art galleries will prove soothing, as will a trip to a locale near the ocean or a river. Some Pisces Moon folks enjoy being near the water (it is their element), so sailing and swimming may help relieve tension. The Pisces Moon female will love feminine clothing, and may have a special fondness for shoes, toe-rings or foot jewelry like a delicate and pretty, silver Indian *payal* or silver anklet. An elegant pair of semi-precious earrings or a pendant made from seashells will wow them; the smaller and more delicate the piece of jewelry, the better. Books and CDs are also a great choice for that sensitive Pisces Moon mate. The best gift for them would be a therapeutic massage from an expert or one session of reflexology a month to help ease their feet. Pisces rules the feet, so this particular gift will be most appreciated.

CPSIA information can be obtained at www.ICGtesting.com
Printed in the USA
LVOW08s0349270614

391888LV00002B/589/A